Critical Essays on John Cheever

Critical Essays on John Cheever

R. G. Collins

G. K. Hall & Co. • Boston, Massachusetts

Copyright © 1982 by R. G. Collins

Library of Congress Cataloging in Publication Data
Main entry under title:

Critical essays on John Cheever.

  (Critical essays on American literature)
  Bibliography
  Includes index.
  1. Cheever, John—Criticism and interpretation—Addresses, essays,
lectures.   I. Collins, Robert G.   II. Series.
PS3505.H6428Z63   813'.52   82-2897
ISBN 0-8161-8623-5   AACR2

This publication is printed on permanent/durable acid-free paper
MANUFACTURED IN THE UNITED STATES OF AMERICA

CRITICAL ESSAYS ON AMERICAN LITERATURE

This series seeks to publish the most important reprinted criticism on writers and topics in American literature along with, in various volumes, original essays, interviews, bibliographies, letters, manuscript sections, and other materials brought to public attention for the first time. This volume on John Cheever, edited by Robert G. Collins, Professor of English at the University of Ottawa, is in many ways a remarkable collection of criticism. It contains reprinted articles by John Wain, Granville Hicks, Cynthia Ozick, Joan Didion, John Gardner, John Hersey, and other notable scholars, and original essays by Frederick Bracher, Robert M. Slabey, Nora Calhoun Graves, Samuel Coale, Frederick R. Karl, Burton Kendle, Richard H. Rupp, John L. Brown, Lynne Waldeland, Theo D'haen, as well as a bibliographical supplement by Dennis Coates. We are confident that this collection will make a permanent and significant contribution to American literary study.

James Nagel, GENERAL EDITOR

Northeastern University

For May

CONTENTS

CRITICISM

INTRODUCTION

John Cheever, An Overview

Despite the endless cascade of fiction published in North America, it is apparent that most of it vanishes like a stone dropped in the sea. The number of known artists who survive through a half century of their own lives without taking on the character of either has-beens or Atheneum monuments is surprisingly few; when one takes the roll of the major American writers of the twentieth century, one discovers only a small feudal aristocracy of men who wield authority over one or another of the imaginative principalities that are the significant definitions of our culture. From Henry James through Faulkner, the list is a small one; and when it is added to, it generally happens only over the fretful objections of those periodical jurists who think for us about literary values. The career of John Cheever is a case in point.

Author of five novels and somewhere around one hundred and fifty published stories, many of them collected in his seven volumes of short fiction, John Cheever was a faithful practitioner of his craft from 1930, when his first story was published in *New Republic*, until his death, June 18, 1982.

In that time, Cheever has become known as the recording angel for a distinct society; as John Leonard phrased it, he is our "Chekhov of the ex-urbs." Or suburbs to use a word that is more familiar and scarcely distinct. In the same sentence, Leonard, editor of *The New York Times Book Review*, made the flat statement, "I happen to believe that John Cheever is our best living writer of short stories."[1] If the belief seems to be a trifle assertive in the phrasing, it suits the situation: John Cheever has been praised by an astonishing number of his peers as one of the greatest writers of the century; at the same time, paradoxically, few writers have been discussed with such ill temper by an important group of reviewers and critics.

In 1966, thirty-six years after the publication of John Cheever's first story, the critic John Aldridge observed "Cheever is one of the most grievously underdiscussed important writers we have at the present time."[2] Eleven years after that, in 1977, John Gardner, himself by that time a distinguished novelist, wrote of his older compeer "John Cheever is one of the few living American novelists who might qualify as true artists.

1

His work ranges from competent to awesome on all the grounds I would count. . . ."[3]

Can this be the same figure described by Irving Howe in 1959: "a toothless Thurber, he connives at the cowardice of contemporary life. . . . "?[4] It is, indeed, and the circumstance illustrates one of the paradoxical situations of the literary world with respect to its prophets and priests.

On the whole, it is difficult to be a living writer. Once a certain body of work has appeared, a text provided, critics prefer to act upon it, judge it, label it, and in most cases dispose of it, without the contradiction of the author's further work which might prove them very wrong. Unlike, say, instrumental performers, in which style is all important but where the artistic vehicle pre-exists, serious writers create the world anew each time they write a story. As a result, writers may be "promising" figures, with praise modified by quibble, for several decades. If sanctified in the highest terms, as in the case of a Nobel Prize, if they retire into confirmed silence, or if they die, then the work becomes "a canon," achieves a fixity that critics feel free to honor. In brief, serious writers generally become acknowledged without demur only in their later years.

In part, at least, this is because they represent their time in its essence, and that essence only crystallizes into unclouded visibility as it begins to pass. Moreover, it is the work of an artist to see things as distinct, as separate and vitally defined within any setting, a quality of imagistic literalness (shared with children and madmen) which both attracts and repels us by its alienating quality. A reader at this surface stage is apt to respond favorably or not in terms of prior tastes and beliefs; to have them confirmed or questioned is the immediate effect of the work. Critics are, basically, social agents, judges operating on behalf of the society in one or another of its parts. Thus, even at their best, they exemplify the tastes and prejudices of one or another particular group. As John Aldridge said in noting that Cheever's first novel had won a National Book Award in 1958, and that he had been the subject of a cover story in *Time* in 1964: "But this scarcely constitutes critical attention. In fact, the receipt of either of these honors may be the best conceivable reason for withholding it."[5] Then, both echoing and anticipating other critics, Aldridge noted that Cheever's fiction was tarred with the brush of the *New Yorker*.

Certainly Cheever's work has been firmly identified with that magazine; in its history, only John O'Hara has had a greater number of stories appear in the *New Yorker* pages. In the popular mythology of modern American publishing, the *New Yorker* writer is a special breed, of which the first generation, E. B. White, James Thurber, Robert Benchley, Woolcott Gibbs, Edmund Wilson, and others, are sanctified as belle-lettristic figures whose wit and judgments of taste were definitive. The fiction writers, on the other hand, have frequently been accused of both preciousness and of acting as apologists for their comfortable middle-class readership, a group that is financially and culturally insulated from American society as a whole. The *New Yorker* writers, particularly Cheever, John O'Hara, J. D. Salinger, and John Updike, have frequently been accused of revolving endlessly around some combination Park Avenue/Madison Avenue/Wall Street urban setting and the suburban domestic enclaves of Westchester and Bucks County; they have been seen as confirming the obtuseness of the modern American middle class even when they reveal it. Cheever, for example, was repeatedly attacked by what might be thought of as socially-conscious critics, who felt that his very subject matter confirmed his irresponsibility, since he failed to involve himself with the social realism of proletarian life.

Ironically, as his image of suburban life in the later stories has become more somber, generally now recognized as what Isa Kapp has called "The Cheerless World of John Cheever,"[6] the criticism has reversed, and he now is charged with having abandoned his proper subject. In fact, the same reaction occurred when Cheever, after having more than a hundred stories in the *New Yorker*, published his first novel. Many of the reviewers deplored his switching from short fiction and assured him that he did not have the depth and endurance for the longer form. He had been branded with the mark of short story writer, which was to say that he was not a heavyweight. In lip service at least, the short story has been honored and respected by serious scholars of literature. In practice, it is regarded as essentially trivial, a diversion, something tucked into the pages of a magazine as a breathing space between current opinion, information, and advertisement, but as ephemeral as such pieces. Yet, when a collection such as *The Stories of John Cheever* appeared in 1978, the achievement within the discipline of the form wiped away at a stroke the easy condescension under which the story has increasingly labored, and one suddenly saw the validity of linking Cheever with Chekhov and Kafka; one realized that a magnificent literary form had been relegated to the back of our mind and that we were the poorer for it, just as we were immeasurably richer for having "The Swimmer," "Torch Song," "The Day the Pig Fell into the Well," "The Country Husband," and dozens of other stories from John Cheever's hand.

"Oh, it is hard to be a Yankee—if only the Wapshots were, if not Braccianis, then Wapsteins—how they might then truly suffer! And we might truly feel" observed Cynthia Ozick,[7] reviewing Cheever's second Wapshot novel in 1964. The criticism is significant; Cheever's subject matter has been time after time leveled as a charge against him. He writes of a mythical New England of absurdity, gentility, and poverty, and is seen as elitist; he writes of a suburban New York society of upper middle class failures, each a solitary isolated from everyone else, and is condemned as an apologist for Westchester. In fact, for half a century, he has traced the metamorphosis of the culture in the northeastern United States through his fiction, discovering the myth elements in our banal and confused reality with laser perception and an exactness of phrase that is surgical. Joan Didion has spoken to the Cynthia Ozick point quite directly in her 1977 review of *Falconer*:

> Some of us are not Jews. Neither are some of us Southerners, nor children of the Iroquois, nor the inheritors of any other notably dark and bloodied ground. Some of us are even Episcopalians. In the popular mind this absence of any particular claim on the conscience of the world is generally construed as a historical advantage, but in the small society of those who read and write, it renders us "different" and a little suspect. We are not quite accredited for suffering, nor do we have tickets for the human comedy. We are believed to have known no poverty except that of our own life-force. We are seen by the tolerant as carriers merely of an exhausted culture, and by the less tolerant as carriers of some potentially demonic social virus. We are seen as dealers in obscure manners and unwarranted pessimism. We are always "looking back." We are always lamenting the loss of our psychic home, a loss which is easy to dismiss—given our particular history in this particular country—as deficient in generality and even in credibility. Yet, in a very real way the white middle-class Protestant writer in America is in fact homeless—as absent from the world of his fathers as he is "different" within the world of letters—and it is precisely this note of "homelessness" that John Cheever strikes with an almost liturgical intensity. . . .[8]

If Cheever has been loved and hated in extraordinary measure, it is probably because the state of domestic life and personal emotional needs in America in the past four decades have been at the very center of our insecurity and regret; as the prose poet of the middle decades of the century, while we were losing our old world, Cheever has been our guide, our conscience, our court fool, and our prosecutor. He is one of those writers that we meet with a sense that he knows all about us in advance; he has thought many of our thoughts already, uttered many phrases that we had assumed were safely buried in our thoughts. Yet, he has done it with so graceful a manner, so mocking and yet gentle a ridicule, that we are teased into acceptance. Or else we don't trust him, not an inch, since he's obviously as much a phoney as we are or he wouldn't have a matching key to the secret strongroom of our mind. Our quondam resentment aside, Cheever, it seems increasingly clear, has been tuned to the successive emotional patterns of his time much more finely than any other writer of the past four decades.

The great writers of modern America have each been landlords of a special territory that has only become defined as their work accumulated. Faulkner may have looked like just another regional writer in 1930; by the 60s Yoknapatawpha, his "postage stamp of a county," had become a living myth that animated the history of the Deep South from its founding before the Civil War to the Roosevelt era. Hemingway's rootless, wounded, faithless men clinging to one illusion of faith roamed the world to avoid going home to an empty house; a major part of one generation was made up of them (although they were disavowed brutally when home faiths returned to their campus-and-cult grandchildren). Steinbeck caught the human tide of the depression and a simple-minded idealism in the westernizing of America just before it was brought to the cauterizing "health" of the Second World War; it would remain forever his doman even though he himself became an absentee landlord in his later years.

John Cheever, in contrast, began with a myth—that of the typical middle-class Manhattanite, an educated, cultivated immigrant from a more stable American setting. Cheever then moved forward and backward: he traced his man back to an old but moribund New England origin, and brought him forward, first to the illusory bourgeois paradise of the suburbs, Shady Hill, then to the richer but bleaker culture of Proxmire Manor and Bullet Park, where empty ceremony hides the inevitable solitude of each individual.

In his third novel, *Bullet Park*, Cheever showed, first, the impossibility of social change or even meaning through action in a world divided between a good-hearted, unquestioning, but emotionally anesthetized Nailles and a half-mad, emotionally helpless but outraged Hammer. In his fourth, *Falconer*, Cheever moved all of us to to a point 190° from where we had begun with him. Society here has been deliberately and completely removed; we exist in myth, among the stylized degenerates and castaways of life, surrounded by degradation, disgusting and at the same time casual brutality, sex reduced to the masturbation and homosexuality that exists outside the clear light of ordered society. All actions now are tokens of a private existence; love itself is relinquishing, the ability to embrace with no claim upon the other being; "prison" is a condition that one enters from society in an unwitting search for purgation, and from which one goes, cleansed, not back to society, but to an undefined and solitary but self-restoring grace. From St. Botolphs, Massachusetts at the turn of the last century, to the anonymous, mad streets beyond Falconer prison, where guilty twentieth century man starts over again, new, cleansed of his anger, relieved of his empty profession, stripped of his predictable—but alien—home, wife, children, having discovered a feeble and pained but real human self beneath his funeral cerements. In 1982, *Oh What a Paradise It Seems* was published. This short novel is both elegaic and evasive, presenting a survivor from the lost world, a grizzled guerilla who fights sporadic engagements, appearing and disappearing, camouflaged in the anonymous glare and shadow of present-day life. This is the mythic history of the twentieth century, with Cheever as our guide, and there is a logic and meaning to it that actuality cannot refute. "The World of Cheever" and "the Cheeveresque" have passed into literary terminology.

In part, perhaps, because Cheever's two chief strengths are language and the use of mythic elements clearly visible under ordinary experience, he has been regarded with unusual respect by other contemporary writers of fiction. Among those who have acknowledged his mastery are Bernard Malamud, John Updike, Joan Didion, John Gardner, Joseph Heller, John Irving, John Wain, John Hersey, Wilfred Sheed, Glenway Westcott, Elizabeth Janeway, Larry Woiwode, Walter Clemons, and others. Significantly, his detractors (most of whom grant him, even if grudgingly, considerable mastery of his material) are apt to be academic critics, particularly those who are themselves natives of New York. Among them are Irving Howe, Alfred Kazin, Stanley Edgar Hyman, Marvin Mudrick, Benjamin De Mott, Anatole Broyard, and Warren Sloat. The "sides" here represent a fascinating division. It almost seems as if the world of the creative mind splits along a center defined by Cheever.

CHEEVER, THE MAN

John Cheever was born on May 27, 1912, in Quincy, Massachusetts, just south of Boston. He was a second son, his brother Frederick some seven years older. His mother, Mary Devereaux (Liley) Cheever, was English; his father, Frederick Lincoln Cheever, was a descendent of the Ezekial Cheever who came to Massachusetts in 1630, an ancestry that plays a significant part in Cheever's first two novels. Cheever's youth was one of shabby gentility, culminating in two apparently significant events. The first was the departure of his father from the family household in 1927, with the subsequent loss of his money in 1929; the second, John's own expulsion from Thayer Academy, in South Braintree, Massachusetts, at the age of seventeen, an event that he has variously described as due to laziness, to his having been caught smoking, and as having been self-engineered because it had become intolerable to him and he did not want to go on to Harvard. At that age, he wrote his first story, "Expelled," which was published by Malcolm Cowley in the *New Republic*, October 1, 1930.[9]

Moving to New York, where he lived with some subsidy from his brother and with a few odd dollars picked up on casual work, John Cheever began a career as a writer that has continued unbroken for a half century; he is proud of the fact that he has never picked up a regular paycheck. (A few brief stints of teaching writing at Barnard, Iowa, and Boston University scarcely invalidate his record, since he was there by virtue of his accomplishment as a free-lance writer.) It was Cowley, apparently, whose good offices first gave Cheever access to publication in the *New Yorker*, a periodical that over the years would publish somewhere around 130 of his stories and would become closely identified with him in the public mind.

During this time, he remained in close touch with his brother, Frederick, whom he has described as a powerful influence in his life, although he was also conscious of the relationship as too confining. His father did not prosper after the loss of his shoe factory in the Depression; he died at the age of 82, in a rented room, where, Cheever notes with somewhat rueful pride, he was apparently in the company of a woman whose lipstick was left on the glass and on cigarette butts, but who "never came forward to identify herself" after the inquest. Leander Wapshot of *The Wapshot Chronicle* is said to be modeled after Frederick Lincoln Cheever, and John has admitted that the famous journal of Leander Wapshot in his novel is based on a similar journal, in similar style, written by his father. (The son has inherited the journal habit from his forebears; he says that all Cheevers have kept journals.) Cheever speaks little of his mother, other than to describe her as "kindly and original." Like Sara Wapshot, in the *Chronicle,* she ran a seaside gift shop to support the family, an enterprise that John did not regard kindly, according to his brother.

Living as an impoverished writer in New York during the '30's, John Cheever published his short stories, polished his style to a fine edge, and developed a close acquaintance with a number of other people in the literary and artistic life of the city. When World War II began, he joined, in his own words, "eagerly"; he was a member of a rifle company. However, when they found out that he was a writer, he was transferred and, as he puts it, the rest of his company was sent out to get killed. He went to the Pacific Theatre but did not see combat. In 1942, he had married Mary Winternitz, daughter of the Dean of the School of Medicine at Yale University. In 1943, his first volume of collected stories, *The Way Some People Live,* was published to favorable reviews.

After the war, he returned to New York for some years. In 1951, he moved out to Scarborough, in Westchester County. In the early 1960s he settled in a 1799 Dutch colonial on six acres in Ossining, New York, within shouting distance of the Hudson. He has had three children: Susan Liley Cowley, Benjamin Hale Cheever, and Federico Cheever, all now grown. His wife, Mary, is a poet and teacher of English at Briarcliff Manor.

Cheever, like most fiction writers, is a morning worker. He arises at dawn, typically takes a bicycle ride of up to two hours on back roads to get his system in tune, then works in one or another of the rooms of his house until lunch time. He claims to have written each novel in a different bedroom of the house as his children have grown and left; he has no formal study or desk. Although he writes regularly, he may be dormant for some time, suddenly "like a cockroach having a fit," he writes a story off in a matter of hours. Cheever has described boiling 150 pages of notes down to a fifteen-page story, in the case of "The Swimmer"; however, on other occasions, he has admitted that he originally wrote that story as a full-length novel. The two views probably are reducible to one, in which the novel was treated as 150 pages of notes once he decided to turn it into a short story, since Cheever is a master at setting a plot and moving it along with scarcely a word wasted.

Over the years, Cheever has had his share of awards and prizes, beginning with a Guggenheim in 1951. He received the Benjamin Franklin Short Story Award in 1954, the O. Henry in 1955 (his stories have been in prize anthologies repeatedly); and the 1956 Award in Literature from the American Academy of Arts and Letters. In 1958 *The Wapshot Chronicle* won the National Book Award; in 1978, *The Stories of John Cheever* won both the Pulitzer Prize for Literature and the National Book Critics Circle Award. In 1979, John Cheever was the recipient of the prestigious Edward McDowell Medal in the Arts. A fellowship holder at the Artists' Colony at Yaddo (Saratoga Springs, N.Y.) in his earlier years, he has since then served on their board; he is also a member of the Selection Committee of the American Academy of Arts and Letters. He has lectured as an American cultural representative in many countries, including Russia, Italy, Bulgaria, Romania, and Canada, and his work has been widely translated.

In the past, Cheever has been a prolific writer of short stories, with a dozen sometimes appearing in a year. More recently, he has concentrated on book publication. He was thirty-one when his first collection, *The Way Some People Live*, containing thirty stories, was published; forty-five, when his first novel, *The Wapshot Chronicle*, appeared. In between, *The Enormous Radio and Other Stories*, made up of fourteen *New Yorker* tales, was published in 1953. In 1958, *The Housebreaker of Shady Hill* was well received, and the 1961 collection of stories, *Some People, Places, and Things That Will Not Appear in My Next Novel* attracted interest for its novel title and approach. In 1964, Cheever's second novel, *The Wapshot Scandal*, continued the saga of the St. Botolphs family, although most of it is set elsewhere. That same year, still another collection of short stories, *The Brigadier and the Golf Widow*, was published. Five years then intervened before the radically different *Bullet Park*, Cheever's third novel, startled critics in 1969. In 1973, the sixth volume of short stories, *The World of Apples*, re-established Cheever's reputation as a master of the short form. Then, in 1977, the novel *Falconer*, with a totally different plot and a very different cast of characters from those to which Cheever's readers were accustomed, created considerable controversy. By this time, it was apparent that Cheever was writing fiction considerably evolved in conception from that of the *New Yorker* stories of the 1950s. Then, in 1978, *The Stories of John Cheever*, a comprehensive collection going back to the period just after World War II, gave his readers a chance to review sixty-one stories, a mature life-time effort, in a single large volume. For the first time in years, a collection of short stories sat on the *New York Times* "Bestseller List" for an extended period, with a third of a million copies sold. The decision was virtually unanimous: Cheever was acknowledged as in the very front rank of living American writers.[10]

INTERVIEWS

It is inevitable, perhaps, that a writer who is so closely identified with a recognizable segment of modern life should become a public figure. Cheever has been extensively interviewed over the years, for television as well as for magazines and newspapers. He seems both to be fascinated by the experience and to be extremely chary of it. Generally, in his interviews, he has disclaimed any critical perception on his own part, and then gone on to speak with penetrating awareness of the nature of literature. He is reluctant to speak about his own writing[11] and clearly engages in diversionary tactics to get the conversation away from reference to specific stories, although he is frank and unabashed in speaking about his bouts with alcoholism, his heart attacks, his family relationships, his past use of drugs and other personal matters.

One of the first interviews with Cheever appeared in the weekly column "In and Out of Books," written by Harvey Breit in the *New York Times Book Review* in 1953.[12] It is interesting in that Cheever, at this time, is still tied closely to the short story as contrasted with the novel. After noting that publishers always want "a novel, or a number of novels . . . then *maybe* they'll take a book of stories," he points out that even Katherine Anne Porter [then in her sixtieth year] "is considered a promising novelist." Short stories are expressions of modern mobility, "determined by moving around from place to place, by the interrupted event." In contrast, he sees the novel as a nineteenth century form, based on a communal life. "The interrupted event" is synonymous with the frustration of the mid-twentieth century; "just as people are about to tell you the secret, they're transferred to another city. There's always the interruption. The way people can drop out of sight. Really drop."

It is a world of aborted relationships, incomplete meanings, frustrated desires, a reaching out of self towards a person who vanishes, a reversion of life back to the self over and over, again. That he was later able to see this world view as capable of extension to the novel indicates how much the novel itself had changed, for a writer such as Cheever, from its "nineteenth century character" to a form parallel to that of the short story by the time he wrote his own first novel.

In the years since then, Cheever has been interviewed by Lewis Nichols (Jan. 1964), and Christopher Lehmann-Haupt (April 1969) for the *New York Times Book Review* in what were essentially profiles of the man behind the books. Alwyn Lee's interview for *Time* (March 27, 1964) was in response to the appearance of *The Wapshot Scandal*, but the review and the interview resulted in a perceptive view of Cheever's art. Annette Grant's interview with Cheever was part of the series "The Art of Fiction" for the *Paris Review* series; later published in the Viking Press collection. [It is included in this volume.]

An interview that reveals as much of the interviewer as of its subject, with the two combining to give a significant response to Cheever, is that of Wilfred Sheed. Entitled "Mr. Saturday, Mr. Monday, and Mr. Cheever," it appeared in *Life,* April 18, 1969, on the occasion of the publication of *Bullet Park.* Sheed found Cheever interesting for his elusiveness. The appearance of *Falconer* resulted in a spate of profiles. A unique exchange with the writer was recorded by Cheever's daughter, Susan Cheever Cowley, herself a writer, for *Newsweek;* as might be expected, it is useful in adding to the picture of Cheever's family background, his personal beliefs, and his working habits. In March of 1977, also, John Hersey, the novelist, reported a long conversation with Cheever on the nature of the writer's craft, a piece published in tandem with the *New York Times Book Review* front page on *Falconer,* reviewed by Joan Didion. [The Hersey interview is also included in this present volume.] The following year, Hersey did a second interview with Cheever the full version of which appeared in the *Yale University Alumni Magazine,* with a substantial section reprinted in the *New York Times Book Review* (March 26, 1978). A shorter interview, by John Firth, was published in *Saturday Review* (also in association with a review of *Falconer*) on April 2, 1977.

The frequent charge that Cheever short-changes female characters may be one reason why *MS.* Magazine profiled him on the appearance of *Falconer,* a work in which appears one of the classic bitches in American fiction; however, Eleanor Munro's "Not Only I the Narrator, but I John Cheever" (April, 1977) is one of the more charming portraits of the Squire of Ossining on his home ground, sending his guest off with a load of apple wood for her fireplace at the end of the visit. During a lecture visit to Canada in the fall of 1978, Cheever was interviewed for *Thalia: A Journal of Literary Humor;* the published transcript is distinctive in that little account of Cheever's personal life intrudes upon the aesthetics of fiction as it does in many of his other interviews. In September, 1978, writing in *Horizon,* Richard Schickel combined what is essentially an overview of Cheever's work, with an interview that cut through Cheever's practical manner and produced some thoughtful response from him. A year later Cheever moved out of the *Book Review* to a full-blown public figure profile feature in the *New York Times Magazine* (October 21, 1979). Written by Jesse Kornbluth and entitled "The Cheever Chronicle," it indicated the greater stature accorded Cheever since his collected *Stories* had brought his past achievement into clearer perspective.

It was to Kornbluth that Cheever uttered a line that defines the chief limitation of the interviews as such: "To discuss one's spiritual life journalistically is impossible" (p. 29). Ten years earlier, Wilfred Sheed had remarked, with some exasperation:

> But if you wish to ferret out these and other symbols [of the inner conflicts of the modern American, in Cheever's work], the essential person *not* to

ask is John Cheever. For Cheever is one of those writers who instinctively deny everything, almost before you've asked it. The town is not his town, the house is not his house, the symbols are your problem.[13]

Sheed is right; John Cheever gives nothing away in an interview. I have watched him fielding questions after giving a reading of his work to a university group, and while he is witty and courteous and immensely well-read, he absolutely refuses to interpret his own work in any way beyond the story line. In fact, he seems to have taken Sheed in, to some extent, for the interviewer observes late in his article "Cheever gives the impression of not understanding his own work too well, and discussing it only out of politeness." On the contrary, Cheever gives the impression that he would just as soon leave *you* with that impression. Although he has taught writing, Cheever perhaps sums up his attitude towards the analysis of art best in the line "Writing well is like having a baritone voice." (Sheed, 40) You have it or you don't. However, what you do with it is another matter, as Cheever well knows.

Certain elements recur in most of the interviews,[14] particularly details of Cheever's life, such as his insistence that the birth of his children was the greatest moment of his life, that his love for his brother was the broadest—if not the deepest and richest he has ever known, that his father was the inspiration for Leander Wapshot. However, of greater ultimate meaning is the recurring of certain attitudes towards art and his own writing. While not pretentious, Cheever accepts without question the seriousness of writing as an art form. As John Leonard noted several years ago,[15] Cheever is unique in his willingness and ability to use the large and meaningful words of human experience—words such as love, virtue, honor, valor, duty—that have been out of fashion for some time, now.

Almost always, the final statement in a Cheever interview is his assertion that he is committed to a search for *radiance* and *illumination*. Personally committed to religion—"it is the legitimate concern of any adult who has experienced love"[16]—Cheever uses it very little in a direct way in his writing, but his belief in radiance is certainly mystical at bottom. Related quite clearly to this search for *illumination* is a view of Art that Cheever frequently refers to with a phrase that he borrows from his own story "The Death of Justina"; it is, he says, the ordering of experience, "the triumph over chaos." To make order out of purposelessness, this is the writer's task; it is, as Cheever repeatedly says, the obligation under which a writer functions. *Service*, then, is the social justification of the writer's work; in this sense, Cheever sees the writer as closely tied to a set of obligations, if not in his personal life, certainly in his art. (Eventually, of course, the two converge more and more.)

Much of Cheever's thought and art is tied to this premise. If creating order from chaos is his task, then the writer is not concerned with *reality*, although he may be very much concerned with *verisimilitude* to create the *illusion* of reality. "In my stories I omit anything that's primarily historical," including two world wars in *The Wapshot Chronicle*, as he told Herbert Mitgang.[17] Wilfrid Sheed has commented on a similar point in his interview with Cheever: "The aim [of Cheever's writing] is a kind of spaceless, timeless fiction in which emotions can have it out unencumbered by circumstance."[18] However, technically speaking, the more important result of this non-historicity is tied to Cheever's concept of fiction as illusion. Fiction, he has several times indicated, is a superior form of a *dream;* both are an ordering of consciousness towards a further end, "but fiction builds towards an illumination—towards a larger usefulness."[19] It is in some such sense that he equates fiction with *light* (illumination) and chaos with *darkness,* using the further equivalencies of good and evil in his second Hersey interview:

> Light and dark, very loosely, of course, mean good and evil. And one is always seeking to find out how much courage, or how much intelligence, or how much comprehension, one can bring to the choice between good and evil in one's life.[20]

Nine years earlier, in describing the "sense of form" in *Bullet Park* to Christopher Lehmann-Haupt, Cheever had mused "It's almost like shaping a dream . . . to give precisely the concord you want . . . the arch, really. It's almost the form of an arch."[21] Lehmann-Haupt reports himself as answering, in an apt phrase, "Caught the dream." It seems an accurate description of Cheever's view of successful fiction, a dream that becomes an arch tying together the universe of the inner being.

The distinction between the *illusion* of reality and reality itself in fiction is given in many variations in the Cheever interviews. In Susan Cheever Cowley's interrogation of her father at the time of the publication of *Falconer,* Cheever, with his customary justness of phrase, defined the difference between journalism and fiction: "Journalism is conscientious to the available facts. In fiction one uses the available facts merely to create a mood, an illusion. . . . [Thus] the essence of literature is always the singularity of the writer."[22]

At the opposite end of experience from illumination is confinement. "All my work deals with confinement in one shape or another, and the struggle for freedom. . . ." he told John Firth in 1977. "Do I mean freedom? Only as a metaphor for a sense of boundlessness, the possibility of rejoicing." He went on to point out (in an identification that should surprise those critics who have regarded him as a sentimentalist about his New England youth) that he had used:

> three metaphors for confinement in my books: the small New England Village [St. Botolphs], the world of affluent exurbia, and now prison. But of course, in our living we are also confined in the various emotional and erotic contracts we have formed, which one may regret, but which it is difficult to find one's way out of.[23]

Almost the exact words were repeated in the interview with Susan Cheever Cowley published the same month, and variations on them have cropped up in some of the others. Clearly Cheever does not agree with those who have seen him as an apologist for either a fake New England or a gimcrack suburbia.[24] Wilfred Sheed has referred to Cheever's assertion that illusion should prevail over reality in fiction as meaning that

> along with the calendar and the maps the author has to go. Cheever is so intent at keeping out of the way of his creations that he almost denies his own existence. . . . you have [from Cheever's stories] just the impression you are supposed to have; that the work is everything, the writer is nothing. All the answers mean the same thing: read my books. A writer's opinion will only distract you from that.[25]

On the other hand, Cheever has firmly rejected any association with the "fabulists,"[26] and is apt to speak, perhaps deceptively, of his preference for traditional authorial approaches. At the same time, he has repeatedly spoken of "nostalgia" as being both "confinement" and "a passion:"

> Nostalgia is the longing for the world we all know, or seem to have known, the world we all love, and the people in it we love. Nostalgia is also a passion, a longing not only for that which is lost to us, or which has been destroyed or burned, or which we've outgrown; it is also a force of aspiration. It is finding ourselves not in the world we love, but knowing how deeply we love, enjoying some conviction that we return or discover it, or discover the way to it.[27]

We are trapped, then, in our very loves, in our own emotional history, but perhaps it is there, too, that redemption lies. In the tension of darkness and light, mentioned earlier, in every man's heart of darkness, in the confusions of life and in tragedy: Cheever has said that in "the case of the successful degenerate, the drive into an ultimate darkness, presumably will result in light."[28] There is, then, a Jungian element in Cheever, and Cheever frequently quotes Cocteau: "Literature is a force of memory that we have not yet understood."

In the long run, the problem with interviews is that they are hunting expeditions for the man; the novelist rather than the novel is the real quarry. That tends to make the fiction a kind of bothersome intrusion; the interviewer wants to keep pushing it aside and say "Yes, but—you, now, what are *you* really like; what do you *really* think?" Interviews, thus, are frequently end-runs around the art, which the author has set up deliberately as a barrier. Cheever's reluctance to comment on his work follows from this situation. Having exposed his innermost thoughts in his writing, he seems to realize that it would result in an obscuring of them to repeat out of context some equivalent statement that must always be a reduction of their fictional and dramatic (that is, living) truth. It is the privilege of a writer, he told his daughter, *not* to have to comment on his work. The writer fulfills himself in the work, and while our interest may pursue him beyond it, Cheever himself points us back to our proper object when he tells us how we may share most fully the writer's creation:

> I know of no pleasure greater than having a piece of fiction draw together disparate incidents so that they relate to one another and confirm that feeling that life itself is a creative process, that one thing is put purposefully upon another, that what is lost in one encounter is replenished in the next, and that we possess power to make sense of what takes place.[29]

THE CRITICISM

As is true of most contemporary writers, the bulk of the criticism on Cheever has appeared in the form of reviews on the publication of one or another of the books. A short story writer whose work was not collected for the first dozen years, he received no serious attention until 1943, when *The Way Some People Live* was published by Random House in the middle of World War II. Struthers Burt, writing in *Saturday Review*, forecast a distinctive future for the writer in Army uniform: "Unless I am very much mistaken, when this war is over, John Cheever . . . will become one of the most distinguished writers; not only as a short story writer but as a novelist."[30] Pointing out in careful and thoughtful manner the difficulties of the genre, he extended high praise to Cheever's short stories, concluding that Cheever "has only two things to fear: a hardening into an especial style that might become an affectation, and a deliberate casualness and simplicity that might become the same. Otherwise the world is his." Burt's anointing of the young writer has proved to be both a blessing and a curse. In the intervening years, it has frequently been quoted, and has probably given direction to any number of critics who have assumed that Cheever did indeed fall into one of the ways of error against which Burt warned. Ironically, no one of the thirty tales in *The Way Some People Live* was revived for the massive 1978 collection of *The Stories of John Cheever*, the oldest of which dated from after the war, the author having eliminated the first sixteen years of his professional production as "embarrassingly immature."

Burt's praise not withstanding, Cheever was writing during the first few decades of what might be called the evolution towards a modern American short story, and his conception of it was more abstract than some other critics of the time appreciated. Diana Trilling, writing in the *Nation* (April 10, 1943) uttered a loud lament at the lack of a well-made plot; to read her review today is to be reminded of how thoroughly our sense of story has changed in the past four decades:

> To read the even better-than-average short story nowadays is to have an experience so tangential to the real thing that it is rather like having a conversation in a language in which one has had considerable training but in which one is still not fluent. John Cheever's stories, which for the most

part have appeared in *The New Yorker* and which are even more talented than the average stories printed in that magazine, are now collected. . . ; to read them one after another is to end with an intense feeling of frustration. Even the best . . . are strongly worded hints rather than completely communicated statements, and I am led to the conclusion that one of the troubles with short story writers today . . . is that they not only choose inarticulate characters to write about but then refuse to be articulate *for* them. It is an artificial and completely self-imposed limitation, of the same order as the fashionable time-limitation in the short story, and I suspect, that the sooner it is got rid of, the better for this branch of contemporary fiction.[31]

Certainly of all of our short story writers in recent decades, Cheever is articulate on behalf of his characters, too much so for many of the critics who followed Mrs. Trilling. Her fretfulness aside, Cheever's first book publication was auspicious enough. However, it was another ten years, in 1953, before his second book *The Enormous Radio and Other Stories* found print. James Kelly, in the *New York Times Book Review*, may have been the first to define "Cheever Country," or at least the original state of it—the author, he said,

has a territory: the correct apartment houses on New York's upper East Side and the tenants, elevator boys, and superintendents who are thrown together for the voyage. He has a subject: the abrasive loneliness of drifting people who uneasily tell themselves that things are bound to work out all right despite personal inadequacy, marital failure, the subtle tortures of genteel poverty. . . . And he has a point of view: life in the Big House is for the most part an uneasy adjustment to alien pressures, a twist of the knife, a complex of human intimacies (both wanted and unwanted) wherein naked emotion sooner or later comes to the surface.[32]

In fact Kelly recognized Cheever's strengths clearly, if not in detail. Writing in a genre that rarely receives review and only through massive achievement ever reaches critical respectability, Cheever had clearly become master of the short story technique by this time. "No American writer in business today is more on top of his genre than Mr. Cheever," said Kelly flatly.

Cheever's oft-quoted line, "The first canon of aesthetics is interest," and his insistence that "story" is a crucial ingredient of fiction for which "[I] would fight . . . with my life" are undoubtedly due to his having written so large a number of short stories over the first three decades of his working life. Where writers of lesser imagination have stretched a brief tale out to a novel a half dozen times over a twenty or thirty-year period, Cheever has poured forth in a year twice that many stories in which both character and circumstance sparkle with vivid interest. Critics are like children in that they like a dependable world; long accustomed to Cheever's identity as a writer of short stories, they were disconcerted by his emergence in the late '50s as a novelist. He was getting out of his depth, it was commonly said. Yet, while none of his novels are excessively long, all are crammed with incident, all fulfill the Cheever First Canon of Aesthetics. He is, in fact, printed proof that a true journeyman in the short story form may become eminently qualified as a novelist. As William Peden, writing in 1956, said of Cheever's miniature saga of middle-class life before and just after the war, "The Day the Pig Fell in the Well:" "This recreation of the Nudd family possesses a variety of character and incident more customarily associated with the novel than with the short story. Around this 'chronicle of small disaster' hovers a kind of Indian summer warmth; like Galsworthy. . . . there is no finer present-day writer of short fiction than John Cheever."[33]

The appearance of *The Wapshot Chronicle* in 1957 and *The Wapshot Scandal* in 1964 led to the first real critical reaction for Cheever; he was now a novelist indisputably, with a National Book Award to certify his status. However, while some of his reviewers, including Joan Didion, Elizabeth Hardwick, Granville Hicks, Elizabeth Janeway, and others, were perceptive in pointing out both his strength and his weaknesses, the limitations of the review, with its few columns of description, meant that such critics scarcely had time to begin to think in any active way about the deeper implications of what they were reading. Even with two novels, even though it was more than thirty years since he had first published fiction, Cheever was labeled with that curse of eternal youthful promise, the condescending passing nod from critics, beyond which few short story writers ever move. Having been recognized as a master in the minor league of the short story, he found himself regarded, perforce, as properly there, as a questionable mutant in the role of novelist.

Among those critics of fiction in the 1960s who considered Cheever's work in a more permanent form than that of periodical reviews, both Ihab Hassan, in his *Radical Innocence* (1961) and John Aldridge (1966) asked a number of serious questions about the import of his work; both, however, addressed their demands more firmly than they looked at his work, and both seemed to be caught in his style.[34] However, some thoughtful analysis was beginning to emerge in the critical journals. In 1963 and 1964, for example, two essays by Frederick Bracher, "John Cheever and Comedy," and "John Cheever: A Vision of the World" placed him in the midst of larger literary concerns than had most of the reviews. Cheever's mythic dimension was recognized and extended, and casual earlier references that linked his name with that of Dante or Kafka suddenly had a justification. (It is a mark, too, of the questionable justice done to serious major writers when they are still at full gallop that we invariably legitimize them by referring to them as "The Dante of the Suburbs," as "our Chekhov" and the like. Certainly Cheever has had more such labels attached to him than any other author of his generation, despite his unique signature as a writer of fiction.)[35]

However, one result of the darker tones in *The Wapshot Scandal* over the *Chronicle*—each of the four first novels has been increasingly complex and abstract—was that the reviewers were pushed towards a more serious critical stance. George Garrett's "John Cheever and the Charms of Innocence: The Craft of *The Wapshot Scandal*" clearly went well beyond description of a new book, as did Joan Didion's "The Way We Live Now," the title of which, playing off that of Cheever's first collection, recognized how fully Cheever had anticipated the shift in modern life over a quarter of a century. By the end of the sixties, Clinton Burhans identified Cheever's concerns as crucial to our time and collective situation:

> This profound and complex sense of the past [i.e. man as a sensitive being shaped by his past] informs the deepest levels of Cheever's apprehensive concerns with the present and future and explains his perplexed feeling of standing "in a quagmire, looking into a tear in the sky." Given man's permanent existential condition and his inescapable relationship to his particular past, what, Cheever wonders, is man doing to himself in the present and what does it forbode for the future? Exploring these questions, Cheever centers on two predominant problems: *one*, the vast and unparalleled changes which characterize the contemporary world; and *two*, the rate of change which these reflect and its frightening significance.[36]

Burhans' essay opens up a vast territory that, despite some interest by a few later critics, has yet to be thoroughly explored. A writer who stands out because of a distinctive style, who works in serious areas of concern and has at the same time a strong sense of the absurdity of reality juxtaposed against the ideal, tends to evoke impatience or even hostility among his contemporaries to a far greater extent than more neutral writers; conversely, they are much easier to love after they are gone, when the writings, displaying a similar character, take the place of the person, in our attention. We love the sweating laborer and distrust the man of easy facility. Throughout his life Cheever has regularly been taken as a lesser thinker because, ironically, he writes too well. It was Austin Warren who somewhere noted, in discussing the suspicion with which rhetoric was regarded in mid-century, that because a thing was well said, it was not necessarily said badly.

In fact, Cheever's masterful style and use of language generally has been noted by virtually every reviewer and critic since he began to receive attention. John Leonard's observation that the English language is lucky to have Cheever writing in it is an opinion that none of Cheever's critics have disputed. Aside from his ability to use "large words" expressive of emotional values without sounding sententious or spurious, Cheever has both an eye and an ear for metaphor that captures meaning very precisely and with that shock of pleasure normally associated with poetry. As John

Gardner has expressed it, "The reason Cheever is a great writer—besides his command of literary form, impeccable style, and unsentimental compassion—is that what he says seems true."[37]

He not only frequently expresses states of mind through striking imagery ("the sound of the dragon's tail moving over dead leaves"), his writing moves in parallel patterns up to the point of overall fable. Granville Hicks may speak of *The Wapshot Scandal* as "in a peculiarly poignant way . . . a novel of and for our time,"[38] but Joseph McElroy is simply nailing down the same point when he says that "Cheever draws a fine line of fable through his fiction and thus claims freedoms—if also license—as magical as the truth told by his exact words and magnetic images. That is why his art seems independent of our 'spatchcocked' American reality yet eerily reflective of it."[39] Richard Rupp brushes against the same quality when he speaks of Cheever's "ceremonial style: the significant action, as ceremonious and vital as it is, works itself out in formal ritualized gestures," and goes on to say that it "reflects the essential need of contemporary life, the need for appropriate forms. . . . the act of writing is itself a ceremonial act that he invites his reader to share."[40] This sharing of creation, as ceremony, takes place in all great literary art, of course; the metaphor or the image or the fable becomes meaning only within the reader, a charge implanted there by the artist to explode according to a certain design.

Where, then, has criticism still to go in the exploration of John Cheever's work? The answer is: almost everywhere. To date, there have been only two books of criticism published on Cheever; appropriate to their purpose, each is general and introductory.[41] [The authors, Samuel Coale and Lynne Waldeland, are represented in this collection with a new essay in each case.] Although a half dozen Ph.D. dissertations have been completed on Cheever's work, none has been published as yet. This present volume includes thirty-five pieces, of which many are new essays written specifically for this collection by scholars who had written on Cheever earlier. While new approaches to the fiction are increasingly apparent, a body of work as large as that created by Cheever represents a mountain of material that will not soon be exhausted. To date, most analyses of his themes remain cursory, most discussion of his style is general, structural and formal approaches to the individual works have been attempted in only a few cases.

It is within that framework of opportunity that *Critical Essays on John Cheever* stands as a seminal collection. The authors who speak here are among the first to recognize formally one of the major writers of modern-day American fiction. Through their insights the work of John Cheever has been preserved and made increasingly accessible to the many thousands of future readers who will find in the unique mind of this master of prose an understanding of an age and themselves that they would be the poorer for not having. If, in John Leonard's phrase, the

English language is lucky that John Cheever writes in it, the truly fortunate are those of us who read through his words of a brighter, deeper, more significant, more human, more passionate, and more visible world, of both chaos and of triumph over chaos.

University of Ottawa (Canada)   R. G. Collins

Notes

1. John Leonard, "Cheever to Roth to Malamud," *Atlantic Monthly*, June 1973, p. 112.

2. John Aldridge, *Time to Murder and Create* (New York: David McKay and Co., 1966), p. 171.

3. John Gardner, "On Miracle Row," *Saturday Review*, 4 (2 April 1977), 20.

4. Irving Howe, "Realities and Fictions," *Partisan Review*, 26 (1959), 131.

5. Aldridge, p. 171.

6. Isa Kapp, "Writers and Writing: The Cheerless World of John Cheever," *The New Leader*, 61 (11 September 1978), 16–17.

7. Cynthia Ozick, "Cheever's Yankee Heritage," *Antioch Review*, 24 (Summer 1964), 267.

8. Joan Didion, "Falconer," *New York Times Book Review*, 6 March 1977, p. 1.

9. Cheever always refers to his "first publication" as having been at the age of seventeen, and most references repeat that statement. Since he was born on 27 May 1912, it is clear that he was well past his eighteenth birthday when "Expelled" appeared in October 1930. Nonetheless, it remains a remarkably early age to achieve significant publication.

10. Already in proofs when Cheever's fifth novel *Oh, What a Paradise It Seems*, appeared in March 1982, this volume necessarily omits consideration of that work.

11. Wilfred Sheed, "Mr. Saturday, Mr. Monday, and Mr. Cheever," *Life*, 8 April 1969, p. 39.

12. Harvey Breit, "Big Interruption," *New York Times Book Review*, 10 May 1953, p. 8.

13. Wilfred Sheed, 39.

14. I have not referred here to the television interviews given by Cheever, notably those on PBS with Dick Cavett, because of the difficulty of securing transcripts. They are, however, listed in the Coates Bibliography and are well worth the watching, if they should be telecast again.

15. "Cheever to Roth to Malamud," 112–116.

16. John Hersey, "John Cheever, Boy and Man," *New York Times Book Review*, 26 March 1978, p. 34.

17. Herbert Mitgang, "Behind the Best Sellers: John Cheever," *New York Times Book Review*, 28 January 1979, p. 36.

18. Sheed, 95.

19. John Hersey, "Talk with John Cheever," *New York Times Book Review*, 6 March 1977, p. 28.

20. Hersey, "John Cheever, Boy and Man," 32.

21. Christopher Lehmann-Haupt, "Talk with John Cheever," *New York Times Book Review*, 27 April 1969, p. 44.

22. Susan Cheever Cowley, "A Duet of Cheevers," *Newsweek*, 14 March 1977, pp. 70, 73.

23. John Firth, "Talking with John Cheever," *Saturday Review*, 2 April 1977, p. 20.

24. See, for example, Warren Sloat, "Bullet Park," *Commonweal*, 90 (9 May 1969), 241–42.

25. Sheed, 45.

26. R. G. Collins and J. Tavernier-Courbin, "An Interview with John Cheever," *Thalia: Studies in Literary Humor*, Autumn 1978, p. 7.

27. Hersey, "Cheever, Man and Boy," 32.

28. Hersey, "Talk with John Cheever," 28.

29. Alwyn Lee, "Ovid in Ossining," *Time*, 27 March 1964, p. 69.

30. Struthers Burt, "John Cheever's Sense of Drama," *Saturday Review*, 30 April 1943, p. 9.

31. Diana Trilling, "Fiction in Review," *Nation*, 10 April 1943, p. 533.

32. James Kelly, "The Have-Not-Enoughs," *New York Times Book Review*, 10 May 1953, p. 21.

33. William Peden, "Four Cameos," *Saturday Review*, 39 (8 December 1956), 16.

34. Ihab Hassan, "Encounter with Possibility—II" in his *Radical Innocence* (Princeton: Princeton University Press, 1961) pp. 187–94; Aldridge, "John Cheever and the Soft Sell of Disaster," in his *Time to Murder and Create*, pp. 171–177.

35. Apropos of Cheever's identification with myth-makers of the past, cf. Richard Gilman, "Dante of Suburbia," *Commonweal*, 69 (19 December 1958), 320; Frank J. Warnke, "Cheever's Inferno," *New Republic* 144 (15 May 1961), 18; among others, Larry Woiwode, "Cheever at His Best: As If He Were Growing Younger," *Times Book Review*, 13 May 1973, pp. 1, 26, draws the comparison with Chekhov in some detail. "Cheever," he says, "seems to be the only present writer able to produce enduring short classics. . . . " Cheever himself frequently refers to Chekhov and has lectured on him. Pressed by John Hersey on his identity as the "American Chekhov," Cheever responded: "I love Chekhov very much. He was an innovator—stories that seemed to the unknowing to have no endings but had instead a whole new inner structure" ("Talk with John Cheever," 26).

36. The Burhans' essay, included in the present volume, originally appeared in *Twentieth Century Literature* 14 (January 1969), 187–98.

37. John Gardner, 3. Gardner has always been a perceptive reader of Cheever's novels; in 1971, two years after the publication of *Bullet Park*, he wrote a thoughtful reconsideration of the book, "Witchcraft in Bullet Park," *New York Times Book Review*, 24 October 1971, pp. 2, 24, which corrected some of the misreadings that had appeared at the time of original publication.

38. Granville Hicks, "Where Have All the Roses Gone?" *Saturday Review*, 47 (4 January 1964), 76.

39. Joseph McElroy, "*Falconer* by John Cheever," *New Republic*, 176 (26 March 1977), 88–89.

40. Richard Rupp, *Celebration in Postwar American Fiction* (Coral Gables, Florida: University of Miami Press, 1970), pp. 27, 39.

41. Samuel Coale, *John Cheever* [Modern Language Monograph Series] (N.Y.: Frederick Ungar Publishing Co., 1977); Lynne Waldeland, *John Cheever* [Twayne American Authors Series] (Boston: G. K. Hall, 1979).

REVIEWS:
SHORT STORIES

John Cheever's Sense of Drama

Struthers Burt*

Unless I am very much mistaken, when this war is over, John Cheever—he is now in the army—will become one of the most distinguished writers, not only as a short story writer but as a novelist. Indeed, if he wishes to perform that ancient triple-feat, not as popular now as it was twenty years ago in the time of Galsworthy and Bennett and their fellows, he can be a playwright too, for he has all the necessary signs and characteristics. The sense of drama in ordinary events and people; the underlying and universal importance of the outwardly unimportant; a deep feeling for the perversities and contradictions, the worth and unexpected dignity of life, its ironies, comedies, and tragedies. All of this explained in a style of his own, brief, apparently casual, but carefully selected; unaccented until the accent is needed. Meanwhile, he has published the best volume of short stories I have come across in a long while, and that is a much more important event in American writing than most people realize.

The short story is a curious and especial thing, a delicate and restricted medium in which many have walked, but few succeeded. It is like the sonnet in poetry; the only artificial (I mean in technique, not content) form of poetry that has ever been able to make itself thoroughly at home within the realms of that magnificent, impatient, sensible, and beautiful mode of human expression, the English language, and, like the sonnet, the short story has, or should have, the same limitations of space, of concentrated emotion, of characters, of theme and events. Never by any chance should it be the scenario, the skeleton, of something longer. Its strength, like the sonnet's, comes from deep emotion and perception, and, when necessary, passion, beating against the inescapable form that encircles it. As in the sonnet, as indeed in all good poetry, not a word or line, or figure of speech, or simile, must be amiss or superfluous. The author has just so many minutes in which to be of value, and the contest—the selection—in his mind is between what he would like to say, and what he should say; the search is for the inevitable phrase and sentence and

*From *Saturday Review*, 26 (24 April 1943), 9. Copyright 1943 by *Saturday Review*.
Reprinted with permission. All rights reserved.

description that contain the final illumination but which, at the same time, seem inevitable and natural.

As a result, probably not more than a score of truly great short stories have ever been written. The same holds true of sonnets. Even the great masters of the short story, Chekhov, Turgeniev, Maupassant, Kipling, O. Henry in his better moments, and others, only reached their culmination in a few instances. The short story, like electricity, gains its power through its amperage. It is a bullet whose penetration is due to a force poured through a narrow channel. Of all forms of writing it is the most difficult.

The present volume consists of thirty short stories most of which have appeared in the *New Yorker*, the *Yale Review*, and *Story* magazine, and one can see the compression used, for the book is only two hundred and fifty-six pages long. Many of the stories are only a few pages in length, a thousand, twelve hundred words; and at least half of them are eminently successful; a quarter are far above the average; all are well done; and only a couple fail. "Of Love; A Testimony," except for its title, is one of the best love stories I have ever read. There is a curious and interesting development in the book, and in the procession of the stories—the way they are placed—that ties the volume together and gives it almost the feeling of a novel despite the inevitable lack of connection between any short stories. The earlier stories have to do with the troubled, frustrated, apparently futile years of 1939 and 1941; and then there are some beautifully told stories of the average American—the average American with a college degree, the same suburbanite—actually at war, but still in this country. This gives the book the interest and importance of a progress toward Fate; and so there's a classic feeling to it.

No one can tell how many artists, musicians, writers, painters, sculptors, are in our armed forces. They will not emerge for some years yet. When they do there should be something interesting, for these younger men have learned a lot, apparently, and apparently it's part of their make-up. They are just as honest and ruthless as their predecessors, perhaps even more so, but they have regained in some mysterious way their belief in irony and pity and the catharsis, which despite the Greeks, and Anatole France, the last who announced their necessity, have for some time been regarded as sentimental clichés.

John Cheever has only two things to fear; a hardening into an especial style that might become an affectation, and a deliberate casualness and simplicity that might become the same. Otherwise, the world is his.

New England and Hollywood

Morris Freedman*

The modern short story ranges from the overinflated bromide, the kind of thing that slicks and certain of the ladies' magazines do so neatly, to the highly concentrated, short novel, complex and ambiguous, which we find sometimes in the little magazines and in *The New Yorker*. The extremes of this gamut may be seen in the collections of Budd Schulberg and John Cheever. Where Schulberg elaborates into a full story the commonplace of a child's discovery of the world's untrustworthiness (which never, in any case, occurs in a moment, as Schulberg with a Hollywood sense of economy would have us believe), Cheever tosses off, in part of a sentence, a far more perceptive comment about a neglected child's premature instinct of self-protection: "[The child and the nurse] quarreled a good deal when they were alone, and they quarreled like adults, with a cunning knowledge of each other's frailties."

Schulberg, the son of a Hollywood producer and born and raised there, seems congenitally unable to see the world except through the special lenses developed by Hemingway (the sentimentalized prize fight and the brutalized deep-sea fishing stories) or Fitzgerald (the beautiful rich girl with a suicidal drive); when he writes of Hollywood it is with the glib cynicism the movies have perfected for self-portraits. His capacity for originality in observation or tone is so meager, so constricted or so undeveloped, that minor perceptions emerge as momentous revelations and obvious flourishes of style betray an excessive labor. Cheever, a product of the Hebraic New England conscience, implacable as a Kafkaesque judge, cuts through the layers of tawdry pretense and elaborate alibi while arraigning his defendants—all of them guilty, often as vaguely and as profoundly as Kafka's people—of some breach against the mysterious deity of honest grace and lightness and self-understanding. Cheever's intelligence is startling and disturbing in its cold superiority as he bares a human problem to the bone, but his fine and controlled compassion is deep and thoughtful and genuine. Schulberg can only give us in the end pale reproductions of the usual contempt for the bully, the anti-Negro sadist, the cheap entertainment celebrity; the stimulus is only of a

*Reprinted from *Commentary*, October 1953, by permission; all rights reserved.

memory of a distant response, long ago buried in the store of attitudes we take for granted. . . .

Cheever's *bête noir* is New York City. It is a place that has the quality of hell, almost literally at some moments: "They sat together with their children through the sooty twilights, when the city to the south burns like a Bessemer furnace, and the air smells of coal, and the wet boulders shine like slag, and the Park itself seems like a strip of woods on the edge of a coal town." The havoc the city works on genuine human beings is Cheever's theme. The insanities connected with city life are simultaneously harrowing and hilarious. Perhaps the most moving story in the book, "O City of Broken Dreams," is also the funniest. A small-town bus driver and his family are lured to the big city by an irresponsible, fancy-talking Broadway producer who has read two acts of a play the driver has written. While the driver is waiting for an executive in a Radio City office, the secretary offers to sell him fresh farm eggs or costume jewelry wholesale; the unpaid butler of a Park Avenue establishment trails a bloody bandage from his finger over the carpets as he berates his employer who, at the moment, is occupied in a floating crap game in Harlem.

At first reading one comes away with a sense that Cheever's characters are sunk in a mire of unrelieved hopelessness. A New England farmer and daughter are permanently and callously corrupted into hard-bitten eccentricity by a New York Communist couple who come to the area one year to help lead a strike. The wife of a placid marriage one day finds her radio tuning in the other apartments in her building; the dirty private activity of her neighbors overpowers her and detonates the buried bomb of secrets in her own life. An unhappy couple obsessively retrace the early events of their marriage in a forlorn attempt to recapture the feelings that originally motivated them.

But the volume as a whole yields the secret of coping with the eternal imminence of disaster which is living. In three stories Cheever transcends the bleakness of Kafka; the other stories, then, must be read as demonstrations not of what Cheever believes life must inevitably be, but of what it should not be, of what we should fight against it becoming. "The Pot of Gold" concludes with the husband turning to his family for richness and away from the mad schemes for success which have driven him for so long. In "The Cure," a husband separated from his wife is slowly disintegrating in his loneliness, succumbing to a series of personal horrors in the improbable and therefore all the more macabre settings of Madison Avenue and suburbia, until he goes back to her and his children to save himself. In "Goodbye, My Brother," the first story, Cheever movingly attacks the narrow-minded enemies of instinct and self-fulfillment. Salvation lies in meeting the unavoidable horror head on, and engaging it with one's best talents, not obscuring it or fleeing from it.

It is no accident, of course, that Cheever should be so much more Hebraically serious, both in his observation and in his prophecy, than

Schulberg. Cheever, by reason of his New England background, has breathed into his system that Biblical concentration on the moral nature of reality, on the inescapable essence of a word or an act, which we find in Hawthorne, Melville, and James; and his good sense has kept him from beclouding his vision with what Steven Marcus criticized in his recent survey of the contemporary American short story, the distorted Puritan search for the overall structural connections in events. Cheever's great advantage over Schulberg is that he has not had to overcome the effect of a wrenching discontinuity with the past.

It is painful to contrast Schulberg with Cheever, for his intentions are so clearly to achieve the urbane subtlety, the sense of self-identity, the intelligent and easy maturity, which are Cheever's—simply by inheritance, as it were. . . .

The Weeding-Out Process

David Ray*

"Fiction can no longer operate as a sixth-rate boardinghouse," John Cheever announces in "Some People, Places, and Things That Will Not Appear in My Next Novel," a volume of stories and satirical notations indicting all that is "sloppy" in American fiction. Readers who object to the sprawling, all-inclusive novels of Thomas Wolfe, or who prefer John O'Hara's stories to his novels, will be happy to see Cheever redirecting the writer to the task of "eviction" of characters who have commanded the artist's involuntary attention, threatening to corrupt his future work.

Though Cheever never refers to total recall as a curse rather than a gift, he clearly feels that both the writer and the mature man—aware of the nearness of madness and death, and thus interested in the "desperate composure" that makes life meaningful, if not altogether tidy—should limit what they allow to claim their attention. Consequently these stories by Mr. Cheever are about people who must be rejected from disciplined lives.

The gallery of "depraved acquaintances" includes a brother whose "aura of smallness" is brought out by his selfishness about an inherited lowboy, his love for which leads to the evocation of family ghosts and his own deterioration; a shipboard friend whose promiscuity represents the lure of "carnal anarchy"; and a drunken, jig-dancing, dish-breaking neighbor who, though inviting pity, threatens to throw into chaos the life of anyone foolish enough to befriend him. Such stories about rejection, frequently of the socially undesirable, might provoke accusations of snobbery if Cheever did not make it clear—by rejecting a few Italian

*From *Saturday Review*, 44 (27 May 1961), 20. Copyright © 1961 by *Saturday Review*.

aristocrats along with American boors—that he is up to something much more serious. He is asking a major question: "Where does responsibility to another end and to one's own life begin?" Just as writers are corrupted when certain characters run away with their stories, lives are corrupted when certain acquaintances, however fascinating, intrude. It takes courage to reject such intrusions in the interests of happiness and sanity. In asserting this theme allegorically, Cheever clearly feels that life is too short to permit disruption and chaos.

Though Cheever "rejects" these characters whose claim on his attention is "intense but not final," he has given them as loving and three-dimensional a life as any possible in his anticipated novel. Even the most obnoxious of them are charmers, and in feeling Cheever's regret as he evicts them one wonders if writing people out of one's system isn't the most courageous of all methods of eviction, and the most charitable. For it is not so much their personalities Cheever rejects as their responses to life. In chronicling the lives of those who foolishly rely on the past, wealth, or travel for salvation, Cheever directs a sacrificial search for firmer values. This is not the search of a snob, but of an enlightened Puritan aware that the victims of such rejections—made in the interests of keeping life meaningful and the search for love successful—often have an easier ability to survive than those who must reject them. In his best story, "The Scarlet Moving Van," Cheever shows that those who would ruin one's life if their demands were met are often self-sufficient and do not need the charities they provoke.

The two themes, then, of the artist's responsibility to control what claims his attention, and man's need to exercise an equivalent concern in his life, mesh beautifully in this book. In rejecting all approaches that seem unworthy, that seem to embrace chaos rather than life as Cheever's (and Thoreau's) God meant it to be lived, the author eloquently insists that the maintenance of sanity is so difficult today that it takes some arranging to manage it. As an investigation of the contemporary writer's search for discipline, this book will stand as a personal and esthetic document of the first magnitude; as a work of fiction dramatizing modern man's search for order it will provide a rich bundle of the wit, insight, and pictorial abilities to which Cheever's readers have long been accustomed.

Literate, Witty, Civilized

John Wain*

I don't know what goes on in the minds of very young people, but to most of us grown-ups there comes a sense, very often, of having started

*Reprinted with permission from *New Republic*, 168 (26 May 1973), 24–26.

our lives amid the outlines of a civilization and having watched them melt away, leaving a featureless desert; quite a suitable environment for prayer and meditation, and also for nameless crimes, but very unfavorable for the practice of ordinary virtues such as tolerance or unselfishness. Goodness knows, the crumbling away of values has been going on for 200 years, but anyone born, as I was, in the 1920s did at least grow up with the feeling that, though metaphysical guidelines had vanished, social ones remained; even though we didn't "believe in God," we accepted a system of values derived from Christianity and our emotions attached to these, so that we recognized love, courage, self-sacrifice, generosity, as virtues and cruelty and meanness as vices. This gave a meaningful basis for action; World War II, for instance, was fought not just from nationalistic competitiveness but from a desire to rid the world of Auschwitz and Buchenwald, the swastika and the goose-step; from the point of view of the new morality, the worship of "alienation" as a principle and the fierce-eyed preaching of meaninglessness and negativism, it is impossible to see how these things could be judged adversely, let alone resisted at the cost of one's life. Can we, in fact, go on inhabiting the planet unless we have something to believe in? As the English critic A. E. Dyson has remarked, "The notes of despair, negation, absurdity, suffering now echo through our literature; and it is probable that when loyalties to everything outside the self have been successfully banished, loyalty to the self will finally fail." In which case, good-bye Charlie.

Mr. Cheever tackles this problem very directly; most directly of all in his title story, "The World of Apples." This tells how an old and famous poet, loaded with honors and near the end of his life, was overwhelmed by an obsession with sexual and defecatory dirt and finally managed to shake it off. The story is told simply and unpretentiously, with nothing much in the way of invention and without the little fanciful melismata that so often enliven the other stories in the book. The old poet has always associated himself with sanity and strength. Of the five other poets of his generation with whom he has customarily been grouped, four committed suicide and the fifth died of drink. He himself has avoided making this kind of mess, not out of adherence to any positive system of belief such as a religion, but just from a personal conviction that it won't do.

> Poetry was a lasting glory and he was determined that the final act of a poet's life should not—as had been the case with Z—be played out in a dirty room with twenty-three empty gin bottles. Since he could not deny the connection between brilliance and tragedy he seemed determined to bludgeon it.

The story is an account of how the poet almost lost that balance and ultimately recovered it. One day a visitor takes him for a trip into the forest. He steps aside from the path to relieve himself and stumbles on a couple making love. The sudden sight puts in motion a train of thoughts and images which he cannot stop. It is not just that he broods on copulation: it is that his broodings are uniformly obscene—what we would call, if the word still had any meaning in the world rigged up for us by the Andy Warhols and the Ken Tynans, "dirty-minded." It is a real crisis; it calls into question the whole of his life's achievement, which at his age he cannot possibly go back over and rework. He has written a famous volume of poems, *The World of Apples* (the Frostian association is obviously quite intentional, even insistent) in which the qualities celebrated are those of sun and air and freshness and soil and patient ripening; the old poet is shown as living in a country villa in Italy, and indeed his imaginative world seems to be that of Virgil in the Georgics. His poems celebrate "the welcoming universe, the rain wind that sounded through the world of apples." Now suddenly these things seem unreal. Has he been a dupe, his life wasted on things which appeared interesting only because of the angle at which they were posed?

> What was it that he had lost? It seemed then to be a sense of pride, an aureole of lightness and valor, a kind of crown. He seemed to hold the crown up to scrutiny and what did he find? Was it merely some ancient fear of Daddy's razor strap and Mummy's scowl, some childish subservience to the bullying world? He well knew his instincts to be rowdy, abundant, and indiscreet and had he allowed the world and all its tongues to impose upon him some structure of transparent values for the convenience of a conservative economy, an established church, and a bellicose army and navy?

At this point, presumably, the most characteristic denizens of the world of today would answer with an emphatic Yes. As they would see it, the old man has at last seen the light of revelation and unchained his Id, liberating it from the domination of Ego and the even more villainous Super-Ego, who between them are responsible for this tribe of monsters—the economy, the church and the armed forces. It may be a little late in the day, but not fatally so, since he is not impotent (the story specifically says that, to try to restore his mental balance, he has intercourse with his housekeeper, who "was always happy to accommodate him"). Presumably there is more rejoicing in the priapic heaven over one sinner who repents than over half-a-dozen saints; this must be one of the sources of the crusading zeal behind contemporary porno-eroticism, where it is not simply concerned with making money.

Mr. Cheever's answer, on the contrary (and I think we are here definitely required to contravene D. H. Lawrence's maxim and identify the "artist" with the "tale") is an equally emphatic No. To him, the poet's collapse into dirty-mindedness is that and nothing more. It is something to be climbed out of, like a depressive illness. The exact steps by which he climbs out of it are, in my opinion, less memorable than the fact that he is determined to climb out, and his inventor, the author, is determined that he shall. If I were in a niggling frame of mind I could even find fault with the way the story is resolved. The old poet hears from his housekeeper about a sacred statue in "the old church of Monte Giordano," the statue of an angel which has the power to purify men's thoughts. He undertakes a pilgrimage to the statue, carrying with him the customary gift; the load begins to lift, and on the way home he comes across a cold, deep hillside stream and suddenly remembers how he saw his father, a Vermont farmer, bathing in such a stream as an old man like himself. He does the same, "bellowing like his father," and seems "at last to be himself." Liberated, he spends the remaining months of his life writing "a long poem on the inalienable dignity of light and air." And the story unequivocally represents this as a happy ending.

I find this story extremely interesting. Not that it is, as an example of literary art, as good as some of the other stories in the volume. But the fact that Mr. Cheever has chosen the title of this story for the masthead of the whole book, and has placed it last in the volume (traditionally a point of emphasis), combined as it is with the air of conviction, of getting down to bedrock, which pervades it, brings the tale firmly into the foreground. Mr. Cheever is *saying* something, and he is evidently not afraid of being laughed at by people who accept the notions currently "in." If you showed this story to the kind of person who keeps the box office happy at the Theater of Total Copulation and Public Masturbation, he or she would have a great deal of superior fun at the expense of such worn-out steps to regeneration as the shrine in a church and the immersion in cold water. Weren't "cold baths," he or she would recall, one of the two bastions against self-abuse in the English public school, the other being "long walks"? And where did it all lead except to frustration, leading in turn to the economy, the church, the army and the navy? We are here in the presence of a genuine difference of opinion, a real fork in the road at which the individual has to declare a choice. Personally I am happy to cast my vote with Mr. Cheever's. His protagonist is not a prude or, in the limiting sense, a self-denier; the episode with the housekeeper is presumably brought in to establish this, and in case it is still in doubt Mr. Cheever has him turn over the pages of Petronius and Juvenal and approve of their "candid and innocent accounts of sexual merriment." What he doesn't do is reach down his well-thumbed copy of the Marquis de Sade's *Les 120 Journées de Sodom* and read the hallowed pages once more, exclaiming reverently over the Divine Marquis' fearless devotion to truth and the scandal of his martyrdom at the hands of a hypocritical society. He doesn't, in other words, equate "sexual merriment" with the infliction of pain, the reduction of other human beings to objects which must be systematically maltreated and destroyed in the search for self-fulfillment. He tries to reconcile the sexual instinct with "the rainy wind that sounds though the world of apples" rather than with "alienation." And in this he surely shows a tenacious hold on human wisdom.

My excuse for devoting so much space to this one story in Mr. Cheever's collection is that it sets the keynote. There is another story just as bedrock and affirmative—and, purely as a story, better written and more convincing—called "Artemis, the Honest Well Digger," which is nothing more nor less than a study in innocence, an attempt to hold our attention with the portrayal of a man with no harm in him. It succeeds brilliantly, in part because of the deftness with which the hero is shown against the backdrop of just about every kind of evil the modern world abounds in—situation follows situation in a rapid and economical series, so skillfully projected that, though Mr. Cheever of course contrived them, they don't seem what one calls "contrived."

Now, because Mr. Cheever has written a volume of stories which tend to show people as being motivated by old-style feelings like love and loyalty and kindness and consideration for others and protectiveness toward the weak (*e.g.*, children), one doesn't want to represent him as preaching. It is merely that every work of art, like every creation of any kind, comes out of a system of values and preferences, and this is a book by a gifted and established writer which doesn't, for once, seem to come out of negativism, alienation, despair of the human condition and frantic self-gratification in whatever horrifying ways suggest themselves. One meets people in everyday life who have these old-fashioned values, and perhaps the shortest way to convey the rare quality of Mr. Cheever's book is to say that here, for a wonder, we have a modern work of literature in which people behave as decently as they generally do in real life, rather than behaving like sick fiends. . . .

The Hero on the 5:42:
John Cheever's Short Fiction

Stephen C. Moore*

Just about ten years ago John Aldridge wrote in *Time to Murder and Create* that Cheever was "one of the most grievously underdiscussed important writers we have at the present time." He had been cursed with a "kind of good housekeeping seal of middlebrow literary approval"; he was said to be "a paid moralist of the button-down-collar Establishment." Of course, as Aldridge added, "Cheever has . . . all along been unfortunate in the company his work has kept." By that he meant *The New Yorker*, a *Time* magazine cover story, the National Book Award; Cheever was recognized as a writer of middlebrow-popular sensibilities. He spoke to, and continues to speak to, an audience that is indeed instructed by *New Yorker* fiction.

*Reprinted with permission from *The Western Humanities Review*, 30, No. 2 (Spring 1976), 147–52.

But Cheever has used the seeming conventions of *New Yorker* fiction to create a form of short fiction that transcends the conventions without quite violating them. His best stories move from a base in a mimetic presentation of surface reality—the *scenery* of apparently successful American middle class life—to fables of heroism. Superficially, his people seem like the gray flannel suited men of another decade; on the surface, they are "antiheroes," stock figures in American popular writing of the recent past. In fact, they are desperate men driven to defending themselves from and against the culture. The stories chronicle a final statement against the decay of youth and the futility of action ("O Youth and Beauty!"), anxiety about failure that is close to the heart of American adult experience ("The Swimmer"), madness ("The Ocean"), the need to exercise some control over one's life ("The Music Teacher"), and the inevitable confrontation in the problem of commitment ("The Scarlet Moving Van"). The stories become fables *about* heroism—even if the central characters are not quite in themselves heroes: directly and obliquely, they must face action, responsibility, anxiety, and failure. Even in the most recent of his published stories, "The World of Apples"—and the battleground is there far removed from the fronts of suburban America, where an old and honored poet fights against a final sickness in his soul, where he finally asserts and triumphs with the forces of health and wholeness over sickness and filth—Cheever is giving us a man who is joined in deadly battle.

Like Randall Patrick McMurphy of Kesey's *One Flew Over the Cuckoo's Nest* and Eliot Rosewater of Kurt Vonnegut's *God Bless You, Mr. Rosewater*, Cheever's people are "mythic," they are exaggerated, caricatures, characters who at first seem "real" and yet who move out of the conventions of middlebrow realistic fiction into another territory. That territory is one of the few ways of suggesting American experience at the present. It is one of Cheever's most telling achievements to have used the machinery of the conventional realistic story—for he is the teller of stories to the middle class—to imply and hint at a quality of experience that defies the limitations of his genre. The Cheever hero faces not the problem of the West, the frontier, the Indian, or the wilderness as it was stated and evoked in American writing of another time; the wilderness is now on the 5:42 for Bullet Park, the third martini, falling in love with the baby sitter, the swimming pools across Westchester County. Cheever's country is mostly dour and disappointing and yet this is not a fashionable restatement, restructuring of the landscape of the Wasteland, now the zombies at the cocktail party, the stupefying accumulation of wealth, the faceless commuters, their paper shuffling jobs, their lives denied nourishing tradition and religion. Against these apparent givens of the culture and of experience itself, aging, the loss of ideals and the impossibility of simplicity of emotion and action, his focal characters in his best short fiction persist in attempting some definition of self when confronted with adversity, inner and outer, that gives a measure to their lives.

"O Youth and Beauty!"—in some ways it is Cheever's "The Short Happy Life of Cash Bentley"—is a chapter in an American life. Bentley, he's forty, is fed up with the routine of his life: domestic fights, he and his wife make up, he feels cut off from life and the life of action, there are money worries at the edge of all he knows now and he finds satisfaction only in hurdling furniture at the country club or parties after he is so drunk that he feels free to express himself. A good part of this story is recognizable terrain; Cash Bentley looks like a version of that middle-aged American male who cannot quite give up his attachment to the robust, athletic life of his youth. Of course, he was a former track star. At the "tag end of nearly every long, Saturday night party," Trace Bearden "would begin to chide" Bentley about his age and thinning hair until Bentley moved the furnitues around the living room and once more ran the hurdle race. His wife Louise knows something of desperation, too: "housework, laundry, cooking and the demands of the children." Her life is no more rich in meaning than is his. One night, racing around a room, he breaks his leg; as he recovers, he becomes aware of the smell of corruption around him, rank meat, rotting flowers, and he is nearly gagged by a spider web in the attic of his house. Discontent, he becomes rude and gloomy. Without the hurdles he is nothing. Then on a summer night, with the smells of life and a new season all around, with his perceptions of the young in one another's arms—"He has been a young man. He has been a hero. He has been adored and happy and full of animal spirits"—when he is fully recovered from the broken leg, he once more tries the hurdles and runs the race successfully. He is exhausted at the finish and his wife "knelt down beside him and took his head in her lap and stroked his thin hair." The following night at home he sets up for the race again; it is a Sunday night—"Oh, those suburban Sunday nights, those Sunday-night blues!" the narrator reminds us—and Bentley gives his wife a pistol to shoot off for the starting gun. But it is a real pistol, "she had never fired it before, and the directions he gave her were not much help." She is confused about the safety on the weapon. "It's that little lever," he tells her. "Press that little lever." Then in his impatience he starts the race anyhow, goes over the sofa. "The pistol went off," Cheever writes, "and Louise got him in midair. She shot him dead."

"The Swimmer," perhaps Cheever's best known story; starts within the conventions of the *New Yorker* tale. Again a Sunday, this time the afternoon "when everyone sits around saying: 'I *drank* too much last night. . . . We all *drank* too much. . . . It must have been the wine.' " The reader seems to be assured that he knows this country well. It looks like what it's supposed to be: a slice of upper crust American affluence. The fiction, however, moves away from its conventions as Neddy Merrill, a slender man but by no means a young man—"he might have been compared to a summer's day, particularly the last hours of one"—decides to swim cross country, via his friends' pools, to his own house. And he names this string of swimming pools, "that quasi-subterranean stream that curved across the county," after his wife Lucinda. Neddy is by no means a "practical joker nor was he a fool but he was determinedly original and had a vague and modest idea of himself as a legendary figure. The day was beautiful and it seemed to him that a long swim might enlarge and celebrate its beauty." Neddy's swim, his odyssey through the mind of a particular kind of modern America, is alive with perils that suggest that his summer afternoon journey is more a species of nightmare than a presentation of daytime reality. Cheever has developed in "The Swimmer" a ghastly presentation of what it means to swim in American values of success, recognition, and status; for as Neddy plunges from pool to pool, encountering rebuff and indifference—and even more, the real suggestion of failure and disaster as the owner of one pool, Mrs. Holloran says to him, "We've been *terribly* sorry to hear about all your misfortunes, Neddy. . . . Why, we heard that you sold the house and that your poor children. . . . " her sentence trails off. But Neddy swims on, enduring even the regimented, chlorine-smelling, "All swimmers must wear their identification disks" indignities of a public pool, finding himself no longer welcome where he was once welcome, out of place where he once felt himself comfortable, only to arrive at his house that "was locked. . . . he shouted, pounded on the door, tried to force it in with his shoulder, and then, looking in at the windows, saw that the place was empty."

The house is empty and it makes little difference whether this story is an angle on madness or a paradigm of deep but rarely uttered American fears about the quality of our life. What is central to this story and a good many more in Cheever's work is that the hero must try to establish who he is in relation to an essentially meaningless—even absurd—world around him. He must try to *act* in some way, be it hurdling over living room furniture perhaps in pursuit of his lost youth or in swimming across the pools of Westchester County, so as to affirm his own being. Drinks, poolwise in Westchester, parties, the rhythms of commuters' lives—part of the ideal of the American good life—are the basis from which the Cheever hero must revolt. It matters not a bit that Cash Bentley or Neddy Merrill fail—fail? there were no goals to begin with—that they are shot or come home to find the house empty. But it matters a great deal that they are disgusted with the limitations of the environment. They find satisfaction not in victory or consolation in defeat but pleasure in action, in making themselves, in expressing a sense of rebellion against a life they can neither control nor understand. Read this way, the Cash Bentley of "O Youth and Beauty!" is not a pathetic middle-aged jock acting out once more the glories of his lost youth; he is a man trying to redefine himself against the contours of smug and shallow values, values that are mainly rotted with drink and acquisitiveness. So too is Neddy Merrill's cross county swim, be it actuality or dream, a gesture of heroic revolt. And if not heroic, something close to that; for Neddy on that swim does seem a fool or madman, no matter whether the swim is in the dark pools of his mind or in the sunlight of that Sunday. It is of the essence that they *do*, not that they win. To perform is to live, is to make a statement about the value of living over the descent into nothingness and even as that nothingness seems rich in good friends, good drink and good food, the pleasures of the family and the recognition of community. Perhaps what is so touching and even old fashioned about these heroes is their belief that there is finally a truth to experiences and that it can be realized in the form of action, no matter how futile or even symbolic.

Foolish or mad as Cash and Neddy might be, their situations are in differing ways resolved, in death or in the nothingness of the empty and abandoned house. Their absurd quests are simple contrasted with the moral ambiguities of Charlie Folkestone in "The Scarlet Moving Van." For Charlie there is a call to action, literally a phone call, a call for help, to which he does not respond and in that failure he loses his life as certainly as Cash shot dead in midair. Charlie and Martha Folkestone—they live in a pleasant town beyond the city, where "in nearly every house there were love, graciousness, and high hopes"; and "schools were excellent, the roads were smooth, the drains and other services were ideal"—welcome their new next-door neighbors whose goods arrive in a scarlet moving van one spring at dusk. They invite the new neighbors, Peaches and Gee-Gee, over for a drink. Peaches is "blond and warm" and Gee-Gee ("They called him the Greek God at college. That's why he's called Gee-Gee") "had been a handsome man, and perhaps still was, although his yellow curls were thin." But Gee-Gee drinks too much, calls the Folkestones stuffy, insults them further, and takes off his clothes. His wife begs him to stop, "Not on our first night." In eight years Peaches and Gee-Gee had lived in eight different houses; invariably Gee-Gee insults people, smashes furniture, and crockery, insisting always "I've got to teach them," until life becomes so uncomfortable that they must move away. And he repeats the pattern in the Folkestones' town. Charlie tries to help, go on the wagon he urges Gee-Gee, but without results. Peaches and Gee-Gee move away to another town, but Charlie later learns that Gee-Gee had broken his hip and one Sunday afternoon in winter—Sunday is the day of horror in Cheever's world—he gets his number from Information and drives over for a drink. Gee-Gee is alone, his wife and children are off to Nassau, he is in a cast and gets around the house in a child's wagon. He lights cigarettes and fumbles with the matches and Charlie wonders that he might burn himself to death. Outside it's snowing heavily and Charlie has a difficult two hour drive home; he wonders about having abandoned "a friend—a neighbor at least—to the peril of death." Safely at home and enjoying the comforts of family life on a snowy night, Charlie receives a phone call from Gee-Gee asking for help, get over here he cries, it took two hours to crawl to the phone. But Charlie will not respond; the roads must be impassable, he thinks; and his children "looked at him calmly, as if they were expecting him to make a decision that had nothing to do with the continuing of a pleasant evening in a snowbound house—but a decision that would have profound effect on their knowledge of him and on their final happiness." But Charlie will not go and it is unimportant that the reader is told that Gee-Gee got help from the fire department in "eight minutes flat." Charlie becomes a drunk, loses his job, becomes abusive of friends and neighbors, and in the end they, too, have their goods carted off in a scarlet moving van; the Folkestones are gone.

Drinks, friends, the suburban town, comfort, and even culture—Charlie and the older children are playing a "Vivaldi sonata" when Gee-Gee calls—this is the scenery of *New Yorker* fiction comforting the reader in his sense that he knows this country well. Yes, of course, the scenery; but the story according to the conventions of realistic fiction is patently absurd, even as it describes an absurd hero. Why does Charlie call in the first place? Why does he not drive back to Gee-Gee, for the desperate cry for help is more important than a difficult drive over snow roads? And certainly no man turns into a drunk and loses his job because he failed to help "a friend," anyhow an ex-neighbor and an obnoxious person? There is a madness to this suburban world of Cheever's, this demand for action, blind, foolish, senseless, even puerile, as it confronts the equally disastrous threats of paralysis that suggests the terrors of Beckett's *The Unnamable*: "I can't go on, you must go on, I'll go on, you must say words, as long as there are any, until they find me. . . . when I am, I don't know, I'll never know, in the silence you don't know, you must go on, I can't go on, I'll go on." The condition of Charlie Folkestone is literally unnamed and unnamable and it is the condition of many of Cheever's heroes.

The man who does not respond to the call is in the world of Cheever's absurd and yet moral fictions the man who has collapsed into the ultimate terror: paralysis. Many of his people experience that. And yet for the aged poet of "The World of Apples" and for Cash Bentley and Neddy Merrill there is still the lovely, legendary, and briefly heroic moments of hurdling living room furniture or swimming cross county, even when the race ends in death or the swim concludes with the man confronting his abandoned home. It is one version of the hero creating his own legend, even if that legend seems pointless, futile, finally absurd. And that may be the last resort of heroism.

Beyond the Cheeveresque: A Style Both Lyrical and Idiosyncratic

George Hunt*

John Cheever has won many awards for his fiction, but the praise and prizes have been reserved for his four excellent novels, *The Wapshot Chronicle, The Wapshot Scandal, Bullet Park,* and *Falconer.* Short stories, by contrast, rarely win important prizes, and collections of stories do not sell well. Cheever persists nonetheless in this neglected *genre,* which he terms "the literature of the nomad." *The Stories of John Cheever* (Knopf, 695 pp, $15), a handsomely designed and printed edition of 61 stories, represents his greatest achievement.

For too long critics have been idly content with the clichés "Cheever country" and "Cheeveresque," a reviewer's shorthand betraying a sensibility less wide and deep than the author's own. Cheever country has become synonymous with the suburbs that abut Route 95 from New York to Boston, a homogenized landscape of semi-elegant cook-outs, drained pools in the winter, parties that begin "Oh, *do* come" and end with forlorn or frantic goodbyes, a place peopled by an upper crust, now moldy or pulpy with desperation, fits of sexual tension, or mere silliness. The implication is that Cheever is something of a sociologist in disguise, a wry and macabre David Riesman who delights in counting the olives in drained martini glasses or the soggy shards of charcoal at aborted cook-outs.

But Cheever is not a sociologist; he is an artist. A social scientist's concern is to so concentrate on particular instances that, accumulatively, a general pattern for understanding the behavior of some segment of society might emerge. The artist, too, begins with the concrete particular, but he *enters* it; a particular experience is thus transformed by his imaginative and compassionate feeling in order that the humanly universal, not the statistically general, might emerge and engage our feeling and imaginative response. The findings of the social sciences are, almost by definition, statable. The results of art elude such definition since the art of fiction, at its best, engages mystery, the mystery of the human and its corollary, the mystery of language.

These twin mysteries are the key to the magic of John Cheever. As this collection demonstrates, the thematic *what* of his fiction is far broader than that of the vicissitudes of megapolis's upper middle class. His central characters range from elevator man to well-digger; the locales include Italy and Russia; and the emotions are rhapsodic and celebratory as often as sad. The recurring place-names like St. Botolphs, Shady Hill, Bullet Park are imaginative constructs not social symbols; they are more

*From *Commonweal,* 106 (19 January 1979), 20–22. Reprinted with permission of Commonweal Publishing Co., Inc.

and less than places on a map. They are, as Cheever has said, "metaphors for human confinement," whether the confinement be that of nostalgia or tradition, or erotic entanglements or of our universal perception of being both travelers and pilgrims and "stuck" somehow, trapped by conflicting aspirations above and below.

That thematic *what*, of course, Cheever shares with many contemporary writers; his distinction lies in the artistic *how*, in his remarkably graceful and lucid prose. We respond to the verbal rhythms of our other two most elegant and versatile stylists, John Updike and Saul Bellow, *inside* our heads. Both Updike and Bellow, though, are difficult to read aloud for a sustained period; Cheever's prose almost demands that it be read aloud. It comes as no surprise, then, to learn in his charming preface to this collection that a good deal of these stories were composed that way and tested with his family as critical audience. Cheever's prose edges closer to the cadences of modern poetry than that of any of his contemporaries.

Cheever's style is both lyrical and idiosyncratic. When lyrical, it is reminiscent of the later poetry of W.B. Yeats and, when idiosyncratic, of the later W.H. Auden. Cheever's stories, in fact, engage many Yeatsian themes: the passion for decorum and ceremonies of innocence in the face of the drowning of decay and disruption; the contrast of man's urge for the "higher" beauties of the artistic and natural order with his lower impulses like the sexually chaotic and the murderous; those emotions of manic desperation that accompany one's realization of aging and its consequence, death. Stylistically, Cheever continually uses the later Yeats technique of direct address to the reader. This technique brings to a story a unique dramatic force; the voice is unabashedly personal and we as readers are encountered, willynilly, by someone grabbing us by the lapels. A good number of his stories begin this way: the voice announces that he is a writer and the variations in his tone of voice prepare us (or so we think) for what will follow—but we had better listen or else. The range possible with this technique is remarkable and Cheever exploits it at the beginning of the following stories:

"The Ocean"—a conspiratorial voice: "I am keeping this journal because I believe myself to be in some danger and because I have no other way of recording my fears."

"The Death of Justina"—a complaint: "So help me God it gets more and more preposterous, it corresponds less and less to what I remember and what I expect. . . . "

"Percy"—quaintly philosophical: "Reminiscence, along with the cheeseboards and ugly pottery sometimes given to brides, seems to have a manifest destiny with the sea."

"The Brigadier and the Golf Widow"—apologetic and inquisitive: "I would not want to be one of those writers who begin each morning by exclaiming, 'O Gogol, O Checkhov, O Thackeray and Dickens, what would you have made of a bomb shelter ornamented with four plaster-of-Paris ducks, a birdbath, and three composition gnomes with long beards and red mobcaps?' "

In addition, there are throughout these stories the Yeatsian long lyric line, iambic in rhythm, merging the abstract impulse with the concrete detail. This is Francis Weed's vision in Cheever's masterpiece, "The Country Husband."

> Up through the dimness of his mind rose the image of the mountain deep in snow. It was late in the day. Wherever his eyes looked, he saw broad and heartening things. Over his shoulder, there was a snow-filled valley, rising into wooded hills where the trees dimmed the whiteness like a sparse coat of hair.

But Yeats was never funny, at least deliberately, and it is here that Cheever parts from Yeats and joins Auden. Like Auden, Cheever is not a satirist, though it might seem so. Instead, he is what Kierkegaard called a "humorist," one whose compassionate understanding of the human comedy with its absurd enthusiasms and low-life urgencies forestalls in his heart the easy, mocking perspective of facile satire. Neither Cheever nor Auden expect or desire a radical change in the human condition, they are content to embrace it, whole and not piecemeal, despite a knowing eye. Is not this Audenesque and Cheeveresque?

> We admire decency and we despise death, but even the mountains seem to shift in the space of a night and perhaps the exhibitionist at the corner of Chestnut and Elm streets is more significant than the lovely woman with a bar of sunlight in her hair, putting a fresh piece of cuttlebone in the nightingale's cage.

Like Auden, Cheever's comic technique will entail: a continual and abrupt shifting of stylistic gears from fantasy to realism, a seeming solemnity of tone that suddenly issues in the mock-heroic catching us unawares, the old juxtaposition of different items in a list, with the last detail a comic climax, a blurring switch from the banal to the shocking and a return to the banal. Throughout, as in Auden, the narrator's voice is ever decorous, detached, urbane; but its tone is never "tsk-tsk," rather it is "well, what do *we* know" and "wait, there's even more to tell."

Fortunately, in Cheever there is always more to tell, and the fertility of his imagination is extraordinary. One critic has described Cheever's style with disfavor as "episodic notation" in that his narratives move swiftly and almost in linear fashion from one glimpse, one incident, one snippet of conversation to another. What is sacrificed here in terms of organic fictional unity—always the stuffy critic's touchstone when he has little else to say—is redeemed by exceptional inventiveness, flexibility and versatility. This apparently loose structure gives his stories the qualities of a yarn and, *sans* dialect and sentimentality, places him firmly in the American tradition of Mark Twain, Ring Lardner and Damon Runyon. Furthermore, a Cheever dialogue is unique in that, while is remains true to our realistic ear, it is always heightened beyond realism to a peculiar brand of poetic speech—and it is this that sets him apart from the genial accuracy of a John O'Hara or Philip Roth.

Finally, the acid test of the comic: Cheever is consistently hilarious. Alone with Peter De Vries's best efforts, Cheever's fiction is not meant to be read among strangers, on planes or trains where suddenly laughing out loud might be thought unseemly or worse. Here, for example, is one narrator's summary account of his eccentric Aunt Percy's marriage:

> Percy and Abbott Tracy met in some such place, and she fell in love. He had already begun a formidable and clinical sexual career, and seemed unacquainted in any way with sentiment, although I recall that he liked to watch children saying their prayers. Percy listened for his footsteps, she languished in his absence, his cigar cough sounded to her like music, and she filled a portfolio with pencil sketches of his face, his eyes, his hands, and, after their marriage, the rest of him.

More famous is the opening paragraph to "The Swimmer." Here the subtle variations on the repetitiveness of human excuses capture not only a specific hangover but a more fundamental, universal experience of misgiving that is beyond all genteel excuse.

> It was one of those midsummer Sundays when everyone sits around saying: "I *drank* too much last night." You might have heard it whispered by the parishioners leaving church, heard it from the lips of the priest himself, struggling with his cassock in the *vestiarium*, heard it from the golf links and the tennis courts, heard it from the wild-life preserve where the leader of the Audubon group was suffering from a terrible hangover. "I *drank* too much," said Donald Westerhazy. "We all *drank* too much," said Lucinda Merrill. "It must have been the wine," said Helen Westerhazy. "I *drank* too much of that claret."

Just as Cheever is not a strict satirist he is not a moralist either. And yet, his work, as his last novel *Falconer* made evident, is deeply Christian in sensibility. Few of his stories, apart from cleverly inserted Biblical allusions, are obviously religious in design. But Cheever's sympathy with his characters' fallen state together with their vague yearnings for personal rebirth, for a virtuous life possibly untrammeled by life's more sordid confusions, betray his sincere Episcopal beliefs. Every artist's endeavor demands an implicit faith-commitment to a world he hopes will reward it, but Cheever has been more religiously specific. He has said in an interview, "The religious experience is very much my concern, as it seems to me it is the legitimate concern of any adult who has experienced love. . . . The whiteness of light. In the church, you know, that always represents the Holy Spirit. It seems to me that man's inclination toward light, toward brightness, is very nearly botanical—and I mean spiritual light. One not only needs it, one struggles for it. It seems to be that one's total experience is the drive toward light."

Unfortunately, despite that inviting light, we are *here* and not there; yet, Cheever, like all great artists consciously committed to religious faith or otherwise, begins here. No other short story in my memory captures better what theologians have called the mystery of Original Sin than his excellent "Seaside Houses." In the story, the narrator, a gentle and reasonable man, has rented a summer cottage for his family. Gradually, he realizes that the Greenwoods who had rented the cottage the previous summer have left ominous moral baggage behind. The narrator discovers a boy's scrawl, "My father is a rat," hidden on a corner baseboard; caches of empty whiskey bottles are found; obscene gossip is later heard about the Greenwoods; soon the narrator begins to dream dreams that he realizes are Mr. Greenwood's dreams. Suddenly, Mr. Greenwood's presence begins to infect him, destroying his relationship with his wife and family. Greenwood has become his counterpart, he divorces, and the story ends with this reflection of his in another seaside house with another wife:

> The shore is curved, and I can see the lights of other haunted cottages where people are building up an accrual of happiness or misery that will be left for the August tenants or the people who come next year. Are we truly this close to one another? Must we impose our burdens on strangers? And is our sense of the universality of suffering so inescapable?

Perhaps those last lines sound faintly cosmic or even pompous, but it is a generous risk that Cheever takes. The other risk is the risk to be hilarious, a risk that the truly pompous regard as lightweight. Like life itself, humor has no weight, only intensity. No one without a sense of humor can deeply enjoy any other of the myriad of human sensations; sadly, for those without, humor and its acolytes offer not mystery but endless mystification. But humor, certainly as often as tragedy, shocks us into truth. Cheever does this again and again; as he has said, "We can cherish nothing less than our random understanding of death and the earth-shaking love that draws us to one another."

REVIEWS: NOVELS

Where Have All the Roses Gone?

Granville Hicks*

Like its predecessor, *The Wapshot Chronicle*, John Cheever's new book, *The Wapshot Scandal* (Harper & Row, $4.95) is distinguished by a remarkable vitality, springing out of the author's fascinated awareness of the variety and unpredictability of human behavior. But in spite of the vigor of the narrative, the tone is elegiac. Leander Wapshot, the dominating figure of the earlier book, died at its close, and his sons, Moses and Coverly, always smaller men, are in bad shape at the conclusion of the present volume. Aunt Honora, the last of the older generation, plays a lively part in the story, but she has quietly met her death before the final chapter. In that final chapter the narrator, coming briefly on stage, says his farewell to St. Botolphs.

Again like its predecessor, *The Wapshot Scandal* is episodic, and rather large parts of it have been published as short stories in *The New Yorker*. There are three principal themes. One concerns Aunt Honora, who has to flee to Italy because she has never bothered to pay an income tax. (One might regard her casualness as implausible if one did not think of Edmund Wilson and James Landis.) The second series of episodes describes Coverly's disillusioning experiences with the new masters of the Space Age. The third portrays the unhappy infatuation of Melissa, Moses's wife, with a grocer's boy.

In all this one feels not merely the decline of the Wapshots but also the decay of a culture. In the opening chapter Cheever describes a Christmas Eve in St. Botolphs, not so very long ago, I take it, but at a time when the traditional values of a small New England community were still alive. Cheever does not take a romantic view of the human condition: in the village that evening there are lust and drunkenness and aridity of the spirit and sudden death. But one nonetheless feels the dignity of man.

It is with the loss of this dignity that Cheever is concerned in most of the novel. The quality of life, he says again and again, has changed. For instance:

---

*From *Saturday Review*, 47 (4 Jan. 1964), 75–76. Copyright © 1964 by *Saturday Review*. Reprinted with permission. All rights reserved.

The Moonlite Drive-In was divided into three magnificent parts. There was the golf links, the roller rink and the vast amphitheatre itself, where thousands of darkened cars were arranged in the form of an ancient arena, spread out beneath the tree of night. Above the deep thunder from the rink and the noise from the screen, you could hear—high in the air and so like the sea that a blind man would be deceived—the noise of traffic on the great Northern Expressway that flows southward from Montreal to the Shenandoah, engorging in its clover leafs and brilliantly engineered gradings the green playing fields, rose gardens, barns, farms, meadows, trout streams, forests, homesteads and churches of a golden past. The population of the highway gathered for their meals in a string of identical restaurants, where the morals, the urinals, the menus and the machines for vending sacred medals were uniform. It was some touching part of the autumn night and the hazards of the road that so many of these travelers pleaded for the special protection of gentle St. Christopher and the blessings of the Holy Virgin.

There is an element of intentional hyperbole in this—note "a golden past"—but I think that Cheever seriously offers the expressway as an example of what he feels to be wrong with our civilization. Another and even more seriously considered example is Dr. Cameron, head of the Missile Research and Development site at which Coverly Wapshot is humbly employed. Cameron, a liar, a monstrous egoist, a bully, and a barbarian at heart, may decide the fate of the world. When he is asked by a Senate investigating committee whether he believes that hydrogen warfare is inevitable, he calmly says, "Yes," and adds that, if we were losing the war, he would be in favor of destroying the planet.

An aged Senator speaks, beginning, "I was born in a small town, Dr. Cameron. I think the difference between this noisy and public world in which we now live and the world I remember is quite real, quite real." He continues:

> We possess Promethean powers but don't we lack the awe, the humility, that primitive man brought to the sacred fire? Isn't it a time for uncommon awe, supreme humility? If I should have to make some final statement, and I shall very soon for I am nearing the end of my journey, it would be in the nature of a thanksgiving for stout-hearted friends, lovely women, blue skies, the bread and wine of life. Please don't destroy the earth, Dr. Cameron. Oh please, please don't destroy the earth.

Even Cheever's humor, and he can be one of the funniest of American writers, is often grim. Aunt Honora's twice crippling a vast steamship by plugging in her ancient electric curling iron is farcical, but it points to the vulnerability of a mechanized society. We laugh at Gertrude Lockhart's struggle with her household appliances, but her frustration ends in suicide. Nothing could be more ludicrous than the story of Emile's hiding the Easter eggs, but what an indictment it is of human greed! There is a lot about sex in the book, and no one is better than Cheever in describing the sexual drive, with all its ridiculous and all its glorious aspects. But even sex, he suggests, is not what it was. Of Emile at the drive-in he writes: "His sitting undressed in the back seat of a car might be accounted for by the fact that the music he danced to and the movies he watched dealt less and less with the heart and more and more with overt sexuality, as if the rose gardens and playing fields buried under the Expressway were enjoying a revenge."

I am afraid that I have not adequately described either the liveliness or the power of the novel, but I have wanted to emphasize the seriousness of Cheever's attitude: he is so serious that he is willing to risk the charge of sentimentality. One does not have to agree with every item in his indictment of contemporary society; what matters is the feeling he has for the world we live in, his sense that, whatever has been gained, much has been lost. As I said at the outset, he is no romantic; he knows that life has always been precarious; but he writes about the special perils of the moment with extraordinary effectiveness. In a peculiarly poignant way this is a novel of and for our times.

John Cheever's Golden Egg

Stanley Edgar Hyman*

When a highly-esteemed short story writer tries a novel and fails at it, in this amazing country, he is rewarded just as though he had succeeded. Thus Katherine Anne Porter's *Ship of Fools* became a rapturously-received bestseller, and J. F. Powers' *Morte D'Urban* and John Cheever's *The Wapshot Chronicle* won National Book Awards. Now, in *The Wapshot Scandal* (Harper & Row, 309 pp., $4.95), Cheever has again tried, and again failed, to make short story material jell as a novel. As a two-time loser, he can probably expect the Pulitzer Prize.

The problem is not any lack of plot. *The Wapshot Scandal* has enough plot for *War and Peace*. In the course of a year, from one Christmas Eve to another, the fortunes of the Wapshots change drastically. (The Wapshots, who are continued from the *Chronicle*, are a family of gentry centered in St. Botolphs, on the Massachusetts coast. They include two young brothers, Moses and Coverly, and their rich maiden aunt Honora.) Coverly's marriage has its ups and downs, as his wife Betsey turns moody or violent, but on the whole he comes off best during the year. Moses is cuckolded and deserted by his wife Melissa, and takes to drink. Honora is exposed as a comic criminal, and dies in contented disgrace. The "scandal" of the title is actually three: Melissa's adultery, Moses' alcoholism, and Honora's banditry.

*Reprinted with permission of *The New Leader*, 3 February 1964. Copyright © the American Labor Conference on International Affairs, Inc.

The changes wrought by a year are most effectively pointed up by the widow Wilston. On the Christmas Eve that begins the book she and an itinerant carpenter named Alby Hooper, both naked and drunk, are trimming a Christmas tree. On the Christmas Eve that ends the book she and Moses Wapshot are naked and drunk in a hotel room, although they seem to have forgotten the tree.

Such a narrative could clearly be a novel if it held together. It breaks into fragments, however, because of inconsistency of character and tone. People change character in the book to accommodate to each new incident. Dr. Lemuel Cameron, the world-famous atomic scientist who is Coverly's boss, is a good example. In one chapter, pursuing his mistress in Rome through a barrage of comic misfortunes and indignities, Cameron is a sympathetic and attractive figure. In another chapter, testifying before a Congressional committee, he is a mad monster. Both figures make perfect sense in their contexts, but they should not have the same name.

The inconsistencies of tone are equally disconcerting. A woman named Mrs. Lockhart is described to Melissa early in the book as a promiscuous slut, too poor to stay in the community now that the neighbors are applying economic pressure. Later Melissa hears that she has hanged herself in the garage. When we are finally told Mrs. Lockhart's story, we discover that the Lockharts are rather well off, and that Mrs. Lockhart is an extremely sympathetic character, an unfortunate victim of circumstances. Fair enough: The woman who told Melissa about Mrs. Lockhart underestimated her husband's income and blackened her character.

However, the circumstances that drove Gertrude Lockhart to promiscuity and suicide are wildly funny; they are her inability to get plumbers and repairmen when the household machinery breaks down. It is this shift in tone that is ruinous. Mrs. Lockhart can kill herself as the tragic victim of uncontrollable lust and consequent scandal, or as the pathetic victim of a neurotic sense of obsolescence and inadequacy, or as the comic victim of the oil burner repairman's bowling team and the washing machine repairman's Florida vacation. She cannot kill herself as all three, as Cheever would have it.

There is a similar failure of tone in the book's wonderful story of Emile the grocery boy and the plastic eggs. To promote the grocery store Emile is to hide a thousand plastic eggs around the village during the night; all contain certificates good for prizes and five gold ones are good for European vacations. In a series of hilarious misadventures, Emile succeeds in rousing the town. A pack of savage housewives in nightgowns pursue him, and he is forced to ditch the eggs in an empty lot, except for a single gold one, which he deposits on Melissa Wapshot's lawn. It is marvelously funny. Unfortunately, Emile is Melissa Wapshot's lover, and all the pity and terror of that affair evaporate in a scramble of plastic eggs.

The gold egg on Melissa's lawn, like Dr. Cameron's realization at the end of his Roman comedy that "there was some blessedness in the nature of things," is a proper end for a short story, not for a chapter in a novel. It does not develop *toward* a final resolution; it *is* a final resolution.

I have perhaps overemphasized one point, and in so doing been unfair to Cheever. If *The Wapshot Scandal* is not a novel, it is a very impressive non-novel. Many things in it are quite fine. Melissa's affair with Emile is convincing and deeply moving (at least until the egg scene). Melissa's feelings for Emile's beauty, her torments of lust, her shame and self-contempt, her progress in degradation from dignified out-of-town weekends with Emile to quick straddles in a shack by the village dump, are all beautifully realized.

One character at least in *The Wapshot Scandal* is both consistent and memorable: the eccentric Honora. In *The Wapshot Chronicle* we learned she throws her mail into the fire unread, and will only pay bus fares by annual check. In the *Scandal*, it turns out that she has other endearing idiosyncracies: she has never been photographed, and she has never paid an income tax. It is this last habit that is her downfall, since the Internal Revenue computers catch her. She is driven first to a suicide attempt, then to flight abroad; brought back to St. Botolphs, she achieves a happy, drunken, and impoverished death. I suspect that Cheever is having a go at Edmund Wilson; in any case Honora Wapshot is one of the true comic creations.

Much of *The Wapshot Scandal* is extremely funny. There is a scene in which Coverly is told by his wife to take her new cleaning woman upstairs and show her how to work the vacuum cleaner. Betsey hears him start the machine, then hears his instructions: "Now we put it in here. That's right. That's the way. We have to get it into the corners, way into the corners. Slowly, slowly, slowly. Back and forth, back and forth." They are of course engaged in a more ancient pastime. This romp is out of character for Coverly, and the scene has been done before (Nelson Algren used a coffee grinder in *A Walk on the Wild Side*, which is closer to the origins of the joke in the double meaning of Negro blues). Out of character and unoriginal the scene may be; it is nevertheless uproarious.

Some of the humor in the book is pure slapstick. The income tax man confronts Honora while she is inspecting a basket of fireworks. Naturally the fireworks go off, and in her efforts to extinguish them she catches him in the face with a vaseful of dirty water and a dozen hyacinths. Other funny scenes are almost surrealistic, as when Emile participates in a male beauty contest in Italy, after which the winners are auctioned off as homosexual concubines (fortunately for Emile, if not for the book's seriousness, he is bought by Melissa, who got to Rome with her golden egg).

Most often, the book's humor is edged, resulting in irony or satire. It is ironic that Norman Johnson, the tax man, throws the book at Honora because he stayed overnight at the Viaduct House, the soup at dinner had a burned match in it, the fight on television was terrible, his breakfast eggs were greasy, and on his way to Honora's house he was attacked by a dog, and some children laughed at him when he ran. It is ironic that the alcoholic Episcopal clergyman displays the only attractive religion in St. Botolphs when, drunk at Mass and unable to remember the service, he improvises a prayer "for all those wounded by rotary lawn mowers, chain saws, electric hedge clippers and other power tools."

A good deal of the satire is directed against bureaucracy. At one point, Coverly is the victim of an airplane robber, as a consequence of which he is given a police questionnaire to fill out, with forty questions ranging from "How often do you take a bath?" to "If you were forced to debase the American flag or the Holy Bible, what would be your choice?" The congressional investigation of Dr. Cameron manages to make nuclear scientists and congressmen seem about equally foolish.

At his best, Cheever is a marvelous writer. Here is the book's last look at Melissa, her hair dyed red, shopping for Emile in a Rome supermarket, and quietly weeping at her fate: "No willow grows aslant this stream of men and women and yet it is Ophelia that she most resembles, gathering her fantastic garland not of crowflowers, nettles and long purples, but of salt, pepper, Bab-o, Kleenex, frozen codfish balls, lamb patties, hamburger, bread, butter, dressing, an American comic book for her son and for herself a bunch of carnations. She chants, like Ophelia, snatches of old tunes. 'Winstons taste good like a cigarette should. Mr. Clean, Mr. Clean,' and when her coronet or fantastic garland seems completed she pays her bill and carries her trophies away, no less dignified a figure of grief than any other."

In "Some People, Places, and Things That Will Not Appear in My Next Novel," Cheever wrote that he was omitting various stereotypes because "they throw so little true light on the way we live." Melissa throws a great deal of true light on the way we live, but it is because of her uncovenanted heart, not because she buys Kleenex and frozen codfish balls. Cheever seems sometimes dazzled by the surface of American life, by its textures and glitters. But his best work shows that at the heart of that golden egg there is darkness and mystery.

John Cheever and the Charms of Innocence: The Craft of *The Wapshot Scandal*

George Garrett*

These stories were no worse than the stories of talking rabbits he had been told as a boy but the talking rabbits had the charms of innocence. — The Wapshot Scandal

The first thing that should be said and not forgotten is that *The Wapshot Scandal* is a very good novel, an outstanding piece of work and craft by any known standard of judgment and it is the best book John Cheever has written. Since his earlier and first novel, *The Wapshot Chronicle*, received the National Book Award for 1957, this means that in the world of prizes and awards and in the circles where there is jostling for the laurel wreath of Success, a game as shrill and chaotic as Drop-the-Handker-chief, it is a book and Cheever is an author who must be taken quite seriously this season. Already *The Wapshot Scandal* has received very good notices and reviews and, what is important, these have been in the most prominent and choice spots, as significant as the fire hydrant in front of a fashionable restaurant where only certain shiny limousines with very special license tags are permitted to park. In the front page lead review for the *Tribune* (and other papers) Glenway Wescott, not only an artist himself but an arbiter with charm, influence, and definite opinions, saluted the publication of the book with high praise, seasoned with just a mere *soupcon* of qualification. He found in the book many of the virtues which he at once celebrates and pleads for in *Images of Truth:* clarity, lucidity, decorum, a fine surface of sensuous aesthetic experience supported on the firm rock strata of meaning and implication. He saw it as tragi-comic, a book thus accurately reflecting the ambivalent feelings of a man of feeling in our time. Elizabeth Janeway in the front page review of *The New York Times Book Review* celebrated the book chiefly in terms of anecdotes she just couldn't resist retelling and by pointing out the extremely clever and "deceptive" use of symbol and analogy employed by Cheever to give the haunting resonance of deep meaning and wide implication. *The Washington Post* offered its highest compliment by stating that the cosmic view of the novel, unflinching honesty lifted by the wings of hope and wisdom, was a fine example of the working philosophy of our late president. Most recently Cheever has received the mixed blessing of a *Time* cover story. It remains to be seen whether or not the celebrated jinx will work.

If there is any justice in this world, *The Wapshot Scandal* is on its way. Whether or not it climbs to a place on the best seller lists and en-

Reprinted with permission from *The Hollins Critic*, 1 (April 1964), 1–12.

dures there for a proper interval remains to be seen, is in the hands of Lady Luck and, of course, that vast, faceless, surging, restive mob, the reading public which, like the voting public and the razor-blade-using public, nobody really knows for sure and practically everybody mistrusts. *The Wapshot Scandal* may or may not sit in the spotlighted position of the best-seller list, but it does not take a gypsy to predict that the book and its author will be much discussed in the coming months, not only in cocktail parties and reading groups, but also in seminar and classroom. High time too. John Cheever has been producing honorable work for more than twenty years and from the beginning he has always threatened to become "a major writer." Perhaps he has at last earned that title. One thing we can be sure of. He has written a good book in a time when good books are few and far between. And that's a cause for celebration. It is, however, at once a better and a *different* book than his reviewers have allowed, and it is quite good enough to be subjected to the kind of inquisition, the rack of speculation and the thumbscrew of questions without easy answers, which only the strong and brave should be asked to endure.

> She loves the fine, the subtle, the non-cliche. . . . from an advertisement in *The New Yorker*

John Cheever is a *New Yorker* writer and may be the best of the bunch. Of course, we all know that both the editors and writers for that distinguished magazine would deny and have denied that a *type* exists. Let us understand the reasons for the denial and ignore it. No use pretending Shakespeare didn't write for the Elizabethan stage. Any magazine worth its weight has a character, one which is partly created by editorial standards and equally by the relationship the magazine enjoys with its readers. *The New Yorker* has a third power haunting, if not dominating the present, a history long enough already to be called a tradition. We know a good deal about the beginning and the early years of *The New Yorker*. The names—Ross, Thurber, E. B. White, Gus Lobrano, Gibbs, and so many others—are celebrated, have been recorded in many a popular, nostalgic reminiscence and have passed beyond mere household familiarity to stand, aloof but never lonely, bronze-like with a nice patina, in the cluttered museum of public mythology. By now at least two generations of Americans have thumbed through *The New Yorker* with pleasure. Didn't we cut our teeth on the magazine's one major contribution to our culture—the cartoons? Still, a popular magazine is a business. Just as the politician must get himself elected, so a magazine must turn a profit to insure its own self-preservation. We have seen magazines come and go, succeed and fail. *The New Yorker* has not only survived, it has prospered, bloomed. Which means, that no matter how adventurous the editorial policy and no matter how well it has been able to adapt itself to the facts of life, change and decay, there is still at heart a basic purpose, that of self-preservation. And thus the preservation of the *status quo* is not just an aim but a duty.

The literary history of *The New Yorker* reflects all these things yet has a general history of its own. And there are a few general things about it which have to be said. One is that over many years *The New Yorker* has been a patron of many writers. More and more steadily than have foundations or colleges or rich old ladies with buzzing hearing aids and ropes of pearls. It is also true that it has specifically patronized the finest second-rate talents of our times. No use arguing. It is simply a fact that none of the acknowledged masters of the art of writing fiction or poetry from the first half of our century has been a regular contributor to the magazine. Maybe this will change, but a literary historian would not bet on it. The remarkable thing is that *The New Yorker* has always maintained a very high level of consistent quality and craftsmanship. Which, of course, is something even, perhaps especially, the masters themselves have not done.

The vintage *New Yorker* story has become a model for the modern short story. Briefly it was the maximum exploration and exploitation of a single dramatically presented incident, more or less strictly observing the unities of time and place and rich in implication, both in depth of characterization and in a larger implied story which had a past and predicated a future. Plot, in the conventional sense, was largely absent, as were the middle class moral dilemmas of slick fiction. In setting the stories were either regional—the East and occasionally the uncorrupted West or the passive and amusing South, or foreign and exotic. Naturally the stories reflected the general moral views of the magazine and its public— reasonably but not ostentatiously well-informed, perhaps a little snobbish, though united against the more common forms of snobbery, more or less liberal politically. It was never, not even in the case of certain religious writers, religious. Its moral fiber, its touchstone was a kind of secular humanism coupled with a gentle intellectual agnosticism. The virtues it honored were all civilized virtues, sedentary, sophisticated and rational, all defended by the curtains (never made of iron) of humor, irony, sensitivity, the skeptical intelligence, and a form of gentility which was *au courant*. Minor figures who entered wearing the white hat signifying a good guy were charming eccentrics, happy-go-lucky losers, cheerful outsiders. Members of the lower classes, those of whom it could be safely said they didn't read *The New Yorker*, and people from other older generations were permitted to display a healthy-minded vulgarity. Those worthy of attention from the class (let's face it—middle) of the readers themselves were usually attractive physically, possessed of charm, and perhaps distinguished by the blessing or burden of a little extra sensitivity and more intelligence than is average. The mortal sins in this universe were, inevitably: vulgarity without the redemption of eccentricity, self-pity, stupidity, hypocrisy, bad manners, complacency, excess of passion, and a lack of good health or physical attractiveness. In short, *New Yorker* fiction was a fiction of manners, and its purpose, classical from tip to toe, was to instruct as it delighted. Nature, or course, was neutral and basically good. It was, however, an idyllic nature, in its own way as formalized and stylish as an 18th Century pastoral. There was a kind of tourist's view of the natural world replete with the names of plants and animals, these, however, always shining like coins or rare stamps in a collector's album. Still essentially progressive, still haunted by the last of the evolutionary analogies, *The New Yorker* viewed the worst excesses of modern civilization with distaste and sometimes with alarm, but never with despair. For, no matter how black the present, how fraught with peril the future or how quaint the past, the fiction and poetry of *The New Yorker* walked forward hand in hand with the advertisements and "The Talk of the Town," always moving toward the vague, but discernible horizon, the glow of which indicated at least the possibility of a Jerusalem of The Good Life somewhere up there among the Delectable Mountains and just beyond the reach of the clean fingernails of the Ideal Reader.

During the Second World War the form of the story began to change. And here we return to John Cheever, who had something to do with changing it.

> *We are no longer dealing with midnight sailings on three-stacked liners, twelve day crossings, Vuitton trunks and the glittering lobbies of Grand Hotels.* —*The Wapshot Scandal*

From the beginning with *The Way Some People Live* (1943) and on through the publication of *The Enormous Radio* (1953) the stories of John Cheever in *The New Yorker* (as of this date he has published more than 100 there) have exhibited an independence of form. Perhaps it was inevitable that this would happen now that the "single event" story has been widely anthologized, taught in schools, and is somewhat less than *chic*. Anyway, for whatever reason, the stories of John Cheever and of some others who appear in that magazine, are now most often much less "dramatic," much more free in the survey of time and space. Cheever, for example, characteristically ranges widely in point of view and also in tense, sometimes past, sometimes present, occasionally even future and conditional. There is a much more positive exploitation of the narrator-writer of the story. He appears openly like the chorus of an early Elizabethan play, does his best to establish an intimacy and rapport with his reader, and then cheerfully re-enters from time to time to point out significant objects or to make intelligent comment. Like a cultivated and slightly superior museum guide, the narrator is clever and witty yet always *sympatico* to the reader because of his slight, pleasing smile, his gentle habit of self-depreciation, and his wry, yet knowing shrug. The narrator is up to date in his allusions, his knowledge of the *things* of this world, and can, if necessary, but not without a wink of misgiving, use the latest slang. His own language is exact, always a model of lucidity and decorum, free from the unrefined extravagance of poetic frenzy, yet able from time to time to reach a modest altitude on the slopes of Olympus, far from the sweaty chaos of the laughing white gods, but anyway a place with a view near timberline where a gourmet picnic might be spread.

Cheever has introduced a new freedom in the form. The meaning of this kind of form is fairly clear. It wants to *say more*, not only about persons, places, and things, but about what these things mean, what patterns they make. Cheever has, for example, from the beginning blithely and easily introduced the world of dreams into his stories. His characters dream a good deal and they do it matter of factly. He has also permitted them to digress, to reminisce, to imagine. And it is one of his special abilities and triumphs that he can lead them (and the reader) step by step credibly from a perfectly "realistic" situation into the areas of farce or nightmare. Perhaps this is what one reviewer meant when he wrote—"It is as if Marquand had suddenly been crossed with Kafka."

Cheever is deeply interested in character and he knows his fictional characters by giving them depth, veils and layers of experience, and the loose ends and untied shoe laces of living, breathing beings. One has only to compare and contrast his treatment of characters with that of Mary McCarthy. Her people are mannequins, shoved in a store window and stripped naked for the amusement of the reader. It would be obscene if her characters were not wooden. It would be cruel if her characters did not in the end seem to be lifted out of somebody else's book or story she is criticizing. Cheever has a good deal of sympathy for his people and if they sometimes fail, in spite of the latest methods of resuscitation and artificial respiration, to breathe the breath of life, it is apt to be because he becomes impatient, quite naturally, with the extremely difficult demands he has set upon himself.

On the early stories, probably the most intelligent critical remarks come from William Peden in his excellent notes to the anthology *Twenty-Nine Stories* (1960). First Peden makes an important comparison, calling Cheever "an urbane and highly civilized social satirist" like Galsworthy. Peden goes on to say, judiciously: "Few writers have depicted more skillfully than he the loneliness and emptiness of certain segments of contemporary society." And he points out that each and all of the stories have been chiefly concerned with "the corrosive effect of metropolitan life upon essentially decent people who are isolated, defeated, or deprived of their individuality in the vastness of a great city." If you wisely include the proliferating suburbs as a part of the great city and if you weigh Peden's words, that is about the long and the short of it.

But we are talking about Cheever the novelist. Even though both his novels have appeared in bits and pieces, slightly re-edited for formal reasons, as stories in *The New Yorker*. And even though his two most recent collections of stories—*The Housebreaker of Shady Hill* (1958) and

Some People, Places, and Things That Will Not Appear in My Next Novel
(1961)—are so constructed as to qualify as novels if the definition of that
form is at last liberated from certain arbitrary restrictions. More and
more *all* the parts of Cheever's work are clearly parts of a whole. What he
has to say to the world has changed a little as the world has changed. But
not so much as one might imagine. And not so much as *The Wapshot
Scandal* intends.

One thing needs to be said here and now. Clearly it is more than difficult, it is a *feat*, to be a serious writer and at the same time to share
without much questioning not only the standards, but also the whole set
of rules and by-laws of a social club as cozy and intimate and proud as
The New Yorker. It is hard not to end up sounding like a tape recording of
clever cocktail party chatter. Yet John Cheever has achieved the delicate
balance and done it with the bravado of the tightrope walker in top hat
and tails, bottle in hand, who seems to stagger across the dangerous wire.
No one can deny that he is a good serious writer. No one can deny the
achievement he has already demonstrated. And this would be true if he
never wrote another line.

The Wapshot Chronicle appeared in 1957 and won the National
Book Award for that year. As in the case of all prizes, it was and will remain debatable whether his first novel was the *best* book of the year, but
it was a fine one and it was a cause for jubilation in the circles of those
who care. More important than prizes, praise, or blame, he created with
economy and dispatch a lively novel which included a town, St. Botolphs,
and its people, a family, the Wapshots, from the *Arabella* up to, almost,
the present; a variety of characters and events, of anecdotes and parables
and fables, and at least two thoroughly memorable and realized
characters—Leander and Miss Honora. It was full of humor ranging from
bathroom jokes (the Wapshot toilet was haunted and occasionally
flushed itself in the middle of the night), to farce (the book *opens* with a
runaway horse-drawn float bearing the Women's Club far from a Fourth
of July parade), to moments of modern sophisticated comedy involving
psychiatrists, crazy castles and the style and tone of Leander Wapshot's
journal, one of the happiest devices of the novel. That Leander has sinned
grievously and has a truly nightmarish vision of a rutting hell before he
drowns himself becomes at least modified by the fact that he is allowed to
have the last word in his journal, a word of advice for those who come
after him.

> Advice to my sons . . . Never put whiskey into hot water bottle crossing
> borders of dry states or counties. Rubber will spoil taste. Never make love
> with pants on. Beer on whiskey, very risky. Whiskey on beer, never fear.
> Never eat apples, peaches, pears, etc. while drinking whiskey except long
> French-style dinners, terminating with fruit. Other viands have mollify-
> ing effect. Never sleep in moonlight. Known by scientists to induce
> madness. Should bed stand beside window on clear night draw shade

before retiring. . . . Avoid kneeling in unheated stone churches. Ec-
clesiastical dampness causes prematurely gray hair. Fear tastes like a rusty
knife and do not let her into your house. Courage tastes of blood. Stand up
straight. Admire the world. Relish the love of a gentle woman. Trust in
the Lord.

In this history of the Wapshots and St. Botolphs Cheever offered a
history of the nation, its growth, bloom, and the question of its possible
decay and corruption. The tone was tolerantly amused and nostalgic
dealing with the past, lyrical about nature and especially about trout
fishing in the unspoiled Canadian wilderness, a little sad about the
decline and decay of the small town, satirical about the excesses of the urban and suburban revolution and the desperate impersonality, the flight
from freedom and responsibility of modern times. A beautiful satirical
point of view was offered by sending Young Moses Wapshot to
Washington and Young Coverly first to New York and then to a missile
site or two, two young rubes against whose bemusement and bafflement
the modern urban *milieu* could be measured.

The book is rich in implication, gained by the "tricks" Elizabeth
Janeway so admires, the time honored method of story tellers from Homer
on of gaining larger implication by allusion, analogy, the echo of an event
or a myth. And, as one might expect, these allusions and echoes are
chiefly from the wellspring, the pure water of our culture, the classics and
the Bible, always used in a way as to be *functional* decoration. Venus is
the reigning deity, yet she is ambiguous, sometimes seen *in bono*,
sometimes *in malo*. There are deaths, births, and entrances. It is truly a
chronicle, giving the impression of sprawling *largesse*, weight and size,
whereas, in fact, it is not really a long novel. A virtuoso performance.

What does the book say? It says all men are sinners, but it is possible
to be good, loving and brave. It says the good old days weren't all that
good, but that, indeed, something has happened to the American dream,
that it is approaching nightmare. It says that the nightmare is there in the
best of us, but it is still possible to hold up your head and "admire the
world." For a book with much pathos and misfortune it ends on a positive
note of instruction, made palatable by the sweetness of Leander's
simplicity and Cheever's irony.

And that could be that. Except that he has chosen to continue the
Wapshot history by continuing it into our time. The books are related,
but not strictly sequential. Though some of the same people appear in
both, they are somehow changed and modified by the times. They are not
quite the same characters. And the world, even its history, is now different. The tone and style are different. (We miss the vitality of Leander's
journal, which only appears once.) Things disintegrate, decay, blur out of
focus, fall apart. The relationship is much like that of *The Rainbow* and
Women in Love or, closer to home, of *The Hamlet* to *The Town*. Which is
to say the two books are Cheever's old testament, written of the time of

myths, the law and the prophets, and his new testament, beginning now on a Christmas Eve and ending, although on Christmas, with a curious last supper to be followed shortly by the last book of the Bible—the Apocalypse. The sins of *Chronicle* are original sin. *Scandal* moves inexorably toward the end of the world. Thus the two books must be taken together; but, as in scriptural exegesis we must not gloss the new law with the old.

The difference between the two can be illustrated by a small thing. Cheever's writing has always been marked by its representative use of the five senses. But in *Chronicle* it is smell, the odors of the world, the flesh and the devil, which predominate. There are great patches and lists of good odors, rich savors. *Scandal* is, by contrast, practically odorless. Most of the odors are bad or sordid and linger to haunt us like ambivalent ghosts. The author-narrator makes this quite explicit, saying that "we leave behind us, in the hotels, motels, guest rooms, meadows and fields where we discharge this much of ourselves, either the scent of goodness or the odor of evil, to influence those who come after us." In another place a character surveys fallen apples: "Paradise must [he thought] have smelled the windfalls." But in contrast to *Chronicle* the predominant sensuous patterns of *Scandal* are all black and white, the presence or the absence of light. " 'Light and shadow, light and shadow,' says old Cousin Honora of the music. She would say the same for Chopin, Stravinsky or Thelonious Monk."

> *I want to put on innocence like a bright new dress. I want to feel clean again!—The Wapshot Scandal*

The Wapshot Scandal begins in St. Botolphs and somehow ends there, after following the young sons of Leander, Moses and Coverly, through many misadventures and following Cousin Honora to Rome and back, fleeing an investigator of the Internal Revenue Service, to her death by self-starvation. It is, however, principally concerned with Coverly, Moses' wife Melissa and Cousin Honora. Moses, the favored and luckier of the two boys, was never fully realized in *Chronicle* and is really no more than a shadow in *Scandal*. Concentrating on these three characters, Cheever keeps the story happily bouncing back and forth, pausing now and then for a wonderfully relevant digression, moving across wide spaces and through patches of time as if waving a passport which reads "freely to pass." Now Cheever is for the most part on his old stamping ground, and Proxmire Manor, where Moses and Melissa exist, is a dead ringer for Shady Hill. The opportunities for satire of the present state of things are manifold and Cheever doesn't miss a trick. It's all there—surburbia, the economy of indebtedness, the religion of the churchs, T.V., space exploration, scientists and missiles, drugs and cancer, repairmen, undertakers, drive-in theaters, superhighways, frozen food, computers, "the sumptuary laws," travel, indifferent clerks and airline stewardesses, a daring airlines robbery, Congressional hearings, security clearance and the income tax, homosexuality, advertising slogans, doctors and the A.M.A., a male beauty contest, blue plastic swimming pools, outdoor barbecues, shabby and unsuccessful adulteries; oh it's all there all right, God's plenty of the outward and visible signs of a time when "Standards of self-esteem had advanced to a point where no one was able to dig a hole," a wild, yet terrifying imitation of "a world that seemed to be without laws and prophets."

The full range of humor is there too. The basic slapstick—"Oh, the wind and the rain and to hold in one's arms a willing love! He stepped into a large pile of dog manure." The irony of character, a wounded veteran thinks: "He could have gotten a deferred job at the ore-loading docks in Superior and made a forture during the war but he didn't learn this until it was too late." The author-narrator's special brand—describing Proxmire Manor as a village which "seemed to have eliminated, through adroit social pressures, the thorny side of human nature."

It is part of the irony and humor of this book that the whole plan of the story is told in capsule in what appears to be an irrelevant digression, the story of a woman, scarcely known by Melissa, whose ruin and downfall began the day the septic tank backed up. Step by step, we follow her into a nightmare of disintegration as, one by one, each of her appliances breaks down and cannot be repaired; she becomes a drunk and an adulteress and ends a suicide. (The book is full of suicides to underline the suicidal inclination of the age.) The pattern of this digression is repeated over and over again. Begin with a credible, typical situation, push it an inch or two into the realm of hilarious farce, then the farce of a sudden becomes dream, and all dreams turn to nightmare. It is typical of Cheever that he backs into his moral plea to the world behind the mask of irony, permitting his mouthpiece to be a decrepit old senator in a Congressional Investigating Committee speaking out to Doctor Cameron, a mad missile scientist:

> "We possess Promethean powers but don't we lack the awe, the humility, that primitive man brought to the sacred fire? Isn't this a time for uncommon awe, supreme humility? If I should have to make some final statement, and I shall very soon for I am nearing the end of my journey, it would be in the nature of a thanksgiving for stout-hearted friends, lovely women, blue skies, the bread and wine of life. Please don't destroy the earth, Dr. Cameron," he sobbed. "Oh, please, please don't destroy the earth."

Yet the earth and the people in it seem inevitably headed for destruction. Even grand old Cousin Honora kills herself. But, like Leander, she leaves a legacy, not a journal but a Christmas dinner to which she has, as always, invited enough strangers to make the magic number twelve. It is Coverly, unlucky and so often defeated, who pulls together, picks up the pieces and keeps the last Christmas dinner in honor of his cousin. He attends a Christmas Eve service performed by a drunken, ineffectual Episcopal priest, and does his duty by staying alone in the Church until the last *amen*. In the morning he collects what is left of the Wapshots and they await the arrival of Honora's eight invited guests. Who turn out to be all inmates of The Hutchins Institute for the Blind, only two of whom are identified, an old testament type muttering the wrath of God on the sinners and a sweet Negress who carries the simple message of love and mercy in a gesture. Of these guests Coverly thinks:

> They seem to be advocates for those in pain; for the taste of misery as fulsome as rapture, for the losers, the goners, the flops, for those who dream in terms of missed things—planes, trains, boats and opportunities—who see on waking the empty tarmac, the empty waiting room, the water in the empty slip, rank as Love's Tunnel when the ship is sailed; for all those who fear death.

It is a profoundly moving conclusion and as close to an explicit statement of Christian faith as I have seen from a *New Yorker* writer, perilously close to religion. Venus has been ubiquitous in this book, too, but here she is clearly the old Venus *in malo*, whose rewards are folly and degradation, who is the first handmaiden of Dame Fortune who gives all who serve her a spin on the wheel. (If this sounds almost Medieval, it is. There is even a mysterious archer, clad all in red, who fires an arrow at Coverly and, fortunately, misses.) In *Scandal* John Cheever makes a firm and definite distinction between false love [*cupiditas*] and the love that moves the stars [*caritas*]. And he ends on the note we are now familiar with, for there is no other song or burden for our times, that "we must love one another or die."

For all these reasons *The Wapshot Scandal* is at once John Cheever's most ambitious work and his finest achievement. Because he is an artist with his own voice and because he has earned the right to speak out in that voice, it is a fine achievement in the art of the novel this year or any year.

> *It seemed incredible to him that his people, his inventive kind, the first to exploit glass store fronts, bright lights and continuous music, should have ever been so backward as to construct a kind of temple that belonged to the ancient world.* [Johnson, an agent of the Internal Revenue Service, views a classic white-steepled New England church.]
> —*The Wapshot Scandal*.

Now the quibbling begins. It will be brief. Yet there are a few things to be said—a few. They will not be exactly objective or fair, for ultimately critical judgment cannot be. It may be that if I break rules and simply state a few personal prejudices and feelings, it will enable the *reader* anyway to judge for himself. First, I am Southern and from as far back as any Wapshot. The Southern background does make a difference. We have never rejoiced in the civilization Mr. Cheever satirizes. In fact it is none of our own. Deep in our hearts, if not in our heads, we feel, perhaps smugly, that it is the end result of all that grand, hypocritical spirit which erupted in New England and would not rest until it had destroyed ours. We feel New England and Mr. Cheever are getting what they asked for and deserved. Perhaps a little more rational is the notion, which is inevitably entertained by those who have had the historical experience of defeat, that disillusionment is a naive posture. There is an air of excitement, urgency and anger, an air of *discovery* about Cheever's treatment of human suffering, of its trinity of devils—poverty, disease and ignorance. One must resist the temptation of the inner smile, the inner voice which says—" 'Tis new to thee."

People do not live like people in *The New Yorker*, try as they will, and they never will. The insulation of that world is foolish and as forlorn as the storm windows Cheever characters are forever putting up and taking down. There may well be a system of election and damnation, but the elect are not necessarily the charming, the gifted, the beautiful, the eccentric or even the innocent. Nor are they necessarily children, cripples, Negroes or victims. There is no text which says that God cannot look with love upon the stupid, the cruel, the vulgar, the hypocritical and the guilty. It is these who need His love most, and it is these whom we have been commanded to love. And that is most difficult. I am not talking about Salinger's Fat Lady. (There's a Fat Lady seen briefly in *Scandal*.) After much trial and error Salinger's Glass family discovered that it is possible to love the Fat Lady. Cheever has come to that conclusion too. But in truth we are not advised to love the unlovable, we are *commanded to*. You don't get medals or merit badges for obeying orders. It is to the point that in Medieval allegories most of the time the devil did not wear red at all. He came in green, camouflaged in the color of faith.

What I am saying is that although this book makes a plea for charity, it does not practice it. Sympathy, yes; compassion, yes, for some characters; and sentimentality is abundant and aplenty. For what is sentimentality but a deep concern for human suffering which disregards the human spirit?

Now a few quibbles in rapid, random order:

(1) *historical—political—social*

Historically the book is very inaccurate precisely because it exists in a vacuum. More obviously in *Chronicle* but also in *Scandal*, both of which intend to deal with the American experience, the *events* of that experience impinge almost not at all upon the characters. It is as if Cheever divided American history into two periods—the Quaint Period, from the *Mayflower* to the middle thirties, and The Vulgar Now, the time of guided missiles and frozen food. Does he really believe that all the Wars and the Depression had *no* influence on the American character? Or is it that "we all know all about that anyway"? Do we really? Have we progressed that far?

(2) *moral-theological*

Have already quibbled once. But we have been told, wisely I believe, by a Pope, that to consider our own age as especially characterized by sin and corruption is a form of spiritual pride and also quite silly. We may be destroyed or destroy ourselves, but it will not be because of our highly developed and high-powered immorality. Morally Cheever appeals to every sane human being. Nobody, even the men at the missile stations, wants to destroy the world or do away with blue skies, trout streams, butterflies, old houses, *The New Yorker* or even the literary *status quo*. It is not likely, on the other hand, that Cheever's moral message will restrain one maniac from pulling a lever or a trigger.

(3) *literary*

Though an innovator of sorts, Cheever has made a *habit* of his innovations. They are altogether acceptable now and, it seems, that suits him fine. At times his method and virtuosity disguises a kind of carelessness and indifference. The verisimilitude he must start with, no matter how deeply into dream or farce he goes, is not always there just because he is able to hang out a list of *things* and current phrases (like the little flags on used car lots). He drops characters who don't interest him and lets others exist in a realm of two-dimensions and cliche. Well, it is his world, isn't it? And one has to admire his bravado. Still, with all admiration, it would be a lie not to admit to the feeling that it is very *safe*. The man on the flying trapeze with a good safe net beneath. The lion tamer cutting a caper in a cage full of toothless lions.

These quibbles don't add up to much. What should one ask of *The Wapshot Scandal*? It is a good book by a good writer, more than good enough and better than we deserve. It is just good enough to be judged against the ideal of greatness. Which may be asking too much.

Cheever's Yankee Heritage

Cynthia Ozick*

What is the difference between a minor and a major writer? Certainly it is not subject-matter: *The Wapshot Scandal* and *Anna Karenina* are both about adultery. Nor is it a question of control—John Cheever has an aerialist's sly command over just how taut the line of a sentence should be, and just how much power must be applied or withheld in the risk of ascent. Nor can the disparity be uncovered, finally, in any theory of what sustains an original characterization—the plain fact is that Leander Wap-

*Reprinted with permission from the *Antioch Review*, 24 (Summer 1964), 263–67.

shot and Honora Wapshot are among those figures who continue to stand even after the novels that housed them have disintegrated into total non-recall. They outlive and overwhelm every artifact and sunset on the premises, and the reason is the premises are exactly that—not merely a farm and a house in a New England port town called St. Botolphs, but the premises and hypotheses of Cheever's idea of America. It is not that major writers work from major premises and minor writers from minor ones—Chekov alone is evidence for the opposite. The difference is simply this: those writers we must ultimately regard (*regard*, not dismiss) as minor do not believe in what they are showing us. Major writers believe. Minor writers record not societies, or even allegories of societies, but vapid dreams and pageants of desire.

Now in an earlier, pre-Wapshot era, Cheever was celebrated as our supreme cicerone and Virgil of the suburbs—conductor on those commuters' trains carrying us to that eery but fine place known as Shady Hill, and, when we arrived, canny conductor once again, this time of the ladies' cocktail orchestra hidden in the forsythia. Everyone applauded, but everyone said: "Limited. Give us more; become major," and those prosperous, self-consciously self-improving communities along the New Haven tracks, with their amiable lusts, lawns, loves, lushes, and of course their babysitters and asembly nights and conjugalities, were abandoned for nothing less than the Yankee Heritage itself. Or so it seemed—*The Wapshot Chronicle* appeared to be both a Departure and a Widening-of-Compass. That Moses and Melissa Wapshot at length settled in Proxmire Manor, Shady Hill under another name, was only accident, and irrelevant; Cheever, in moving from the short story to the novel, had given up the breadth of a finger-nail for the roominess of all the Russian steppes. And as if that were not bravery enough, we have in *The Wapshot Scandal* a sequel, suggesting perhaps an American cycle, family epic, documentary, even, of the national or free-world tone: it is true that the *Scandal* chases us all the way from a missile center (with gantries on the horizon) somewhere in the "real" American West to a sale of male prostitutes just on the other side of the Bay of Naples, where Melissa buys her old lover (who happens also to be her old grocery-boy), to Rome, where, in good Yankee-heritage Edmund Wilson style, Honora is caught up with for non-payment of Federal taxes. The canvas looks wide enough at last—surely Shady Hill is finally too specialized to count, surely St. Botolphs is left far behind, veiled in its miasma of not-being-with-it?

But the canvas, just because it *is* so "contemporary," is deceptive; you can turn it upside-down and see something else, perhaps the very note the artist most needed to hide from himself and us—that suddenly clear figure in the abstraction which gives everything away. The *Chronicle* began overtly as an idyll, so that it might end cunningly as an idyll mocking at its own elements. But the *Scandal*, to prove its even shrewder ironies, begins with the mockery itself: Coverly Wapshot, spending the night in the empty house of his childhood, thinks he sees the ghost of Leander. "Oh, Father, Father, why have you come back?" he cries, and cries it still, even when he is safely back in the missile center which is his home, and which, like all appurtenances of the up-to-date, is thoroughly ghost-free.—"Oh, Father, Father, why have you come back?"

The answer is that in Cheever Father (Father Time, in fact) always comes back because he only pretended not to be there in the first place. Cheever's suburbs are not really suburbs at all; they are a willed and altogether self-deluding reconstruction of a dream of St. Botolphs. And St. Botolphs is not really what we are meant to take it for, a dying New England village redolent of its sailing-glory days—it too is a fabrication, a sort of Norman Rockwell cover done in the manner of Braque: Cheever's deliberately wistful, self-indulgent and sleight-of-hand dream of a ruined history and temperament. It is the history and temperament of the "quaint," commemorated and typified in fake widow's walks on top of those ubiquitous antique shoppes which seek to reproduce Our New England Legacy in places like Mojave Desert naval stations or the Florida swamps. Under this system of pretense we all landed at Plymouth Rock, and that is why Dr. Cameron, the missile master of the *Scandal*, is shamed by having to reveal that he was born not a Cameron, but a Bracciani. Cheever's Yankee Heritage, for most Americans, never existed, and even the few who are entitled to it have long ago repudiated it for the acceptable salvations of our coast-to-coast parking lot, with its separate traffic lanes for shopping carts and baby carriages. This is the supermarket America we all daily smell, and this is the America which the suburbs, those stage-sets of our grassy and decently small-town beginnings, play at forsaking and often denying. The trouble is not just homesickness, but meretricious homesickness. We long for the white clapboard house behind the picket fence, we have need of going to Grandma's for Thanksgiving, and in our plasterboard-walled version of the American Dream Past we tell each other lies about the land around us. The suburbs are not St. Botolphs, they cannot be St. Botolphs, because there is no St. Botolphs any more—and for most of us there never was. We too were born Bracciani.

All of this Cheever knows, and his knowledge is his irony—but there is no iron in it. The problem stems partly from the beauty of his prose—I can think of only four or five other novelists who match his crystal and perfectionist dedication to the weight of a word, and, except for Nabokov, they are all embossers, cameo-workers in the extreme. Cheever's is a prose on which the ironic has been forced by conscience and will: so that often enough the second half of a sentence will contrive to betray the first half—whether by anti-climax, an unexpected intrusion of the mundane or a sly shift of tonality from the oratorical to the humble, or a shudder of fatalism suddenly laid on the glory of the perceived world. "The maples and beeches had turned," he will begin, "and the moving lights of that afternoon among the trees made the path ahead of him seem like a chain of corridors and chambers, yellow and gold consistories and vaticans," and then the completion with "but in spite of this show of light he seemed still to hear the music from the television, and see the lines at Betsey's mouth and to hear the crying of his little son. He had failed. He had failed at everything." Or an elderly Senator at a Congressional investigatory hearing will rise and speak thus:

> Come, come, let us rush to the earth. It is shaped like an egg, covered with fertile seas and continents, warmed and lighted by the sun. It has churches of indescribable beauty raised to gods that have never been seen, cities whose distant roofs and smokestacks will make your heart leap, auditoriums in which people listen to music of the most serious import and thousands of museums where man's drive to celebrate life is recorded and preserved. Oh, let us rush to see this world! They have invented musical instruments to stir the finest aspirations. They have invented games to catch the hearts of the young. They have invented ceremonies to exalt the love of men and women. Oh, let us rush to see this world!

The next words are: "He sat down," and immediately afterward we learn that the witness, who is Dr. Cameron, is a sadist who has tortured his own son into idiocy. It is all chiaroscuro, all febrile play: play derived from the hints and darts of fantasy, from a yearning for the brightness that precedes disillusionment.

"This was the place where he [Coverly] had been conceived and born, where he had awakened to the excellence of life," Cheever says of St. Botolphs, "and there was some keen chagrin at finding the scene of so many dazzling memories smelling of decay; but this, he knew, was the instinctual foolishness that leads us to love permanence where there is none." This explicit rebuttal of all his charge of instruments, games, ceremonies, and exaltations of love is rare in Cheever; he eschews statement and leaves it to the falling tread of his elegiac lines. Among these his disbelief must be *detected*, for he covers everything over with a burden of beauty and sensibility. Exquisite apprehension of one's condition cancels failure; "some intensely human balance of love and misgiving" cancels brutality. Eloquence cancels all things inscrutable. All the same it is no surprise that Cheever does not believe in St. Botolphs and its cardboard replicas, including the houses and lives girdled by the gantries. He does not pretend to believe in them; he only wishes they were real. The luminiferous quality of his wishing follows his sentences like a nimbus, and in the end he fails to move because he moves us *all the time*, from moment to moment, from poignancy to poignancy. In Cheever, even adultery is less an act than an emblem of promise and peace. In every instance rapture overwhelms chagrin; over every person and incident he throws his coruscating net of allusion: to the past, to other lives, other possibilities, other hopes—so that his novels have no unitary *now* out of which the next event can naturally rise. I mentioned Chekhov as an example of a writer who, though self-limiting, is not minor, and it is Chekhov who gives the final word on the relation of manner to emotion. For language to be moving, Chekhov said, coldness is essential—a style should always be colder than its material. Cheever's infirmity is not that he is often episodic (he progresses like a radiant yet never static mediaeval triptych), and not even that his people are frequently tiresome innocents (through whom he has the terrifying trick of making evil seem picturesque); but he has not heeded Chekhov. It is no use arguing that he has justified and ameliorated his nostalgia by mocking it. The mockery is weaker than the nostalgia and is in every case overcome by it. And the nostalgia, like those wagon-wheels on suburban lawns, like old Mr. Jowett, the stationmaster of St. Botolphs with his yellow lantern, is fraudulent and baseless, a lie told not out of malice or self-interest, but worse, out of sentiment and wholesale self-pity.

It is all a part of the American piety. It is a ritual exercise in an emptied-out culture—the so-called Yankee Heritage has no willing legatees. "Oh, Father, Father, why have you come back?" But in reality, and in America especially, he does not come back, and Cheever, in his anguish over this absence, this unyielding and mutilating absence, settles for ghosts. There is no Yankee sociology, there is no Yankee anthropology, there is only a Yankee archaeology, and, perhaps, a Yankee mythology, more comic-strip cliché than compelling legend. The latter subsumes an image of a Europe ruined, brilliant, erotic, and past. It is on account of the abundant yet barren supermarket present that Cheever needs this sensuous and fertile make-believe past—how else can he complicate and enrich? Mere eccentricity, like Honora Wapshot's, will not do—eccentricity is a function of a secure and complacent society, but Cheever is so out of sorts and so out of sympathy with Happy America that he has been driven to invent a Happier America. It is a sad country where a decision—a return, a renewal, a reprieve—is made not because anything has *happened*, but because something is all at once *felt*: an epiphany of the spirit, a revelation without relevance. Smell the rain! see how the light slants!—and suddenly restoration is achieved, forgiveness flows from the spleen. It is a country so splendid and melancholy, so like an artificial (though thoroughly artistic) rose, that anyone writing in it can measure his stature by the inchworm. Oh, it is hard to be a Yankee—if only the Wapshots were, if not Braccianis, then Wapsteins—how they might then truly suffer! And we might truly feel.

The Way We Live Now

Joan Didion*

*I think all Americans who have wandered from their birthplace—and
that includes most of my generation—carry with them a guilty feeling
often disguised as 'nostalgia.' They wouldn't dream of returning to roam
in the house where they were born (even if it hasn't been torn down) but
they sometimes feel that 'life would have been simpler' if they had.*

T. E. Matthews

When did music come this way?
Children dear, was it yesterday?

Matthew Arnold

Let me tell you something first: I am in my late twenties, a relatively
articulate member of the most inarticulate segment of the middle class,
the kind of woman who sets store by her great-grandmother's orange
spoons, by well-mannered children, by the avoidance of chic and by a
sense of sin. I remember learning more about orange spoons than about
sin from the Episcopal Church, in which I was christened and confirmed
(and in which I was told, when I said I feared death, that there was no
hell; "only different levels of heaven"); I learned even less from the
Catholic Church, in which I was married (the boundary between mortal
and venial sin, I was told when I expressed concern, "differs from parish
to parish"). It has sometimes occurred to me that sin, as a helpful abstract
in these bountiful times, is pretty much left to those of us who prize it.

In those ways, if in no others, I might be one of John Cheever's
characters, those driven creatures who categorize their sins of omission
and commission with as much satisfaction as those of more faith count off
their beads; a heightened interest in good and evil is what is left of those of
us who prize faith but lack it. *There is sin in fear, sin in sloth, how many
angels on the head of a fat man*: the pervasive importance of sin is the
fragment we shore against our ruin. Cheever's one great story—told and
retold in all its variations, in all its inversions, through his short stories,
through *The Wapshot Chronicle,* and now through *The Wapshot Scandal*—is of children led astray by natural error and inflexibly punished,
banished from the Eden that lies all around us.

He writes about the kind of man who burns with sad pure lust for the
babysitter, about the kind of woman who cries for her errors when she
overhears a stranger ordering flowers for a funeral, because it occurs to
her that one day she will herself be "the subject of some such discussion in
a flower shop, and close her eyes forever on a world that distracted her
with its beauty." (To forestall this fate, Melissa Wapshot runs of to Rome
with a grocery boy, and it is Cheever's genius that she seems less absurd
than tragic, grieving in a *Supra-Marketto Americano* and "gathering her

*Reprinted with permission from *National Review*, 16 (24 March 1964), 237–40.

fantastic garland not of cornflowers, nettles and long purples, but of salt, pepper, Bab-o, Kleenex, frozen codfish balls, lamb patties, hamburger, bread, butter, dressing, an American comic book for her son and for herself a bunch of carnations.") Life has somehow bewildered these Cheever people, left them bereft of something—they forget just what it is—once promised. One thinks of W. H. Auden's line: *Lost in a haunted wood, children afraid of the night who have never been happy or good.*

But there is a difference between Auden's children and Cheever's children, and the difference is vital to understanding Cheever. Cheever's children *have* been happy or good, or think they have been; they remember it, or believe they do. It has something to do with their childhood, something to do with where they came from. The narrator of "Torch Song" is disturbed to see, with a drunk in Grand Central Station, a girl with whom he had grown up in Ohio; "it troubled Jack to see in these straits a girl who reminded him of the trees and the lawns of his home town." The wife in "A Season of Divorce" tends her sick children and recalls a more promising time, when she was at Grenoble and wrote a paper in French on Charles Stuart. "A professor at the University of Chicago," she adds, "wrote me a letter." In *The Wapshot Scandal*, Coverly Wapshot wonders whether, when he arrives home for dinner, his unhappy wife will be watching television, whether his son will be in tears, whether in fact there will be any dinner, and "some vision of St. Botolph's in the light of a summer evening" appears to him: "It was that hour when the housewives called their children in for supper with those small bells that used to be used for summoning servants to the table. Silver or not, they all had a silvery note and Coverly recalled this silvery ringing now from all the back stoops of Boat Street and River Street, calling the children in from the banks of the river."

It is not merely of St. Botolph's that Coverly mourns—St. Botolph's, where Wapshots had always lived until Coverly and his brother Moses banished themselves from its summer light; it is something larger than St. Botolph's, and Coverly is not alone in mourning it. As the narrator of "A Season of Divorce" explains, of himself and his wife: "We both come from that enormous stratum of the middle class that is distinguished by its ability to recall better times. Lost money is so much a part of our lives that I am sometimes reminded of expatriates, of a group who have adapted themselves energetically to some alien soil but who are reminded, now and then, of the escarpments of their native coast."

Lost money, the recollection of better times, silver bells ringing children in from play: the twilight world of the old American middle class is indeed a lost world, as lost as Czarist Russia or the antebellum South, and like both those countries of the mind it has become a dream that in some respects never was, an imagined territory capable of paralyzing its exiles.

Paralyzed, they wonder why their circumstances had "appeared to offer something better," wonder what stands between them and "what they deserved." They sense in themselves, as a character in *The Wapshot Scandal* senses in herself when she can get no one to repair a sewer line, a kind of "tragic obsolescence."

Adrift in "a world that seemed to be without laws and prophets," they try with an almost superstitious fervor to apply the standards they learned as children; they fail. Like Coverly Wapshot, they try to judge themselves "along traditional lines," and end up yearning only for the immortality of someone like Honora Wapshot, for the constant presence of someone who will "punish his and his brother's wickedness with guilt, reward their good works with lightness of heart, pass judgments on their friends and lovers." Banished from paradise, Cheever's children count their sins, try for goodness in a world they fail to understand, and love life the more because they so fear death. I can think of no other writer today who tells us so much about the way we live now.

The Road Through Nightmare

George Greene*

Old Leander Wapshot, one of the most bumbling yet shrewd men in recent fiction, cries out in a rare moment of panic, "I only want to be esteemed." Apparently his creator has been spared such doubts, which says a good deal for his valor. If one had to choose the most underrated man of our American literary scene, one could close the competition by citing John Cheever. *Time* acknowledges his skill at conveying "the masked anxieties of the 'have-not-enoughs.' " The majority of "major" judges, though, rank him as yet another horse in the *New Yorker* stable, authors they suspect, I think wrongly, of exhibiting more expertise than depth. No silencer quite eliminates the noise of a hidden revolver.

After two volumes of stories, in 1957 John Cheever published *The Wapshot Chronicle*, his first novel and still his best-known book. Cheever never lapses into what he might have settled for, a facile imitation of John Marquand. The sage of the Wapshots praises the values of Cheever's ancestors, seeking in their life style what might still prove serviceable to an exiled, urbanized son. It is one milieu ripe for orgies of memorializing. Forestalling our question about the distance between St. Botolphs and Marquand's North Shore—*Wickford Point* comes to mind most readily— Cheever sets us straight. "They are not like this" (he proceeds to identify the Wapshots) "—these are country people. . . ."

If *The Wapshot Chronicle* is a canticle of praise, *The Wapshot Scandal* (1964) is a cry of dismay. Now Leander's sons take the center of the stage as they fumble to maintain their identity in an era of Cold War. The

*Reprinted with permission of the author from the *Kenyon Review*, 31, No. 4 (1969), 564–70.

book is Cheever's most pessimistic report, and it shows what ensues when the computerized nightmares accessible to modern technology are controlled by men who have never participated in that fallible yet forgiving world made possible by shared ideas. In most of its public forms modern science has crippled man's response to those realities which are nonetheless real for being unseen. The worst of our scandals is the progressive diminution of man's imagination as well as his soul. Although he had always been drawn to the revelations inherent in fantasy, it may well have been at this point that Cheever became fully committed to that program which distinguishes him as our most sensitive mediator between the empirical and the miraculous.

In a sense, everything Cheever has written grows out of the threat of human extinction and how we may combat it while still remaining sane. This accounts for one favorite tactic of rehabilitating characters by making them eligible for expansions of consciousness which soar beyond statistical solutions to merely quantitative problems. The wildest leaps of imagination are more wholesome than a world where machines control men and where flesh stifles the legitimate cries of spirit. In a rare statement about his craft Cheever conceded his tie with the Puritan past. "My aim as a writer," he went on, "has been to record a moderation of these attitudes—an escape from them if this seemed necessary. . . ."

One suspects that observation as well as innate need have strengthened a preference for sifting over abandonment. Cheever's characters may work on Madison Avenue or Wall Street, yet their memories almost always include the Boston Massacre, the Declaration of Independence, and the family Bible. When reality itself becomes surrealistic the most efficacious method by which to preserve sanity is to widen the range of one's own masks. Such antics may suggest persiflage which has grown unmanageable because of too many martinis. Yet was it not Freud who taught that all human behavior is a form of language? In this age of synthetic need and synthetic emotion there still survives the urge to give allegiance to those immemorial charities which qualify us for the category of human beings.

Initially *Bullet Park* may seem to stand outside this canon. Its characters are far more isolated than the Wapshots. There are no references to unity, energizing if narrow, of old New England. One person comes from as far afield as Indiana. The structure, rapid yet intense, owes as much to theme as to narrative strategy. The spare note proves functional nonetheless, for it throws beleaguered suburbanites more irreversibly on their own resources. Clearly Cheever has become wary of falling into the trap of elegy. The perils of retreat are underscored when one character dreads "the greasy green waters of the Lethe. . . ."

Bullet Park starts with a sentence which seems to endorse Westchester as the Elysian Fields. "Paint me a small railroad station then, ten minutes before dark." Eliot Nailles, a chemist whose firm markets mouthwash, resents the national game of chopping away at the suburbs. He lives saturated by virtuous love for a comely wife and their teenage son. Cheever's eye for village spectacles is as adroit as ever. Backed-up septic tanks display the caprice of Wagnerian deities. There is a sociable meeting of amateur firemen as vain as guild members in Chaucer. Cultural status seekers invoke John O'Hara and, more rarely, Camus (mispronounced). It takes little time before we sense all is not well. The cost of every house in Bullet Park is public knowledge, but its suicide rate is a secret. We knock against empty whiskey bottles, "ranged . . . like the gods in some pantheon of remorse." Railroad waiting rooms look as if they had been sacked. There is one droll scene where, over a Sunday roast, communication halts when the son brings home a Manhattan war widow with whom he has slept. Mr. Nailles loses his wallet, and his wife and he search with the passion of those who are pursuing their true grail. "Sitting at their breakfast table Nailles and Nellie seemed to have less dimension than a comic strip. . . ."

Yet disorder stalks this fashionable milieu like a sex maniac drooling outside the picture window. One man burns to death when a charcoal igniter explodes during a barbecue. Nailles stands by helpless when a neighbor is sucked under a rushing express train. The villain encourages a woman whose house he covets to drink and get pulverized on the highway. Tranquilizers make Mr. Nailles feel like Zeus floating on a cloud. Hazzard is the name of a local realtor. For hungover commuters a Monday morning train feels like Gethsemane. A teacher fears she may be the victim of a conspiracy of psychopaths. Vacationers standing on a beach seem trapped in a solitude nothing less than apocalyptic. One alcoholic readies bar equipment "as a dentist prepares his utensils for an extraction." In none of Cheever's prior works have we strayed so far onto the steppes of hysteria.

The bucolic note veers toward the plaintive, then dives abruptly into the fearful. Unknown to himself, Nailles has been chosen as a murder victim by one newcomer. The link between Hammer and Nailles is as tenacious as the urge to make a stale joke about their names, and it functions more subtly than any tip insinuating a clash between evil vs. good. Nailles stands at that point in time when he must either acquire self-knowledge or become a paunchy cipher. Even his religious practice expresses a fear of heights or depths. "The trout streams open for the resurrection": he assimilates the liturgical cycle only by localizing it. "The crimson cloths at Pentecost and the miracle of the tongues meant swimming." Nailles's sense of reality is not so much obtuse as it is parochial. Success has dulled him. In church one neighbor wears a monstrously oversized suit. Automatically Nailles thinks of our version of catastrophe immeasurable, cancer. Then he realizes that the man's father died in an airplane crash—the neighbor is wearing his parent's clothes. Nailles's narrow range is such that he "beamed at this triumph of practicality over death."

Eliot Nailles is the only hero in recent American fiction who utters the word "scandalous," expecting to be taken seriously. He rhapsodizes about guarding his family in some "clear amber fluid that would surround them, cover them, preserve them. . . ." It is as if we were embalming a corpse. Nailles cannot face the fact that his mother lies paralyzed in an anonymous, immaculate—and remote—nursing home. When his son suffers bouts of melancholy and takes refuge in bed Nailles is first forced to re-examine his assumptions. What saves him from smugness are those surges of puzzlement when he senses that pain is not, as he had hitherto thought, "a principality, lying somewhere beyond the legitimate borders of western Europe." He is blind to the fact that terror has finally qualified for American citizenship. He spends weekends felling diseased elm trees, yet he feels uncomfortable when the odor of dead wood intimates "the unease of all change." Inevitably he resists the fact that his son's malaise is spiritual rather than physical, cataloguing it as mononucleosis. At last he owns up. "Without his son he could not live." This visceral admission dislodges and makes visible the core anxiety. "He was afraid of his own death."

Ultimately the stamina of the text depends on Mr. Hammer, a figure some readers will doubtless reject as implausible because he discloses the obstinacy of unreason in a society which has always assumed that demons are exorcised once one reaches a minimum level of income. Indeed when we first meet him his face is "scrubbed, decent, and bright." Hammer's loveless childhood, his wealth, his agitation bespeak the risks of affluence without reciprocity. His travels constitute their own insane liturgy of famous hotels. He enjoys mobility to the point of vertigo. Hammer's need to counter dehydration of self makes for Cheever's most risky yet timely pages. At Yale Hammer unsuccessfully petitions a court to change his name to Levy. The choice confirms a faulty analogy between elation as the quintessence of living and the drama of those on whom turmoil has been thrust by others. In Rome he joins a funeral for a dead Communist, staring hungrily at signs bearing words like *pace, speranza, amore.* "I felt the strongest love for these strangers" (his sympathy is as transient as it is ominous) "for the space of three city blocks."

Hammer becomes obsessed with a haven symbolized by yellow walls. One senses a tug toward some act of cleansing destruction not unlike that of Van Gogh. Hammer cannot tolerate the "inoffensive improvisation" of his days. His quest for landscapes as supportive as they are unreal is paralleled by the feverish scope of his sexual drives. At a London revival meeting he enjoys one short remission. "Life was natural and we, together, were natural men and women." Both Nailles and Hammer want the "sense of sanctuary that is the essence of love." Whereas Nailles's mistake is to delay (nail down?) temporal flux, Hammer worships at a more insidious altar. He tries to reach the eye of a hurricane, meanwhile molding (hammering?) the world in order to buttress the faltering contours of his own identity. For all his stock responses, Nailles is bolstered by outside forces (wife, son, church). Hammer's compulsion to seize, exploit, then pass beyond whatever he touches eventually reaches the pitch of a peevish child lost in a thunderstorm. A mounting muddle between survival and velocity unleashes the crowning nightmare. "The fear was not of falling" (one bolt illuminates the bottom of his pit) "but of vanishing."

Hammer seeks to absolve himself by means of a scapegoat, attacking the manipulation of false hopes symbolized by American advertising. By accident he has seen a photograph of Nailles in a trade magazine, and with the counsel of his bizarre mother he develops a plan to murder a man of executive status. Somewhere along the line Hammer shifts his choice from father to son, possibly one further mark of sexual imbalance. He kidnaps the youth and drives him to an Episcopal church for immolation on the altar. With that wryly appropriate do-it-yourself Excalibur, a chain saw, Nailles breaks down the door just in time. When Hammer is taken into custody a newspaper reports one ostensible motive. "He intended, he claimed, to awaken the world."

We cannot escape the inference about who are the true awakeners in Bullet Park. The disturbing fact is that professionals in a number of categories come off badly. Nailles resents the local pastor because his breath smells. One woman, a convert from Unitarianism, is so belligerent in her observation of ritual that she promotes "competitive churchmanship." Tony Nailles is treated unsuccessfully by a number of medical experts. Finally the parents call in a guru, a calm and purposeful black man who once cleaned toilets in Grand Central. The guru encourages meditation on words like "love," a therapy which invites smirks but which rouses the patient. As he listens to the cries from upstairs Nailles suspects voodoo may have invaded his enlightened household. "His lawns and the incantations came from different kingdoms." Yet it is Nailles's kingdom which stands in need of quickening. For one opportunist who uses dinner parties as a trick to get a tax exemption thunder signifies nothing more than a massive orgasm. For Hammer the sound implies that an airplane has broken the sound barrier. For Nailles it contains a more human impact: "thunder always reminds me of what it felt like to be young." No wonder Eliot Nailles is so anxious about those encroaching highways. In Bullet Park one gets back on the path toward order by submitting to the rage as well as to the bequests of nature. Institutions and traditions are not so much irrelevant as lost in the din. "Someone has to observe the world," Nailles insists. We take heart at his readiness to accept the job, especially when one of the most apropos terms to define that world is "outrageous."

Vanity as well as individual fervor may account for the fact that we have so many American reports about youth. At the other end of the scale our society is so frightened by the prospect of growing old that this stage remains the least well-charted area in the national imagination. In between lies that only slightly less ominous plateau, middle age. It is there that Cheever stands, one of our most reliable scouts about the tribes inhabiting that risky expanse. The heartening thing is that, despite its special quandaries, he points it out as exciting as well as inevitable. In Eliot Nailles's suburb, bewildering, unclassifiable, poise resides in responding to reality as it gallops past our wary eyes. Yet the existential loneliness of Westchester may be productive of good, forcing Cheever's characters to recognize that the reciprocity they seek and the fumbling they so often exhibit are surer verifications of humanity than any safety zone insured by parochial forbearance and institutionalized by family chronicles.

Cheever rests his case on man as he finds him, anonymous, deracinated, breathing the unwholesome vapors of the metropolis. Elegy is no solution. Survival has come to depend on perception far more than on pedigree. "How can a people who do not mean to understand death," he writes in an earlier story that prefigures the theme of *Bullet Park*, "hope to understand love, and who will sound the alarm?" Yet the most distinctive strength of this man's art is the way in which rigor of scrutiny produces so many examples of the tenacity, if not the triumph, of our hunger for wholeness. Leander, that racy Ulysses of the South Shore, has sailed for the Happy Isles. Yet his fidgety descendants still testify to what was most deathless in him, that mixture of erosion of purpose and human sweetness which is the most permanent characteristic of our nature and which will survive all systems, Puritan and computerized as well. Psychologically, at least, Eliot Nailles is one such heir. He refuses to lapse into dementia by howling that he has lost control or that society, in any meaningful way, has ceased to exist. His definition of being alive depends on the effort, binding no matter how imperfect, "to bridge or link the disparate environments and rhythms of his world. . . ." Even in our decade of the bullet, the only passable road out of nightmare is through it.

Falconer by John Cheever

Joseph McElroy*

Degenerate or intact, our rituals are close kin to parody; for the formal recollection of a shared present imitates as it reenacts, and the imitation is at best some communal fiction. In *Bullet Park* John Cheever brought together by violence in a suburban church two complementary characters Hammer and Nailles whose collision course he had plotted with poignance and bizarre wit. Now in *Falconer* he reconciles the parts of one character, one person—a man in prison. Once again Cheever draws a fine tone of fable through his fiction and thus claims freedoms—if

*Reprinted with permission from *New Republic*, 176 (26 March 1977), 31–32.

also license—as magical as the truth told by his exact words and magnetic images. This is why his art seems independent of our "spatchcocked" American reality yet eerily reflective of it.

Here again are his familiar themes: escape, anodyne, marital enmity, the strange touch invading some safe or resigned routine, a love for what is graspable and palpable, the need for ceremony, the conflict between brothers, the pleasures of that Nabokovian trinity egotism, nostalgia, and, as Cheever puts it, the "speechless genitals." Likewise familiar is the haunted gap in which *Falconer* is not only marvelous and tantalizing in its inner correspondences and innuendoes, it is new for Cheever in the curious labor with which prisoner's progress emerges.

Ezekiel Farragut, whose grandmother rounded the Horn and whose image "for a big orgasm" is "winning the sailboat race," has been convicted of killing his brother. He has been sentenced to up to 10 years in Falconer (called here a Correctional Facility not because Cheever wants mere accuracy but because the euphemism like the rundown state of the place may seem to mark some unknown decline, perhaps "the last days of incarceration," a time recalling the ambiguous desuetude of tradition to be found in Kafka's "A Hunger Artist" or "In the Penal Colony").

Farragut believes he has been convicted because he is a drug addict and "sexual adventurer." Like De Quincey in *Confessions of an English Opium-Eater*, echoed here and in *Bullet Park*, Farragut acknowledges no guilt. Or that is what he thinks. Farragut's wife, visiting him, remarks that "it's nice to have a dry toilet seat," and she is rough on him in other ways; but she has had a "rotten marriage" and Farragut knows it and knows her; loves her, desires her, sees her as she is, burdened by him and by history. If the world seems unjust, his own inconsistencies are what he must gather together and live with. Entering the prison he thinks he is resigned to dying there. But "Then he saw the blue sky and nailed his identity to it" and to his immediate plans. He brings Descartes with him, but the clarity and distinctness with which he must come to himself will seem more mysterious than methodical.

Why is he an addict? Farragut's recollections take us back over Cheever's work and beyond any real focus on the symptoms or cure of heroin addiction. His father and brother tried at their different distances to get him killed; the family lost its money, and certain incongruities arising from this have been especially confusing in the person of Farragut's mother. She is nothing like his ideal image of "mother," a serene woman in a Degas painting; and even at 48 he finds this discrepancy too painful. "Why had the universe encouraged this gap?"

Further and further from that too quaint New England Eden of the Wapshot books, Cheever has shown us again and again the resorts of the unequal self as it seeks sanctuary in our middle-class wastelands. The people of his stories commute between barbecue and communion-rail; they translate themselves from country-club masquerade (knightly visor propped open with a train timetable) to the sacraments of the marriage bed. Somewhere there is a good, firm tree-house, like those formal sentences Cheever writes; but in search of solace and "self-esteem" (a recurrent word), his characters dose themselves to get to the end of the turnpike or into the next week. Like the missile base in an earlier novel, our computed landscapes are inhuman for Farragut, and, simplistic or not, his views must find in science and technology "murderous contradictions" that lead only to the poppy.

Denied his methadone, Farragut becomes a "withdrawal show" for a sadistic warden to watch those labor pains DeQuincey speaks of. Recovering from injuries, Farragut plots his retaliation. He completes three magnificently rational letters to his wife, his bishop, and the Governor, expounding with pomp, flair and intellect his principles, rights and identity. But the letters can't help him, except as their writing is one part of a growing meditation by turns as vivid and articulate as it is all the time turning about old fragments and intimations and turning about a truth whose well-worn words are moving becaused earned: "He did not know himself. He did not know his own language."

So he lets go; but he remains at the mercy of his memory, and, falling toward himself, he lives some new half-heard argument whose tendrils of twined wonder and inquiry surpass anything in Cheever's thought heretofore. And as Farragut listens to himself he lives with others, listens to men who may seem so different from him in their mad American monologues that the intimacy with which he comes to feel these men in the routines they all share grows upon the reader.

Farragut has a love affair, passes into it with a need that is like the grace of Cheever's unselfconscious presentation of it. Sexual feeling overflows, and Farragut is in love. And when his beloved withdraws—escaping disguised as an acolyte in a Cardinal's helicopter powered by that matchless old invention which Cheever has transcended in the miracles that really interest him—Farragut lives the loss.

Engrossed in his new life, he discovers one day that he is "clean." He had felt the walls vanishing and was afraid—for in this book about "the mystery of imprisonment" prison itself may be an escape. Now, out of chance and death, he must make his own bodily escape along a route as risky as it is ritually familiar.

But first—controlled perhaps too neatly by his creator's final flashbacks into a theme that has been with Cheever since his story "The Brothers" 40 years ago—Farragut must find again that mystery of the first murder whose contradiction he could reenact and embody more than know. Cheever says in *The Wapshot Scandel*, "A mythology that would penetrate . . . the density of the relationship between brothers seems to stop with Cain and Abel and perhaps this is as it should be." In "Good-bye, My Brother," which stands behind *Falconer* in other ways as well, the narrator at last can't bear his brother's narrow, negative nature and strikes him down. But resisting the impulse to finish the job, he feels "like two men, the murderer and the Samaritan," divided as brothers may be divided by an organic opposition to which the right response may not necessarily be love. Farragut's impulse to brain his cruel, stupid, sanctimonious brother turns out to be some turning of the stair, some way for Farragut to become one with himself.

Often in Cheever's stories the authorial power seems to have understood everything in advance; but in *Falconer*, the style often coincides with Farragut's groping pain and strength and moves as he moves. Among several other writers, Yeats and Eliot are allusively present not only because Farragut was an English professor, but because Cheever humbly, if quizzically, places his novel in a humane tradition where ceremonies of experience are honored as they should be. *Falconer* should be so honored. It will last.

Crying in the Wilderness

John Leonard*

A John Cheever character has wandered into the wrong novel and doesn't know how to get out. Where am I? Here, Céline's hospital; there, Kafka's penal colony; yonder, some William Burroughs; back aways, the Bible, with God in a bad mood and the sun-crazed desert prophets explaining why. Whatever happened to suburbia?

Certainly Ezekiel Farragut *is* a Cheever character—an upper-middle-class Wasp with marital problems, a professor of discrepancies, a disappointed romantic. Indeed, his disappointments amount almost to ecstasies. He thinks like this:

> What he felt, what he saw, was the utter poverty of erotic reasonableness. That was how he missed the target and the target was the mysteriousness of the bonded spirit and the flesh. He knew it well. Fitness and beauty had a rim. Fitness and beauty had a dimension, had a floor, even as the oceans have a floor, and he had committed a trespass. It was not unforgivable—a venial trespass—but he was reproached by the majesty of the realm.

Trespass, borders, contours, "that sense of sanctuary that is the essence of love" have always been important to Cheever characters. The mundane itself is a principality, with a rueful lyric for its anthem. The sadness in rumpus rooms is somehow political, a condition of citizenship in Cheeverdom. Typically, Ezekiel's feelings are chaotic, "and he might have cried, but he might have cried at the death of a cat, a broken shoelace, a wild pitch." He is decency at an impasse.

*Reprinted with permission from *Harper's*, 254 (April 1977), 88–89.

What does Ezekiel want? Not much: "A little kindness." "Some oneness . . . some contentment." "He would settle for the stamina of love, a presence he felt like the beginnings of some stair." Perhaps he doesn't want enough; Cheever people are often punished for not having wanted more boldly. Still: "Almost everyone I love has called me crazy." And that's typical, too. Cheever people care with such passion for the ordinary—"the chords, the deep rivers, the unchanging profundity of nostalgia"—that they seem wacky, wrong for this world, waiting for an accident.

From previous experience with Cheever, then, one expects that Ezekiel's luck, or charm, will run out. Gusts of chance—in Cheever country, chance is a sort of secular substitute for evil—will unmoor him. He will consult himself, like a compass: surely inside this mess of memories and desires there is a moral pole toward which the knowing needle swings and points. Something will be required of him: an extravagance, a surprise, a rhapsody, a proof.

But hold on. Ezekiel is also a heroin addict. Ezekiel murders his own brother with a fire iron. Ezekiel is sent to prison, gets beaten up, has a homosexual love affair, and busts out. Wow. We are, in the Falconer Correctional Facility, a long way from Shady Hill, St. Botolphs, and Bullet Park. It is as if our Chekhov—and some of us believe Cheever to be our Chekhov—had ducked into a telephone booth and reappeared wearing the cape and leotard of Dostoevsky's Underground Man. Modernism, the literature of fire alarms, has caught up with him.

It's not that violence and death have been missing from Cheever in the past. Men drown, and crack up cars, and fall off mountains in his stories. Children eat ant poison. Fifteen-year-old prodigies commit suicide. A wife shoots her husband as he is about to hurdle the living-room couch. Someone is devoured by his own dogs. People burn to death when cans of charcoal igniter explode at barbecue parties.

But always in the past these have seemed to be accidents, arranged so as to throw into relief the fragility of all that Cheever holds most dear: the sanctuaries of love, "the perfumes of life: sea water, the smoke of burning hemlock, and the breasts of women," "the ear's innermost chamber, where we hear the heavy noise of the dragon's tail moving over the dead leaves." He seemed to be reminding us of how foolish we were in our tacit claim "that there had been no past, no war—that there was no danger or trouble in the world."

He did his reminding in a prose at once evocative and dreamy. (Does it still need saying that the English language is lucky John Cheever writes in it?) The accidents could be thought of as dreams, to which the dreamer responded as if "to a memory that I had not experienced." All accidents, all dreams in Cheever country—of infidelity, revenge, escape, rum punch, scarlet moving vans, full-page spreads in national magazines, fathers, castles, hydrogen bombs, supermarkets—seemed to have equal weight and a similar purpose. They were preparations for an eruption of mind and spirit. Even in *Bullet Park*, when Hammer called upon Nailles to sacrifice his own son, it was possible to believe that Hammer was a manufactured darkness, a stand-in for malign chance, a bad dream by which Nailles might find a way to prove his love for Tony.

Not so inside the walls of *Falconer*. The violence and death are real, and to accommodate them the prose occasionally coarsens. Ezekiel dwells among jewel thieves, check-forgers, hijackers, kidnappers, wife-killers, human cigarettes stubbed down to the last coal of their being. As they lie about and explain themselves, as they scream in their sleep, as they listen to radio reports on what appears to be the Attica uprising, as they stand at night to masturbate in a long tunnel called the Valley, they don't sound like Coverly Wapshot. They are experiencing extremity, not dreaming it; their accidents are permanent. A prisoner whose eardrums have been pierced with an ice pick isn't going to hear any chords or dragons' tails. The massacre of the cellblock cats isn't lyrical; it is stomach-turning.

Outside the walls, the sweet prose is still at work. Cheever hasn't forgotten how. There are flashbacks—flares, really, or grenades—by whose bright brief light we see something of Ezekiel's soulscape. There is his family, "his hated origins:" his father wanted him aborted; his brother, Eben, liked to remind him of this fact; I think I would have hit Eben with a fire iron myself. There are snapshots of his marriage. ("You are the biggest mistake I ever make," says his beautiful wife), of his foray into drug addiction ("murderous contradictions"), and of his career as a college professor ("no philosophical suture").

And there are swatches of that surpassing tenderness, that respect for the intimacy and the mystery of men and women together, that Cheever alone among male American writers seems capable of producing: Ezekiel's letter to his girlfriend, "exalted by the diagnostics of love;" his safari for fox grapes in the hoarfrost to prepare his wife's favorite jelly; notations on the loneliness of single men in Chinese restaurants; the irony of Christmas; rain dripping from gun towers.

Very well. Cheever has left Shady Hill in a black van through the twilight zone and into hell. (He has, in fact, taught at Sing Sing.) Inside Falconer, Ezekiel is unknowingly cured of his addiction, subdues the past and, with the help of a miracle, escapes—just as, with the help of an earlier miracle, his lover Jody had escaped. This strikes me as being at least one miracle too many, especially as it comes on top of several improbabilities: Ezekiel's shooting up before college lectures, his having an affair with Jody, the presence of so many good Samaritans at so many crucial moments, et cetera. But what was implicit in *Bullet Park*—the imagery of a kind of muscular Episcopalianism—runs rampant in *Falconer*. Ezekiel's durance vile is full of miracles and prophets, mechanical and plastic Holy Ghosts, ciboriums and chalices, the Eucharist, and "fallen men" in "the white light" beyond redemption. And Ezekiel himself is almost literally resurrected from the dead, bloody but unbowed.

Is this symbolism necessary? I'm not sure. It sent me to the Bible to read up on Ezekiel (which in Hebrew means "God strengthens"), and God *was* in a bad mood in that book, wrathing at the mouth, tossing around the twelve tribes, rattling dry bones. It also sent me to William Butler Yeats to read up on falcons: "Turning and turning in the widening gyre. . . . the centre cannot hold. . . . Mere anarchy is loosed upon the world." I'm still not sure. And yet a certain anarchy is proposed.

Into what does Ezekiel escape? Into, apparently, an idea of love not as a sanctuary but as a relinquishing. Sanctuaries are prisons. Those whom we love, we liberate (or evict) into the pursuit of their self-interest. Ezekiel and Jody will never meet again. Out of extremity, Cheever seems to be saying, emerges an irreducible and persevering *me*, and a laissez-faire economy of the emotions. Where he's going, Ezekiel won't have much use for his wife, son, brother, father, or heroin. There is no country but the self, and its anthem is a whistle.

Sentence by sentence, scene by scene, *Falconer* absorbs and often haunts. As a whole, it confounds. Shady Hill has been reversed, turned inside out like a glove or one of those stars that ends up, under pressure of gravity, a black hole in space: the cell. And like a black hole, it transmits mysterious signals. It seems more asserted than felt, more willed than imagined, and an odd valedictory tone predominates, as if everything must be left behind in order for the self to forage for a new connection . . . with what? Angels, moons, freedom? Since any Cheever is better than most of what passes for adult fiction nowadays, he is entitled to make his departures when he wants to, in whatever direction he chooses. It is sad, though, that one of the few novelists who knows how to write about the dialectic between men and women (and their children) with a gentle seriousness, a palpable joy, should have made himself a stranger.

On Miracle Row

John Gardner*

John Cheever is one of the few living American novelists who might qualify as true artists. His work ranges from competent to awesome on all the grounds I would count: formal and technical mastery; educated intelligence; what I call "artistic sincerity," which implies, among other things, an indifference to aesthetic fashion, especially the tiresome modern fashion of always viewing the universe with alarm, either groan-

*Reprinted with permission of the author from *Saturday Review*, 4 (2 April 1977), 20–23.

ing or cynically sneering; and last, validity, or what Tolstoi called, without apology, the artist's correct moral relation to his material. I will not spell out in detail what all that means, especially the unspoken premise here that some opinions on life are plain right and some plain wrong, nor will I waste space explaining why nearly all the rest of our respected novelists seem to me either mediocre or fake. I will simply try to explain why Cheever's *Falconer*, though not long or "difficult," not profound or massive, devoid of verisimilitude's endless explanations on the one hand, and of overwrought allegorical extension on the other—though in fact merely a dramatic story of character and action accessible to the most ordinary sensitive reader—is an extraordinary work of art.

Falconer is a prison. The novel tells the story of one man's imprisonment there, and of his quietly miraculous escape. The man is Zeke Farragut, a college professor and heroin-methadone addict who accidentally, for good reason, has killed his brother, a man who was truly murderous, but the kind you can never put in jail because although he cruelly persecutes his family and friends and causes attempted suicides, he does it all legally.

Structurally, the novel is a set of Browningesque monologues by prisoners, guards, and passing strangers, along with a few dialogues, some funny (as when the prisoners play dumb), some chilling (as when Farragut's wife comes to visit). The novel moves like an opera built almost entirely of arias and comic, tragicomic, or tragic duets. Cheever has a gift for catching the emotional nuances in the speech of murderers, drug addicts, petty larcenists, pious and deadly "good" people, people full of contradictions—like the killer guard who means no harm and loves his plants—like all of us.

Everywhere, the writing is convincing, more authoritative than any tape recording, and it shows us what is wrong with Philip Roth's notion that literature can never hope to compete with the craziness of life. One of the things a great writer can do, in a mad time, is simply write things down as they are, without explanation, without complicated philosophical, sociological, or psychological analysis of motivation, simply trusting the authority of his voice, because he knows that all he's saying is true, that his ear is infallible, and that in a world bombarded by "communications" he can trust the reader's experience and sensitivity—or can at least trust the best of his readers.

Such writing is of course risky, but that's the wonder of it. All true art takes risks, and all true fiction assumes a reader of intelligence and goodwill.

Farragut has a wife, Marcia, who wanted to be a painter but was no good—an infuriating fact she refuses to face. She is a beautiful, intelligent woman who once loved Farragut but loves him no more, since in her view his drug addiction, casual philanderings, and, now, imprisonment have ruined her life. The things she says when she visits Farragut in prison are unbelievably cruel and could come from no one but an injured wife, though many readers—lucky people—will surely cry, in the face of such cruelty, "Impossible!" Cheever simply copies down reality at its fiercest, making no excuses—sets down as unjudgmentally as any machine the crackle of fire in the angry woman's voice, the fake disinterest and specious objectivity, the undying murderous jealousy toward a girl with whom Farragut had long ago had a brief, sweet affair:

> "So tell me how you are, Zeke. I can't say that you look well, but you look all right. You look very much like yourself. Do you still dream about your blonde? You do, or course; that I can easily see. Don't you understand that she never existed, Zeke, and that she never will? Oh, I can tell by the way you hold your head that you still dream about that blonde who never masturbated or shaved her legs or challenged anything you said or did. I suppose you have boyfriends here?"

One could write for pages on the terrible cunning and cruelty in that speech. No one, I think, has ever written down a more deadly wife than Farragut's.

Yet for all her unutterable viciousness, Marcia comes off in *Falconer* as an understandable human being, not a mere bitch, yet also not—as she might have been in someone else's novel—one of those pitiful people "more sinned against than sinning." We simultaneously despise her and understand why Farragut once loved her, even loves her still. The achievement—the mature nonsentimentality of it—is remarkable, for Marcia, like Farragut's brother, is one of those true murderers the law cannot punish. It's pure accident that she hasn't killed her husband. Cheever writes:

> At a rehabilitation center in Colorado where Farragut had been confined to check his addiction, the doctors discovered that heroin had damaged his heart. . . . He must avoid strenuous changes in temperature and above all excitement. Excitement of any sort would kill him. . . . Farragut flew east and his flight was uneventful. He got a cab to their apartment, where Marcia let him in. "Hi," he said and bent to kiss her, but she averted her face. "I'm an outpatient," he said. "A salt-free diet—not really salt-free, but no salt added. I can't climb stairs or drive a car and I do have to avoid excitement. It seems easy enough. Maybe we could go to the beach."
> Marcia walked down the long hall to their bedroom and slammed the door. The noise of the sound was explosive and in case he had missed this she opened the door and slammed it again. The effect on his heart was immediate. He became faint, dizzy, and short-winded. He staggered to the sofa in the living room and lay down. He was in too much pain and fear to realize that the home-coming of a drug addict was not romantic.

No two ways about it, Marcia has become a terrible human being. But Farragut, though we grow immensely fond of him for his sensitivity and wit, above all for his suffering, is no angel either. We get only glimpses, since the novel is mostly from Farragut's point of view, of how painful it is to live with him. But Cheever hints at the evidence—Farragut's many mistresses, his neurosis and floating detachment from his family and work, his own disgust at his more blatantly cruel brother, who, in the socially acceptable way, cuts out and kills by means of vodka.

No one is simply good in *Falconer;* the novel convinces us that in point of fact no one in the world is really good. Yet *Falconer* has nothing in common with the typical contemporary novel about how life is garbage. Life, for Cheever, is simply beautiful and tragic, or that's how he presents it, and both the beauty and the tragedy in *Falconer* are earned. Cheever finds no easy enemies, as William Gaddis would, no easy salvation for the liberated penis and spirit, as Updike would. He finds only what is there: pathos and beauty, "the inestimable richness of human nature."

The pathos can strike surprisingly, as if from nowhere. There is a minor character known only as "Chicken Number Two," a petty thief and killer who bullies and brags and makes trouble throughout the novel, a creature of bottomless stupidity who at the time of Falconer's minor riot demands that visitors be allowed to sit with their prisoner friends at a table, not separated from them by a counter. A guard points out that Chicken hasn't had a visitor in twelve years; nobody out there knows or cares about him. Cheever writes:

> Chicken began to cry then or seemed to cry, to weep or seemed to weep, until they heard the sound of a grown man weeping, an old man who slept on a charred mattress, whose life savings in tattoos had faded to a tracery of ash, whose crotch hair was sparse and gray, whose flesh hung slack on his bones, whose only trespass on life [now, Cheever means] was a flat guitar and a remembered and pitiful air of "I don't know where it is, sir, but I'll find it, sir," and whose name was known nowhere, nowhere in the far reaches of the earth or in the far reaches of his memory, where, when he talked to himself, he talked to himself as Chicken Number Two.

It is familiar theory that people outside prisons are as bad as the people inside, but Cheever makes the argument stick, and in his statement of the old opinion there is nothing liberal or slogany. He does not pretend that the prisoners are really wonderful people; and the outside citizens, all hypocrites. He says what is true, that we're a miserable pack, yet a pack capable of vision, like Farragut, who "even in prison . . . knew the world to be majestic." Throughout the novel, in one prisoner's story after another, and in the continuing story of Farragut's life, evil falls on evil—in flat, sometimes half-comic prose, disaster on disaster, shot by shot. Here, for instance, a mere parenthesis in a larger disaster: "Mrs. Farragut was not an intentionally reckless driver, but her vision was failing and on the road she was an agent of death. She had already killed one

Airedale and three cats." No one who has not happened to live un-luckily—many people have—will believe such a catalog of small and large disasters: except for the maniac who believes life "wonderful" (as Nailles used to, in Cheever's *Bullet Park*), Cheever's catalog, because of the authority of his writing, will convince.

What is more, the catalog of disasters here is tolerable, not inconsis-tent with an affirmation of life and love. What redeems this miserable, ghastly world is miracle—the small miracles of humor and compassion that we may without lunacy extend to universal principle, even to a lov-ing though somewhat feeble God. *Falconer* contains numerous minor miracles (the occasional, half-unwitting generosity of prison guards, the prison humor that gives brutalized men dignity) and two major miracles—two escapes from prison. In the first major miracle, a friend and homosexual lover of Farragut's escapes in disguise as a priest and is—for no reason—helped by the local bishop. Tolstoi would give us the bishop's reasons, but that is unnecessary in Cheever's kind of novel. Mostly, the world is inexplicably bad, bad beyond all probability: children die, or even purposely cause others to die. (Farragut's brother once casually tried to kill him.) But also, on rare occasions, the world is mysteriously good. That is enough. To emphasize the miracle of the friend's escape and the bishop's whimsical assistance, Cheever breaks point of view, shifting from Farragut's consciousness to the friend's—it's the only time he does it in the novel, and the effect is like a wall magically opening, letting in light.

The second major miracle is Farragut's own escape or, rather, resur-rection. A prison friend dies, either of influenza or from the new vaccine being tired out on prisoners. Farragut takes the place of the corpse in its death sack, gets carried out through the prison gates, and walks away.

The novel's end is a masterpiece of poetic prose, not only stylistically but also because it rings true. Farragut has nowhere to go—his wife hates him, his heart is bad. Nevertheless, Farragut escapes prison, joyfully breathes free, garbage-scented air, and meets, in bald-faced miracle, a generous, odd creature who gives him a coat and offers him a place to stay. Habitual cynics will scoff at such miracles, as the sentimentally op-timistic will purse their lips on hearing of the misery inside and outside Falconer. But that is how it is, Cheever says. Cheever proves what we are always forgetting: that great art is not technical trickery, novelty of ef-fect, or philosophical complexity beyond our depth, but absolute clarity: reality with the obfuscating wrappings peeled away. The reason Cheever is a great writer—besides his command of literary form, impeccable style, and unsentimental compassion—is that what he says seems true.

INTERVIEWS

John Cheever:
The Art of Fiction LXII

Annette Grant*

The first meeting with John Cheever took place in the spring of 1969, just after his novel *Bullet Park* was published. Normally, Cheever leaves the country when a new book is released, but this time he had not, and as a result many interviewers on the East Coast were making their way to Ossining, New York, where the master storyteller offered them the pleasures of a day in the country—but very little conversation about his book or the art of writing.

Cheever has a reputation for being a difficult interviewee. He does not pay attention to reviews, never rereads his books or stories once published, and is often vague about their details. He dislikes talking about his work (especially into "one of those machines") because he prefers not to look where he has been, but where he's going. Where he has been is impressive.

His collections of short stories are *The Way Some People Live* (1943), *The Enormous Radio and Other Stories* (1953), *Stories and Others* (1956), *The Housebreaker of Shady Hill* (1958), *Some People, Places and Things That Will Not Appear in My Next Novel* (1961), *The Brigadier and the Golf Widow* (1964), and *The World of Apples* (1973). His novels are *The Wapshot Chronicle* (1957), *The Wapshot Scandal* (1964), and *Bullet Park* (1969). He has recently finished another, due out in the spring of 1977.

For the interview Cheever was wearing a faded blue shirt and khakis. Everything about him was casual and easy, as though we were already old friends. The Cheevers live in a house built in 1799, so a tour of buildings and grounds was obligatory. Soon we were settled in a sunny second-floor study where we discussed his dislike of window curtains, a highway construction near Ossining that he was trying to stop, traveling in Italy, a story he was drafting about a man who lost his car keys at a nude theatre performance, Hollywood, gardeners and cooks, cocktail parties, Greenwich Village in the thirties, television reception, and a number of other writers named John (especially John Updike, who is a friend).

While Cheever talked freely about himself, he changed the subject when the conversation turned to his work. Aren't you bored with all this talk? Would you like a drink? Perhaps lunch is ready, I'll just go

*Annette Grant's interview with John Cheever from *Writers at Work, The Paris Review Interviews*, Fifth Series, edited by George Plimpton. Copyright © 1981 by The Paris Review, Inc. Reprinted with permission of Viking Penguin, Inc.

downstairs and check. A walk in the woods, and maybe a swim afterwards? Or would you rather drive to town and see my office? Do you play
backgammon? Do you watch much television?

During the course of several visits we did in fact mostly eat, drink,
walk, swim, play backgammon or watch television. Cheever did not invite us to cut any wood with his chain saw, an activity to which he is
rumored to be addicted. On the day of the last taping, we spent an afternoon watching the New York Mets win the World Series from the
Baltimore Orioles, at the end of which the fans at Shea Stadium tore up
plots of turf for souvenirs. "Isn't that amazing," he said repeatedly,
referring both to the Mets and their fans.

Afterwards we walked in the woods and as we circled back to the
house, Cheever said, "Go ahead and pack your gear. I'll be along in a
minute to drive you to the station. . . ." upon which he stepped out of his
clothes and jumped with a loud splash into a pond, doubtless cleansing
himself with his skinny-dip from one more interview.

Grant: I was reading the confessions of a novelist on writing novels:
"If you want to be true to reality, start lying about it." What do you
think?

Cheever: Rubbish. For one thing the words "truth" and "reality"
have no meaning at all unless they are fixed in a comprehensible frame of
reference. There are no stubborn truths. As for lying, it seems to me that
falsehood is a critical element in fiction. Part of the thrill of being told a
story is the chance of being hoodwinked or taken. Nabokov is a master at
this. The telling of lies is a sort of sleight-of-hand that displays our deepest
feelings about life.

Grant: Can you give an example of a preposterous lie that tells a
great deal about life?

Cheever: Indeed. The vows of Holy Matrimony.

Grant: What about verisimilitude and reality?

Cheever: Verisimilitude is, by my lights, a technique one exploits in
order to assure the reader of the truthfulness of what he's being told. If he
truly believes he is standing on a rug you can pull it out from under him.
Of course verisimilitude is also a lie. What I've always wanted of
verisimilitude is probability, which is very much the way I live. This table
seems real, the fruit basket belonged to my grandmother, but a mad-
woman could come in the door any moment.

Grant: How do you feel about parting with books when you finish
them?

Cheever: I usually have a sense of clinical fatigue after finishing a
book. When my first novel, *The Wapshot Chronicle*, was finished I was
very happy about it. We left for Europe and remained there so I didn't see
the reviews and wouldn't know of Maxwell Geismar's disapproval for
nearly ten years. *The Wapshot Scandal* was very different. I never much
liked the book and when it was done I was in a bad way. I wanted to burn
the book. I'd wake up in the night and I would hear Hemingway's

voice—I've never actually heard Hemingway's voice, but it was conspicuously his—saying, "This is the small agony. The great agony comes later." I'd get up and sit on the edge of the bathtub and chain-smoke until three or four in the morning. I once swore to the dark powers outside the window that I would never, *never* again try to be better than Irving Wallace. It wasn't so bad after *Bullet Park* where I'd done precisely what I wanted: a cast of three characters, a simple and resonant prose style and a scene where a man saves his beloved son from death by fire. The manuscript was received enthusiastically everywhere, but then Benjamin Demott dumped on it in the *Times*, everybody picked up their marbles and ran home. I ruined my left leg in a skiing accident and ended up so broke that I took out working papers for my youngest son. It was simply a question of journalistic bad luck and an over-estimation of my powers. However, when you finish a book, whatever its reception, there is some dislodgement of the imagination. I wouldn't say derangement. But finishing a novel, assuming it's something you want to do and that you take very seriously, is invariably something of a psychological shock.

Grant: How long does it take the psychological shock to wear off? Is there any treatment?

Cheever: I don't quite know what you mean by treatment. To diminish shock I throw high dice, get sauced, go to Egypt, scythe a field, screw. Dive into a cold pool.

Grant: Do characters take on identities of their own? Do they ever become so unmanageable that you have to drop them from the work?

Cheever: The legend that characters run away from their authors—taking up drugs, having sex operations and becoming President—implies that the writer is a fool with no knowledge or mastery of his craft. This is absurd. Of course, any estimable exercise of the imagination draws upon such a complex richness of memory that it truly enjoys the expansiveness—the surprising turns, the response to light and darkness—of any living thing. But the idea of authors running around helplessly behind their cretinous inventions is contemptible.

Grant: Must the novelist remain the critic as well?

Cheever: I don't have any critical vocabulary and very little critical acumen and this is, I think one of the reasons I'm always evasive with interviewers. My critical grasp of literature is largely at a practical level. I use what I love, and this can be anything. Cavalcanti, Dante, Frost, anybody. My library is terribly disordered and disorganized; I tear out what I want. I don't think that a writer has any responsibility to view literature as a continuous process. I believe that very little of literature is immortal. I've known books in my lifetime to serve beautifully, and then to lose their usefulness, perhaps, briefly.

Grant: How do you "use" these books . . . and what is it that makes them lose their "usefulness?"

Cheever: My sense of "using" a book is the excitement of finding myself at the receiving end of our most intimate and acute means of communication. These infatuations are sometimes passing.

Grant: Assuming a lack of critical vocabulary, how, then, without a long formal education, do you explain your considerable learning?

Cheever: I am not erudite. I do not regret this lack of discipline but I do admire erudition in my colleagues. Of course, I am not uninformed. That can be accounted for by the fact that I was raised in the tag-end of cultural New England. Everybody in the family was painting and writing and singing and especially reading, which was a fairly common and accepted means of communication in New England at the turn of the decade. My mother claimed to have read *Middlemarch* thirteen times; I dare say she didn't. It would take a lifetime.

Grant: Isn't there someone in *The Wapshot Chronicle* who has done it?

Cheever: Yes, Honora . . . or I don't remember who it is . . . claims to have read it thirteen times. My mother used to leave *Middlemarch* out in the garden and it got rained on. Most of it is in the novel; it's true.

Grant: One almost has a feeling of eavesdropping on your family in that book.

Cheever: The *Chronicle* was not published (and this was a consideration) until after my mother's death. An aunt (who does not appear in the book) said, "I would never speak to him again if I didn't know him to be a split personality."

Grant: Do friends or family often think they appear in your books?

Cheever: Only (and I think everyone feels this way) in a discreditable sense. If you put anyone in with a hearing aid, then they assume that you have described them . . . although the character may be from another country and in an altogether different role. If you put people in as infirm or clumsy or in some way imperfect, then they readily associate. But if you put them in as beauties, they never associate. People are always ready to accuse rather than to celebrate themselves, especially people who read fiction. I don't know what the association is. I've had instances when a woman will cross a large social floor and say, "Why did you write that story about me?" And I try to figure out what story I've written. Well, ten stories back apparently I mentioned someone with red eyes; she noticed that she had bloodshot eyes that day and so she assumed that I'd nailed her.

Grant: They feel indignant, that you have no right to their lives?

Cheever: It would be nicer if they thought of the creative aspect of writing. I don't like to see people who feel that they've been maligned when this was not anyone's intention. Of course, some young writers try to be libelous. And some old writers, too. Libel, is, of course, a vast source of energy. But these are not the pure energies of fiction, but simply the libelousness of a child. The sort of things one gets in freshman themes. Libel is not one of my energies.

Grant: Do you think narcissism is a necessary quality of fiction?

Cheever: That's an interesting question. By narcissism we mean of course clinical self-love, an embittered girl, the wrath of Nemesis and the rest of eternity as a leggy plant. Who wants that? We do love ourselves from time to time; no more, I think, than most men.

Grant: What about megalomania?

Cheever: I think writers are inclined to be intensely egocentric. Good writers are often excellent at a hundred other things but writing promises a greater latitude for the ego. My dear friend Yevtushenko has, I claim, an ego that can crack crystal at a distance of twenty feet; but I know a crooked investment banker who can do better.

Grant: Do you think that your inner screen of imagination, the way you project characters, is in any way influenced by film?

Cheever: Writers of my generation and those who were raised with films have become sophisticated about these vastly different mediums and know what is best for the camera and best for the writer. One learns to skip the crowd scene, the portentous door, the banal irony of zooming into the beauty's crow's feet. The difference in these crafts is, I think, clearly understood and as a result no good film comes from an adaptation of a good novel. I would love to write an original screen play if I found a sympathetic director. Years ago René Clair was going to film some of my stories but as soon as the front office heard about this they took away all the money.

Grant: What do you think of working in Hollywood?

Cheever: Southern California always smells very much like a summer night . . . which to me means the end of sailing, the end of games, but it isn't that at all. It simply doesn't correspond to my experience. I'm very much concerned with trees . . . with the nativity of trees, and when you find yourself in a place where all the trees are transplanted and have no history, I find it disconcerting.

I went to Hollywood to make money. It's very simple. The people are friendly and the food is good but I've never been happy there, perhaps because I only went there to pick up a check. I do have the deepest respect for a dozen or so directors whose affairs are centered there and who, in spite of the overwhelming problems of financing film, continue to turn out brilliant and original films. But my principal feeling about Hollywood is suicide. If I could get out of bed and into the shower I was all right. Since I never paid the bills, I'd reach for the phone and order the most elaborate breakfast I could think of and then I'd try to make it to the shower before I hanged myself. This is no reflection on Hollywood, but it's just that I seemed to have a suicide complex there. I don't like the freeways, for one thing. Also, the pools are too hot . . . 85°, and when I was last there, in late January, in the stores they were selling yarmulkes for dogs—My God! I went to a dinner and across the room a woman lost her balance and fell down. Her husband shouted over to her, "When I told you to bring your crutches, you wouldn't listen to me." That line couldn't be better!

Grant: What about another community—the academic? It provides so much of the critical work . . . with such an excessive necessity to categorize and label.

Cheever: The vast academic world exists like everything else, on what it can produce that will secure an income. So we have papers on fiction, but they come out of what is largely an industry. In no way does it help those who write fiction or those who love to read fiction. The whole business is a subsidiary undertaking, like extracting useful chemicals from smoke. Did I tell you about the review of *Bullet Park* in *Ramparts?* It said I missed greatness by having left St. Boltophs. Had I stayed, as Faulkner did in Oxford, I would have probably been as great as Faulkner. But I made the mistake of leaving this place, which, of course, never existed at all. It was so odd to be told to go back to a place that was a complete fiction.

Grant: I suppose they meant Quincy.

Cheever: Yes, which it isn't. But I was very sad when I read it. I understood what they were trying to say. It's like being told to go back to a tree that one spent fourteen years living in.

Grant: Who are the people that you imagine or hope read your books?

Cheever: All sorts of pleasant and intelligent people read the books and write thoughtful letters about them. I don't know who they are but they are marvelous and seem to live quite independently of the prejudices of advertising, journalism, and the cranky academic world. Think of the books that have enjoyed independent lives. *Let Us Now Praise Famous Men. Under The Volcano. Henderson The Rain King.* A splendid book like *Humboldt's Gift* was received with confusion and dismay but hundreds of thousands of people went out and bought hard-cover copies. The room where I work has a window looking into a wood and I like to think that these earnest, loveable and mysterious readers are in there.

Grant: Do you think contemporary writing is becoming more specialized, more autobiographical?

Cheever: It may be. Autobiography and letters may be more interesting than fiction, but still, I'll stick with the novel. The novel is an acute means of communication from which all kinds of people get responses that you don't get from letters or journals.

Grant: Did you start writing as a child?

Cheever: I used to tell stories. I went to a permissive school called Thayerland. I loved to tell stories and if everybody did their arithmetic—it was a very small school, probably not more than eighteen or nineteen students—then the teacher would promise that I would tell a story. I told serials. This was very shrewd of me because I knew that if I didn't finish the story by the end of the period, which was an hour, then everyone would ask to hear the end during the next period.

Grant: How old were you?

Cheever: Well, I'm inclined to lie about my age, but I suppose it was when I was eight or nine.

Grant: You could think of a story to spin out for an hour at that age?

Cheever: Oh, yes, I could then. And I still do.

Grant: What comes first, the plot?

Cheever: I don't work with plots. I work with intuition, apprehension, dreams, concepts. Characters and events come simultaneously to me. Plot implies narrative and a lot of crap. It is a calculated attempt to hold the reader's interest at the sacrifice of moral conviction. Of course, one doesn't want to be boring . . . one needs an element of suspense. But a good narrative is a rudimentary structure, rather like a kidney.

Grant: Have you always been a writer, or have you had other jobs?

Cheever: I drove a newspaper truck once. I liked it very much, especially during the World Series when the Quincy paper would carry the box scores and full accounts. No one had radios, or television—which is not to say that the town was lit with candles, but they used to wait for the news; it made me feel good to be the one delivering good news. Also I spent four years in the Army. I was 17 when I sold my first story "Expelled" to *The New Republic*. *The New Yorker* started taking my stuff when I was 22. I was supported by *The New Yorker* for years and years. It has been a very pleasant association. I sent in twelve or fourteen stories a year. At the start I lived in a squalid slum room on Hudson Street with a broken window pane. I had a job at MGM with Paul Goodman doing synopses. Jim Farrell, too. We had to boil down just about every book published into either a three, five, or a twelve page précis for which you got something like five dollars. You did your own typing. And, oh, carbons.

Grant: What was it like writing stories for *The New Yorker* in those days? Who was the fiction editor?

Cheever: Wolcott Gibbs was the fiction editor very briefly and then Gus Lobrano. I knew him very well; he was a fishing companion. And of course Harold Ross, who was difficult but I loved him. He asked preposterous queries on a manuscript—everyone's written about that—something like thirty-six queries on a story. The author always thought it outrageous, a violation of taste, but Ross really didn't care. He liked to show his hand, to shake the writer up. Occasionally he was brilliant. In "The Enormous Radio" he made two changes; a diamond is found on the bathroom floor after a party. The man says "Sell it, we can use a few dollars." Ross had changed "dollars" to "bucks" which was absolutely perfect. Brilliant. Then I had "the radio came softly" and Ross pencilled in another "softly." "The radio came softly, softly." He was absolutely right. But then there were twenty-nine other suggestions like, "This story has gone on for 24 hours and no one has eaten anything. There's no mention of a meal." A typical example of this sort of thing was Shirley Jackson's "The Lottery" about the stoning ritual. He hated the story; he started turning vicious. He said there was no town in Vermont where there were rocks of that sort. He nagged and nagged and nagged. It was not surprising. Ross used to scare the hell out of me. I would go in for lunch. I never knew Ross was coming, until he'd bring in an egg cup. I'd sit with my back pressed against my chair. I was really afraid. He was a scratcher and a nosepicker, and the sort of man who could get his underwear up so there was a strip of it showing between his trousers and his shirt. He used to hop at me, sort of jump about in his chair. It was a creative, destructive relationship from which I learned a great deal, and I miss him.

Grant: You met a lot of writers during that time, didn't you?

Cheever: It was all terribly important to me since I had been brought up in a small town. I was in doubt that I could make something of myself as a writer until I met two people who were very important to me: One was Gaston Lachaise and the other was E.E. Cummings. Cummings I loved and I love his memory. He did a wonderful imitation of a wood-burning locomotive going from Tifflis to Minsk. He could hear a pin falling in soft dirt at the distance of three miles. Do you remember the story of Cummings' death? It was September, hot, and Cummings was cutting kindling in the back of his house in New Hampshire. He was sixty-six or seven or something like that. Marion, his wife, leaned out the window and asked, "Cummings, isn't it frightfully hot to be chopping wood?" He said, "I'm going to stop now, but I'm going to sharpen the axe before I put it up, dear." Those were the last words he spoke. At his funeral Marianne Moore gave the eulogy. Marion Cummings had enormous eyes. You could make a place in a book with them. She smoked cigarettes as though they were heavy, and she wore a dark dress with a cigarette hole in it.

Grant: And Lachaise?

Cheever: I'm not sure what to say about him. I thought him an oustanding artist and I found him a contented man. He used to go to the Metropolitan—where he was not represented—and embrace the statues he loved.

Grant: Did Cummings have any advice for you as a writer?

Cheever: Cummings was never paternal. But the cant of his head, his wind-in-the-chimney voice, his courtesy to boobs and the vastness of his love for Marion were all advisory.

Grant: Have you ever written poetry?

Cheever: No. It seems to me that the discipline is very different . . . another language, another continent from that of fiction. In some cases short stories are more highly disciplined than a lot of poetry that we have. Yet the disciplines are as different as shooting a twelve-gauge shotgun and swimming.

Grant: Have magazines asked you to write journalism for them?

Cheever: I was asked to do an interview with Sophia Loren by the *Saturday Evening Post.* I did. I got to kiss her. I've had other offers but nothing as good.

Grant: Do you think there's a trend for novelists to write journalism, as Norman Mailer does?

Cheever: I don't like your question. Fiction must compete with first-rate reporting. If you cannot write a story that is equal to a factual account of battle in the streets or demonstrations, then you can't write a story. You might as well give up. In many cases, fiction hasn't competed successfully. These days the field of fiction is littered with tales about the sensibilities of a child coming of age on a chicken farm, or a whore who strips her profession of its glamour. The *Times* has never been so full of rubbish in its recent book ads. Still, the use of the word "death" or "invalidism" about fiction diminishes as it does with anything else.

Grant: Do you feel drawn to experiment in fiction, to move toward bizarre things?

Cheever: Fiction *is* experimentation; when it ceases to be that, it ceases to be fiction. One never puts down a sentence without the feeling that it has never been put down before in such a way, and that perhaps even the substance of the sentence has never been felt. Every sentence is an innovation.

Grant: Do you feel that you belong to any particular tradition in American letters?

Cheever: No. As a matter of fact I can't think of any American writers who could be classified as part of a tradition. You certainly can't put Updike, Mailer, Ellison or Styron in a tradition. The individuality of the writer has never been as intense as it is in the United States.

Grant: Well, would you think of yourself as a realistic writer?

Cheever: We have to agree on what we mean before we can talk about such definition. Documentary novels, such as those of Dreiser, Zola, Dos Passos—even though I don't like them—can, I think, be classified as realistic. Jim Farrell was another documentary novelist; in a way, Scott Fitzgerald was, though to think of him that way diminishes what he could do best . . . which was to try to give a sense of what a very particular world was like.

Grant: Do you think Fitzgerald was conscious of documenting?

Cheever: I've written something on Fitzgerald, and I've read all the biographies and critical works, and wept freely at the end of each one—cried like a baby—it is such a sad story. All the estimates of him bring in his descriptions of the '29 Crash, the excessive prosperity, the clothes, the music, and by doing so, his work is described as being heavily dated . . . sort of period pieces. This all greatly diminishes Fitzgerald at his best. One always knows reading Fitzgerald what time it is, precisely where you are, the kind of country. No writer has ever been so true in placing the scene. But I feel that this isn't pseudo-history, but his sense of being alive. All great men are scrupulously true to their times.

Grant: Do you think your works will be similarly dated?

Cheever: Oh, I don't anticipate that my work will be read. That isn't the sort of thing that concerns me. I might be forgotten tomorrow; it wouldn't disconcert me in the least.

Grant: But a great number of your stories defy dating; they could take place anytime and almost any place.

Cheever: That, of course, has been my intention. The ones that you can pinpoint in an era are apt to be the worst. The bomb shelter story ("The Brigadier and the Golf Widow") is about a level of basic anxiety, and the bomb shelter, which places the story at a very particular time, is just a metaphor . . . that's what I intended anyhow.

Grant: It was a sad story.

Cheever: Everyone keeps saying that about my stories, "Oh, they're so sad." My agent, Candida Donadio, called me about a new story and said, "Oh, what a beautiful story, it's so sad." I said, "All right, so I'm a sad man." The sad thing about "The Brigadier and the Golf Widow" is the woman standing looking at the bomb shelter in the end of the story and she sent away by a maid. Did you know that *The New Yorker* tried to take that out? They thought the story was much more effective without my ending. When I went in to look at page proofs, I thought there was a page missing. I asked where the end of the story was. Some girl said, "Mr. Shawn thinks it's better this way." I went into a very deep slow burn, took the train home, drank a lot of gin and got one of the editors on the telephone. I was by then loud, abusive and obscene. He was entertaining Elizabeth Bowen and Eudora Welty. He kept asking if he couldn't take this call in another place. Anyhow I returned to New York in the morning. They had reset the whole magazine—poems, newsbreaks, cartoons—and replaced the scene.

Grant: It's the classic story about what *The New Yorker* is rumored to do—"remove the last paragraph and you've got a typical *New Yorker* ending." What is your definition of a good editor?

Cheever: My definition of a good editor is a man I think charming, who sends me large checks, praises my work, my physical beauty and my sexual prowess, and who has a stranglehold on the publisher and the bank.

Grant: What about the beginning of stories? Yours start off very quickly. It's striking.

Cheever: Well, if you're trying as a story-teller to establish some rapport with your reader you don't open by telling him that you have a headache and indigestion and that you picked up a gravelly rash at Jones

Beach. One of the reasons is that advertising in magazines is much more common today than it was twenty to thirty years ago. In publishing in a magazine you are competing against girdle advertisements, travel advertisements, nakedness, cartoons, even poetry. The competition almost makes it hopeless. There's a stock beginning that I've always had in mind. Someone is coming back from a year in Italy on a Fulbright Scholarship. His trunk is opened in Customs and instead of his clothing and souvenirs, they find the mutilated body of an Italian seaman, everything there but the head. Another opening sentence I often think of is, "The first day I robbed Tiffany's it was raining." Of course, you can open a short story that way, but that's not how one should function with fiction. One is tempted because there has been a genuine loss of serenity, not only in the reading public, but in all our lives. Patience, perhaps, or even the ability to concentrate. At one point when television first came in no one was publishing an article that couldn't be read during a commercial. But fiction is durable enough to survive all of this. I don't like the short story that starts out "I'm about to shoot myself," or "I'm going to shoot you." Or the Pirandello thing of "I'm going to shoot you or you are going to shoot me, or we are going to shoot someone, maybe each other." Or the erotic thing, either "He started to undo his pants, but the zipper stuck . . . he got the can of three-in-one oil . . . " and on and on we go.

Grant: Certainly your stories have a fast pace, they move along.

Cheever: The first principle of aesthetics is either interest or suspense. You can't expect to communicate with anyone if you're a bore.

Grant: William Golding wrote that there are two kinds of novelists. One lets meaning develop with the characters or situations, and the other has an idea and looks for a myth to embody it. He's an example of the second kind. He thinks of Dickens as belonging to the first. Do you think you fit into either category?

Cheever: I don't know what Golding is talking about. Cocteau said that writing is a force of memory that is not understood. I agree with this. Raymond Chandler described it as a direct line to the subconscious. The books that you really love give the sense, when you first open them, of having been there. It is a creation, almost like a chamber in the memory. Places that one has never been to, things that one has never seen or heard, but their fitness is so sound that you've been there somehow.

Grant: But certainly you use a lot of resonances from myths . . . for example, references to the Bible and Greek mythology.

Cheever: It's explained by the fact that I was brought up in Southern Massachusetts where it was thought that mythology was a subject that we should all grasp. It was very much a part of my education. The easiest way to parse the world is through mythology. There have been thousands of papers written along those lines—Leander is Poseidon and somebody is Ceres, and so forth. It seems to be a superficial parsing. But it makes a passable paper.

Grant: Still, you want the resonance.

Cheever: The resonance, of course.

Grant: How do you work? Do you put ideas down immediately, or do you walk around with them for a while, letting them incubate?

Cheever: I do both. What I love is when totally disparate facts come together. For example, I was sitting in a cafe reading a letter from home with the news that a neighboring housewife had taken the lead in a nude show. As I read I could hear an Englishwoman scolding her children. "If you don't do thus and so before Mummy counts to three," was her line. A leaf fell through the air, reminding me of winter and of the fact that my wife had left me and was in Rome. There was my story. I had an equivalently great time with the close of "Goodbye My Brother" and "The Country Husband." Hemingway and Nabokov liked these. I had everything in there: a cat wearing a hat, some naked women coming out of the sea, a dog with a shoe in his mouth and a king in golden mail riding an elephant over some mountains.

Grant: Or ping-pong in the rain?

Cheever: I don't remember what story that was.

Grant: Sometimes you played ping-pong in the rain.

Cheever: I probably did.

Grant: Do you save up such things?

Cheever: It isn't a question of saving up. It's a question of some sort of galvanic energy. It's also, of course, a question of making sense of one's experiences.

Grant: Do you think that fiction should give lessons?

Cheever: No. Fiction is meant to illuminate, to explode, to refresh. I don't think there's any consecutive moral philosophy in fiction beyond excellence. Acuteness of feeling and velocity have always seemed to me terribly important. People look for morals in fiction because there has always been a confusion between fiction and philosophy.

Grant: How do you know when a story is right? Does it hit you right the first time, or are you critical as you go along?

Cheever: I think there is a certain heft in fiction. For example, my latest story isn't right. I have to do the ending over again. It's a question I guess of trying to get it to correspond to a vision. There is shape, a proportion and one knows when something that happens is wrong.

Grant: By instinct?

Cheever: I suppose that anyone who has written for as long as I have, it's probably what you'd call instinct. When a line falls wrong, it simply isn't right.

Grant: You told me once you were interested in thinking up names for characters.

Cheever: That seems to me very important. I've written a story about men with a lot of names, all abstract, names with the fewest possible allusions: Pell, Weed, Hammer, and Nailles, of course, which was thought to be arch, but it wasn't meant to be at all. . . .

Grant: Hammer's house appears in "The Swimmer."

Cheever: That's true, it's quite a good story. It was a terribly difficult story to write.

Grant: Why?

Cheever: Because I couldn't ever show my hand. Night was falling, the year was dying. It wasn't a question of technical problems, but one of imponderables. When he finds it's dark and cold, it has to have happened. And, by God, it did happen. I felt dark and cold for some time after I finished that story. As a matter of fact, it's one of the last stories I wrote for a long time, because then I started on *Bullet Park*. Sometimes the easiest seeming stories to a reader are the hardest kind to write.

Grant: How long does it take you to write such a story?

Cheever: Three days, three weeks, three months. I seldom read my own work. It seems to be a particularly offensive form of narcissism. It's like playing back tapes of your own conversation. It's like looking over your shoulder to see where you've run. That's why I've often used the image of the swimmer, the runner, the jumper. The point is to finish and go on to the next thing. I also feel, not as strongly as I used to, that if I looked over my shoulder I would die. I think frequently of Satchel Paige and his warning that you might see something gaining on you.

Grant: Are there stories that you feel particularly good about when you are finished?

Cheever: Yes, there were about fifteen of them that were absolutely BANG! I loved them, I loved everybody—the buildings, the houses, wherever I was. It was a great sensation. Most of these were stories written in the space of three days and which run to about thirty-five pages. I love them, but I can't read them; in many cases, I wouldn't love them any longer if I did.

Grant: Recently you have talked bluntly about having a writer's block, which had never happened to you before. How do you feel about it now?

Cheever: Any memory of pain is deeply buried and there is nothing more painful for a writer than an inability to work.

Grant: Four years is a rather long haul on a novel, isn't it?

Cheever: It's about what is usually takes. There's a certain monotony in this way of life, which I can very easily change.

Grant: Why?

Cheever: Because it doesn't seem to me the proper function of writing. If possible, it is to enlarge people. To give them their risk, if possible to give them their divinity, not to cut them down.

Grant: Do you feel that you had diminished them too far in *Bullet Park?*

Cheever: No I didn't feel that. But I believe that it was understood in those terms. I believe that Hammer and Nailles were thought to be social casualties, which isn't what I intended at all. And I thought I made my intentions quite clear. But if you don't communicate, it's not anybody else's fault. Neither Hammer nor Nailles were meant to be either psychiatric or social metaphors; they were meant to be two men with their own risks. I think the book was misunderstood on those terms. But then I don't read reviews, so I don't really know what goes on.

Grant: How do you know when the literary work is finished to your satisfaction?

Cheever: I have never completed anything in my life to my absolute and lasting satisfaction.

Grant: Do you feel that you're putting a lot of yourself on the line when you are writing?

Cheever: Oh yes, oh yes! When I speak as a writer I speak with my own voice—quite as unique as my fingerprints—and I take the maximum risk at seeming profound or foolish.

Grant: Does one get the feeling while sitting at the typewriter that one is godlike, or creating the whole show at once?

Cheever: No, I've never felt godlike. No, the sense is of one's total usefulness. We all have a power of control, it's part of our lives: we have it in love, in work that we love doing. It's a sense of ecstasy, as simple as that. The sense is that "this is my usefulness, and I can do it all the way through." It always leaves you feeling great. In short, you've made sense of your life.

Grant: Do you feel that way during or even after the event? Isn't work, well, work?

Cheever: I've had very little drudgery in my life. When I write a story that I really like, it's . . . why, wonderful. That is what I can do and I love it while I'm doing it. I can feel that it's good. I'll say to Mary and the children, "All right, I'm off, leave me alone. I'll be through in three days."

Talk With John Cheever

John Hersey*

One end of the living room in a house built in 1799, in Ossining, N.Y. A table has been pushed against the lefthand wall, under a large print of Hadrian's tomb spouting frenetic fireworks. Cheever, in a brown pullover, is seated beyond the table, with a window at his back. He is 64; looks like a man of 34 who has been to a hilarious but awfully late party

*Reprinted with permission from *New York Times Book Review*, 6 Mar. 1977, pp. 1, 24, 26–28.

the night before. Face flushed: recent skiing in Utah mountains. Nut brown hair. Sharp eyebeams. The brilliant glow behind him is mist-filtered sunlight. Two large glasses of dark amber liquid on the table—iced tea. Cheever is smoking.

Seated at the outer edge of the table, facing the wall, is a visitor, at whom Cheever is looking with some alarm. This bastard is fiddling with a cassette tape machine.

Center and right: the rest of a living room that doesn't seem to have jumped out of any known Cheever story. Lived-in. Two comfortable chairs. Chinaware brought from Canton by Cheever's seafaring grandfather. On far wall, a Paxton, a painting of a woman on a summer's verandah. Right, a wide reach of pine paneling (restored) over a fireplace; a Seth Thomas clock. Fire of applewood logs cut by twice-warmed Cheever. Wood smoke in the air. A golden retriever, Edgar, settles down for a nap.

JOHN HERSEY: Could we test your voice?

JOHN CHEEVER: Three, five, seven.

RECORDER (playing back): Three, five, seven.

(Hearing this, Cheever performs one of his remarkable repertory of groans.)

JH: Sing Sing? If a crow flew from here. . . .

JC: About five miles. Approximately 15 minutes by car.

JH: I remember it from my boyhood, at the Ossining station, the walls and lookout towers looming near the tracks. You've been here 20 years. Has it seemed to you to loom as a presence all that time?

JC: Not particularly.

JH: Did we hear some time ago that you were working in the prison?

JC: I taught at Sing Sing for two years. Falconer is *not* Sing Sing. I used the imaginary prison of Falconer principally as a metaphor for confinement. It would be the third large metaphor I've used. The first is St. Botolphs, a New England village which has the confinement of traditional values and nostalgia; the second was the suburban towns, Bullet Park and Shady Hill, again areas of confinement; and the third is Falconer. *Not* Sing Sing. My students—some of whom are still in prison and some of whom I continue to see—are *not* characters in the novel.

JH: Of course not.

JC: I feel very strongly about this. Fiction is not crypto-autobiography. Fiction seems to me a much more important means of communication. St. Botolphs never existed. Nor did Bullet Park. Nor Falconer. The smells, sounds, noises and lights are all there, but from a variety of places.

JH: How did you happen . . .

JC: I taught in prison because at a party someone said there were two thousand inmates and six teachers. One doesn't marry in order to write about women nor have children to write about children nor teach in prison to write about prisoners.

JH: What do you mean by confinement?

JC: I think I mean the confinements of the impoverished sense of right and wrong that, socially, we are in agreement on. My first-hand experience with confinement, on a surface level, has been of sorts we're all familiar with, such as being in in-transit areas—in airports—during blizzards, when you're in for 32 or 36 hours, in places where you can't speak the language and are not sure what plane you're supposed to be on. Being stuck in elevators, and particularly, again, in countries where you don't know how to yell "Help!" or "The elevator won't work!" Being stuck in sentimental or erotic contracts that are extraordinarily painful and difficult to extricate oneself from.

(Cheever stubs out a butt and at once lights a new cigarette. An illusion: the coils and swirls of brilliantly backlit cigarette smoke seem not to move; they hover, as if painted on the air—seem to have been hung out on purpose to hide the restless animation of the face beyond. As the conversation goes on, this motionless blue-white curtain blurs quick facial shots of surprise, puzzlement, delight, annoyance, explosive amusement.)

JH: Besides confinement, one finds in "Falconer" many vivid, small recurrences from other books of yours: An older man endangered by the sea. Yard work. Figures seen in the buff. Sailboat races. Family turmoil. Glimpses of the sky. Beaches. . . .

JC: This is obviously the mortal furniture of one's life—what one lives with and dreams of. The strong reprises, though, have been, I think, the confinements of an impoverished society and the thrust of life in determining to vary them. Escape is not the word one means. There doesn't seem to be any word for eliminating confinement. It is the effort to express one's conviction of the boundlessness of possibility.

JH: Mind if I check to see if this damn thing is recording? It makes me so nervous.

JC: Not half as nervous as it makes me.

RECORDER: . . . conviction of the boundlessness of possibility.

(The dog, Edgar, leaps to his feet, alarmed that his beloved, voluble Cheever seems to be throttled in the box in the guest's hands. The golden-retriever temperament immediately translates concern, however, into licking and tail-wagging.)

JC: (delighted): His master's voice in the Victrola! *(Cheever's laughter comes in a rush, like the few chugs of an outboard motor not quite catching.)*

JH: (resuming): Where do the sounds in your written voice in "Falconer" come from? We know you read: there's that dentist in the "Chronicle," Bulstrode, wonderful name you ripped off from "Middlemarch."

JC: It seems to me that the people of my generation, and yours, when asked for influential books, cannot stop at a thousand. Well.The sound of my grandmother's voice, perhaps, reading to me. She was an Englishwoman. In my day it was customary to have almost all of Dickens read to you as a child. My father was a north-shore Yankee. He did not have a marked accent. He had, I should think, a very good prose style—he wrote some of Leander's journal in the "Chronicle." The voices of southern Massachusetts, and of course of the people one loves. Literary voices? Surely this is the most intimate of all the choices a writer makes. One hopes one has chosen those that are strongest and most radiant. I consider myself lucky, for example, to have read Donne when I was very young.

JH: What about Chekhov? You're well known as the American Chekhov.

JC: If I'm known, it's as the oldest living short story writer. *(He laughs.)* No, I love Chekhov very much. He *was* an innovator—stories that seemed to the unknowing to have no endings but had instead a whole new inner structure.

JH: Your voice has a blurted quality—shifts, ellipses, disjunctions.

JC: I have always felt there is some ungainliness in my person, some ungainliness in my spiritual person that I cannot master. Perhaps you mean that.

JH: No. It's fascinating. A matter of form-speed.

JC: I do find myself more concise than I would like to be. There are paragraphs which had been chapters. For instance, the Cuckold's jewelry business. It's simply in three sentences which could have gone on and on. There were other situations. I could not accept them. The line was there, and I have to throw everything out and keep it concise. When I was younger I could run all over the pasture and come back. Now I seem to be going much more directly to what I have to say. I was unable to be digressive in this case. I trust I'm more mature. *(He laughs again.)* My father's speech was most precise. I can recall that he'd never had a dry martini. I made him one, and he drank a good deal of it, and all he said was, "Strong enough to draw a boat." Which is a very good example of his powerful laconic speech.

JH: Your spiritual person. . . .

JC: I have been a church-goer for most of my adult life—a liturgical churchgoer. I am very happy with Cranmer's "The Book of Common Prayer." The current schisms of the church concern me not at all. It seems to be one of God's infinite mercies that the sexual disposition of the priest has never been my concern. The religious experience is very much my concern, as it seems to me it is the legitimate concern of any adult who has experienced love.

JH: Any desk rituals?

JC: As a matter of fact, I seldom have a desk. At the moment I am working in a third-floor room with a broken television set, a Miro print and a chair that is bound together with picture wire. That should be a source of petulance. But it really doesn't matter. When I finish a book in one room, then I don't particularly want to get back into that room. Since the house has seven rooms, I have a couple to go. I'm very fond of ceremony, but as far as writing goes—just this: I work in the morning, I work with the light. I come down to breakfast very early, in the dark, before the light. The cats want their breakfast at once. I truly never have been cruel to a cat, but when they start climbing up and down my legs, I say to them *(he speaks now in a sharp tone, leaning down to the edge of the table)*, "I'm celebrated for my cruelty to cats!" The intelligent ones stop.

JH: Does confinement start with the body? Have you felt confined since your heart attack four years ago?

JC: I like to think of it as no more than a part in the stream of experience. Cardiomyopathy is, along with much medical science, still in an investigative stage. Little is known. For example, altitude. I was cross-country skiing at Alta in Utah, last week, and I didn't know how high I could go. I thought I wasn't supposed to go over six, but we started at six, so I got on the lift and went to nine, and it was perfectly all right, so I went up to twelve.

JH: Testing?

JC: I was testing! *(Here he laughs most mischievously.)* To live physically is extremely important to me. I was brought up to take some of the responsibilities in maintaining a house. Cutting firewood, for example. I bicycle, skate, ski, walk, swim. It's very, very important to me to be continuously in touch with my environment.

JH: You once said, "I chain smoke. I chain drink. I chain everything." I know you've stopped drinking.

JC: I stopped drinking two years ago. I was an alcoholic. It was something of a struggle to stop drinking. But it has been accomplished.

JH: Any connection with Farragut's getting clean in the book?

JC: There may be. But no. I've had clinical trouble with alcohol and also with drugs, but that really was not, I think, what I was concerned about. I wanted to use *that* as a metaphor, too, as the prison was to be, for confinement.

JH: Is love a confinement? Family?

JC: Mary and I have been married for 38 years, I think. That two people—both of us temperamental, quarrelsome and intensely ambitious—could have gotten along for such a vast period of time is for me a very good example of the boundlessness of human nature.

JH: Any children?

JC: *(Another small groan, hardly more than a sigh.)* I have not been very good as a sedate parent. I'm particularly aware of this for my two sons. I've offered, for example, to wear a hat and take commuting trains if they would be more comfortable about it, and they said that really wouldn't make the difference. They felt that there was a lack, and then I said to both of them, "Coming of age, when you find a lack in me, you'll be able to find plenty of other men who'll be able to play out the role of father for you." The most exciting thing in my life *(the cadence changes, the voice is suddenly brisk)* has been the birth of my children and watching them grow and take up their lives. I want them to walk away from me without rancor. One has gotten to be defensive about the enormous pleasures and diversity, the richness of life in a family, because, God, beginning with Samuel Butler the family was thought to be the shield of hypocrisy, and it's taken us that long, nearly two centuries, to be candid about the enormous pleasure we take in one another and the enormous richness in our relationships.

JH: The book is dedicated to your son Federico?

JC: It is to my son Federico, yes. He's a freshman at Stanford. I went out last week, after Utah. I said, "Do you want this kind of book dedicated to you, Fred?" He had read it, and considering the nature of the book. . . . As I finished large sections of it, I would read them to Mary, Suzie [Cheever's daughter], Fred, by the open fire. They were all very pleased with it. It did seem rather a curious performance. What I wanted, of course, was a very dark book that possessed radiance. And they seemed to feel that's what it was.

JH: You spoke of fiction as an important means of communication.

JC: Writing is for me a means of communication. It is for me my ultimate—as far as I know—usefulness. It is talking with people whose company I think I would enjoy if I knew them. And it's speaking to them about my most intimate and acute feelings and apprehensions about my life, about our lives. *(Cheever leaves the room to refill the iced-tea glasses. Comes back talking.)* The point of this communication is that it is a *useful* performance. The force of reality in fiction and the force of reality in a dream are very much the same. You find yourself on a sailing boat that you do not know—don't know the rig—going along a coast that is totally strange to you, but you're wearing an old suit, and the person beside you is your wife. This is in the nature of a dream. The experience of fiction is similar: one builds as if at random. But whereas the usefulness of the dream, in a rudimentary sense, is only for your own analyst to interpret, fiction builds toward an illumination—toward a larger usefulness.

JH: For parties on both ends of the communication?

JC: Yes. It is a mutual enterprise. I have something to say, and I would like your response. *"Ich habe etwas gesagen."* I said that yesterday, and somebody said, "Why do you say it in German?" The imperative implication in English is not very strong. "I have something to say." But it *is* an imperative. *(Cheever is talking very loud now.)* I have something to say, and if you are interested, I would like your response. We can't quite say it in English. *"Ecoute!"*—you know. "Listen" isn't sharp enough. But it is an imperative: "I would like your response to what I have to say."

JH: Do you visualize a reader to whom you're saying this?

JC: I always think of the reader as being in the woods. *(He seems to love this idea. It sounds as if the outboard is really going to start this time.)* Now and then you see a form. Not hidden, actually—but readers don't, for an American novelist, *appear.* I think perhaps Mrs. Woolf and the English novelists knew pretty much the income group, the sartorial tastes and the education of the people they addressed. The American novelist does not. We have no idea where they come from, where they went to school, what they wear, eat, do. But they are numerous enough to support—modestly, in any case—a novelist. There are enough of them so that fiction is quite independent of commercialism—commercial interests—commercial power or influence. The readers are interested, and they seem to be intelligent. This is an astonishing and marvelous thing.

JH: If your pleasure in writing is the usefulness of this communication, what is the pain?

JC: Pain? I have no memory for pain.

JH: You spoke of darkness and radiance. There is a lot of darkness in "Falconer," all right. It makes the light in the book seem specially intense. A patch of sky. . . .

JC: Oh, sky! How I miss it, in anyone's fiction, when there is no sky! I look through chapter after chapter, thinking, well, there *may* be some sky.

JH: The light in the prison courtyard. . . .

JC: Radiance and light, I suppose, originate with fire. I suppose it's one of the oldest memories man has. In my church, the mass ends, of course, not with a prayer, not with an amen. It ends with the acolyte extinguishing the candles. Which goes back, probably to the close of the most savage congregation, which was the scattering of fire. Light, fire—these have always meant the possible greatness of man.

JH: Fire suggests fear. I see another kind of light in your writing—more joyous.

JC: The whiteness of light. In the church, you know, that always represents the Holy Spirit. It seems to me that man's inclination toward light, toward brightness, is very nearly botanical—and I mean spiritual light. One not only needs it, one struggles for it. It seems to me almost that one's total experience is the drive toward light. Or, in the case of the successful degenerate, the drive into an ultimate darkness, which presumably will result in light. Yes. My fondness for light is very very strong and, I presume, primitive. But isn't it true of us all?

CRITICISM

John Cheever and the Grave of Social Coherence

Clinton S. Burhans, Jr.*

I

Many qualities make John Cheever's writing appealing and in-teresting. Sinuous, mellow, evocative, capable of a surprising range of ef-fects, his prose moves without apparent effort and convinces without fireworks. He has a keen eye for the bizarre and the eccentric; for the left-overs, the left-behinds, the left-outs; but more than this, a quiet accep-tance of them all growing from an understanding that everyone is warped by life either more or less and in one way or another. He is a major chronicler of contemporary absurdity, especially in its upper middle-class urban and suburban manifestations; and he is a trenchant moralist who sees all too clearly into the gap between men's dreams and what they make of them. But in illuminating this absurdity and uncovering this gap, he neither derides the human beings trapped in both nor belittles their dreams. He has the long view of man: he sees what we call progress has only drawn man deeper into the quicksand of his basic condition; that men are born more than ever into a world of chance, complexity, and ultimate loneliness; and that whatever the contemporary terminology; harpies still hover over man and devils ride his back. Cheever reflects this world in whimsy and fantasy, in irony and extravagance, but never at the cost of his deep compassion for those who must live in it with him; an unobtrusive decency shines everywhere in his writing.

Beyond these values and closely related to them, a provocative and significant theme seems to be emerging in Cheever's work, especially in the stories and novels of the past ten years or so. Writing in 1959, he pin-points a shaping change in the attitudes underlying his thought and art:

> The decade began for me with more promise than I can remember since my earliest youth. . . . However, halfway through the decade, something went terribly wrong. The most useful image I have today is of a man in a quagmire, looking into a tear in the sky. I am not speaking here of despair, but of confusion. I fully expected the trout streams of my youth to

*Reprinted with permission from *Twentieth Century Literature*, 14 (Jan. 1969), 187–98.

fill up with beer cans and the meadows to be covered with houses; I may even have expected to be separated from most of my moral and ethical heritage; but the forceful absurdities of life today find me unprepared. Something has gone very wrong, and I do not have the language, the imagery, or the concepts to describe my apprehensions. I come back again to the quagmire and the torn sky. (*Fiction of the Fifties*, ed., Herbert Gold, Dolphin Books, Doubleday & Company, Garden City, New York, p. 22.)

The image is a powerful one; and Cheever's writing since the mid-fifties, especially in the Wapshot novels and in the stories collected in *The Brigadier and the Golf Widow*, seem at their deepest levels of meaning and value to be his groping both for a conceptual framework to explain his apprehensions and also for a language and forms to express them.

II

As Cheever's feeling that "something has gone very wrong" has deepened, so too has his sense of the past and of the indelible relationship between human beings and their socio-cultural matrix. His concern with contemporary absurdity is not that of an existentialist; his vision is not that of a Sartre or a Camus. He has the traditionalist's sense of a human nature and of its continuance in time and in experience; and he increasingly views man as a creature industriously but blindly cutting away the roots from which he grows and tearing up the soil which nurtures him.

In "Metamorphoses," Cheever updates Ovid, and the ease with which Actaeon and Orpheus wear modern dress illustrates Cheever's sense of the past and of the permanence of the human condition. In similar ways, Cheever's sense of the past—geological, historical, social, and familial—recurs constantly throughout the Wapshot novels. Looking out over a ski trail he is about to descend, Coverly Wapshot sees that "it would be dark very soon but all the mountain peaks, all of them buried in snow, still stood in the canted light of day like the gulfs and trenches of an ancient sea bed. What moved Coverly in the scene was its vitality. Here was a display of the inestimable energies of the planet; here in the last light was a sense of its immense history" (*The Wapshot Scandal*, Bantam Books, 1965, pp. 107–08. Subsequent page references will be to this edition). Cheever traces the Wapshots back to Norman antecedents and sketches in the history of the family and of the town of St. Botolphs for two hundred years preceding the mid-twentieth-century events of the novels. These center not only on Moses and Coverly and on their leaving the backwater town to make their way in the world and produce sons to carry on the family name but equally on their father, Leander, and their aunt, Honora, and on the old town itself.

In his journal, Lorenzo Wapshot, Honora's uncle, stresses the value of reading history, "which I find very interesting. . . . By a retrospective view of the past may I find wisdom to govern and improve the future more profitably" (*The Wapshot Chronicle*, Bantam Books, 1958, p. 13. Subsequent page references will be to this edition). Honora admires "all sorts of freshness: rain and the cold morning light, all winds, all sounds of running water in which she thought she heard the chain of being . . . " (*WS*, 64). Leander "would never take his sons aside and speak to them about the facts of life. . . . If they looked out of the window for a minute they could see the drift of things. It was his feeling that love, death, and fornication extracted from the rich green soup of life were no better than half-truths, and his course of instruction was general. He would like them to grasp that the unobserved ceremoniousness of his life was a gesture or sacrament toward the excellence and the continuousness of things" (*WC*, 53–54). Away from St. Botolphs, caught in the bewildering incomprehensibility of the contemporary world, Leander's son Coverly tries desperately to retain "his conviction that the devastating blows of life fell in some usable sequence" (*WS*, 60).

St. Botolphs and its history, its people and its ways, haunt the novels from beginning to end. It "was an old place, an old river town," Cheever writes. "In a drilling autumn rain, in a world of much change, the green at St. Botolphs conveyed an impression of unusual permanence" (*WC*, 3). Returning to his boyhood home, Coverly stands in the upstairs hallway, "and here, in the dark, he seemed to yield to the denseness of the lives that had been lived here for nearly two centuries. The burden of the past was palpable . . . " (*WS*, 23). Inescapably, Coverly feels, "we are all . . . ransomed to our beginnings" (*WS*, 53).

For Cheever, then, man is a creature of the past both in his unchanging and unchangeable existential conditions and also in the tissue of historical, social, and familial forces and relationships which shape his responses to these conditions. Cheever's increasing concern with the past thus leads him to a growing emphasis on the influence of such environmental forces and relationships. In "Marito in Città," Mr. Estabrook's wife and children go to the mountains for the summer, leaving him alone in the city. Lonely, he becomes involved in a love affair which seems increasingly romantic until conversation with a neighbor inadvertently reminds him that his life is not simply his own, that it is a complex fabric of relationships and responsibilities utterly foreign to his paramour:

> The authority with which she spoke astonished him. Here was the irresistibility of the lawful world, the varsity team, the best club. Suddenly, the image of Mrs. Zagreb's bedroom, whose bleakness had seemed to him so poignant, returned to him in an unsavory light. He remembered that the window curtains were torn and that those hands that had so praised him were coarse and stubby. . . . Sitting in the summer night, in his clean clothes, he thought of Mrs. Estabrook, serene and refreshed, leading her four intelligent and handsome children across some gallery in his head. Adultery was the raw material of farce, popular music, madness, and self-

destruction (*The Brigadier and the Golf Widow*, Bantom Books, 1965, p. 211. Subsequent page references will be to this edition.)

Honora Wapshot, on her way to exile in Europe to escape prosecution for failure to pay income taxes, thinks not of where she is going but of St. Botolphs and of all that it has meant to her:

> She had lived out her life there, and each act was a variation on some other act, each sensation she experienced was linked to a similar sensation, reaching in a chain back through the years of her long life to when she had been a fair and intractable child, unlacing her skates, long after dark, at the edge of Parson's Pond, when all the other skaters had gone home and the barking of Peter Howland's collies sounded menacing and clear as the bitter cold gave to the dark sky the acoustics of a shell. The fragrant smoke from her fire mingled with the smoke from all the fires of her life. Some of the roses she pruned had been planted before she was born. . . . She did not want to leave her home and move on into an element where her sensations would seem rootless, where roses and the smell of smoke would only remind her of the horrible distances that stood between herself and her own garden (*WS*, 111).

Away from home, Cheever feels, Americans are unmistakably identifiable; they wear the marks of the native background which shaped them. They walk "unlike the Italians, as if they accommodated their step to some remembered and explicit terrain—a tennis court, a beach, a plowed field—and seemed set apart by an air of total unpreparedness for change, for death, for the passage of time itself" (*WS*, 225).

Time and place and their particular cultural forces shape man, then, and one aspect of this shaping which especially concerns Cheever is its stocking of the mind with the images in which man thinks, the language of the imagination with which he tries to structure and understand his world. "We are born between two states of consciousness," Cheever writes; "we spend our lives between the darkness and the light, and to climb in the mountains of another country, phrase our thoughts in another language or admire the color of another sky draws us deeper into the mystery of our condition" (*WS*, 110). Noting the ease and speed of contemporary travel, he points out that "we can have supper in Paris and, God willing, breakfast home, and here is a whole new creation of self-knowledge, new images for love and death and the insubstantiality and the importance of our affairs" (*WS*, 111). Coverly Wapshot realizes that Honora will survive and influence him in his images of her, and he is "consoled to think that she would not, after all, ever die:"

> She would stop breathing and be buried in the family lot but the greenness of her image, in his memory, would not change and she would be among them always in their decisions. She would, long after she was dust, move freely through his dreams, she would punish his and his brother's wickedness with guilt, reward their good works with lightness of heart,

pass judgment on their friends and lovers even while her headstone bloomed with moss and her coffin was canted and jockeyed by the winter frosts. The goodness and evil in the old woman were imperishable (*WS*, 234).

In still another dimension of his view that man is indelibly marked by particular backgrounds in time and place, Cheever suggests that man in turn marks these backgrounds and thereby influences those who come after him. Beginning a summer vacation in a rented house is exciting, Cheever writes:

> But as strong as or stronger than this pleasant sense of beginnings is the sense of having stepped into the midst of someone else's life. All my dealings are with agents, and I have never known the people from whom we have rented, but their ability to leave behind them a sense of physical and emotional presences is amazing. Our affairs are certainly not written in air and water, but they do seem to be chronicled in scuffed baseboards, odors, and tastes in furniture and paintings, and the climates we step into in these rented places are as marked as the changes of weather on the beach. Sometimes there is in the long hallway a benignness, a purity and clearness of feeling to which we all respond. Someone was enormously happy here, and we rent their happiness as we rent their beach and their catboat. Sometimes the climate of the place seems mysterious, and remains a mystery until we leave in August (*BGW*, 180–81).

Back in his childhood home, now empty, Coverly Wapshot is deeply affected by a strange but inescapable sense that the rooms somehow reflect the generations who lived and died in them. "He knew that we sometimes leave after us, in a room, a stir of love or rancor when we are gone. He believed that whatever we pay for our loves in money, venereal disease, scandal or ecstasy, we leave behind us, in the hotels, motels, guest rooms, meadows and fields where we discharge this much of ourselves, either the scent of goodness or the odor of evil, to influence those who come after us" (*WS*, 24).

As the complex product of this tissue of interrelationships, of an immutable existential condition shaped by particular backgrounds in time and place, man pays a price and often a terrible one, Cheever feels, if he tries to deny his backgrounds and become something different or if he is cut off from these sources of his identity and values. Self-exiled from America because of a scandal, Anne Tonkin in "A Woman Without a Country" tries to make herself into an Italian, "but the image was never quite right. It seemed like a reproduction, with the slight imperfections that you find in an enlargement—the loss of quality. The sense was that she was not so much here in Italy as that she was no longer there in America" (*BGW*, 144). Refusing to be taken as a tourist, she claims to be Greek, and "the enormity, the tragedy of her lie staggered her. . . . Her passport was as green as grass, and she traveled under the protectorate of the Great Seal of the United States. Why had she lied about such an important part of her identity?" (*BGW*, 145).

Cheever's interest in the problems of the expatriate appears in greater detail in two other stories which function like contrasting sides of a single coin. "The Bella Lingua" centers on Americans living in Rome. Wilson Streeter "was keenly conscious of the fact that he was making his life in a country that was not his own, but this sense of being an outsider would change, he thought, when he knew the language" (*BGW*, 95). He is not a tourist gathering memories to take home with him; "instead of accumulating memories, the expatriate is offered the challenge of learning a language and understanding a people" (*BGW*, 96). Streeter accepts the challenge, but he finds it impossible either to learn Italian like a native or to understand the Italians and their ways.

His teacher, Kate Dresser, is an American left widowed in Rome. She remains there, partly from unhappy memories of her small-town childhood and partly from an obsessive clinging to the illusion that other cultures are somehow finer than her own. But, despite her fluency in the language, she stays and will immutably stay an outsider. Ironically, her son, Charlie, who has never seen America, is aggressively American. He has grown up among the expatriate American colony and taken his identity from it; he has even refused to learn Italian. " 'Even if I had,' " he argues, " 'it wouldn't make any difference. It would still sound strange. I mean it would still remind me that it wasn't my language. I just don't understand the people, Mama. I like them all right, but I just don't understand them' " (*BGW*, 116). He insists on going "home" and does; " 'if I was with people who spoke my language, people who understood my, I'd be more comfortable' " (*BGW*, 117). Streeter and Kate remain in Rome, each trying pathetically to nourish infertile roots in an alien soil.

In "Clementina," Cheever examines the other side of the coin. An Italian peasant girl who comes to America, Clementina has a cousin who has seen the Devil, and she herself has seen wolves trotting through the streets. "She was terrified and she was rapt, as if the sight of the wolves moving over the snow was the spirits of the dead or some other part of the mystery that she knew to lie close to the heart of life" (*BGW*, 120). She becomes a servant for an American family who are "generous and ignorant" (*BGW*, 122) and who do "not believe in the dead" (*BGW*, 124). They offer to take her to America with them, "and for once the world where she had lived and had been so happy seemed to her truly to be an old world where the customs and the walls were older than the people, and she felt that she would be happier in a world where the walls were all new, even if the people were savage. . . . But on the morning when they sailed she felt a great sadness, for who can live out a good life but in his own country?" (*BGW*, 126).

Clementina finds life in America strange and often superficial, but she soon grows to love its comforts and the machines which do so much of the domestic work. When her visa expires, she thinks about returning home and telling everyone about America, "but then she saw gathering in the imagined faces of her townsmen a look of disbelief. Who would believe her tales? Who would listen? They would have admired her if she had seen the Devil, like Cousin Maria, but she had seen a sort of paradise and no one cared. In leaving one world and coming to another she had lost both" (*BGW*, 131). In the end, unable to relinquish her comfortable and youth-preserving new life, she marries a sixty-three-year-old Italian milkman and stays in America. But she cannot escape her past, and there are times when she sees "the white snow and the wolves of Nascosta, the pack coming up the Via Cavour and crossing the piazza as if they were bent on some errand of that darkness that she knew to lie at the heart of life, and, remembering the cold on her skin and the whiteness of the snow and the stealth of the wolves, she wondered why the good God had opened up so many choices and made life so strange and diverse" (*BGW*, 139–40).

For Melissa Wapshot and Honora, the attempt to live in an alien culture is far more fruitless. Melissa sees some Roman portrait busts, "but instead of feeling some essence or shade of Imperial power she was reminded of that branch of her family that had gone north to Wisconsin to raise wheat." Walking in the Borghese Gardens, she feels "the weight of habit a woman of her age or any other age carries from one country to another; habits of eating, drinking, dress, rest, anxiety, hope and, in her case, the fear of death" (*WS*, 212). She buys her food at the American supermarket "on the Via Delle Sagiturius. Here she disengages one wagon with a light ringing of metal from a chain of hundreds and begins to push her way through the walls of American food. Grieving, bewildered by the blows life has dealt her, this is some solace, this is the path she takes" (*WS*, 235). Honora, utterly homesick, accepts extradition from her self-exile with complete joy. Returning to St. Botolphs and suicide by starving herself is for her infinitely preferable to living wealthy and free in foreign lands in which she has no roots.

III

This profound and complex sense of the past informs the deepest levels of Cheever's apprehensive concern with the present and the future and explains his perplexed feeling of standing "in a quagmire, looking into a tear in the sky." Given man's permanent existential condition and his inescapable relationship to his particular past, what, Cheever wonders, is man doing to himself in the present and what does it forebode for the future? Exploring these questions, Cheever centers on two predominant problems: *one*, the vast and unparalleled changes which characterize the contemporary world; and *two*, the rate of change which these reflect and its frightening significance.

In "The Angel of the Bridge," the narrator recounts his mother's, his brother's, and his own bizarre responses to a contemporary world whose changes they find incomprehensible and subliminally unbearable. At seventy-eight, his mother skates at Rockefeller Center dressed like a young girl; she had "learned to skate in the little New England village of St. Botolphs . . . and her waltzing is an expression of her attachment to the past. The older she grows, the more she longs for the vanishing and provincial world of her youth. She is a hardy woman . . . but she does not relish change" (*BGW*, 20–21). She is afraid to fly, and "her capricious, or perhaps neurotic, fear of dying in a plane crash was the first insight I had into how, as she grew older, her way was strewn with invisible rocks and lions and how eccentric were the paths she took, as the world seemed to change its boundaries and become less and less comprehensible" (*BGW*, 21). Reflecting similar deep-seated anxieties, the narrator's brother is unable to use elevators because he is afraid the building will collapse while he is riding in one.

At first amused by these aberrations and feelings superior to them, the narrator suddenly finds himself terrified by large bridges. Convinced they will fall if he tries to drive across them, he goes out of his way to find "a small old-fashioned bridge that I could cross comfortably" (*BGW*, 25) and he feels "that my terror of bridges was an expression of my clumsily concealed horror of what is becoming of the world":

> The truth is, I hate freeways and Buffalo Burgers. Expatriated palm trees and monotonous housing developments depress me. The continuous music on special-fare trains exacerbates my feelings. I detest the destruction of familiar landmarks, I am deeply troubled by the misery and drunkenness I find among my friends, I abhor the dishonest practices I see. And it was at the highest point in the arc of a bridge that I became aware suddenly of the depth and bitterness of my feelings about modern life, and of the profoundness of my yearning for a more vivid, simple, and peaceable world (*BGW*, 27–28).

Even more than by the nature of contemporary change, Cheever is disturbed by its velocity, by the rate of change and its chasmal incoherence. Shopping at a supermarket, the narrator of "A Vision of the World" thinks that "you may need a camera these days to record a supermarket on a Saturday afternoon. Our language is traditional, the accrual of centuries of intercourse. Except for the shapes of the pastry, there was nothing traditional to be seen at the bakery counter where I waited" (*BGW*, 215). Later, at the country club, he watches the daughter of a millionaire funeral director dancing with an indicted stock-market manipulator who had paid his fifty-thousand-dollar bail from the money he carried in his wallet. The band plays songs from the 1920's, and "we seemed," the narrator remarks, "to be dancing on the grave of social coherence" (*BGW*, 218).

The Wapshot novels center on the rapidly widening gap between the anachronistic village of St. Botolphs and the incomprehensibly changing contemporary world. Born and brought up in St. Botolphs, Moses and Coverly Wapshot leave it to make their way in a world not only different in every way from their background but also without any relationship to it whatever, a world symbolized by "the great Northern Expressway that flows southward from Montreal to the Shenandoah, engorging in its clover leaves and brilliantly engineered gradings the green playing fields, rose gardens, barns, farms, meadows, trout streams, forests, homesteads and churches of a golden past" (WS, 90). Cheever heightens this contrast throughout *The Wapshot Scandal* by juxtaposing the gantries of the missile center where Coverly works and the abandoned farm which they have so suddenly and so incoherently superseded. Beyond the administration building, "one could see some flat pasture land and the buildings of an abandoned farm. There was a house, a barn, a clump of trees and a split-rail fence, and the abandoned buildings with the gantries beyond them had a nostalgic charm. They were signs of the past, and whatever the truth may have been, they appeared to be signs of a rich and a natural way of life. The abandoned farm evoked a spate of vulgar and bucolic imagery—open fires, pails of fresh milk and pretty girls swinging in apple trees—but it was nonetheless persuasive" (WS, 30).

For Coverly, the total lack of continuity between the contemporary world and the past becomes increasingly bewildering: "to create or build some kind of bridge between Leander's world and that world where he sought his fortune seemed to Coverly a piece of work that would take strength and perseverance. The difference between the sweet-smelling farmhouse and the room where he lived was abysmal. They seemed to have come from the hands of different creators and to deny one another" (WC, 119). After going to night school, he takes a Civil Service job at a rocket installation; and in its scientists he discovers a further lack of coherence. "It was the first time that Coverly had associated with men of this echelon and he was naturally inquisitive but he couldn't understand their language. . . . It was another language and one that seemed to him with the bleakest origins. You couldn't trace here the elisions and changes worked by a mountain range, a great river or the nearness of the sea" (WS, 140–41).

The price contemporary man pays for too much and too rapid change appalls Cheever. The urban-suburban sprawl and the moral-esthetic collapse which the narrator of "The Angel of the Bridge" ultimately cannot stomach are more than simple ugliness evoking a good-old-days nostalgia: they reflect a way of life without roots or meaning or values, a quantitative life lacking any qualitative dimension. Similarly, in a drive-in movie near the Northern Expressway, the young man who later becomes Melissa Wapshot's lover engages in the casual sexuality of his time. "His sitting undressed in the back seat of a car might be accounted for by the fact that the music he danced to and the movies he watched dealt less and less with the heart and more and more with overt sexuality, as if the rose gardens and playing fields buried under the Expressway were enjoying a revenge" (WS, 91).

For Cheever, then, the major casualties in the disruption of social coherence are traditional human values and relationships and the process by which they are sustained and extended. In "A Vision of the World," the narrator is constantly struck and increasingly disturbed by the meaninglessness and incoherence of the contemporary world. Its chaotic discontinuities have the quality of a dream world; and, paradoxically, only in his dreams can he establish any relationship to the past and its traditional values. Feeling "that our external life has the quality of a dream and that in our dreams we find the virtues of conservatism" (BGW, 217), he wants to identify "not a chain of facts but an essence—something like that indecipherable collision of contingencies that can produce exaltation or despair. What I wanted to do was to grant my dreams, in so incoherent a world, their legitimacy" (BGW, 218).

His dreams are largely of past events or people and traditional figures; and in each dream, someone speaks the words, "*porpozec ciebie nie prosze dorzanin albo zyolpocz ciwego.*" These apparent nonsense syllables are actually broken Polish and other Slavic derivatives from which relevant meaning can be extrapolated: "there are many good things in life; you should not search for the things that do not exist in life," or perhaps, "you have a good and pleasant life and should not cry for things you do not need." The relevance of these strange words becomes clear in the narrator's last dream:

> I dream that I see a pretty woman kneeling in a field of wheat. Her light-brown hair is full and so are the skirts of her dress. Her clothing seems old-fashioned—it seems before my time—and I wonder how I can know and feel so tenderly toward a stranger who is dressed in clothing that my grandmother might have worn. And yet she seems real—more real than the Tamiami Trail four miles to the east, with its Smorgorama and Gigantic-burger stands, more real than the back streets of Sarasota (BGW, 221).

She begins to speak the mysterious eight words, and he suddenly awakes to the sound of rain. Sitting up, he too speaks eight words: " 'Valor! Love! Virtue! Compassion! Splendor! Kindness! Wisdom! Beauty!' The words seem to have the colors of the earth, and as I recite them I feel my hopefulness mount until I am contented and at peace with the night" (BGW, 222). The strange unfocussed words have become sharp and clear; they are "the virtues of conservatism," the "good things in life," the traditional values the narrator wants to make legitimate "in so incoherent a world."

Whatever else it may lack, St. Botolphs continues to live by such human values and relationships; and throughout the Wapshot novels, Cheever contrasts with this aspect of the old town a vigorous and incredibly changing contemporary world whose people face the unchanging and inescapable existential problems stripped of the values, beliefs, and relationships which traditionally have sustained human life. Emile is dissatisfied with his date's casual attitude towards sex: "in her readiness she sometimes seemed to debase and ridicule the seat of desire, toward which he still preserved some vague and tender feelings." He has a deep and undefined yearning for something better, "something that would correspond to his sense that life was imposing; something that would confirm his feeling that, as he stood at the window of Narobi's grocery store watching the men and women on the sidewalk and the stream of clouds in the sky, the procession he saw was a majestic one" (WS, 92). Emile's mother is disturbed by "the covert moral revolution that was being waged by men of Emile's age. . . . In her own youth she had seen some wildness but the world had seemed more commodious and forgiving. She had never been able to settle on who was to blame. She feared that the world might have changed too swiftly for her intelligence and her intuition. She had no one to help her sift out the good from the evil" (WS, 188–89).

Coverly's wife, Betsey, roams the novels 'ike a lost soul, seeking forever in unappeased longing for friends and neighbors. No matter where she goes, in the huge impersonal cities or in the uniform rows of suburban housing developments, she remains a stranger. She comes " 'from a small town . . . where everybody's neighbors' " (WS, 31), and all she asks is to be part of a community. But in the world of rockets and nuclear energy, in which she and Coverly live, there is no community; no one has the time or the inclination for friendship or neighborliness. Absorbed in their work or turned inward by its oppressive security regulations, they isolate themselves from all but those who share their particular jobs. For Betsey, the contemporary world is therefore an endless limbo unwarmed even by Coverly's unfailing love and care. She needs also to belong to the tribe, but there is no longer any tribe to include her.

Even more terrible is the plight of Gertrude Lockhart. She lives in an expensive suburban house full of the conveniences and machines designed to make life easier and better. But the conveniences defeat her efforts to use them, and the machines keep breaking down. Her husband is at work in the city, repair men are out of town or busy, and even the unemployed refuse to do manual labor. "She cried for her discomforts but she cried more bitterly for their ephemeralness, for the mysterious harm a transparent bacon wrapper and oil burner could do to the finest part of her spirit; cried for a world that seemed to be without laws and prophets" (WS, 85). Utterly miserable and alone in the midst of plenty, she seeks escape in alcohol and sex: "she could not educate herself in the maintenance and repair of household machinery and felt in herself that tragic obsolescence she had sensed in the unemployed of Parthenia who needed work and money but who could not dig a hole. It was this feeling of obsolescence that pushed her into drunkenness and promiscuity and she was both" (WS, 86). From her neighbors she receives neither understanding nor help but only scorn and a campaign to drive her away; and in the end, an absurdly tragic figure, she hangs herself.

In a different but equally shattering way, Melissa Wapshot is unable to adapt to the contemporary world. In the midst of her rich, comfortable, and apparently happy life, she is suddenly stricken by the oldest of human ills: the awareness of her own inevitable extinction. "The pain in her chest seemed to spread and sharpen in proportion to her stubborn love of the night, and she felt for the first time in her life an unwillingness to leave any of this; a fear as senseless and powerful as her fear of the dark when she went down to shut the door; a horror of death" (WS, 74–75). But in the infinite progress and material magnificence of the contemporary world, death is inconsistent, something vaguely shameful and unmentionable. "Most maladies have their mythologies, their populations, their scenery and their grim jokes . . . but here was the grappling hand of death disinfected by a social conspiracy of all its reality" (WS, 75). Nothing in her world had prepared Melissa for this basic existential awareness; a society that hides the reality of death cuts itself off from traditional ways of living with that reality nor is it likely to evolve new ones. Forced to cope with death in terrifying emptiness and loneliness, she turns to its apparent antithesis in the immediate life of the senses, to a desperate escape into sex. She takes a young boy as her lover and becomes a bewildered and pathetic casualty of a world of infinite energies and headlong change grown careless of continuity and direction and of the human values they serve.

IV

In this complex feeling for the past, for man's relationship to his backgrounds and his deep need for social coherence, Cheever is neither a nostalgic traditionalist nor a naturalistic determinist. He is thoroughly aware that man cannot return to or repeat the past, especially an imaginary past, however tempting an escape it may seem; and he views man in more than animal terms. To Cheever, man is the complicated product of his past, of heredity shaped by natural and cultural environment, and he is convinced that the identity and the values man lives by are rooted with him in that past. If man cannot return to or repeat the past, neither can he with impunity move very far beyond a coherent relationship to it. Deeply disturbed by his perceptions of vast change exploding in an apparently geometric progression, Cheever senses that man may be incurring a catastrophic penalty for progress, that the brilliance and power which have given man dominion over the earth may finally be operating to eliminate him from it.

Working at the heart of Cheever's complex concern with the past, then, is a profound insight into the contemporary human condition, a potentially tragic view of man which seems both electrifyingly relevant and poignantly accurate. As Cheever implicitly defines him, man is a biological creature who survives, like all organic life, by adapting to his environment. But man is also a cultural creature, a unique being who changes his environment; and in this uniqueness lies the potential for tragedy which Cheever has sensed. For if man changes his environment faster than he is capable of adapting to it, he is inevitably and self doomed.

Here is the "something" which for Cheever "has gone very wrong" in our time; man has released energies and developed technologies which together are changing his world far beyond his capacity to endure such change. Listening to a group of scientists, Coverly is struck by a frightening contradiction. He "supposed that the palest of them could smite a mountain but they were the most unlikely people to imagine as being armed with the powers of doom-crack. They spoke of lightning in their synthetic language but with the voices of men. . . . They were men born of women and subject to all the ravening caprices of the flesh. They could destroy a great city inexpensively, but had they made any progress in solving the clash between night and day, between the head and the groin? Were the persuasions of lust, anger and pain any less in their case?" (WS, 141). What can save a world, Cheever wonders, in which the needs and angers once vented in spears and arrows can now find outlet in nuclear missiles?

But life can end with a whimper as well as with a bang; and man can destroy himself just as surely, if more slowly, by violating the organic relationship to his natural and social environments through which he understands himself and his world and derives the values he lives by. At a lecture on space technology, Coverly can find no point of contact between the world implied in the lecture and the world in which he had grown up:

> The . . . lecture dealt with experiments in sending a man into space in a sack filled with fluid. The difficulty presented was that men immersed in fluid suffered a grave and sometimes incurable loss of memory. Coverly wanted to approach the scene with his best seriousness—with a complete absence of humor—but how could he square the image of a man in a sack with the small New England village where he had been raised and where his character had been formed? It seemed, in this stage of the Nuclear Revolution, that the world around him was changing with incomprehensible velocity but if these changes were truly incomprehensible what attitude could he take, what counsel could he give his son? Had his basic apparatus for judging true and false become obsolete? (WS, 140–41.)

How, Cheever asks, can man adapt to a world he is changing faster than his capacity for comprehending and humanizing change?

In this provocative insight, which seems increasingly to be shaping his recent work, Cheever becomes more than the whimsical *New Yorker* satirist of urban and suburban absurdities, more than an austere but compassionate New-England moralist, and certainly far more than Ihab Hassan's maker of an "affirmative statement" detached from "the disagreeable aspects of reality in order to *create* a metaphor of the excellence and continuity of things" (*Radical Innocence*, Harper Colophon Books, New York, 1966, p. 194). Cheever is seeking precisely the opposite metaphor. Fearing that contemporary man in his obsession with progress is destroying "the excellence and continuity of things," Cheever sees that he may ultimately pay the price of survival for the very brilliance of his own success. Emerging in Cheever's thought and art, this insight suggests a thoroughly contemporary and potentially major tragic vision of man and the human condition. If Cheever has not yet fully articulated it, if he has not yet found the most effective forms to express it, the promise is rich and worth exploring.

O'Hara, Cheever & Updike

Alfred Kazin*

    John Cheever found in suburbsville almost as many cruel social differences as O'Hara had always known in Gibbsville. But the overwhelming sensation that a reader got from Cheever's special performance of the short story was of a form that no longer spoke for itself. It was not even a "slice of life," as O'Hara's stories were, but had become a demonstration of the amazing sadness, futility, and evanescence of life among the settled, moneyed, seemingly altogether domesticated people in Proxmire Manor. As Cheever said in two different pieces of fiction, Why, in this "half-finished civilization, in this most prosperous, equitable and accomplished world, should everyone seem so disappointed?" It is a question that earlier writers of "*The New Yorker* story" would not have asked openly, with so much expectation of being agreed with, and twice. But Cheever's brightly comic charming, heartbreaking performances always came out as direct points made about "the quality of life in the United States," or "How We Live Now."

    Cheever—Salinger and Updike were to be like him in this respect—began and somehow has remained a startlingly precocious, provocatively "youthful" writer. But unlike Salinger and Updike, he was to seem more identifiable with the rest of *The New Yorker*, just as his complaint about American life was more concrete and his fiction more expectable. As I've written before, his stories regularly became a form of social lament-writing never hard to take. What they said, and Cheever openly *said* it, was that America was still a dream, a fantasy; America did not look lived

*Reprinted with permission from *The New York Review of Books* (19 April 1973), pp. 14–18. Copyright © 1973 Nyrev, Inc.

in. Americans were not really settled in. In their own minds they were still on their way to the Promised Land. In story after story Cheever's characters, guiltily, secretly disillusioned and disabused with their famous "way of life" (always something that could be put into words and therefore promised, advertised, and demonstrated), suddenly acted out their inner subversion. They became "eccentrics," crazily swimming from pool to pool, good husbands who fell in love with the baby sitter. Sometimes, like "Aunt Justina," they even died in the living room and could not be moved because of the health laws and restriction by the zoning law on any funeral parlors in the neighborhood.

Acting out one's loneliness, one's death wish—any sudden eccentricity embarrassing everybody in the neighborhood—these make for situation comedy. Life is turning one's "normal" self inside out at a party. The subject of Cheever's stories is regularly a situation that betrays the basic "unreality" of some character's life. It is a trying-out of freedom in the shape of the extreme, the unmentionable. Crossing the social line is one aspect of comedy, and Cheever demonstrates it by giving a social shape to the most insubstantial and private longings. Loneliness is the dirty little secret, a personal drive so urgent and confusing that it comes out a vice. But the pathetic escapade never lasts very long. We are not at home here, says Cheever. But there is no other place for us to feel that we are not at home.

In these terms the short story becomes not the compression of an actual defeat but the anecdote of a temporary crisis. The crisis is the trying-out of sin, escape, the abyss, and is described by Cheever with radiant attention: *there* is the only new world his characters ever reach.

> . . . They flew into a white cloud of such density that it reflected the exhaust fires. The color of the cloud darkened to gray, and the plane began to rock. . . . The stewardess announced that they were going to make an emergency landing. All but the children saw in their minds the spreading wings of the Angel of Death. The pilot could be heard singing faintly, "I've got sixpence, jolly jolly sixpence. I've got sixpence to last me all my life. . . ."

The "country husband" in this most brilliant of Cheever's stories returns home to find that his brush with death is not of the slighest interest to his family, so he falls in love with the baby sitter. He does not get very far with the baby sitter, so he goes to a therapist who prescribes woodworking. The story ends derisively on the brainwashed husband who will no longer stray from home.

But who cares about this fellow? It is Cheever's clever, showy handling of the husband's "craziness," sentence by sentence, that engages us. Each sentence is a miniature of Cheever's narrative style, and each sentence makes the point that Cheever is mastering his material, and comes back to the mystery of why, in this half-finished civilization, this most prosperous, equitable, and accomplished world, everyone should seem so disappointed. So there is no mastery in Cheever's story except Cheever's. It is Cheever one watches in the story, Cheever who moves us, literally, by the shape of his effort in every line, by the significance he gives to every inflection, and finally by the cruel lucidity he brings to this most prosperous, equitable, and accomplished world as a breaking of the heart.

My deepest feeling about Cheever is that his marvelous brightness is an effort to cheer himself up. His is the only impressive energy in a perhaps too equitable and prosperous suburban world whose subject is internal depression, the Saturday night party, and the post-martini bitterness. Feeling alone is the air his characters breathe. Just as his characters have no feeling of achievement in their work, so they never collide with or have to fight a society which is actually America in allegory. All conflict is in the head. People just disappear, as from a party. Cheever's novels— *The Wapshot Chronicle, The Wapshot Scandal, Bullet Park*—tend to muffle his characters in meaning even more than the short stories do. Cheever is such an accomplished performer of the short story that the foreshortening of effect has become second nature with him. There is the shortest possible bridge between cause and effect. *The New Yorker* column is still the inch of ivory on which he writes. Cheever always writes about "America." He is an intellectual. The Wapshot novels are wholly allegories of place showing the degeneration of the old New England village, "St. Botolph's," into the symbolic (but spreading) suburb that is "Proxmire Manor. . . ."

The Domesticated Stroke of John Cheever

Eugene Chesnick*

Our life is not so much threatened as our perception," Emerson says early in "Experience," his essay on his own disturbed serenity. For the Transcendentalist the possibility of any diminishment or confusion of his sensory powers was the source of greatest distress, especially since the knowledge of the beautiful and the knowledge of the good were understood as together making up the moral sentiment. Thoreau's journals are filled with prescriptions for cultivating sensory awareness. When he goes walking in the woods but cannot forget the aggravations of life in town, he is genuinely disgusted. He is not at one with himself. "I am not where my body is," he complains; "I am out of my senses." If John Cheever, with the familiar New England name, is a legitimate heir in more than

*Reprinted with permission from *The New England Quarterly*, 44 (Dec. 1971), 531–52.

name only to this way of looking at things, the heir to the individualistic way of Emerson and Thoreau, then the question is: What good is this inheritance of a carefully cultivated sensibility for a novelist trying to do his work in our time? Can it serve him at all when the pressures working for the destruction of one's perceptions are so great?

With Thoreau and Emerson moral declarations often seem very much a matter of mood. Emerson grants the power of mood. "Our moods do not believe in each other," he says in "Circles." Our conviction of the illusoriness of life is strongest when we recognize our changes in moods, each mood casting doubt on the reality of every other. But our demands for a various life make such changes in mood necessary, he argues again in "Experience." "Our love of the real draws us to permanence, but health of body consists in circulation, and sanity of mind in variety or facility of association. We need change of objects." A moral structure dependent upon a balance of moods is obviously a delicate one. Thoreau associates questions about personal guilt with Puritan gloom of which in his opinion we have had too much already. His shifts in mood defeat any feeling of profound guilt, which, of course, depends upon a continuity of feeling from past to present. With their new freedom, Thoreau and Emerson can set about merrily teasing churchgoers and advising them that their time would be more wisely spent out-of-doors on a Sunday morning. Thoreau is never in the mood to go to church. Similarly, when Leander Wapshot near the end of *The Wapshot Chronicle* finally does decide to attend church one Sunday, it is, according to him, a sight to "make the angels up in heaven start flapping their wings." He is the latest in a long line of New England orthodoxy baiters. What he observes at church, as might be expected from his sort, are the old pine needles on the carpet and "these cheered him as if this handful of sere needles had been shaken from the Tree of Life and reminded him of its fragrance and vitality." Eliot Nailles, resident of Bullet Park, somehow still possesses the smallest portion of the old sensibility. For Nailles religion remains connected with the seasons of the year and the motions of the spirit.

> His sense of the church calendar was much more closely associated with the weather than with the revelations and strictures in Holy Gospel. St. Paul meant bizzards. St. Mathias meant a thaw. For the marriage at Cana and the cleansing of the leper the oil furnace would still be running although the vents in the stained glass windows were sometimes open to the raw spring air. Abstain from fornication. Possess your vessel in honor. Jesus departs from the coast of Tyre and Sidon as the skiing ends.

With both Thoreau and Cheever immersion in water indicates full sensory vitality. Leander's cold morning bath is the ritual equivalent to Thoreau's dip in Walden Pond. Johnny Hake in "The Housebreaker of Shady Hill" is kept from further crime by being caught in a rainstorm and so having his love of life restored. Cheever uses a similar device more than

once as a way of ending a story. At times one is ready to swear that all his
characters are saved simply by being caught out in the rain. During events
of significant emotional intensity we are almost always made aware of the
rain outside or of water nearby. The sea evokes the loneliness which is
likewise always nearby in Cheever's work. It is here that he is most
vulnerable, vulnerable to being dismissed as a mere illustrator as soon as
he resorts to the easily available landscape and seascape values. What! the
critical reader complains, you would have us take seriously all this
business about the cold bath and the dip in the pond? Next, you will want
us to consider the aesthetics of the swimming pool. In Cheever's case, that
is precisely what the matter does come down to eventually.

Even the stories in *The Way Some People Live*, a collection published
in 1943, long before the appearance of some of the better-known stories in
Cheever's war-interrupted career, although often slight, contain the
recognizable form of his fiction: the depiction of what appears to be a
more or less satisfactory life and the abrupt revelation of genuine frustration. Some people live, it would seem, in a condition of considerable anxiety. The loss of the cat on moving day triggers a woman's outburst over
never having a child; a man is unable to forget an early love affair. In *The
Enormous Radio*, ten years later, Cheever explores the disturbances of our
well-being in greater detail. The narrator in one story, "Goodbye, My
Brother," explains the pleasure he takes in the annual reunion at the family summer cottage: the late-at-night swims, family doubles, backgammon, the costume parties, and everything enjoyed the more by being
shared with his mother and wife and his brothers and sisters. Only one
brother, Lawrence, looks upon the family games with stern disapproval.
The Pommeroys have a long Puritan background, including one ancestor
who was eulogized by Cotton Mather for his "untiring abjuration of the
Devil," and Lawrence, the sole representative of this Puritan conscience,
lectures everyone on the universality of guilt and the unreality of their
lives. Finally in an argument over all this gloominess, Lawrence is hit
over the head with a sea-root by his brother and he leaves in indignation.
But the narrator feels no remorse for his violence and is in no mood to
worry. "Jesus what a morning!" he says. "The wind was northerly. The
air was clear. In the early heat, the roses in the garden smelled like
strawberry jam." He gives up on Lawrence and his unwanted dreariness.

"The Enormous Radio" depends upon an out-and-out gimmick. Jim
and Irene Wescott buy an expensive radio but instead of getting great
music on their new set they find themselves by some mysterious freak of
circuitry turned into all the other apartments in their building. They find
out about illicit love affairs, terrors of fatal illnesses, shady business deals.
The story is pure Cheever in its narrative unfolding. A family is subjected
to a breakdown of its routine happiness and is exposed to a new knowledge of evil. From the first, Irene is afraid of her radio. She is sure that
something has gone wrong when she hears the noices of kitchen appli-

ances coming through the set. "The powerful and ugly instrument, with its mistaken sensitivity to discord, was more than she could hope to master, so she turned the thing off and went into the nursery to see her children." The value of "sensitivity to discord" is what Cheever will try to decide in many books to come.

Listening in gets to be a habit and a source of some delight. But eventually the new insight becomes too much to bear. "Oh, don't, don't, don't," she cried. "Life is too terrible, too sordid and awful. But we've never been like that, have we, darling?" Irene needs greater reassurance that her own life will not deteriorate. Jim gets the radio fixed to work properly. But the next day the two of them have an argument over her spending and his apprehensiveness about money so that the radio obviously has had time to do its work. Jim mocks his wife and recites to her her own crimes, the theft of her mother's jewelry before the will could be probated, the abortion she insisted upon having. The quarrel continues while in the background the voice from the repaired radio tells of more distant tragedies, a train accident in Tokyo, a fire in a hospital for blind children in Buffalo, and reports of the temperature and the humidity.

Even in his short stories Cheever shows some recognition of the need to establish a fictional place for himself. Other stories in *The Enormous Radio* are stories in which the apartment-house setting is insisted upon, pieces about life as seen by the elevator operator in the building or by the superintendent. But an apartment house is a terrible place to have to start from. So it is in *The Wapshot Chronicle*, Cheever's first novel, that he finds his place, the small dying New England seaport town of St. Botolphs, the one spot on earth from which he can define his values. It is Leander Wapshot who will have to be the carrier, if there is to be a carrier, of the principles of New England individualism. If the fictional Leander seems a peculiar heir to Thoreau, Thoreau was a peculiar heir to Jonathan Edwards. Peculiarity is the whole point.

Eccentricity abounds in St. Botolphs but in no case does it have the potential to turn into destructive grotesqueness. The small-town types that Cheever describes are all harmless enough. The more important eccentrics, however, are Leander and his cousin, Honora Wapshot. Leander's only visible occupation is that of captain of a summer excursion steamer, the *S.S. Topaze*. Honora, who has what is left of the Wapshot money, throws away all her mail without opening it, sends the bus company a check once a year, boards its buses as she pleases, and refuses to waste any of her life's energies on the world's pointless routines. Cheever sees her as some admirable "naked human force, quite apart from dependence and love." He describes life in St. Botolphs itself with a kind of exclamatory innocence. The beauty and mystery of life overcome him. "The house is easy enough to describe but how to write a summer's day in an old garden? Smell the grass, we say. Smell the trees!" When Leander breaks down and fakes a suicide because his boat has been taken away from him and is being converted into a floating gift shop, Cheever exclaims, "What a tender thing, then, is a man." Happiness is fragile and Cheever wants to depict the life of a man with a delicate and gentle art.

Leander keeps a journal, partly because Wapshots have always kept journals. The diary is a "meteorological journal of the mind," as Thoreau calls his. As recorded in the journal, the happiest time of Leander's life began oddly enough with an act of treachery against him. When he was a young man, his boss, under threat of firing and blackmailing, forced him to marry a girl whom the old man has made pregnant. With the girl, Clarissa, on a farm where they have gone for the birth of the baby, Leander feels intensely alive. "Long after nightfall, departure of rain, embrace of wife returns to writer all good things. Magic of haying weather. Heat of sun. Chill of storm." But, brooding because the baby is to be taken from her, Clarissa drowns herself in the river. The final passage dealing with the episode, with the emotions under control and emerging naturally from the remembered details, will stand up under the most demanding critical observation:

> Overcast day. Not cold. Variable winds. South, southwest. Hearse at station. Few rubbernecks watching. Father Frisbee said the words. Old man then; old friend. Purple face. Skirts blowing in wind. Showed old-fashioned congress boots. Thick stockings. Family lot on hill above river. Water, hills, fields restore first taste of sense. Never marry again. Roof of old house visible in the distance. Abode of rats, squirrels, porcupines. Haunted house for children. Wind slacked off in middle of prayer. Distant, electrical smell of rain. Sound amongst leaves; stubble. Hath but a short span, says Father Frisbee. Full of misery is he. Rain more eloquent, heartening and merciful. Oldest sound to reach porches of man's ear.

Leander blames no one for what has happened, neither his boss, nor Clarissa, nor himself. The rain promises an eventual return to life so that all feelings of guilt and betrayal can be put aside. Even in his old age, when the possibilities of pleasure are considerably diminished, Leander has no quarrel with his past. He never does attempt to discover the moral contour of events. What Leander has to teach both his sons, Moses and Coverly, pertains not to responsibility or to guilt but rather to the significance of ceremony, a set of lessons that may or may not help them in their own times.

> It was his feeling that love, death, and fornication extracted from the rich green soup of life were no better than half-truths, and his course of instruction was general. He would like them to grasp that the unobserved ceremoniousness of his life was a gesture or sacrament toward the excellence and continuousness of things. He went skating on Christmas Day—drunk or sober, ill or well—feeling that it was his responsibility to the village to appear on Parson's Pond.

Moses and Coverly grow up and leave St. Botolphs to make their way in the world. Cheever alternates journal chapters with chapters describing their adventures. Both have their troubles. Moses is more his father's son and had early "found in himself a taste for the hair and grain of life." But in Washington where he goes to work for a federal agency his zest for living gets him involved with a married woman and he is dismissed as a security risk. True to his heritage, Moses goes fishing to think things out. Coverly, always the more timid son, is having difficulties that could prove more permanent. In his technician's job he is assigned first to a military installation in the Pacific and then to a rocket-launching site in the United States called Remsen Park. Coverly's newly acquired wife, Betsey, is restless and unhappy there and soon leaves him.

Moses falls in love with a girl named Melissa. Melissa, recently divorced, is living under the protection of Justina Scaddon, who also happens to be a Wapshot. The old decaying mansion where she is staying is both a castle and a prison for her, the just representation of both her own and Justina's fears. Justina makes it so difficult for Moses to see Melissa that he finally has to resort to crawling naked across the rooftops of the old house to get to Melissa's bedroom. These women troubles of Moses and Coverly are important for the novel. Honora's will stipulates that both of them produce male heirs before her money can pass over to their side of the family.

The castle burns down in a fire caused by defective wiring so that Moses and Melissa are freed. In an immediately juxtaposed scene, Coverly comes home and finds Betsey back. Happiness is recovered that quickly. Ihab Hassan in *Radical Innocence* (1961), trying to evaluate Cheever's career up to that point, found him unwilling to confront the depths of his myth. "The spectacle of history and nature, the panorama of people, towns, seascapes, and countryside, finds a kind of unity in the marvellous state of mind the author wishes to impress upon us. But character and action seem always to fall short of the fabulous evocation of time, place, and archetype," Hassan argued. The fault is in too much playing around. It is hard not to concede Hassan his point about Cheever then and since then, especially when one has in mind the easy juxtaposition that is made to stand for a conclusion to *The Wapshot Chronicle*, but perhaps a truer estimate of Cheever's career might be reached, not by focusing upon instances of his evasiveness, but by considering him as a writer of some talent but who is struggling to make his fictional meanings in an increasingly frantic world, a point I shall try to make more convincing as I go along. Cheever's talent is vulnerable, but one wonders if in the future only the toughest and eventually only the crudest talents are to survive.

With the publication of the short-story collection, *The Housebreaker of Shady Hill*, Cheever's setting becomes the suburb. If storytelling ability is any criterion, then the pieces in this volume must be respected. Both the title-story and the widely anthologized "The Country Husband," for example, utilize fine control of narrative pace and considerable technical ingenuity in demonstrating how discontents can pile up for the previously happy suburbanite. Cheever usually manages to contrive an energetic opening. "The Housebreaker of Shady Hill" begins,

> My name is Johnny Hake. I'm thirty-six years old, stand five feet eleven in my socks, weigh one hundred and forty-two pounds stripped, and am, so to speak, naked at the moment and talking into the dark. I was conceived in the Hotel St. Regis, born in the Presbyterian Hospital, raised on Sutton Place, . . .

Cheever's idea of story at this stage leads him toward fairly free forms that will allow considerable intimacy with the narrator. Cheever's narrative experiments here consist of technical ingenuity and small adjustments in method. He does not seem yet to desire a drastically new form. The story moves from summary into the immediate crisis. Johnny is forced out of his job with the company he has been with all his business career and must strike out on his own. His soft life in the prosperous suburb of Shady Hill has left him with little equipment to deal with his impending financial problems.

Just as the checks are about to start bouncing, Johnny sees his opportunity for relief. He and his wife Christina are invited to a party at the Warburtons', one of the richest of their Shady Hill neighbors. Mrs. Warburton brags about how much money her husband usually has on him and later that night after the party, Johnny sneaks back into the house and takes nine hundred dollars from the wallet in Warburton's pocket while everyone is asleep. His knowledge of himself as a thief causes a premature *ubi sunt* of the senses. "Where were the trout-streams of my youth and other innocent pleasures?" he asks. All of a sudden the world seems filled with petty corruptions. He observes a customer in a restaurant pocketing the waitress' tip; he overhears the man in the office next to the one he has rented trying to sell phoney uranium stock; he himself is offered a chance by a friend to come in on a deal to swindle some rich young people. Johnny resents the loss of his joys. Identification with small-time losers has not been one of his instincts. The happiness in his family gets lost in quarreling as the strain of the theft begins to tell on him and he is forced to prowl around at night looking for more neighbors to victimize. Exposure and permanent expulsion from respectable society seem inevitable but he is saved by nature's grace. On his way to another attempted housebreaking, he is drenched by a thundershower.

> I wish I could say that a kindly lion set me straight, or an innocent child, or the strains of distant music from some church, but it was no more than the rain on my head—the smell of it flying up my nose—that showed me the extent of my freedom . . .

The renewed sensory vitality makes Johnny aware of his freedom from the past. He is not guilty since nothing has yet been done that cannot be undone. The old firm invites him back to work. He leaves nine hundred dollars on the Warburtons' kitchen table.

In similar fashion, Francis Weed in "The Country Husband" is let off easily when he develops a mad passion for his children's teen-age baby-sitter. The psychiatrist he consults advises woodworking. For the reader who wants to know what would happen if these men were caught in their crimes and who demands a more thorough follow-through on the implications of always threatening disaster in the prosperous suburbs, the endings of the stories are, of course, not in the least satisfactory. Cheever knows plenty of sad stories, though, and most of the action in Shady Hill takes place with drunks and bankrupts and elderly lovers in the background. Johnny Hake and Francis Weed are merely the lucky ones, still alive by chance, a fact which they acknowledge and which makes them tremble.

Perhaps *Some People, Places, & Things That Will Not Appear in My Next Novel,* a collection published in 1961, can be made out to be more than an assemblage of items admittedly belonging together only by default. Nothing is to be gained by perversely overstating the significance of this thin volume as the turning point in a career except that Cheever himself uses the occasion to declare that he has grown impatient with many of the themes of our literature and is determined to seek out new ones. The last piece in the volume, "A Miscellany of Characters That Will Not Appear," lists methods of description and characterization that are rejected from this time forward. The book is the only extended process-fiction we get from Cheever. To his immense credit he does not bog down in complaints about the inadequacy of art, but instead makes a serious attempt to define what can still be done in fiction and produces a few worthwhile stories as he does so.

"The Death of Justina," does, in fact, suggest a new tact on Cheever's part, a search for a way of describing the upheaval he sees around him. The narrator is named Moses but neither he nor the Justina of the story seems further identifiable with the characters from *The Wapshot Chronicle.* Justina is killed off early before being given a chance to be realized as anything but a dying old woman. When she expires in Moses' living room, the mayor of Proxmire Manor tells him that Justina cannot be buried from his home since the zoning laws forbid funeral parlors in the neighborhood. Unfortunately the zoning laws of perception are not being guarded so carefully. Moses complains, "We admire decency and we despise death but even the mountains seem to shift in the space of a night and perhaps the exhibitionist at the corner of Chestnut and Elm streets is more significant than the lovely woman with a bar of sunlight in her hair, putting a fresh piece of cuttlebone in the nightingale's cage." Returning from the office on the commuter local the evening of Justina's death, Moses studies the scenery along the way but finds it unintelligible, suggestive of great wealth but meaningless.

I stand, figuratively, with one wet foot on Plymouth Rock, looking with some delicacy, not into a formidable and challenging wilderness but onto a half-finished civilization embracing glass towers, oil derricks, suburban continents and abandoned movie houses and wondering why, in this most prosperous, equitable, and accomplished world—where even the cleaning women practice the Chopin preludes in their spare time—everyone should seem so disappointed.

That night after his argument with the mayor over Justina's burial, Moses has a dream. He is in a supermarket. The customers seem to have so much to choose from. But at the checkout counter the clerks tear open all the packages and ridicule everyone for his choices. One by one the customers are thrown out into the darkness beyond the supermarket. In the land of plenty death can never make any sense.

The Wapshot Scandal is another kind of farewell—this time to St. Botolphs. But Cheever is obviously troubled that imminent chaos rather than transition to a new order of civilization may be what the novelist now is recording. Coverly is continually subjected to panic alerts at Talifer, another missile site where he is stationed, where world conflagration presents itself as always real and "total disaster seemed part of the universal imagination." At a Senate investigation one old Senator embarrasses everyone in the room by jumping up in the middle of the questioning and begging Cameron, a ruthless scientist in charge of Talifer, not to destroy the earth. He pathetically recites a list of the beauties of nature and the wonderful works of man. Early in the novel Melissa is sent to the hospital. She is feverish and her cold may be turning into pneumonia. She realizes how much she loves life and is afraid of death. But the presentiment of death is general. "Now that was the year when the squirrels were such a pest and everybody worried about cancer and homosexuality," Cheever says. Cheever, like Coverly, who during one of the alerts recalls the Adventists back in St. Botolphs climbing a hill to await the end, tries to keep up his comic spirit by maintaining that fears of dissolution are seasonal but there is nothing in the structure of his narrative that supports this. He is able to resolve no one's problems.

Incident and outcome in human lives seem now totally disproportionate so that the storyteller is always dealing with the incredible. Out of the hospital, Melissa becomes dissatisfied with her life in the suburbs and, afraid of death and missing out on life, takes the grocery boy as a lover. They go off on weekends together until the boy's mother discovers what is happening and complains to Moses. Moses leaves his wife and becomes a drunk. Melissa goes to Italy. The delivery boy, Emile, eventually takes a job as a seaman. He jumps ship and becomes a contestant in a male beauty contest which turns out to be a flesh sale. The highest bidder for his body is Melissa. They set out again to see what ultimate in sensibility they might discover.

The Wapshot Scandal provides us with three separate returns to St. Botolphs in the first three chapters: first, St. Botolphs on a Christmas Eve now; then a glimpse back at the old days when the whole Wapshot family was still together; and finally Coverly coming back to visit Honora and to look in at his old home. Cheever claims close knowledge of the Wapshots of this town. "I knew them well," he says. "I made it my business to examine their affairs, indeed I spent the best years of my life, its very summit, on their chronicle." He introduces one more chapter from Leander's diary. Honora comes upon it in her attic. The discovery is like the discovery of Thoreau's lost journal, another addition after the record has been assumed to be complete. The recorded observations seem as sharp as ever. "Also fine weather. Bright sun. Warm air. Breeze up and down the mast. Wouldn't blow a butterfly off your mainsail," Leander had written. We are reminded that the invention of this diary may well have been Cheever's supreme fictional achievement.

Honora herself has come upon bad days. One is able to ignore the claims of the world only so long, and now the Internal Revenue Service wants to prosecute her for never having filed an income tax return. Convinced that she will land at the dreaded poor farm, she goes up to the attic to hang herself but after reading in Leander's journal, where she finds herself being called a skinflint and where Leander describes another amorous adventure which ended badly for him but which he refuses to weep over, she is convinced that she should not take herself so seriously and that life is worth living. Among the other characters from the earlier Wapshot novel, Coverly is still the most attractive: sensitive if ineffective. The rest are no longer likable. Moses, once he has lost his youthful gusto, has little left. He is borrowing on his presumed inheritance from Honora and seems petty and selfish even before the disclosure about Melissa's affair. Betsey, Coverly's wife, is truly tiresome with her complaints that everywhere she goes people are unfriendly to her and with her constant punishment of Coverly for her loneliness.

Coverly is trying to connect the old and the new but the old farmhouse that stands at the edge of the Talifer base and the site itself just cannot be connected. His government service has occasionally brought Coverly close to the sources of power and it is his knowledge of the dullness and vulnerability of the powerful men that he meets that keeps him from conceding the inferiority of his own more provincial vision. But it is also precisely such knowledge of weakness that is the source of so much unhappiness all around. Mr. Applegate in St. Botolphs is beginning to imagine that he can tell what is really going on in the minds of his parishioners at communion time but such knowledge, he suspects, might be enough to make him lose his faith. Melissa, at one point in the story, thinks to herself how "mistaken it was to assume that the exceptions—the drunkard and the lewd—penetrate, through their excesses, the carapace of immortal society." She asks who does understand the naked truth about them, the priest, the doctor, the psychiatrist, and "What was the penetration worth?" Too great consciousness is extracting its price.

At the end of the novel, Moses is back in St. Botolphs, supposedly for one last Christmas celebration. He is a complete drunk. His knowledge of his wife's infidelity and the treacherousness of all existence has helped do him in. "The brilliance of light, the birth of Christ, all seemed to him like some fatuous shell game invented to dupe a fool like his brother while he saw straight through to the nothingness of things." With such knowledge he awaits his final destruction. Coverly insists upon preserving Honora's custom of inviting to Christmas dinner all the lost souls that can be found and he seems the happier for his effort. Cheever himself says farewell. St. Botolphs has been the place from which his fiction had to start. "I pack my bags and go for a last swim in the river. I love this water and its shores; love it absurdly as if I could marry the view and take it home to bed with me."

After such farewells Cheever's next two works, *The Brigadier and the Golf Widow* and *Bullet Park* should be examples of a new sensibility. Cheever says in the lead story in *The Brigadier and the Golf Widow* that he will not strain to stay in Eden. "I would not want to be one of those writers who begin each morning by exclaiming, 'O Gogol, O Chekhov, O Thackeray and Dickens, what would you have made of a bomb-shelter ornamented with four plaster-of-Paris ducks, a birdbath, and three composition gnomes with long beards and red mobcaps?' " He will not be such a writer if he can help himself. Cheever is determined to discover the beauty in this scene, in this land of impoverished prosperity. But what more unpromising material could there be than the brigadier who strides up and down the country club locker room shouting, "Bomb Cuba! Bomb Berlin! Throw a little nuclear hardware at them. Show them who's boss!" and who takes as his latest mistress shopworn Mrs. Pastern? Mrs. Pastern, for her part, demands a key to his bomb shelter in return for her favors.

"Hang-up" may be the modern word for it; "dead set" is what Thoreau called it when we cannot get the accumulated furniture of our lives through the doorway into the place where we wish to live; but, whatever the phrase, it is this inability to cross over from one place to another that Cheever describes in "The Angel of the Bridge." The narrator of the story was sure he was invincible. He had always enjoyed the sensation of flying and the conviction of being part of a changing world. But then the bridges begin to loom up in front of him and to sway underneath him when he tries to drive across them. Modern technology has erected a great many forms but the bridge is the one shape on the landscape that terrifies him. He has been compassionate in his judgment of the modern world, but now he must admit to his contempt.

> The truth is, I hate freeways and Buffalo Burgers. Expatriated palm trees and monotonous housing developments depress me. The continuous music on special-fare trains exacerbates my feelings. I detest the destruction of familiar landmarks, I am deeply troubled by the misery and drunkenness I find among my friends, I abhor the dishonest practices I see. And it was at the highest point in the arc of a bridge that I became aware suddenly of

the depth and bitterness of my feelings about modern life, and of the profoundness of my yearning for a more vivid, simple and peaceable world.

The solution is again an instance of unexpected grace. A more attractive figure from the new world, a young girl with a guitar, turns up as a hitchhiker at the foot of a bridge. She seems not at all afraid of confronting the risks of life. She sings the frightened man across the bridge.

In "The Swimmer," Cheever provides a complete map of a suburban place. The swimmer is Neddy Merrill, who on one Sunday afternoon in Bullet Park decides to return to his own home and children from the Westerhazys' by way of all the neighborhood swimming pools, an eight-mile hike and swim.

> He seemed to see with a cartographer's eye, that string of swimming pools, that quasi-subterranean stream that curved across the county. He had made a discovery, a contribution to modern geography; he would name the stream Lucinda after his wife. He was not a practical joker nor was he a fool but he was determinedly original and had a vague and modest idea of himself as a legendary figure.

If he succeeds Neddy will have proved that the terrain is still test enough to be worth conquering and naming, that man-made pools and streams can supply the imagination as natural ones once did. Moreover, it is the quality of his own life with his family and neighbors that will be specified. His choppy crawl stroke will be a handicap. "It was not a serviceable stroke for long distances but the domestication of swimming had saddled the sport with some customs and in his part of the world a crawl was customary." The story is the best possible parable of Cheever's predicaments as a writer. American life has moved from ocean-side to pond-side to pool-side and Cheever must write of it in short stories and episodic novels with his own domesticated stroke, perhaps good for short distances but not for long journeys of the imagination.

At first Neddy's escapade goes well enough. He feels strong and he is strengthened even further by the drinks he is offered at every pool-side party he comes upon. But he is soon beset with troubles. He is caught on the interstate highway divider, unable to find a break in the traffic that will let him get to the other side. People shout insults at him as they drive by and someone throws a beer can at him. There are hints of worse disasters in his life. At the Hallorans' pool, Mrs. Halloran tells him she is sorry to hear about his misfortunes, about his having to sell his house and about what happened to his children, and all. Neddy is beginning to wonder just how much he has forced himself to forget. Each new house he comes to presents its own disappointment. He is almost exhausted at last by the long swim. His old mistress greets him cruelly at her pool. She asks him if he will ever grow up and tells him she will not lend him more money. What exactly has happened with her is something else he seems to have forgotten. He swims the final pool and arrives home but he is too worn out for the victory to mean anything. The house is deserted. His children are not there. His wife has not come over from the Westerhazys'. The house is locked up and has the appearance of not having been lived in for a long time. The epic journey has been a journey to nowhere at all.

The energy of the opening of *Bullet Park* is the energy of counterattack. Discouraged as he is himself at times, Cheever is unwilling to accept the prophets of a radically new morality who ridicule his world. Least of all, is he willing to take the word of children as critics. An introductory tour of the community reveals to us how the "lights of Powder Hill twinkled, its chimneys smoked and a pink plush toilet-seat cover flew from a clothes-line," all of which "Seen at an improbable distance by some zealous and vengeful adolescent, ranging over the golf links, the piece of plush would seem to be the imprimatur, the guerdon, the accolade and banner of Powder Hill behind which marched, in tight English shoes, the legions of wife-swapping, Jew-baiting, booze-fighting spiritual bankrupts." But, Cheever says, "the adolescent, as adolescents always are, would be mistaken."

Cheever sincerely believes that fathers should be able to pass down knowledge to their children. The fact that they are no longer able to do so does not allow one to assume a reversal of the flow of wisdom. Tony Nailles, the adolescent, has a problem. He cannot get out of bed in the morning because the world seems so sad. He resents the sounds of love he hears coming from his parents' room. He takes to his bed when his father raises his golf putter to him for calling him a phoney mouthwash pusher. Nailles can only try to make it up to his son by telling him rather timidly about his own feelings. "I love to see leaves blowing through the headlights. I don't know why. I mean they're just dead leaves, no good for anything, but I love to see them blowing through the light." But Tony requires another landscape. "Give me back the mountains," he cries from his bed. His father is helpless. Only the guru can help. He teaches the boy the old mystic formulas for letting one's imagination take him to a new place. He has him repeat after him, "I am in a house by the sea. It is four o'clock and it is raining." Then he teaches him the love cheer, "Love, love, love," and Tony is cured. But, by then, Nailles is having his own problems. He cannot finish the trip into the city on the commuter train. He keeps jumping off at every stop and then must wait for another train to reboard, only to get off again at the next chance. At the end of the first part of the novel Tony may be cured all right, but his father is still in trouble. The problems of an adult civilization are not so easily cured by the chants of a guru. Cheever knows a gimmick when he sees one.

Part Two introduces Paul Hammer, the prophet of the new awakening. If we are indeed living in a fragmented world, then perhaps Nailles and Hammer might go together, their lives joined to form some kind of meaning not present in either life separately. But Hammer has come to kill Nailles. He has picked him as the typical suburbanite, someone whose innocence can be assaulted as a way of making a whole culture acknowledge the presence of evil and thus preparing for a new morality. In his part of the book, Hammer tells about his career before he came at last to Bullet Park. He is a bastard, named for a tool being carried past the window by a gardener at the time of his naming, given a name by fate and so named as to indicate that he might be right in thinking of himself as a power more than as a person. His father instead of marrying his mother merely provided for her and made it possible for her to wander around the world pursuing her various pastimes. His mother has visions. Sleeping in hotel rooms she believes she can absorb the spirit of all the previous occupants from their impress on the mattress. It is she who first suggests the idea of an execution to Hammer. She advises him, "I would single out as an example some young man, preferably an advertising executive, married with two or three children, a good example of life lived without genuine emotion or value."

Hammer's wife, Marietta, the granddaughter of a perfume chemist turned alchemist, shifts madly from mood to mood, a more dangerous Melissa. Their marriage took place soon after they met and somehow the thread she always seems to have hanging onto her clothes is for Hammer the only adequate token of the instability of their passion. Violence, like the violence of a thunderstorm, makes her feel vulnerable and loving. Disasters reported from some far-off place she absorbs for the sake of her own emotional life. Hammer says of her, "She seemed to think of love as a universal dilemma, produced by the convulsions of nature and history. I will never forget how tender she was the day we went off the gold standard and her passion was boundless when they shot the King of Parthia." At other times she is cold and hostile. Their pointless wandering around Europe ends only after Hammer comes across a parade for a dead communist hero in Italy. He joins the parade and feels much better. "We flew back to New York soon afterwards and it was sitting on a beach that following summer (I had already seen the picture in the dental journal) that I decided, on the strength of a kite string, that my crazy old mother's plan to crucify a man was sound and that I would settle in Bullet Park and murder Nailles. Sometime later I changed my victim to Tony." The decision is just so much a matter of mood. The kite string, the string on the coat, the narrow thread on which happiness in the suburbs depends all are images of Cheever's sense of the modern fate. The turns in his stories, though, cannot be dismissed as tricks but must be given their due as repeated statements of the lack of connection between cause and effect.

Nailles apparently is the perfect choice for Hammer's revenge on a class. His ignorance of the evil around him seems absolute. To be unfaithful to his wife has never occurred to him. Despite his quarrels with his son, he does want the two of them to get along well together. Nailles is not all that innocent, however, as it turns out. He would really have liked to brain Tony with his golf putter that time; and when Hammer suggests to him on a fishing trip that he should get rid of his old faithful dog, Nailles is resentful enough to feel quite murderous himself towards Hammer. So Hammer is not just the threatening external Other but one side of Nailles, and we have in *Bullet Park* a modern American novel on the anarchist part of the self.

The point is that Cheever is trying to handle his knowledge of human nature in the still recognizable Transcendentalist way. For Emerson, evil is an illusion; it is the lack of good and how can the lack of something be real? The argument can sound like a sophistical gimmick, the philosophical equivalent of Cheever's tricky endings. The voice of authorial wonder in Cheever's fiction is his device for refusing to acknowledge the finality of evil. Cheever focuses on the changes of mood within the individual. The thought of killing Nailles gives new zest to Hammer's days. Cheever describes his mood with exactly the same exclamatory innocence that he has employed for the enthusiasms of Leander and Coverly. "Have you ever waked on a summer morning to realize that this is the day when you will kill a man? The declarative splendor of the morning is unparalleled. Lift up a leaf to find a flaw and there is none. The shade of every blade of grass is perfect." Hammer's plan is to burn Tony on the altar of Christ Church to awaken the world. The guru, to whom Hammer has told his plan, tips off Nailles, who rushes from a party when he finds out what is happening to his son. He cuts through the locked front door of the church with his chain saw, the same saw he ordinarily uses for felling trees for firewood as his own form of therapy. The Transcendentalist preference for outdoors over the inside of the church has taken a peculiar turn. Tony is saved in time and Hammer is committed as insane. No one is awakened.

What becomes clearest perhaps from the survey of the career of John Cheever, one filled with achievements of considerable substance but inconclusive still, is the drastic change in the nature of individualism that has taken place. Thoreau and Emerson protested against the follies of modern life with a contrariness that they insisted amounted to no more than reasonableness. The unlived life was what Thoreau opposed. But he never believed otherwise than that we could only have so much of one kind of life as we were willing to give up of another. The economy of the universe did not allow for having everything. Hence the solitary disciplined existence at Walden. This principle of economy provided Thoreau's moral intuition: the fixed point among the variable moods. But how small a band the Concord reformers seem now! Their formulas for living we could almost take as only literary parables although we know better. We are tempted to do so because looking back we most notice that there were fewer prophets then and fewer disciples and fewer opponents and fewer people altogether on the earth. The delicate balance of aesthetic and moral perceptions had not yet been subjected to the pressure of great numbers. The Cheever world, on the contrary, is bulging with people who have discovered the value of life and who suffer harsh agonies at the thought of its loss or diminishment, so that it is hard to tell whether their sense of the apocalypse is any more than a heightened awareness of individual mortality. Cheever, for his part, has never been able to trust preachers who would claim the right to deprive us of our fictions and to force the hard realities upon us. Even though we may acknowledge to ourselves the unreality of our lives, we cannot tolerate those who would claim to possess reality unto themselves. It is no wonder that Cheever's career as a writer of fiction is difficult to appraise.

The Machines in Cheever's Garden

Scott Donaldson*

Certainly, Lewis Coser is right that "the life of art illuminates the social life of man" (1972, pp. xv–xix). Certainly, one agrees with Paul Blumberg that literature does provide "a rich form of social documentation, illuminating the norms and values and entire culture of our own and previous eras" (1969, pp. 291–92). But the plain fact is that most classical 19th-century American literature qualifies rather better as romance than as realism, so that only in the 20th century, after the white whales were hunted down at sea and the demons exorcised from Puritan forests, have the nation's serious writers begun to supply the kind of picture of everyday, contemporary, middle-class society that has been the staple subject matter of the English novel for the last 200 years.

Following the lead of William Dean Howells in *Criticism and Fiction* (1891), however, American writers have moved in this century toward more realistic rendering of the surfaces of American life, particularly as it was lived in the city or small town. Curiously, however, very few of our best writers have concentrated their gaze on the suburbs, despite their burgeoning population. Still fewer have descended beneath the suburban surface to discover "the formative but largely submerged currents" in the life of this time, currents which go undetected by all but the most perceptive of artists (see Hoggart 1966, p. 279). This is the accomplishment of the novelist and short-story writer John Cheever (1912–   ),[1] who during the past two decades has sketched in his fiction an exceedingly disturbing portrait of what it is like to live in the postwar, upper-middle-class American suburb. Whether purposefully or not, Cheever has come to function as the Jeremiah of our suburban age.

To a substantial extent, Cheever's method has been one of implicit contrast among city, country, and suburb. Thus his earliest stories, such as the well-known "The Enormous Radio" (1953), brilliantly evoke "the

*Reprinted from *The Changing Face Of The Suburbs*, ed. Barry Schwartz by permission of The University of Chicago Press. Copyright © University of Chicago Press, 1976.

corrosive effect of metropolitan life upon essentially decent people who are isolated, defeated, or deprived of their individuality in the vastness of the great city:"[2] people afflicted, in short, by urban *anomie*. Then in Cheever's first novel, *The Wapshot Chronicle* (1957), the scene shifts to the seaside town of St. Botolphs, Massachusetts, heavy with tradition and populated by eccentrics—the exhibitionist Uncle Peepee Marshmallow, Doris the male prostitute, even (on a more respectable plane) the peculiar Wapshots themselves—who are affectionately tolerated by their neighbors.

Clearly, the author's preference is for this small town of the past, since, as he asks in celebration (but with the final phrase undercutting the sentiment), "Where else in the world were there such stands of lilac, such lambent winds and brilliant skies, such fresh fish?"[3] One critic has objected that nobody's grandfather ever lived in a place so idealized as St. Botolphs.[4] However that may be, Cheever certainly realizes that his country town is an anachronism and underlines the point in the anecdote of the young girl who, having run away from home, finds herself among the carolers on the St. Botolphs village green on Christmas eve and calls home to wish her mother Merry Christmas. The carolers are singing "Good King Wenceslas," but, as Cheever comments, the voice of the girl, "with its prophecy of gas stations and motels, freeways and all-night supermarkets, has more to do with the world to come than the singing on the green" (Cheever 1963, p. 11).

Attractive though it is, St. Botolphs emits an air of sadness as well, "for while the ladies [of the town] admired the houses and the elms they knew that their sons would go away. Why did the young want to go away? Why did the young want to go away?" Off go the Wapshot boys, Moses and Coverly, to their separate suburban destinations, aiming to make what fortunes are unavailable in the country town of their youth and no more aware of the significance of their departure than the most temporary summer visitor: "We have all parted from simple places by train or boat at season's end with generations of yellow leaves spilling on the north wind as we spill our seed and the dogs and the children in the back of the car" (Cheever 1957, pp. 21, 92).

In effect, Cheever followed the young men of the Wapshot clan south to their Connecticut and Westchester suburbs, for his fiction since the mid-1950s has consistently been set in suburban communities, variously called Shady Hill, Proxmire Manor, Maple Dell, and Bullet Park. Cheever himself has lived for some years in the up-the-Hudson exurb of Ossining, New York (also the site, incidentally, of Sing Sing prison), and understands as well as anyone writing today the style of life that predominates in the upper-middle-class suburb. His reputation, in fact, has suffered because to some critical eyes he appears to play the role of apologist for the suburbs, and because to others the milieu seems so bland as to be incapable of supplying the stuff of fiction.

Both charges are nonsensical. It is true, to be sure, that Johnny Hake glowingly invokes the joys of cooking meat outdoors, of looking down the front of his wife's dress as she salts the steaks, of growing roses and gazing at the lights in Heaven: "Shady Hill is, as I say, a *banlieue* and open to criticism by city planners, adventurers, and lyric poets, but if you work in the city and have children to raise, I can't think of a better place." But even as he reflects on the pleasures of suburban living, Hake is plotting to burglarize a neighbor's house in order to maintain his place among the expensive people (Cheever 1958*b*, pp. 3, 12). Similarly, Eliot Nailles in *Bullet Park* inveighs against those who are always "chopping at" the suburbs ("I can't see that playing golf and raising flowers is depraved"), but something surely has gone wrong in the suburb where he lives and whose commuting life he can face only by taking daily, massive doses of drugs (Cheever 1969, p. 66).

"It goes without saying," Cheever once remarked in an interview, "that the people in my stories and the things that happen to them could take place anywhere" (Waterman 1958, p. 33). People live and love and suffer and die in all locations, but one difference is that they try very hard, in the suburbs of Cheever's fiction, to ignore suffering and death. Proxmire Manor, he writes, "stood on three leafy hills north of the city, and was handsome and comfortable, and seemed to have eliminated, through adroit social pressures, the thorny side of human nature." It is known "up and down the suburban railroad line as the place where the lady got arrested." It is also the place where it is illegal to die in Zone B, so that it is necessary to take the body of "the old lady and put her into the car and drive her over to Chestnut Street, where Zone C begins" (Cheever 1966, pp. 682–84; 1961, pp. 10–11).

The town of St. Botolphs, though sometimes ridiculous, had at least evolved through the natural order of things which shaped it as an organic community. The inhabitants of Proxmire Manor, by way of contrast, do everything in their limited power to subvert nature, to create an artificial community surrounded by paper fences and legal boundaries. But they cannot legislate death away, or crime, or the peculiar boredom that afflicts the well-to-do suburban housewife. In "The Embarkment for Cythera," Jessica Coliver begins—and ends—a casual affair with her grocery boy principally out of boredom. "Loneliness was one thing," she muses, "and she knew herself how sweet it could make lights and company seem, but boredom was something else, and why, in this most prosperous and equitable world, should everyone seem so bored and disappointed?" (Cheever 1966, p. 685). Perhaps it is because they have no roots, no true home—only a house in Maple Dell where "the houses stand cheek by jowl, all of them built twenty years ago, and parked beside each was a car that seemed more substantial than the house itself, as if this were a fragment of some nomadic culture" (*Time* 1964, p. 69). But if the suburb has no future, its greater sin is neglecting or repudiating the past, as in Shady Hill's "tacit claim that there had been no past, no war, that there was no danger or trouble in the world" (Bracher 1963, p. 75).

The consequences of so short-sighted an attitude Cheever has depicted in increasingly apocalyptic terms. As George Garrett has observed, Cheever's 1964 novel, *The Wapshot Scandal*, like many of his stories in the last 10 years, "moves inexorably toward the end of the world." Like Thoreau's mass of men, his suburbanites lead lives of quiet (because suffering is not to be acknowledged) desperation. There is laughter in Cheever, for he will not repudiate his gift of wit, but at the end the corners of the mouth turn down in dejection. A characteristic Cheever story thus begins with a credible, realistic situation, proceeds to farce or satire, and finally descends to nightmare. "It is," a critic has commented, "as if Marquand had suddenly been crossed with Kafka" (Garrett 1964, pp. 4, 8, 9–10).

In part, it is the dusky aspect of modernity itself which supplies the shadow side of Cheever's fiction. It is at first merely amusing when the housewife cannot cope with the formidable dials on her labor-saving appliances, but less funny when she gives up in despair, turns to drink and adultery, and finishes in suicide (his stories are full of suicides). Technological progress, he warns, has swept away all received values in its wake. Left with nothing to guide them, the young joylessly copulate on a double date at the drive-in movie near the Northern Expressway where, as Cheever comments, the young man's "sitting undressed in the back seat of a car might be accounted for by the fact that the music he danced to and the movies he watched dealt less and less with the heart and more and more with overt sexuality, as if the rose gardens and playing fields buried under the Expressway were enjoying a revenge" (Burhans 1969, pp. 194–95).

However, John Cheever does not write his tales out of sentimental nostalgia or latter-day Comstockism. Unlike Jay Gatsby, he is under no illusions about any man's ability to repeat or recapture the past, but "he is convinced that the identity and the values man lives by are rooted with him in that past." In his fiction he is warning us against ourselves, against the "catastrophic penalty" we may have to pay for what passes for progress (ibid., p. 197).[5]

The symbols which stand for such heedless progress in Cheever's fiction are almost invariably associated with transportation, a theme which links his concern with modern suburbia to a concern with modernity in general. One of his most famous stories, "The Angel of the Bridge," specifically focuses on the relationship between modern means of travel and the dispiriting quality of contemporary existence. The story is built around three phobias. The first is that of the narrator's 78-year-old mother, who came from St. Botolphs and who insists on skating on the Rockefeller Center rink at the lunch hour, "dressed like a hat-check girl." She used to skate in St. Botolphs, and she continues to waltz around the ice in New York City "as an expression of her attachment to the past." For all her seeming bravado, however, she panics and is utterly unable to board an airplane. The second phobia is that of the narrator's successful older brother, who because of his fear of elevators ("I'm afraid the building will fall down") is reduced to changing jobs and apartments. Finally, the narrator himself, who had felt superior to both his mother and his brother, finds that he is quite unable, because of an unreasonable, unshakable conviction that the bridge will collapse, to drive across the George Washington Bridge. On a trip to Los Angeles (for he does not mind flying), it comes to him that this

> terror of bridges was an expression of my clumsily concealed horror of what is becoming of the world. . . . The truth is, I hate freeways and Buffalo Burgers. Expatriated palm trees and monotonous housing developments depress me. The continuous music on special-fare trains exacerbates my feeling. I detest the destruction of familiar landmarks, I am deeply troubled by the misery and drunkenness I find among my friends, I abhor the dishonest practices. And it was at the highest point in the arc of a bridge that I became aware suddenly of the depth and bitterness of my feelings about modern life, and of the profoundness of my yearning for a more vivid, simple, peaceable world.

His problem is resolved when a young girl hitchhiker, carrying a small harp, sings him across a bridge with "folk music, mostly." "I gave my love a cherry that had no stone," she sings, and he can once again negotiate the trip across the Hudson, the sweetness and innocence of the music from the past restoring him to "blue-sky courage, the high spirits of lustiness, and ecstatic sereneness" (Cheever 1964a, pp. 23–35).

In *Bullet Park* (1969), the novel in which Cheever most acutely dissects suburban life-styles, the principal characters seek a similar angel to restore them to spiritual and psychological health. Once more, the dominant symbol for their ills comes from the world of transportation. In letting railroads, airlines, and freeways—which shrink space, distort time, and confuse perceptions—stand for a deep psychological alienation, he uncovers a malaise inherent not only in modern life but more specifically in that portion of it lived in the commuting suburb. His contemporary suburbanites are terrified by the hurtling freeway automobiles, high-speed trains, and jet airplanes which make is possible for them to sleep in Bullet Park and work in New York or office in New York and fly across the continent on a business call.

This emphasis grows naturally out of Cheever's fictional concentration of the journey motif. The concept of life as a journey is probably as old as the earliest legends, but in Cheever's work the theme is obsessive. His characters are forever in transit; the dominant metaphor of his fiction is that of the risky journey that modern man takes each day (Bracher 1964, p. 49). There are some—"the losers, the goners, the flops" that

Cousin Honora Wapshot annually invites to Christmas dinner—who manage to miss the "planes, trains, boats and opportunities," but such derelicts are the exception (Garrett 1964, p. 10). Normally, the Cheever protagonist has, in the eyes of the world, "made it": the house in Bullet Park stands as emblem of his success, and so does the daily trip into the city and back.

But no one who lives that disconnected life, one foot on Madison Avenue and the other in Westchester or Connecticut, manages to stay happy for long. His daily commutation, by means of technologically wonderful highways or railbeds, only takes him on a fruitless circular voyage. He stays in motion, and goes nowhere but down. He comes home to roost, but can sink no roots. Neddy Merrill, in "The Swimmer," conceives of a Sunday voyage: he sets out to cross eight miles of suburban space by water—or, more specifically, by the swimming pools that dot the landscape. Neddy "seemed to see, with a cartographer's eye, that string of swimming pools, that quasi-subterranean stream that curved across the county." He decides to swim home by this stream, which he names after his wife Lucinda. Neddy's trip becomes to him a quest undertaken in the spirit of "a pilgrim, an explorer, a man with a destiny." But reality keeps intruding (the whistle of a train brings him back to reality, reminding him of the time), and when he finally reaches home, after being insulted and ignored and rejected en route, he discovers (what he had been trying to forget) that the house has been sold and his wife and four beautiful daughters have moved on (Cheever 1964b, pp. 61–76).

Though his voyaging is fanciful and his plight extreme, Neddy Merrill is symptomatic of the restless and rootless denizens who inhabit Cheever's fictional suburbs. "The people of Bullet Park," for instance, "intend not so much to have arrived there as to have been planted and grown there," but there is nothing organic or indigenous or lasting about their transplantation. The evenings call them back to "the blood-memory of travel and migration," and in due time they will be on their way once more, accompanied by "disorder, moving vans, bank loans at high interest, tears and desperation (Cheever 1969, pp. 4–5). They are, almost all of them, but temporary visitors, and they will find themselves, most of them, in the same boat (or commuter train) every morning.

To further underline the rootless quality of Bullet Park, the narrator adopts the pose of an anthropologist looking back on what is, in fact, current American society. Though it is not raining, Eliot Nailles turns on his windshield wipers. Why? "The reason for this was that (at the time of which I'm writing) society had become so automotive and nomadic that nomadic signals or means of communication had been established by the use of headlights, parking lights, signal lights and windshield wipers." For the power of speech, for face-to-face communication, contemporary society substitutes mechanical symbols. One character in the book is convinced that her windshield wipers give her "sage and coherent advice" on the stock market; Nailles is urged by the diocesan bishop "to turn on [his] windshield wipers to communicate [his] faith in the resurrection of the dead and life of the world to come" (ibid., pp. 21, 155).

The technology of rapid movement (which is both a cause and effect of the development of places like Bullet Park) attempts, in short, to provide a convenient, painless substitute for true affirmation of one's spiritual faith. So Lent passes with only Nailles himself remembering the terrible journey of Paul of Tarsus: "Thrice was I beaten with rods, once was I stoned, thrice I suffered shipwreck, a night and a day I have been in the deep; in journeyings often, in perils of waters, in perils of robbers, in perils by mine own countrymen, in perils by the heathen, in perils in the city, in perils in the wilderness, in perils in the sea, in perils among false brethren; in weariness and painfulness, in watchings often, in hunger and thirst, in fastings often, in cold and nakedness" (ibid., p. 39). But what possible analogy can be drawn between the trials of Paul and the seemingly placid surface of the life which Eliot and Nellie Nailles lead in Bullet Park?

Eliot Nailles, the principal figure in the novel, is a middle-aged businessman with a job he would rather not talk about: though educated as a chemist, he is now employed to merchandise a mouthwash called "Spang." He is kind, uxorious, a conventional family man old-fashioned in his values. If he had talent, he would write poems celebrating his wife Nellie's thighs. He loves her, as he loves their only child Tony, possessively and protectively, his love seeming "like some limitless discharge of a clear amber fluid that would surround them, cover them, preserve them and leave them insulated but visible like the contents of an aspic." He thinks "of pain and suffering as a principality, lying somewhere beyond the legitimate borders of western Europe," and hardly expects any distressing foreign bodies to penetrate his protective fluid (ibid., pp. 25, 50).

But in suburbia there is only a false security: Neither Nailles nor Nellie nor their son Tony, a high school senior, can escape the ills of modern society. Nellie goes to New York to see a matinee in which a male actor casually displays his penis; outside the theater college-age youngsters are carrying placards which proclaim four-letter words; on the bus one young man kisses another on the ear. She returns from her disconcerting afternoon "bewildered and miserable." In an hour, she thinks during the train ride home, she will be herself again, "honest, conscientious, intelligent, chaste, etc. But if her composure depended upon shutting doors, wasn't her composure contemptible?" (ibid., pp. 30–33). She decides not to tell Nailles about her experience, and it is just as well; absolutely monogamous and faithful himself, he is shocked and disturbed by promiscuity or homosexuality.

Thus, nothing much to trouble Eliot Nailles comes of Nellie's day in the city. The case is quite different when Tony, suffering through a prolonged spell of depression, refuses to get out of bed or to eat normally.

Physically, there is nothing wrong with the boy; psychologically, he is consumed by a sadness which remains impervious to the ministrations of the family doctor, the psychiatrist, and the specialist on somnambulatory phenomena. His is a radical instance of the more common "suburban sadness." After Tony has been in bed for 17 days and it begins to look as though he will not survive his depression, Nailles also cracks and finds himself unable to ride the commuter train into the city without a sedative.

The locomotive, screaming across the countryside, was the preeminent machine invading the 19th-century American Garden of Eden. We have constructed an Atropos, a fate which will soon slip beyond our control, Thoreau warned. Do we ride upon the railroad or the railroad upon us? Emerson wondered. Dickinson's seemingly playful iron horse stuffed itself on nature as it hooted its way, paradoxically "docile and omnipotent," to its stable door. And Hawthorne, in "The Celestial Railroad," made clear (as the folk song affirmed) that you can't get to heaven in a railroad car.[6]

Disturbing though it may have been in 1860, the railroad has been supplanted in the mid-20th century by other, still more frightening technological monsters. Take, for example, the jet airplane which enables one "to have supper in Paris and, God willing, breakfast at home, and here is a whole new creation of self-knowledge, new images for love and death and the insubstantiality and the importance of our affairs" (Burhans 1969, p. 190). This is no conventional paean to the wonders of progress, for "God willing" emphasizes the risk attendant upon jet travel, and if our "affairs" which cause us to hurtle across oceans and continents are truly insubstantial, without body, they are hardly important enough to justify the trip. Just how trivial these affairs are, in fact, is emphasized in Cheever's much anthologized "The Country Husband." In that story, Francis Weed survives a crash landing on the flight from Minneapolis to New York and that same evening attempts, unsuccessfully, to interest anyone—his wife, children, neighbors, friends—in what has happened. For nothing in his suburb of Shady Hill "was neglected; nothing had not been burnished" (Cheever 1958a)—and the residents want things to stay that way. They do not wish to hear of disasters, much less disasters narrowly averted; they shut tragedy, especially potential tragedy, out of their consciousness. Cheever's fiction, however, tries to wake them up, to point to the thorns on the rosebushes, to call attention to the hazards of the journey.

The trains of today, by way of contrast, play a somewhat ambiguous role in Cheever's gallery of horrors. To the extent that they are reminiscent of a quieter past, they summon up a certain nostalgia. "Paint me a small railroad station then," *Bullet Park* begins, and by no accident, for the "setting seems to be in some way at the heart of the matter. We travel by plane, oftener than not, and yet the spirit of our country seems to have remained a country of railroads." The train mistily evokes loneliness and promise, loss and reassurance:

> You wake in a pullman bedroom at three a.m. in a city the name of which you do not know and may never discover. A man stands on the platform with a child on his shoulders. They are waving goodbye to some traveler, but what is the child doing up so late and why is the man crying? On a siding beyond the platform there is a lighted dining car where a waiter sits alone at a table, adding up his accounts. Beyond this is a water tower and beyond this is a well-lighted and empty street. Then you think happily that this is your country—unique, mysterious and vast. One has no such feelings in airplanes, airports and the trains of other nations.

A romantic aura envelops any journey, by night, along the tracks of the continent. But in the small suburban railway station at Bullet Park, designed by an architect "with some sense of the erotic and romantic essence of travel," the windows have been broken, the clock face smashed, the waiting room transformed into a "warlike ruin" (Cheever 1969, pp. 3-4, 14).

The train trip is one thing; commutation is something else. The commuter station is the site of the sudden death, one perfectly normal morning, of Harry Shinglehouse, who is introduced on page 60 and disposed of on page 61 of the novel. Shinglehouse stands on the Bullet Park platform, like Nailles and Paul Hammer (who has determined, in his madness, to crucify Tony Nailles) waiting for the 7:56, when "down the tracks came the Chicago express, two hours behind schedule and going about ninety miles an hour." The express (a deadly product of technological progress) rips past, its noise and commotion like "the vortex of some dirty wind tunnel," and hells off into the distance. Then Nailles notices one "highly polished brown loafer" lying amid the cinders and realizes that Shinglehouse has been sucked under the train.

The next day, troubled by his memory of this incident and by Tony's refusal to get out of bed, Nailles misses his usual connection, takes a local which makes 22 stops between Bullet Park and Grand Central Station, and finds that he has to get off the train every few stops to summon up the courage to go on. "Nailles's sense of being alive was to bridge or link the disparate environments and rhythms of his world, and one of his principal bridges—that between his white house and his office—had collapsed." To restore this sense of continuity and to alleviate his commutation hysteria, Nailles starts taking a massive tranquilizer with his morning coffee, a drug which floats him into the city like Zeus upon a cloud. The day the pills run out, however, Nailles discovers that the doctor who prescribed them has been closed down by the county medical society and desperately turns to a pusher to get an illegal supply of the magic gray and yellow capsules. Even after Tony is miraculously restored to health by the unlikely angel of this novel, one Swami Rutuola, his father continues, each Monday morning, "to meet his pusher in the supermarket parking lot, the public toilet, the laundromat, and a variety of cemeteries." And even after Nailles, with the help of the Swami once more, manages to rescue Tony from crucifixion, "Tony went back to school on Monday [these are the final words of the novel] and Nailles—drugged—went off to work and everything was as wonderful, wonderful, wonderful as it had been" (ibid., pp. 60–65; 121–26; 142, 245).

Cheever's suburbanites drink and smoke and party a great deal, while their children stare fixedly at television. Clearly, they stay drugged to ward off reality. Having a few drinks with the neighbors ("You can look all over the world but you won't find neighbors as kind and thoughtful as the people in Bullet Park") who come to commiserate with her about her husband's suicide, Mrs. Heathcup "almost forgot what had happened. I mean it didn't seem as though anything had happened" (ibid., p. 12). On his way from Boston to Kitzbühl to see his mother, suburbanite Paul Hammer first loads up on martinis to cross the Atlantic in a drunken haze and then gets thoroughly stoned in a pub when he is delayed in London. He is a victim of the economy which his mad mother (once a militant socialist) characterizes, with wisdom characteristic of the Shakespearean fool, as having degenerated "into the manufacture of drugs and ways of life that make reflection—any sort of thoughtfulness or emotional depth—impossible." It is advertising, she maintains, that carries the pernicious message: "I see American magazines in the cafe and the bulk of their text is advertising for tobacco, alcohol and absurd motor cars that promise—quite literally promise—to enable you to forget the squalor, spiritual poverty and monotony of selfishness. Never, in the history of civilization, has one seen a great nation singlemindedly bent on drugging itself." If she were to go back to the States, she tells her son, she would crucify an advertising man in some place like Bullet Park in an attempt to "wake the world" (ibid., pp. 164–69). Hammer takes over her mission, changes his victim from Eliot Nailles to his son, and only fails because he pauses to smoke a calming cigarette before immolating Tony on the altar of Christ's Church. For Cheever, then, the step between the drug culture of youth and the drugged culture of suburbia is a short one.

Drugging also facilitates driving on the freeways and turnpikes which represent, in Cheever's fiction, the most damnable pathways of contemporary civilization. Among the machines in his garden, none has wrought so cruelly or so terrifyingly as the bulldozers and road builders which have gouged out unnatural and inhuman roads. Poor Dora Emmison, for example, cannot negotiate the New Jersey turnpike unless she's drunk: "That road and all the rest of the freeways and thruways were engineered for clowns and drunks. If you're not a nerveless clown then you have to get drunk. No sensitive or intelligent man or woman can drive on those roads. Why I have a friend in California who smokes pot before he goes on the freeway. He's a great driver, a marvelous driver, and if the traffic's bad he uses heroin. They ought to sell pot and bourbon at the gas stations. Then there wouldn't be so many accidents." Fifteen minutes after this speech, well fortified with bourbon, Dora is killed in a crash on the Jersey pike (ibid., pp. 193, 196–97).

The suicide rate aside, the most shocking statistic in Bullet Park has to do with casualties on the highway; these "averaged twenty-two a year because of a winding highway that seemed to have been drawn on the map by a child with a grease pencil" (ibid., p. 10). A brief story in Cheever's latest book, *The World of Apples*, vividly portrays the cost, to one particular woman, of the technological wonder of Route 64. One Saturday morning Marge Littleton loses her husband and children when on returning from a shopping trip their automobile is demolished by a gigantic car carrier. Next she campaigns, unsuccessfully, against widening Route 64 from four to eight lanes. Then, upon recovering from her bereavement, she marries a "handsome, witty, and substantial" Italian named Pietro Montani who is decapitated by a crane as he drives down 64 in his convertible. Subsequent to these tragedies, curious accidents begin to occur on the highway. "Three weeks after Pietro's death a twenty-four wheel, eighty-ton truck, northbound on Route 64 . . . veered into the southbound lane demolishing two cars and killing their four passengers." Then the truck caught on fire. Two weeks later another 24-wheeler "went out of control at the same place," struck an abutment, and although there was no fire this time, the two drivers "were so badly crushed by the collision that they had to be identified by their dental work." Twice more trucks swerve out of control at the same spot, and in the last case the truck comes to rest peacefully in a narrow valley. When the police get to the oversized vehicle, they discover that the driver has been shot dead, but they do not find out that Marge has done the shooting. Finally, in December "Marge married a rich widower and moved to North Salem, where there is only one two-lane highway and where the sound of traffic is as faint as the roaring of a shell" (ibid., pp. 132–37).

Marge Littleton's one-woman vendetta hardly provides the harried suburban traveler with a practical way of expressing his objections against heedless technological progress. Nor can he find much consolation in the prayers of a drunken priest, in yet another story, for "all those killed or cruelly wounded on thruways, expressways, freeways and turnpikes . . . for all those burned to death in faulty plane landings, mid-air collisions, and mountainside crashes . . . for all those wounded by rotary lawn-mowers, chain saws, electric hedge clippers, and other power tools" (Bracher 1964, p. 53).

Unless it is halted, Cheever's fiction suggests, progress will not only kill large numbers of human beings but will also destroy the quality of life for those who survive. The world which Moses and Coverly Wapshot leave St. Botolphs to conquer is symbolized by the vast Northern Expressway which takes them south, "engorging in its clover leaves and brilliantly engineered gradings the green playing fields, rose gardens, barns, farms, meadows, trout streams, forests, homesteads and churches of a golden past." Similarly, Bullet Park's Route 61, "one of the most dangerous and in appearance one of the most inhuman of the new highways," is a road which has "basically changed the nature of the Eastern landscape like some seismological disturbance," a freeway on which at least 50 men and women die each year. The simple Saturday drive on Route 61 becomes warlike, and Nailles fondly recalls the roads of his young manhood: "They followed the contours of the land. It was cool in the valleys, warm on the hilltops. One could measure distances with one's nose. There was the smell of eucalyptus, maples, sweet grass, manure from a cow barn and, as one got into the mountains, the smell of pine. . . . He remembered it all as intimate, human and pleasant, compared to this anxious wasteland through which one raced the barbarians" (Cheever 1969, pp. 228–29).

Significantly, it is the mountains that Nailles's son Tony inchoately longs for as he lies in deep depression. Nailles rouses him from bed one fine morning, takes him to the window, shows him how bright and beautiful it is outside, tells him that "everything's ahead of you. Everything. You'll go to college and get an interesting job and get married and have children." But Tony sinks to the floor and then howls out, "Give me back the mountains." What mountains? The White Mountains in New Hampshire that he and his father climbed together one summer? The Tirol where, Nailles later remembers, he had been awfully happy climbing "the Grand Kaiser and the Pengelstein" (ibid., pp. 59–60, 241)? Tony does not know (and will not know until Swami Rutuola comes to work his cure) that the mountains are symbolic.

The Swami had first discovered his ability as a healer while employed to clean the washrooms at Grand Central Station. There he had been accosted, very early one morning, by a desperate man certain that he was going to die momentarily. The Swami took him up to the concourse where they gazed together at the "great big colored picture that advertises cameras" and which showed a man and a woman and two children on a beach, "and behind them, way off in the distance, were all these mountains covered with snow." Then, Swami Rutuola tells Tony, he had asked the dying man "to look at the mountains to see if he could get his mind off his troubles," and the therapy had worked. As part of his treatment for Tony, Rutuola recites "cheers of place" for pleasant, unspoiled places: "I'm in a house by the sea at four in the afternoon and it's raining and I'm sitting in a ladderback chair with a book in my lap and I'm waiting for a girl I love who has gone on an errand but who will return" (ibid., pp. 133–34, 139–40). These cheers, and others, miraculously restore Tony to health.

In a malaise similar to Tony's, Paul Hammer is overtaken "on trains and planes" by a personal *cafard*, or carrier of blues, whom he can escape only by summoning up images that represent to him "the excellence and beauty" he has lost. The first and most frequent of such images which counterpoint the realities of Bullet Park is that of a perfect, snow-covered mountain, obviously Kilimanjaro. In attempting to ward off his *cafard*, Hammer also calls up a vision of a fortified medieval town which, "like the snow-covered mountain, seemed to represent beauty, enthusiasm and love." Occasionally he glimpses a river with grassy banks—the Elysian fields perhaps—though he finds them difficult to reach and though it seems "that a railroad track or a thruway [has] destroyed the beauty of the place" (ibid., pp. 174–75).

In Tony's malaise, in Rutuola's cheers, in Hammer's visions, Cheever indirectly expresses his yearning after unspoiled nature and his conviction that mankind can stand only so much technological progress. Now that the walls of the medieval town have been breached, the Elysian fields invaded by freeways, space obliterated and time brought very nearly to a stop, Cheever joins Mark Twain in lamentation that "there are no remotenesses, anymore" (Tanner 1964, p. 183).

The depiction of the machine—particularly the railroad locomotive—as villain was, as has been noted, a commonplace in mid-19th-century American literature. In the first half of this century the theme reemerged in such writers as Steinbeck, Hemingway, and Faulkner. The Joads, in *The Grapes of Wrath*, are driven from their land by the tractor and painfully make their way west via broken-down automobile; Robert Jordan and the Spanish guerrillas, in *For Whom the Bell Tolls*, face "mechanized doom" from the sophisticated aircraft of the Fascists; Ike McCaslin, in *Go Down, Moses*, watches despairingly as the wilderness he loves is transformed into "flashing neon, speeding automobiles, sheet iron, and hooting locomotives." In the world these writers contemplate, "not only life and dignity, but human moral, spiritual, and rational processes are opposed by unreasoning forces of anonymous brute mechanism."[7] So, as Kurt Vonnegut would say, it goes.

The theme, then, is hardly original with John Cheever. His unique contribution has been, first, to point to the engines of the transportation revolution as the particular devil-machines in the contemporary garden, and next, to localize the issue in that place—the upper-middle-class suburb—whose inhabitants he knows and understands and whose dependence, for its very survival, upon thruways and commuter lines most aptly qualifies it to exemplify the rootlessness and artificiality of contemporary life. In his fiction, Cheever warns, Jeremiah-like, against the boredom and depression, drugs and suicide, that will surely follow the suburbanite on the cruel journey of commutation, unless. . . . But the answers he leaves to us.

References

Blumberg, Paul. 1969. "Sociology and Social Literature: Work Alienation in the Plays of Arthur Miller." *American Quarterly* 21 (Summer): 291–310.

Bracher, Frederick. 1963. "John Cheever and Comedy." *Critique* 6 (Spring): 66–77.

———. 1964. "John Cheever: A Vision of the World." *Claremont Quarterly* 11 (Winter): 47–57.

Burhans, Clinton S. 1969. "John Cheever and the Grave of Social Coherence." *Twentieth Century Literature* 14 (January): 187–98.

Cheever, John. 1957. *The Wapshot Chronicle*. New York: Bantam.

———. 1958a. "The Country Husband." Pp. 48–83 in *"The Housebreaker of Shady Hill" and Other Stories*. New York: Harper.

———. 1958b. "The Housebreaker of Shady Hill." Pp. 3–31 in *"The Housebreaker of Shady Hill" and Other Stories*. New York: Harper.

———. 1961. "The Death of Justina." Pp. 1–19 in *Some People, Places and Things That Will Not Appear in My Next Novel*. New York: Harper.

———. 1963. *The Wapshot Scandal*. New York: Bantam.

———. 1964a. "The Angel of the Bridge." Pp. 23–35 in *The Brigadier and the Golf Widow*. New York: Harper & Row.

———. 1964b. "The Swimmer." Pp. 61–76 in *The Brigadier and the Golf Widow*. New York: Harper & Row.

———. 1966. "The Embarkment for Cythera." Pp. 682–705 in *First Prize Stories 1919–1966 from the O. Henry Memorial Awards*, with introduction by Harry Hansen. Garden City, N.Y.: Doubleday.

———. 1969. *Bullet Park*. New York: Knopf.

———. 1973. *The World of Apples*. New York: Knopf.

Coser, Lewis A. 1972. *Sociology through Literature*. Englewood Cliffs, N.J.: Prentice-Hall.

Garrett, George. 1964. "John Cheever and the Charms of Innocence: The Craft of *The Wapshot Scandal*." *Hollins Critic* 1 (April): 1–12.

Greene, Beatrice. 1971. "Icarus at St. Botolphs: A Descent to 'Unwonted Otherness,' " *Style* 5 (Spring): 119–37.

Hoggart, Richard. 1966. "Literature and Society." *American Scholar* 25 (Spring): 277–89.

Marx, Leo. 1964. *The Machine in the Garden*. New York: Oxford University Press.

Ozick, Cynthia. 1964. "America Aglow." *Commentary* 38 (July): 66–67.

Peden, William. 1964. "Jane Austens of Metropolis and Suburbia." Pp. 45–85 in *The American Short Story: Front Line in the Defense of Literature*. Boston: Houghton Mifflin.

Tanner, Tony. 1964. *The Reign of Wonder*. New York: Harper & Row.

Time. 1964. "The Metamorphoses of John Cheever." (March 27).

Waldron, Randall H. 1972. "The Naked, the Dead, and the Machine: A New Look at Norman Mailer's First Novel." *PMLA* 87 (March): 271–72.

Waterman, Rollene. 1958. "Literary Horizons." *Saturday Review* (September 13).

Notes

1. See Peden (1964), p. 46. Peden calls Cheever "perhaps the most distinguished" among recent "chroniclers of the non-exceptional."

2. See Garrett (1964), p. 6. Garrett's is an exceptionally insightful and well-written essay.

3. Greene (1971) demonstrates that this pattern, "the systolic pulse of sublime and prosaic juxtaposed," occurs frequently in Cheever's writing. The quotation is from Cheever
(1963), p. 111.

4. E.g., Ozick (1964), pp. 66–67.

5. Burhans perceptively isolates a theme which Cheever had yet to elaborate in *Bullet
Park* and *The World of Apples*.

6. For a brilliant analysis of this idea, see Marx (1964).

7. Though one could cite many other examples, for felicitously suggesting these I am in-
debted to Waldron (1972), pp. 271–72.

Icarus at St. Botolphs:
A Descent to
"Unwonted Otherness"

Beatrice Greene*

"The image of a locomotive replaces the angel."[1]

Of the many reviews of *The Wapshot Scandal* which appeared at the
time of its publication, it was, I think, Cynthia Ozick alone, writing for
Commentary magazine, who drew attention to one of the most obvious
propositions of John Cheever's tale: "Nobody can inherit St. Botolphs
because nobody had a grandfather who lived there."[2] It is largely true
that the characters of Cheever, from a present of "unwonted otherness,"
turn with nostalgia to a past where no one has been, to an ideal where no
one can go. Always audible to their ear is a rhapsody which dazzles and
eludes with the abstract, self-inverted unapproachability of Platonic
perfection. The narrator of Cheever's short story, *The Death of Justina*,
expresses the yearning:

> I seemed to hear the jinglebells of the sleigh that would carry me to
> grandmother's house although in fact grandmother spent the last years of
> her life working as a hostess on an ocean liner and was lost in the tragic
> sinking of the S. S. *Lorelei* and I was responding to a memory that I had
> not experienced. But the hill of light rose like an answer to some primitive
> dream of homecoming.

So too, the weightlessness of Cheever's novels, *The Wapshot Chronicle*
and *The Wapshot Scandal*, tends substantially towards a conclusion that
tradition never was and dreams are mist.

The passage from *The Death of Justina* continues:

> On one of the highest lawns I saw the remains of a snowman who still
> smoked a pipe and wore a scarf and a cap but whose form was wasting
> away and whose anthracite eyes stared out at the view with terrifying bit-
> terness. I sensed some disappointing greenness of spirit in the scene. . . .

*Reprinted with permission from *Style*, 5 (1971), 119–37.

Cheever's Wapshot novels similarly are dominated by a central motif of falling—descent. "Icarus, Icarus," mourns Leander when Coverly, his son, has disappointed him—"as if the boy had fallen away from his heart." Icarus, relates the fable, together with his father Daedalus fleeing the tyrant Minos at Crete, flew too near to the sun, melted the wax joints of his wings and fell into the sea. Cheever's downward movement is from fable to floor, and ultimately the floor itself is gone and we find ourselves falling still in the glare of the mythic element indigenous to Cheever's work and latent beneath the surface of all his character and event. In Cheever's Wapshot novels myth and fable are a constant charged energy whose playing lightning not only reveals to us the heights of the dream, but searches out in the grey bones of normality the skeleton of nightmare.

The themes and meanings adhering to *The Wapshot Chronicle* and *The Wapshot Scandal* may be studied in larger, more encompassing contexts of plot, character, and incident. Or they may be discussed in terms of their comment on the traditional paradox of the American condition: the American dream versus the monumental vulgarity that proliferates with our generations. It will, however, be the purpose of this study to show that theme and meaning are as well revealed in the more subliminal minutiae of the total art of Mr. Cheever to which the reader is exposed. Because it is in Mr. Cheever's management of the smallest units of language and image that the texture is created in which overall meaning is constantly being born, reinforced, and defined.

Cheever manipulates the language of fable in twofold manner and for twofold purpose. By means of imagery, allusion, archaic language—the language and imagery of historical heritage, of myth, heraldry and the Bible—by the use of literary devices of trope and elaboration, those elements that comprise the "majestic and elevated combination or composition" of Longinus's criteria for sublimity in art, Cheever raises us to the alien, the dream, the tradition which is lost and gone: from which there is to be the subsequent lapse and falling off to the ordinary and commonplace. The descent is from elevated image to homely image. A language of *literary* sublimity subsides to one of broad general *oral* usage, a colloquial speech so relaxed as often to be cliché or slang. The sharply divergent polarities are consistently sustained in a partnership of closest juxtaposition. And conversely, again and again the dreamlike forces of myth are used to invest the commonplaces of contemporary urban life with the malevolence of generating forces of mischief, so that the myth itself descends to malignity.

It is this pervasive play of myth and mundane, the systolic pulse of sublime and prosaic juxtaposed, over and over the grandeur and the deflation, the wavelike cresting and subsiding of glorious to inglorious, a modulation of dignity to confusion on through the flow of life and generations, each disabused of its dream, that tempers the Wapshot novels of John Cheever with that texture of disbalance which sends us falling, suspends us line by line from ravelling threads. Viewed against the background of the short stories, this quality of dis-equation is one so distinctive in Cheever's work as to identify it perhaps as the salt of his writing and the mark of his hand. Thus:

> He could only watch and admire the vast barrel of night fill up to its last shelf and crevice with the fair light of day and all the birds singing in the trees like a band of angels whistling to their hounds . . .
>
> *The Wapshot Scandal*

is a sentence neither mannered nor precious; yet the image of the birds singing *like a band of angels whistling to their hounds* is one sharply characteristic of Cheever's wit. As is (my italics):

> Where else in the world were there such stands of lilac, such lambent winds and brilliant skies, *such fresh fish?*
>
> *The Wapshot Scandal*

Or, as in the following sample, where the bawdy song is juxtaposed with heroic classic imagery:

> "Oh, who put the overalls in Mrs. Murphy's chowder" Mr. Jowett sang loudly, although he knew that it was all wrong for the season, the day and dignity of a station agent, the steward of the town's true and ancient boundary, its Gate of Hercules.
>
> *The Wapshot Scandal*

So, too, in the following passage from the short story, *The Country Husband*, we may clearly identify this characteristic quality of Cheever's writing. The hero, Francis, struggling to overcome his infatuation for the babysitter, is having a troubled dream:

> Down the mountain he swung, matching his speed against the contours of a slope that had been formed in the first ice age, seeking with ardor some simplicity of feeling and circumstance. Night fell then, and he drank a Martini with some old friend in a dirty bar.
>
> In the morning, Francis' snow-covered mountain was gone, and he was left with his vivid memories. . . . He had been bitten gravely. He washed his body, shaved his jaws, drank his coffee, and missed the seven-thirty-one.

Some essential truth is sought in the movement of the climatic forces of geologic antiquity "against the contours of a slope that had been formed in the first ice age." The purity of "simplicity of feeling and circumstances" is sought with "ardor," a word of heroic connotation. Immediately thereupon we plummet to the lesser platform of martinis with a friend "in a dirty bar." And still we fall. The elevated literary prose of the first paragraph lapses to the colloquial "He had been bitten gravely" in the second, followed by a cataloguing of severely prosaic event: "He washed his body, shaved his jaws, drank his coffee, and missed the seven-thirty-one."

The long winding horn of olden times sounds the openings of both *The Wapshot Chronicle* and *The Wapshot Scandal*. We begin, in *The Wapshot Chronicle*, at the birthtime of our national origins. It is the Fourth of July. Already in the first paragraph of the novel may be clearly sensed the characteristic texture of this prose. Disequilibrium, deflation, the drop from fable to floor is manifest in a close-spun dichotomy of *then* and *now*, in a juxtaposition of national heritage—the schoolboy's dream—with a present reality that somehow represents decline.

> St. Botolphs was an old place, an old river town. It *had been* an inland port in the great days of the Massachusetts sailing fleets and *now it was left with a factory that manufactured table silver and a few other small industries*. The natives did not consider that it had *diminished much* in size or importance, but the long roster of the Civil War dead bolted to the cannon on the green, *was a reminder of* how populous the village *had been* in the 1860's. St. Botolphs *would never muster as many soldiers again*. The green was shaded by a few great elms and loosely enclosed by a square of store fronts. The Cartwright Block, which made the western wall of the square, had along the front of its second story a row of lancet windows, as *delicate and reproachful* as the windows of a church. Behind these windows were *the offices of the Eastern Star, Dr. Bulstrode the dentist, the telephone company and the insurance agent. The smells of these offices—the smell of dental preparations, floor oil, spittoons and coal gas*—mingled in *the downstairs hallway* like *an aroma of the past. In a drilling autumn rain, in a world of much change* the green at St. Botolphs conveyed an *impression* of unusual permanence. On Independence Day in the morning, when the parade had begun to form, the green looked prosperous and festive.
>
> *The Wapshot Chronicle*

My italics underscore Cheever's language of distilled dissolution. The sense of falling off from "great days of the Massachusetts sailing fleets" is heightened in overall structural significance by the placement of the depicted scene in the time scheme of the novel. For the lapsed "present" of the paragraph is in actuality Fourth-of-July past. It is a scene from blurry brown mezzotint photographs of the American dream of small-town childhood, a vignette from the boyhood of Moses and Coverly Wapshot upon which they will look with nostalgia once they are grown up into the missile and supermarket culture of the present-day world in which the novel actually takes place. And even then, the "unusual permanence" which the scene at St. Botolphs conveys is only an "impression."

The flag of history and tradition—"the great days of the Massachusetts sailing fleets" and "the long roster of the Civil War dead"—is dropped to the far less ceremonious half-staff of mock heroic in the depiction of Sarah Wapshot's role in the Fourth of July procession:

> Thus above the heads of the crowd, jarred a little by the motion of the truck or wagon, exactly like those religious images that are carried

through the streets of Boston's north end in the autumn to quiet great storms at sea, Mrs. Wapshot appeared each year to her friends and neighbors, and it was fitting that she should be drawn through the streets for there was no one in the village who had had more of a hand in its enlightenment. It was she who had organized a committee to raise money for a new parish home for Christ Church. It was she who had raised a fund for the granite horse trough at the corner and who, when the horse trough became obsolete, had had it planted with geraniums and petunias. The new high school on the hill, the new fire house, the new traffic lights, the war memorial—yes, yes—even the clean public toilets in the railroad station by the river were the fruit of Mrs. Wapshot's genius.

The Wapshot Chronicle

The expression is literary and elaborate—*over* elaborate and orotund. "Thus above the heads of the crowd,' "It was fitting," "It was she" and "it was she" repeated, "enlightenment," "the fruit of Mrs. Wapshot's genius," "drawn through the streets," "—yes, yes—" and metaphors of religious images "carried through the streets . . . to quiet great storms at sea." In the discrepancy between high-flown expression and humble content ("even the clean public toilets in the railroad station by the river") we experience our descent.

With the broadly colloquial opening sentence of the succeeding paragraph, "Mr. Wapshot—Captain Leander—was not around," we are on the floor. The colloquial, the prosaic, dominates the first half of this ensuing paragraph: "He had been a partner in a table silver company," "nothing much stuck to his fingers," "to keep him out of mischief," "a sixty-foot water line," "an old Harley engine with a single screw," "She was an unseaworthy hulk that moved . . . like real estate." And then follows a passage of rise and fall, of sublimity and commonplace interwoven in the characteristic technique of disbalance of Cheever's narrative:

But the voyage seemed to Leander, from his place at the helm, glorious and sad. The timbers of the old launch seemed held together by the brilliance and transitoriness of summer and she smelled of summery refuse—sneakers, towels, bathing suits and the cheap fragrant matchboard of old bathhouses. Down the bay she went over water that was sometimes the violet color of an eye to where the land wind brought aboard the music of the merry-go-round and where you could see the distant shore of Nangasakit—the scrim of nonsensical rides, paper lanterns, fried food and music that breasted the Atlantic in such a fragile jumble that it seemed like the rim of flotsam, the starfish and orange skins that came up on the waves.

The Wapshot Chronicle

In *The Wapshot Scandal* it is again shades of olden time which is the mustering position for our swift descent. The opening scene is a framed sampler of traditional Christmas cheer pricked out in the dutiful cross-stitch of auld lang syne:

The snow began to fall into St. Botolphs at four-fifteen on Christmas eve.

We are in disbalance almost at once:

> It was a conservatively dressed population that performed this tree-trimming ceremony. All the men wore trousers and all the women wore skirts, excepting Mrs. Wilson, who was a widow, and Alby Hooper who was an itinerant carpenter. They had been drinking bourbon for two days and wore nothing at all.
>
> *The Wapshot Scandal*

Immediately the polarities are set in their characteristic juxtaposition. (My italics):

> *The rector was about to bless the carolers* who stood in his living room. *A rancid and exciting smell of the storm* came from their clothes. The room was *neat and clean and warm,* and *had been—before* they entered in their snowy clothes—*fragrant.* Mr. Applegate had *cleaned* the room himself. . . . With his spectacles on he gave the impression of *a portly and benign ecclesiastic,* but when he removed his eyeglasses to *clean* them his gaze was *penetrating and haggard and his breath smelled of gin.*
>
> *The Wapshot Scandal*

There ensues a piling on of juxtaposition—*forlorn* and *transfigured, dumpy* and *gracefully, angel* and *misspent*—until, in the unhesitating and characteristic direction of Mr. Cheever's prose, the scaffolding of grandeur must collapse for the whittling away at its supports, and we are on the floor: (My italics)

> In the *dark, mixed* clothing they had put on for the *storm,* carollers looked uncommonly *forlorn,* but the moment they began to *sing* they were *transformed.* The *Negress* looked like an *angel,* and *dumpy* Lucille *lifted* her head *gracefully* and seemed to cast off her *misspent* youth in the *rainy* streets around Carnegie Hall. This *instantaneous transformation* of the company was *thrilling,* and Mr. Applegate felt his *faith renewed,* felt that *an infinity of unrealized possibilities lay ahead of them, a tremendous richness of peace, a renaissance without brigands, an ecstasy of light and color, a kingdom! Or was this gin!*
>
> *The Wapshot Scandal*

It is not alone from canonized ideals of heritage and tradition that the reader's fall is designed, but also from the innocence of idyll, where we may in Cheever's work always regard as implicit the lurking snake-in-the-grass: (My italics)

> From this dark pool he (Moses) waded through *white water* again to a place with *meadowy banks* where *Turk's-cap lilies* and *wild roses* grew and where it was *easy* to cast. While he was fishing this pool *the sun came up and out—a flood of golden light* that *spread* all through the woods and sank into the water so that every *blue* stone and *white* pebble showed—*flooded* the water with *light* until it was *as golden as bourbon*

whiskey—and the instant this happened *he got a strike*. . . . His rod was bent . . . and then *the trout surfaced with a crash* . . . *zooming* this way and that and the *thrill of his life* shooting up into Moses' arms and shoulders. Then, as the fish tired and he got his landing net, he thought: *What a life; what a grand life!* He admired the *rosy* spots in the fish, broke its back and wrapped it in *fern, ready now* for *a big day*. . . .

Looking down to the pool below, Moses discovers that Rosalie is there bathing: (My italics)

> He snapped his reel so that she *would not hear him take in the line* and waded *carefully, not to make any noise,* to the banks of the pool where she *could not* see him and where he could see her through the leaves. He watched his gleaming Susanna, *shamefaced,* his *dream of simple pleasure replaced by some sadness, some heaviness* that *seemed* to make his mouth taste of *blood* and his teeth *ache.* . . . His head was *confused* and *the smell of the dead trout in his pocket seemed* like something from his *past.* He *unwrapped* the fish and washed it in the running water, *but it looked like a toy.*
>
> *The Wapshot Chronicle*

The italicized words in this pair of consecutive paragraphs, the first of the pair significantly in a diction of purity, celebration, joy, full of noisy movement of life, the second in language of confusion, disillusion and pain, falling over all a hush of shame and death, are illustrative of the constant thematic juxtaposition of up-down, up-down which establishes the narrative tone of Cheever's Wapshot novels.

What is to be emphasized is that this is not the ever-broadening upward-scaling registers of *now* to *then*, such movement as characterized, for instance, seventeenth century art, not moving mass of mortal corporeality rising, but always a lapsing from *then* to *now*, mass of mortal corporeality weighted and falling. All that comprises that collective property, the common memory of the lost dream, all the ingredients of the Western ancestral soul, are pressed into service as timber for the rapid succession of scaffoldings which are cast up to represent the golden *then*. Greys of painful or prosaic circumstance, or—simply—a more broadly colloquial language, manifest the sunless *now* to which the splendor of the scaffolding predictably will tarnish.

National heritage and tradition, the innocence and purity of idyll are, as we have seen, richly utilized by Cheever in the Wapshot novels as building materials for the setting up of the *then*, the dream. No less heavily drawn upon in the construction of these scaffoldings from which the fall will be perpetrated is the language and imagery of classical myth and fable. Examples of such imagery are frequent in the short stories: (I have italicized the elements of juxtapositon.)

> The sleeping car compartments with *their soiled bed linen trailed* through *the fresh morning* like *a string of rooming house windows.* Then

> he saw *an extraordinary thing;* at one of the bedroom windows sat *an unclothed woman of exceptional beauty, combing her golden hair.* She passed like an *apparition* through Shady Hill *combing and combing her hair*, and Francis followed her with his eyes until she was out of sight. *Then old Mrs. Wrightson joined him on the platform and began to talk.*

When Mrs. Wrightson and her pedestrian difficulties with living room curtains are disposed of, the author returns to his image:

> A *wonderful* feeling enveloped him, as if *light were being shaken about him*, and he thought again of *Venus combing and combing her hair* as she *drifted* through *The Bronx*.
>
> *The Country Husband*

The unclothed woman "combing and combing" her "golden hair" is a figure of legend with whom is juxtaposed garrulous Mrs. Wrightson and her uninteresting curtains. The dream figure is then more specifically identified as Venus, and from this realm of classic beauty we are brought down to the more prosaic geography of the Bronx.

When the old Topaze, Leander's boat, is converted by his wife to a gift shoppe, it is language and imagery of classic inheritance which is made to serve as the height from which the descent is to be made:

> The taste of alum in the rind of a grape, the smell of the sea, the heat of the spring sun, berries bitter and sweet, a grain of sand in his teeth—all of that which he meant by life seemed taken away from him. Where were *the serene twilights* of his old age? He would have liked to *pluck out his eyes.* Watching the candlelight on his ship—he had brought her home through *gales and tempests*—he felt ghostly and emasculated. Then he went to his bureau drawer and took from under the dried rose and the wreath of hair his loaded pistol. He went to the window. The fires of the day were burning out like a conflagration in some industrial city and above the barn cupola he saw the evening star, as sweet and round as a human tear. *He fired his pistol out of the window and then fell down on the floor.*
>
> *The Wapshot Chronicle*

For the sake of clarity I have italicized only those phrases comprising the encompassing juxtaposition—the classic heroic imagery and the act, verging on farce, of extravagant non-heroism to which the narrative eventually descends. The fine counterpointing of juxtaposition—juxtaposition *within* juxtaposition—however, distinguishes the texture of this paragraph as it does all the prose of the Wapshot novels, and should not be overlooked in our study of these samples. We want to be aware, for instance, of the contributory effect upon the whole of "berries bitter and sweet," the loaded pistol under the "dried rose and wreath of hair," "the fires of the day" and the "evening star, as sweet and round as a human tear," "industrial city" contrasted with "above the barn cupola," and "fires" and "conflagration" as against the "sweet and round" fluid of "a human tear."

Similarly, it is in the golden light of a porticoed classic world that the following passage has its origin. The encompassing juxtaposition takes us from the light, clean, orderly beginnings of a world to the kitchen where the rolls are burning. My italics here outline the busy subcounterpointing of juxtaposition contained within the framework of the larger juxtaposition:

> How *orderly, clean and sensible* the world seems; above all how *light*,
> as if these were the *beginnings* of a world, a chain of *mornings*. It is *late* in
> the day, *late* in the history of this part of the world, but this *lateness* does
> nothing to *eclipse* their ardor. Presently there is a *cloud of black smoke*
> from the kitchen—the rolls are *burning*.
>
> *The Wapshot Scandal*

From Leander's journal we have this excerpt, also illustrating Cheever's use of classic imagery to raise the height of the dream:

> Travertine Mansion House ranked with wonders of the ages. Compared
> in free literature to monuments in Karnak, Acropolis in Greece, Pantheon
> in Rome. Large, frame, brine-soaked fire trap with two-story piazzas,
> palatial public rooms, 80 bedrooms, 8 baths. Wash basins and chamber-
> pots still widely in use. Accounted for poignant smell in hallways. . .
>
> *The Wapshot Scandal*

Always the tight counterpointing of juxtaposition is the means. The medium varies, and often it is the romance and heraldry of feudal tradition that fabricates the height of the upper axis of the juxtaposed elements. The quest is a central image of the Wapshot novels. Knight errantry, modern style, in a sense constitutes the action of these novels. The adventures of the boys, Moses and Coverly, displaced from their natural environment, are the substance of these novels, which have their affinities with the structure of the epic. Minutiae everywhere parallels overall form, and the diction of the Wapshot novels is tapestried with the language and imagery of heraldry. Significantly, Moses wins his bride Melissa from a castle. In the railroad station waiting room

> There was a large photograph on the wall, framed in oak, of his destina-
> tion. Flags flew from the many towers of Clear Haven, the buttresses
> were thick with ivy, and considering what he went there for it seemed far
> from ridiculous. Justina seemed to have had a hand in the waiting room
> for there was a rug on the floor. The matchboard walls were stained the
> color of mahogany and pipes that must heat the place in winter rose
> gracefully, two by two, to disappear like serpents into the holes in the ceil-
> ing. The benches around the walls were divided at regular intervals with
> graceful loops of bent wood that would serve the travellers as arm rests
> and keep the warm hams of strangers from touching one another.
>
> *The Wapshot Chronicle*

Flags, buttresses, towers and thick ivy are juxtaposed with the word "ridiculous." The pipes that "rose gracefully," an image that we are brought, in this context, to associate with gothic spires, is juxtaposed with the lowness of "serpents," itself a word of medieval connotation, disappearing into "holes." The crenellated grandeur of the original image lapses to a most homely and inglorious base against "the warm hams of strangers."

In *The Wapshot Scandal* Cheever turns to the dream heights of feudal tradition to help silhouette the drabness of life at the missile site at Talifer. Coverly, now working here, is invited for dinner. He is served "frozen meat, frozen fried potatoes, and frozen peas." The dreariness of the meal is juxtaposed against heraldic imagery: (My italics)

> It was the monotonous fare of *the besieged*, it would be served everywhere on the site that night, but where were *the walls, the battering rams*, where was *the enemy* that could be accounted for this tasteless *porridge?*

In another sample, the hijacker in the airplane is described in terms of an image of medieval tradition, against which the comparative tawdriness of the modern event is to be inferred: (My italics)

> He wore a felt hat and black handkerchief tied over his face with holes cut for the eyes. It was, except for the felt hat, *the ancient mask of the headsman.*
>
> *The Wapshot Scandal*

Similarly the language and imagery of Christian tradition and the Bible are used to revive atavistic dreams of better times past, from which there is to be the awakening. "What kind of tidings were these to carry from house to house?" Melissa is brought to wonder when her neighbor comes in for a glass of sherry in order to tell her that "Gertrude Lockhart is a slut." "What was this testiness of his flesh?" thinks Coverly to himself, loathing the touch of the policeman who holds him by the arm. From this statement evoking Biblical echoings our path is downward: (My italics)

> Rising before him was the Central Police Headquarters—a yellow-brick building with a few halfhearted architectural flourishes and a few declarations of innocent love written in chalk on the walls. *The wind blew dust and papers around his feet.*
>
> *The Wapshot Scandal*

I continue with samples, like those above, all from *The Wapshot Scandal*, in order to illustrate with greater weight the marked frequency of imagery from Christian tradition and the Bible. In the two samples following, the italics mark the polarities of the encompassing juxtaposition.

> (They) roared out of the Moonlite onto the Expressway, jeopardizing their lives and the lives in every car they passed (men, women, and children in

arms), *but gentle St. Christopher or the mercies of the Holy Virgin spared them*, and they got Emile safely home. He climbed the stairs, kissed his mother good night—*she was reading an article in 'Reader's Digest' about the pancreas. . .*

The plane was losing altitude rapidly, and then below them they could see *the roofs of a city that seemed like the handiwork of a marvelously humble people going about useful tasks and raising their children in goodness and charity*. The moment when they ceased to be airborne passed with a thump and roar of the reverse jets, and out of the ports they could see that industrial wilderness that hedges airstrips. *Scrub grass and weeds, a vegetable slum, struggled in the sandy bottom soil that formed the banks of an oily creek.*

In the following sample, still from *The Wapshot Scandal*, Melissa brings her problems to the minister. Here the italics underscore the diction evocative of Christian tradition:

What touched her as he leaned toward the fire, was *the antiquity of his devotions*. No *runner* would ever come to his door with the news that the *head of the vestry* had been *martyred* by the local police and had she used the name of *Jesus Christ* out of its *liturgical context*, she felt that he would have been terribly embarrassed. He was not to *blame*, he had not chosen this moment of *history*, he was not alone in having been overwhelmed at the *task* of giving *the passion of our Lord ardor and reality*. He had failed, he seemed sitting by his fire to be a failure as she was and to *deserve*, like any other failure, *compassion*. She felt how *passionately* he would have liked to avoid her troubles; to discuss the *church* fair, the World Series, the covered dish supper, the high price of *stained glass*, the *perfidy* of communism, the comfortableness of electric blankets, anything but her trouble.

From the banalities of "the covered dish supper," "the comfortableness of electric blankets," the juxtaposition of "stained glass" with notions of "price" to which we are sunk from heights of language sacred to Christian tradition, we are brought quickly to a height again:

"I have sinned," Melissa said. "I have sinned and the memory is grievous, the burden is intolerable."

The language, for dialogue, is ornate, uncommon, not natural to our day. It serves, though, Cheever's technique of juxtaposition, the method of construction of the novel. Melissa's extraordinary manner of expression, with its strong connotations of Christian tradition, forces us back once again upon the pinnacle, from which we are instantly brought down by the shocking banality of the minister's reply in the glassy-surfaced impersonalities of common jargon:

He shielded his eyes with his hands and she saw that he was shocked and disgusted. "In matters like this," he said, his eyes still shielded, "I work with Dr. Herzog. I can give you his telephone number or I'll be happy to call him myself and make an appointment."

Also employed by Cheever to evoke the upper polarity of the juxtaposition is language with the coloration of archaism—words like *bruit, impuissant, puissant, brigands, the green, porridge, smite, despoil, devotions, miscreants.*

> He stood at the table, covering her with his wide gaze, and she wondered what would happen if she reached out to him. Would he run out of the kitchen? Would he shout, "Unhand me!"? . . .
> He wondered if she hadn't *lost her marbles*. . . . He didn't want *to fool around with a woman who had lost her marbles*.
> *The Wapshot Scandal* (My italics)

From the stagey fustiness of "Unhand me!" we descend to the broadly colloquial and slangy "fool around with" and "lost her marbles."

Abstract moral words with their aura of the old-fashioned, uncommon in today's fiction, also make a reappearance in Cheever's Wapshot novels, with the evocations of irrecoverable good old days to connote the upper axis of juxtaposed polarity: words like *honor, noble, order, sensible, orderly, clean, pride, goodness, love, humble.* Or it is simply the repeated use of *old, oldest* that evokes for the reader the juxtaposition of a golden past, the corruptibility of time:

> St. Botolphs was an old place, an old river town.

> Moses looked at the old launch tied up at the wharf. . . . His father came down the path with the groceries and an old man followed him. It was the old man who took off the lines.

> This is one of the oldest houses in St. Botolphs and our bathroom is the oldest in the county.

> Beautiful scenery. Milky blue hills in distance. Old lakes. Old mountains.

> Where were the serene twilights of his old age?

> She is the image of an old pilgrim. . . .

The heritage of literature is also used for purposes of casting up the structure that will represent the dream. Thus the retrospect of a younger purer America is evoked in its literary inheritance to be juxtaposed against a more tawdry present actuality in *The Wapshot Chronicle* when the burlesque girls at the village fair climb up onto the ramshackle platform "shyly, shyly, as children called on to recite 'Hiawatha' or 'The Village Blacksmith.' " But Cheever does not confine himself to American literature. His characters read *David Copperfield, The Count of Monte Christo, Middlemarch,* and these are used in their place to help establish the upper standard of the polarity. In the same manner, and for the same purpose, the legacy of Shakespeare becomes Cheever's own. There is strong evocation of Mercutio's Queen Mab speech in

> one of those legendary tramps who were a part of the local demonology and who were supposed to inhabit the empty farms, leaving traces of fire, empty snuff cans, a dry cow and a frightened spinster.
>
> *The Wapshot Scandal*

And Melissa, shopping at the Supra-Marketto in Rome, where she is living with her grocery-store delivery boy, last appears to us as Ophelia "gathering her fantastic garland not of cornflowers, nettles and long purples, but of salt, pepper, Bab-o, Kleenex . . ."

Often an interspersed poetic canvas signalizes the peak from which the symbolic descent is to take place. Here the dream is evoked by a marked and poignant lyricism in abrupt change of tone from the surrounding prose patternment, or alternatively, by the distinctive poetic device of iteration and refrain:

> Honora glances at the pile of envelopes, picks them up and throws them into the fire. Now we wonder why she burns her mail without reading it, but as she goes away from the fireplace back to her chair the light of a very clear emotion seems to cross her face and perhaps this is explanation enough. Admiring that which is most easily understood we may long for the image of some gentle old woman, kind to her servant and opening her letters with a silver knife, but how much more poetry there is to Honora, casting off the claims of life the instant they are made. *When she has stowed away her breakfast . . .*
>
> *The Wapshot Chronicle*

My italics underscore the device of the author here, as the lyricism of the antecedent lines gives way to the broadly colloquial diction, the prosaic incident of *stowed away her breakfast.* Or the similar juxtaposition:

> On the other half was the farm at St. Botolphs, the gentle valley and the impuissant river and the rooms that smelled now of lilac and hyacinth. . . .

Here we have the height of the *then.* The paragraph immediately following drops us to prosaic *now:*

> His father poured himself some whisky and when the stove was hot he took some hamburgers and cooked them on the lid. . . .
>
> *The Wapshot Chronicle*

Similarly in the following excerpt, the lyricism of the antecedent paragraph is to be contrasted with the tone of ordinary prose of the lines immediately following: (My italics)

> We have all parted from simple places by train or boat at season's end with generations of yellow leaves spilling on the north wind as we spill our

seed, and the dogs and the children in the back of the car, but it is not a fact that at the moment of separation a tumult of brilliant and precise images—as though we drowned—streams through our heads. We have indeed come back to lighted houses, smelling on the north wind burning applewood, and seen a Polish countess greasing her face in a ski lodge and heard the cry of the horned owl in rut and smelled a dead whale on the south wind that carries also the sweet note of the bell from Antwerp. . . .
    Sarah began to cry when Moses kissed her. . . .

The Wapshot Chronicle

The device of poetic repetition or refrain is also used to establish the height which defines the juxtaposition. In *The Wapshot Scandal*, it is to the refrain of "Oh, the wind and the rain and to hold in one's arms a willing love," a refrain sustained for a chapter's length, that the scientist Cameron enacts the tawdry adventure that he hopes will reunite him with his sluttish Italian mistress; (My italics)

> *Oh, the wind and the rain and to hold in one's arms a willing love!* He was suffering, as he would put it, from a common inflammation. . . . The pilot announced in two languages that they were taking the plane into a hangar to wait for their clearance. . . . *Oh, the wind and the rain and to hold in one's arms a willing love!* There was the day to kill. . . . There were four women in a front pew and a priest in soiled lace was celebrating mass. He looked around him anxious to appreciate the art treasures, but there seemed to be a roof leak above the chapel on his right and while he guessed that the painting there must be valuable and beautiful it was cracked and stained with water like the wall of any furnished room. . . . *Oh, the wind and the rain and to hold in one's arms a willing love!* . . . He saw himself stumbling over wet cobblestones under old-fashioned street lamps, falling, falling, falling from usefulness into foolishness, from high spirits into crudeness. . . . *Oh, the wind and the rain and to hold in one's arms a willing love!* He stepped into a large pile of dog manure. . . .

The Wapshot Scandal

Always we come to the empty iron pot at the end of the long violet light. Deposited on the floor of commonplace in the continuous slippage of *then* to *now*, surprisingly we do not cease to fall. For though the floor is down from the heights of the dream, it is a floor which has no substance, it is not ground. We strike it, we discover, only in passing, and like Icarus plunging into the sea, find ourselves falling still. The dream is cobweb, the present foundationless, and down, down in unterminating descent we continue to fall.
    There is no hospitality in the present. Attempting to sustain soul and life in the housing development he inhabits at the missile site, Coverly perceives in his environment an "unwonted otherness." Cheever's secure control of his craft is evident in the manner in which he continues to sustain the form of juxtaposition to string the rigging of prosaic existence

with those same forces of myth and fable—which are now made to represent an endemic mischievousness and malignity in the everyday machinery of modern life. The italics in the following samples are mine:

The transparent wrapper that *imprisoned* the bacon seemed *like some immutable transparency in her life, some invisible barrier of frustrations* that stood between herself and what she deserved.

> *The Wapshot Scandal*

His sitting undressed in the back seat of a car might be accounted for by the fact that the music he danced to and the movies he watched dealt less and less with the heart and more and more with overt sexuality, as if *the rose gardens and playing fields buried under the Expressway were enjoying a revenge.*

> *The Wapshot Scandal*

Moses and Melissa Wapshot lived in Proxmire Manor, a place that was known up and down the suburban railroad line as the place where the lady got arrested. The incident had taken place five or six years before, but it had *the endurance of a legend,* and the lady had seemed briefly to be *the genius of the pretty place.*

> *The Wapshot Scandal*

Mr. Freeley walked home. So did Emile but they took different routes. Emile cut through some back yards to Turner Street and started up the hill. *The scene was apocalyptic. Foresaken children could be heard crying in the empty houses and most of the doors stood open in the dawn as if Gabriel's long trumpet had sounded.* At the top of Turner Street he cut over onto the golf links, climbed to the highest fairway and sat down, waiting for the day.

> *The Wapshot Scandal*

After the staple words have been accounted for, those ubiquitous workers that cement the syntax of the language, one of the next most frequently recurring groups of word clusters in *The Wapshot Chronicle* and *The Wapshot Scandal* might well reveal themselves to be *fall, falling, fallen* and their synonyms. It is hardly inappropriate that this should be so. Writing is for use. The words of the novelist no less than those of the poet must serve their function. In these novels of the downfall of a family within the context of a societal structure in which human life grows increasingly impossible, it is the letter which informs the overall spirit of decline. The anatomy of decline pervades this pair of novels. As a broader study would indicate, decline is made manifest in the schematic ordering of the successive chapters, in the nature and juxtaposition of incident, in the introspective lives of the characters, in the corroboration of imagery. And as our present study has demonstrated, even on the most elemental level of the relationship of word to word, as closely as in poetry structure and theme are made to coalesce. The force of these novels, their clarity of effect, is a direct function of the craft with which they are contrived, so that to describe their form is to define their meaning.

Notes

1. John Cheever, *The Wapshot Chronicle* (New York, 1954), p. 30.
2. Cynthia Ozick, "America Aglow," *Commentary* (July 1964), p. 66.

John Cheever's Vision of the World

Frederick Bracher*

The writings of John Cheever fall readily into two groups. In his early stories and first novel, Cheever, for the most part, uses his remarkable gifts to catch and record, without explicit criticism, the ephemeral quality of middle-class life on the Atlantic seaboard. The later stories, increasingly somber in tone and experimental in technique, are sharply critical of today's mechanized society. In them Cheever uses exaggeration and fantasy to contrast the stable world of Leander Wapshot with the violent changes that have taken place in our own time. (*Bullet Park* and *Falconer* may possibly represent still another stage in Cheever's career.)

The dividing line between the early stories with their celebration of life in city and suburb and the later satirical fantasies lies somewhere in the early sixties. *The Wapshot Chronicle* (1957) and the stories in *The Housebreaker of Shady Hill* (1958) are good representatives of the early period. *The Brigadier and the Golf Widow* and *The Wapshot Scandal*, both published in 1964, are typical of the later period, in which Coverly Wapshot, Leander's son, finds his life determined, not by the traditions of his fathers, but by chance and accident. It is a computer error that puts him to work as a public relations man at an underground plant devoted to missile research and development, and chance encounters determine most of his subsequent career. Cheever's awareness of his own change of direction is indicated by the title *Some People, Places, and Things That Will Not Appear in My Next Novel* (1961). This collection of stories announced the author's dissatisfaction with the sardonic accounts of upper-middle-class life that had established his reputation as a professional author and burdened him with the label "*New Yorker* writer," entertaining but not to be taken seriously.

Two brief descriptions in *The Wapshot Scandal* pinpoint the contrast

*This essay, written especially for this volume and used with permission of the author, incorporates material from two earlier articles of his, "John Cheever and Comedy," *Critique: Studies In Modern Fiction*, 6 (Spring 1963), 66–77 and "John Cheever: A Vision of the World," *Claremont Quarterly* 11, No. 22 (Winter 1964), 47–57, with acknowledgement herewith made.

between the stable life of St. Botolphs and the random uncertainty of the society parodied in the later books. A relic of Leander's world is "the railroad station at St. Botolphs with its rich aura of arrivals and departures, its smells of coal gas, floor oil, and toilets, and its dark waiting room, where some force of magnification seemed brought to bear on the lives of the passengers waiting for their train."[1] A contrasting symbol of the new world in which Coverly tries to find his bearings is the International Airport, "this loft or palace, its glass walls open to the overcast sky, where spaciousness, efficiency, and the smell of artificial leather seemed not to magnify but to diminish the knowledge the passengers had of one another" (WS, p. 185). A central aim of the early stories is to create an air of verisimilitude; the title of Cheever's first book indicates its purpose: to show *The Way Some People Live.* The later works, mainly published in the sixties, use introspection, incongruity, and parody to proclaim the absurdity of the modern world.

Moral earnestness is a pervasive element in all of Cheever's writing, as Morris Friedman noted in 1953. "By reason of his New England background, Cheever has breathed into his system that Biblical concentration on the moral nature of reality . . . which we find in Hawthorne, Melville, and James."[2] Like the nineteenth century Russian writers whom he particularly admires, Cheever is infected "by the worm of moral thirst," and the importance of his fiction comes from his moral insights. The weight of his early writing is usually on the side of affirmation; instead of ridiculing man's weakness and limitations, Cheever holds up for admiration the virtues and potentialities of his fellow men. His celebration of life is not achieved by a facile ignoring of man's dark destiny. On the contrary, it is a pervading sense of the fragility of life that makes his moments of illumination possible. Shady Hill hangs by a thread over moral and economic chaos, but it does hang there in the evening light. In the stories, only those who feel their insecurity can ever burst joy's grape, and by his own account, Cheever writes "to make some link between the light in the sky and the taste of death." Taken as a whole, Cheever's early fiction constitutes, like the life of Leander Wapshot, "a gesture or sacrament toward the excellence and continuousness of things."

In this respect, Cheever's early stories approximate the original assumptions of comedy, a moral vision of continuity in which disaster is not necessarily an unhappy ending but may be, also, a new beginning in the never-ending cycles of human existence. If tragedy deplores the death of Dionysus, comedy celebrates the renewal of life that follows the death, "the epiphany or manifestation of the risen hero. . . . No logic can explain this magic victory over Winter, Sin, and the Devil."[3] Cheever seems to be saying, yes, the heart of man is crooked and false, his opportunities are limited by social barriers and personal traumata, and his end is tragic. We know this, but we do not have to live by it. What we live by is "clear emotion toward other people," and an uninhibited experience of "the harsh surface beauty of life." The element of harshness is inescapable—the beach is full of sand burrs and the reviving water is shockingly cold at first—but the man who accepts initiatory pain is rewarded by the capacity for beauty, a sense of freedom, and the power to love. These are all signs and privileges of maturity.

The basic conflict between those who are confirmed in life and those who, for whatever reason, renounce their possibilities is made explicit in a remarkable early story, "Goodbye, My Brother" (1951). Lawrence, the youngest brother in the story, diminishes things by categorizing them with his "baleful and incisive mind." He and his whole family reject life; the scared, unhappy children will not go outdoors because they have seen a snake under the doorstep, and the drab wife spends her time in the steam of the laundry, washing clothes with an expiatory passion while the other brothers and sisters are out on the thundering beach, swimming in the cold green water of the Atlantic. The sea here, as in most of Cheever's writing, is a symbol of primal energy, "the rich green soup of life." The youngest brother, characteristically, ignores the sea except when it feeds his morbid appetite for partings and decay and the falling away of things. He notices the eroding fields, the termites in the shingles, the cracks in the seawall. The waves break on the beach "with a sound like 'hurrah, hurrah, hurrah,' but to Lawrence they would say 'Vale, vale.' " On the "vast and preternaturally clean and simple landscape of the beach," Lawrence announces that he has returned to Laud's Head only to say good-bye. It is his most characteristic gesture. He has said good-bye to his drowned father, to college friends and Yale, to his "dishonest" first employer, to the Episcopal church, to private enterprise, to the Roosevelt Administration, and now to the sea.

The brother who tells the story, a secondary school teacher, is the Manichean opposite of Lawrence, with a genius for simple happiness—for clear emotion toward his charming, foolish mother, his gracefully aging wife, his healthy, active children. He turns naturally to direct experience of the world: the bracing shock of the Atlantic waves, the smells of wood smoke and salt air, the quality of light on a summer morning. He enjoys the family tennis and family cocktails, the after-dinner gambling at backgammon, the light-hearted silliness of a costume dance at the Club, the beauty of his divorced sister. He has, in short, made the effort of spirit necessary to reject the Puritan inheritance of a family which goes back to the time of Cotton Mather: "the habits of guilt, self-denial, taciturnity, and penitence." Lawrence affects him strongly. "When I woke in the morning, I felt sick, as if I had suffered a great spiritual loss while I slept, like the loss of courage and heart." But he has rituals for exorcizing such evil spirits: sailing, picnics with his wife and children, the party at the Club, and above all, swimming in the sea. The ritual efficacy of salt water, "as if swimming had the cleansing force claimed for baptism," is stressed throughout the story.

The latent hostility between the two brothers reaches a climax during a walk on the beach. In an excess of revulsion—the kind of reflex that makes one stamp on a spider or batter a venomous snake—the narrator strikes his brother with a piece of driftwood. It is a treacherous and possibly murderous blow from behind, but it is also a moral protest, a denial of the death-wish in all its forms. The ritual gesture is followed by a purifying dip in the sea and the evil spell is broken. Lawrence and his dreary family leave the next day.

> The buoys would toll mournfully for Lawrence, and while the grace of the light would make it an exertion not to throw out your arms and swear exultantly, Lawrence's eyes would trace the black sea as it fell astern; he would think of the bottom, dark and strange, where full fathom five our father lies.[4]

The story ends with a lyric restatement of the theme. The narrator rejects the symbols of death and decay which have determined his brother's character, and the mythical overtones announce his confirmation in "the new, strange, vivid world around him."

> Oh, what can you do with a man like that? What can you do? How can you dissuade his eye in a crowd from seeking out the cheek with acne, the infirm hand; how can you teach him to respond to the inestimable greatness of the race, the harsh surface beauty of life; how can you put his finger for him on the obdurate truths before which fear and horror are powerless? The sea that morning was iridescent and dark. My wife and my sister were swimming—Diana and Helen—and I saw their uncovered heads, black and gold in the dark water. I saw them come out and I saw that they were naked, unshy, beautiful, and full of grace, and I watched the naked women walk out of the sea. (SC, p. 23)

Cheever's dismissal of the morbid and infantile is not escapist; his stance is not so much turned away from as turned toward something else. At Leander Wapshot's funeral, Prospero's words acknowledge the transience of our little life, but Leander's "Advice to My Sons," written out and inserted in the volume of Shakespeare where the sons will surely find it, honors the values by which healthy men live:

> Fear tastes like a rusty knife and do not let her into your house. Courage tastes of blood. Stand up straight. Admire the world. Relish the love of a gentle woman. Trust in the Lord.[5]

For all their verisimilitude of speech, dress, and decor, many of Cheever's early stories have a legendary quality; they are full of strange happenings, and some, like "The Enormous Radio," or "The Death of Justina," shift imperceptibly into the casual fantasy of the märchen. *The Wapshot Chronicle* is loosely situated in time and space. St. Botolphs is reminiscent of Newburyport according to Cheever, but it is as detached from actual topography as Trollope's Barsetshire. It is impossible to determine when the main action of the novel occurs. Incidental references to security checks and to rocket launching sites indicate a period after World War II, but there is no mention of the War, nor of the depression which preceded it. The events take place in a mellow twilight, once upon a time. Cheever has indicated in a letter that this is deliberate:

> I have carefully avoided dates in order to give my characters freedom to pursue their emotional lives without the interruptions of history. . . . A sense of time that revolves around the sinking of ships and declarations of war seems to me a sense of time debased. We live at deeper levels than these and fiction should make this clear.[6]

The deeper levels are personal, and the important events of the novel lack an ideological as well as a temporal setting. Except for a pervasive flavor of Freudian thought, Cheever ignores the major trends in the intellectual history of our times. No one in *The Wapshot Chronicle* shows any interest in politics or in the implications of the rocket base where Coverly works as a programmer. Economic factors influence the lives of the Wapshots on the practical, rather than the theoretical level. The community of St. Botolphs is not analyzed in the manner of J. P. Marquand; its way of life is given, not explained. The weird menage of Justina on the Hudson is an appropriate setting for social comedy, but the improbable and diverting events that go on there are innocent of social satire, and the motivations of the characters are simple. Moses undertakes his preposterous, hazardous midnight traverse of the roofs for an elementary, indisputable reason: he wants to sleep with his fiancée.

Even in the full-length novels, the characters are picturesque rather than profound, and whatever psychological interest may be implied by their odd behavior is not elaborated. The stories often have no plot, in the traditional sense. They are sequences of feeling, rather than casually linked events; they depend on the logic of the imagination to supply a felt unity. Francis Weed, in "The Country Husband," goes through a series of unrelated traumatic experiences and develops a helpless, hopeless passion for a young girl, the new baby-sitter. His airplane has made a crash landing in a cornfield; at dinner he recognizes a neighbor's new French maid as the woman whom he had seen, years before, stripped and shaved for collaboration with the enemy. The odd events of the day, unexorcised by the normal rites of family life, have "opened his memory and his senses, and left them dilated." The reader feels his complete vulnerability to the girl's dark, troubled beauty, his frustrating knowledge of the possibilities and dangers of the situation, and the almost ludicrous efficacy of a primitive cure: wood-working and "the holy smell of new wood."

Cheever knows that nothing recreates the past like a whiff of perfume or the smell of an old familiar house, and he frequently uses this device to evoke a scene. In both a literal and a figurative sense, Cheever's principal subject matter is "the perfumes of life," and Leander Wapshot regrets their diminution in a more sanitary era:

> More savory world then, than today. Smell of ship's-bread bakery. Green coffee beans roasted once a week. Perfumery of roasted coffee floated miles downriver. Lamp smoke. Smell of cistern water. Lye from privy. Wood fires. (*WC*, p. 25)

The feel of rain on his head, "the smell of it flying up to his nose," breaks the spell of guilt and despair for the amateur housebreaker of Shady Hill, reminding him that he can still possess the gifts of life if he will only turn toward them.

For his first novel, Cheever found the stable, unselfconscious life of St. Botolphs an ideal parochial background. Past generations of the Wapshot family are described in some detail, and there are indications that they are traced from originals in Cheever's own family. The name "Wapshot" is a corruption of the Old French "Vaincre-Chaud," as "Cheever" is an Anglicized version of Old French "Chievre." The American branch of the fictional family was founded by Ezekiel Wapshot, who came to Boston in 1630, where he taught Latin, "abominated periwigs, and had the welfare of the Commonwealth always upon his conscience." These details, as well as the encomiastic sermon preached after his death by Cotton Mather, are taken direct from the account, in Samuel Sewall's *Diary*, of Ezekiel Cheever, who came to Boston, in fact, in 1633. The borrowing serves to underline Cheever's feeling for the continuity of a family. One of the troubles with Shady Hill is its ignoring of any living link with past civilizations, its "tacit claim that there had been no past, no war, that there was no danger or trouble in the world." *The Wapshot Chronicle* shows that there is plenty of trouble and danger in St. Botolphs today, just as there was in the seventeenth century.

The hero of the *Chronicle* is Leander Wapshot. He is the most fully developed character (his journal is a masterpiece of characterization and Dickensian humor), and he has survived the change from the lamplit world of 1890 to the 1950s. Leander's sturdy assertion of his own humanity defies historical process, and "the unobserved ceremoniousness of his life is a gesture or sacrament toward the excellence and continuity of things." His ancestors have all been shipmasters or schoolteachers, he boasts in his journal; and he recapitulates in his own time and his own way the experience of earlier Wapshots who were familiar with Calcutta and Java and China, and who refreshed themselves en route with the willing girls of Samoa. True, times have changed, and instead of a square-rigged clipper, Leander is master of a decrepit 60-foot launch used for ferrying tourists on the bay. His Samoa is the gritty railroad embankment where he discovers sex with the aid of a middle-aged prostitute, or the matchboard cottages and seaside girls of the amusement park at

Nangasakit across the bay. Though the limitations of New England life do not afford the apparatus for heroic adventures in the grand manner, in spirit Leander belongs with Odysseus and his companions.

By the end of the book, Leander has taken on legendary stature. "Smelling powerfully of the sea salts in the old sponges that he used," he is a kind of sea god, with hairy nostrils and a hearty, perpetual lecherousness. He passes on to his sons the traditional rites and skills of a seaport village: "to fell a tree, pluck and dress a chicken, sow, cultivate and harvest, catch a fish, save money, countersink a nail, make cider with a hand press, clean a gun, sail a boat, etc." And like a god or culture hero, his disappearance from earth is mysterious and ceremonious.

One Sunday, after a ominous dream, he surprises everyone by going to church, "not convinced of the worth of his prayers, but pleased with the fact that on his knees in Christ Church he was, more than in any other place in the world, face to face with the bare facts of his humanity." The pine needles on the carpet, left there since Advent, "cheered him as if [they] had been shaken from the Tree of Life and reminded him of its fragrance and vitality." Next morning he goes alone to the beach.

> The surf spoke in loud voices of wrecks and voyages and the likeness of things; for the dead fish was striped like a cat and the sky was striped like the fish and the conch was whorled like an ear and the beach was ribbed like a dog's mouth, and the movables in the surf splintered and crashed like the walls of Jericho. (WC, p. 378)

His preliminary gesture of wetting his wrists and temples looks from a distance as though he were crossing himself, and he swims with his old-fashioned sidestroke out into the Atlantic and is never seen again.

If Leander reminds one, increasingly, of Neptune, his patient wife suggests Demeter-Ceres. Standing on a float, she is drawn by horses through the streets of the town, smiling sadly among the fruits of her labors—the new parish house, a granite horsetrough now planted with petunias—and yearning for a daughter. Rosalie, a stray from the City, arrives in St. Botolphs one night accompanied by Death. (Her boyfriend has just been killed in an auto crash.) She is taken in by the Wapshots and spends a season in the light and warmth of West Farm, but then she is reclaimed by her black-suited father in his long black car and returned to the netherworld of a Boston parsonage.

In "The Scarlet Moving Van" Gee-Gee (Greek God) recalls Bacchus and his car. His alcoholic efforts "to teach them" not the beneficent culture of the vine but "some vision of the suffering in life" make it necessary for him to move every year from one hill town to another in the gaudy van. As an "advocate for the lame, the diseased, the poor," he merges with the figure of the scapegoat god, annually sacrificed to free the town of evils. Brimmer, in the story of that name, looks like a satyr—one of the older ones "with lined faces and conspicuous tails." An epigone of the Great God Pan, Brimmer lives on in the heart of every man who can imagine the feel of a hairy tail coiled in the seat of his pants.

The women of the early stories show a startling aptitude for metamorphosis. Moses Wapshot's golden Melissa can transform herself between dinner and bedtime into a sour frigid spinster in a long woolen nightshirt. Following her lovemaking in the dunes, Rosalie ceremoniously washes in the ocean, as Aphrodite renewed her virginity in the sea at Paphos. Aphrodite, sometimes surnamed Pandemos (sensual lust) and Anadyomene (rising from the sea) is, in another metamorphosis, Melaenus (the black one, Goddess of Death-in-life). She appears in Cheever's "Torch Song" as a handsome girl always dressed in black who has a vulture's eye for the moribund—drunks, consumptives, dope addicts—and who renews her own vitality by tending her lovers till they die.

In a talk in San Francisco in 1960, Cheever said that he writes to make sense out of his experience. "Art is the triumph over chaos," he insists, and order is achieved "by the most vigilant exercise of choice" (SC, pp. 505–6). But in a world where "even the mountains seem to shift in the space of a night," how can a writer make with confidence the choices that will order our feelings and throw a true light on the way we live? The writer's choices are apt to be as precarious as those of the people in the dream sequence in "The Death of Justina," the motley shoppers who select, with agonizing care, unlabeled, unrecognizable packages in a monstrous supermarket, only to be overcome with guilt and cast into outer darkness when their packages are opened at the checkstand.

In *Some People, Places, and Things That Will Not Appear in My Next Novel*, Cheever explicitly turns his back on some elements of his earlier writing. The superficial trappings of social comedy—glamor girls, scornful descriptions of the American scene, explicit accounts of sex, drunks, and homosexuals—are among the things that will not appear, if one takes the title at face value, in his subsequent writing. They "throw so little true light on the way we live." Cheever singled them out to demonstrate "the unimportance that threatens fiction," if it continues to concern itself chiefly with the external look of society.

The later stories often use a realistic setting only as a point of departure for an expedition into the inner world of dream and fantasy. If successful, such explorations may arrive at truths that can redeem and give some reality to the preposterous surface of our mechanized suburbia. The writer's perpetual struggle "seems to be to tell the truth without surrendering the astringent atmosphere of truthfulness." Cheever's later stories are full of images of confusion: a housewife in a raincoat, carefully watering her lawn in a thunder shower; Proxmire Manor, a suburb so respectable that burial and even death are illegal within its boundaries; TV commercials advertising "Elixircol for wet-fur-coat-odor"; "highways lined with Smorgorama and Giganticburger stands." To discover a vision of the world that has the atmosphere of truthfulness, the writer must turn inward. "What I wanted to do," says the narrator in "A Vision of the World," "was to grant my dreams, in so incoherent a world, their legitimacy" (SC, p. 607).

Cheever's later fiction is reminiscent of Kafka, or of T. S. Eliot's unreal city. The stories exploit the sense of dissociation induced by modern living, and two key images are the supermarket and the freeway—two inhumanly efficient devices for satisfying basic human needs. The setting has changed from the comfortable, if transitory, security of Shady Hill to the sinister irrationality of Proxmire Manor. In the supersuburb, where the Moonlight Drive-In has replaced old churches and homesteads, life is disjointed and discontinuous; and the structure of the stories makes a virtue of accidental associations, the "broken lines of communication in which we express our most acute feelings."

The events which make up the action of "A Vision of the World" have no logical or rational connections: a message from the past found in a tin can dug up in the garden, a copperhead disappearing into the stone wall, a dance with a stranger in the supermarket, an inexplicable parade led by a drum majorette wearing bifocals, a dinner at the Gory Brook Country Club, where the guests "seemed to be dancing on the grave of social coherence." Any order imposed on such events will be an order of feelings, not a rational order. Cheever unifies the story by interpolating a series of intensely real and somehow reassuring dreams, in each of which a sentence in an unknown language recurs: "Porpozec ciebie nie prosze. . . ." It is a kind of incantation, which makes the dream setting "real, vivid, and enduring" and gives the dream experience the healing quality of a benediction.

When the sentence crops up in the narrator's waking life, as an involuntary answer to the question of what he wants for breakfast, he recognizes it as an acute symptom of neurosis, and agrees to go for a rest to Florida. There the sound of the rain on his cabin brings release; it reminds him of smiling farmers and lovers awake in the night, and sitting up in bed he says aloud some of the ancient words of his own language: "Valor! Love! Splendor! Kindness! Wisdom! Beauty!" (SC, pp. 610–11). The night blots out the Tamiami Trail, rain links him to the lovers, and the words now "seem to have the colors of the earth" and bring him contentment and peace.

The difficulty of an adequate emotional response to our blaring mechanized environment is at least an implicit theme in Cheever's later stories. One of the feelings evoked by his acute and rebellious sensibility is dismay at "a new hue in the spectrum of human pain": a sense of emotional impotence like that of the wife who has "this terrible feeling that I'm in black and white and that I can be turned off by anybody." She is "sad because her sadness is not a sad sadness"; she sorrows "over the inadequacies of her sorrow."

Before we can feel truly, we must be able to define the people, places, and things toward which our feeling is directed. In the past, language and literature have helped man to make some order out of the chaos of his external environment; but what language can do justice to the violence of recent change, the unreality of the supermarket? The hero of "The Bella Lingua" studies Italian in an effort to comprehend the confusion of present-day Rome:

> Here comes Cardinal Micara with the True Finger of Doubting Thomas—that much is clear—but is the man beside us in the church asleep or dead, and what are all the elephants doing in the Piazza Venezia? (SC, p. 361)

Not even the *bella lingua* can provide an answer. "Our language is traditional, the accrual of centuries of intercourse," but in the supermarket nothing is traditional except the shapes of the pastry. Neither Shakespeare nor the Twenty-Third psalm nor "the resonance of the Mass" seems relevant, and a drunken priest prays finally for "all those killed or cruelly wounded on thruways, expressways, freeways and turnpikes, . . . for all those burned to death in faulty plane landings, mid-air collisions, and mountainside crashes, . . . for all those wounded by rotary lawn-mowers, chain saws, electric hedge clippers, and other power tools," and hurries back to his gin bottle in the vestry.

To sustain a vision of a world in which life flows freely, Cheever has relied more and more on the mythopoeic imagination. "What I wanted to identify then was not a chain of facts but an essence—something like that indecipherable collision of contingencies that can produce exaltation or despair." In "The Embarkment for Cythera," a long story originally published in the *New Yorker* (3 November 1962),[7] Cheever distilled such an essence out of a series of the inexplicable events and contingencies that make up contemporary life. The story is developed from the myth of a voyage to the Blessed Isle, as it is given nostalgic embodiment in Watteau's great painting. Arnold Hauser has noted that Watteau's profundity is due to "the ambivalence of his relation to the world, to the expression of both the promise and the inadequacy of life, to the always present feeling of an inexpressible loss and an unattainable goal," a concept which might serve to define the essence of Cheever's later writing. The painting shows couples of elegant ladies and gentlemen in langorous procession through a dreamlike sylvan landscape to the ship which will presumably carry them to ineffable delight on the island sacred to Aphrodite. But the mood of the painting is melancholy; the unearthly light suggests that the paradise of Cythera can hardly be achieved in this life. "In all his pictures [Watteau] describes a society menaced by the unrealizable nature of its desires."[8]

Cheever's story concerns two people who discover in themselves a longing for a voyage to Cythera. One is a rich and cultivated married woman, whose boredom with the conventional life of Proxmire Manor, with her husband, and with "the importunate, cheerful, and vulgar demands of his body" arouse in her "a profound nostalgia for some emotional island or peninsula that she had not even discerned in her dreams." The other is a teenage delivery boy who wants "something that would correspond to his sense that life is imposing." In a superb pardoy of a *fête champêtre* by Watteau—the half-nude girls in the car at the drive-in movie giggling and drinking whiskey out of paper cups—Cheever justifies the boy's feeling that there should be more to love than the back-seat seduction of Louise Mecker, that all-too-willing tomato. The story traces, with the casual haphazardness of a dream and with the aid of several dreams, the convergence of the two, driven by their congruent but different aspirations: she to experience a more "real" emotional life, he to escape from the brute realities of back-seat sex.

The central and climactic scene occurs early in the story. Jessica is feeding the baby in the kitchen; the atmosphere is charged with "an intimacy so intense that it seemed to her as if she and the baby were the same flesh and blood." The feeling of secure intimacy is broken by a symbol of death, a glimpse of an old man "craning his neck like an adder." A loud pounding on the door leads her to hug the baby protectively. But it is only the grocery boy, "beaming and with a kind of radiance that seemed to liberate her from this absurd chain of anxieties." She offers him food, and as the three sit in comfortable silence, she feels the first stirring of desire for this son of the "real world."

The rest of the story is anticlimax. In reality, the airplane that carries the pair to the island (Nantucket) is dented and grimy, the cottage on the bluff seems to the boy cold and barren, the surf is chilling. Jessica's step, returning to the bed after closing windows against a storm, "sounded heavy and old." The boy would have preferred, he confesses later, to spend the weekend driving to a football game in a sleek convertible. Subsequent voyages to hotels in Boston and New York are more desperate; the boy's innocence and inexperience make him invulnerable. The realization that a Voyage to Cythera is impossible for so ill-matched a pair is brought about by exploiting the ancient symbolism of food and love. The boy is perpetually hungry (he is still growing, he explains), and the final scene in which he rejects his mistress in favor of roast-beef sandwiches recalls ironically the intense intimacy of the earlier scene in which Jessica feeds the baby sweet canned figs. Trying to reconstruct the absurd chain of events that has brought her to this dead end, Jessica finds her mind a blank. "She had wanted to bring into her life the freshness of a journey and had achieved nothing but a galling sense of moral shabbiness."

The sardonic conclusion, however, does not invalidate the legitimacy of the dream or the relevance of the myth. Modern life, from the super-highway to the missile-launching site, seems illogical and incomprehensible; but is Coverly Wapshot, programming on a South Pacific atoll, more at sea than his ancestor who floated for three days on a spar in the Java Sea, kicking at the sharks with his heels? Man is born unto trouble, as the sparks fly upward; to live in any period, one must learn to roll with the punch, immerse in the destructive element, accept change and abnormality as normal.

For model and guide, Cheever reminds us, we have always had the dream—a nightly vision of the world which flouts the limitations of the waking mind and yet has its own authenticity. To grant our dreams their legitimacy means, ultimately, to accept the incomprehensible, as myth has always done, and to adapt ourselves, with the sanction of ritual if possible, to the next stage of the cycle. A voyage to Cythera which ends in a moral blind alley is still better than the dehumanized life of Proxmire Manor. Whether our desires are realizable or not, the important thing is to move ahead, to continue the voyage. On the moral level, Cheever would seem to agree with T. S. Eliot's imperative: "Not fare well, but fare forward, voyagers."

The last of the characters to be ousted in Cheever's "A Miscellany of Characters That Will Not Appear" is an aging writer in a shabby *pensione* in Venice. In an account of what this writer has lost, Cheever gives a strong hint of his own intentions. He will try to preserve and exercise "the gift of evoking the perfumes of life: sea water, the smoke of burning hemlock, and the breasts of women." But this is not enough. "To celebrate a world that lies spread out around us like a bewildering and stupendous dream" one must manage to comprehend it through the imagination. The nearly impossible task of the writer is to make the world of the supermarket and the missile site, in which we must live, congenial to the sensibility that makes life worth living. To reestablish the continuity of human experience, the writer must fare inward as well as forward, to a territory in which the senses and the sensibility are reinforced by "the ear's innermost chamber, where we hear the heavy noise of the dragon's tail moving over the dead leaves."

Notes

1. *The Wapshot Scandal* (N.Y.: Harper and Row, 1964), p. 184. Subsequent references, in the text, will be identified as *WS*.

2. New England and Hollywood," *Commentary* 16 (October 1953), 390.

3. Wylie Sypher, *Comedy* (N.Y.: Doubleday, 1956), p. 220.

4. *The Stories of John Cheever* (N.Y.: Ballantine Books, 1978), p. 23. Subsequent references, in the text, will be identified as *SC*.

5. *The Wapshot Chronicle* (N.Y.: Time-Life Books, 1965), p. 365. Subsequent references, in the text, will be identified as *WC*.

6. Unpublished letter to Frederick Bracher, July 15, 1962.

7. The story, expanded and adapted to fit Melissa, the flighty wife of Moses Wapshot, was incorporated as a major segment of *The Wapshot Scandal*, but with considerable distortion of its original emotional impact.

8. Arnold Hauser, *The Social History of Art: Rococo, Classicism and Romanticisim* Vol. III (London: Routledge and Kegan Paul, 1962), p. 14.

John Cheever: The "Swimming" of America

Robert M. Slabey*

. . . the story of Rip Van Winkle has never been finished, and still awaits a final imaginative recreation.

—Constance Rourke

Indeed, the central fact about America in 1970 is the discrepancy between the realities of our society and our beliefs about them. The gap is even greater in terms of our failure to understand the possibilities and potential of American life.

—Charles A. Reich

I

More than a century after Washington Irving described the Catskills as "fairy mountains" with "magical hues" produced by seasonal and diurnal atmospheric changes, John Cheever has taken that enchanted vicinity as the setting for some of his best fiction. In this continuation of Hudson River mythology, Cheever's territory, like Irving's, is somewhere between fact and fantasy, the mundane and the marvelous, "modern" life and ancient legend. And while both writers mix comedy and sadness, Irving's vision gravitates towards the first pole, Cheever's towards the second. They are both in the company of American writers who suggest the existence of a level—mysterious and mythic—beyond the middle range of experience and find "reality" at the crossroads of actuality and myth. In addition, Cheever's magical transformations have cultural roots in Ovid and Cotton Mather as well as in American Romanticism. Like Irving, Hawthorne, Mark Twain, and Faulkner, Cheever has taken a region and a time and, without diminishing their importance, has made them stand for the larger meanings of American experience; he can see the meaning of the country in the way ordinary people live their daily lives.

In a career spanning five decades Cheever has published over one hundred short stories (most of them in the *New Yorker*), six story-collections, and four novels. A conscious craftsman and a brilliant stylist,

*This essay was written specifically for this volume and is published here for the first time with permission of the author.

he has encountered substantial success but only spare attention by academic critics. "The Swimmer," a fifteen-page tale which will be the focus of the present study, is, according to its author, the product of two months' work and 150 pages of notes.[1] He is, I think, the most underestimated—and sometimes misunderstood—of contemporary fictionists: Cheever's mastery of art and theme places his best work in touch with basic forms of existence as well as in the center of our culture. He charts the peregrinations of American life—from town to city to the suburbs to Europe to "America." His special theatre, however, is suburbia where the metamorphosis is not of Irving's sleepy Dutch into busy Americans but of work-day city businessmen into weekend "country gentlemen."

On one level, Cheever's fictions are comedies of manners recording the objects and occasions of suburban life: supermarkets, swimming pools, commuter trains, thruways, cocktail parties. Behavioral nuances function as in manners fiction; for example, a "loss of social esteem" can be discerned when a hired bartender gives rude service at a party.[2] In spite of satiric possibilities too numerous to be resisted, Cheever's primary impulse is not to ridicule the silly surfaces. He suggests and sometimes depicts loneliness and despair as well as mysterious and sinister realities. Suburbia is built over the abyss from which disaster and darkness occasionally emerge. For example, in *Bullet Park* a commuter waiting on a station platform is sucked under the wheels of the Chicago express; Cheever's reality here and elsewhere is closer to Kafka than O'Hara. He exposes the nightmare behind Norman Rockwell's *Saturday Evening Post* "America." Though Cheever's alma mater is the Romance-tradition, his vision (though not his style) resembles William Dean Howells's depiction of the troubled day-to-day existence of the middle class: people living on the thin surface hiding terror and violence and pain attempting to plug along with honor in a chaotic world.[3] Cheever depicts the "more smiling aspects of life," which (according to Howells) were the more, American—and sometimes the more terrifying.

Cheever's people are ordinary, weak, foolish, shallow; for the most part lonely, sad, disappointed, inarticulate, they muddle through after barely avoiding catastrophe. But since they have a capacity for love and goodness, to their creator their lives are finally worth saving. Cheever has sympathy for his people but contempt for their false values. Life, he writes, is "a perilous moral journey;" the freaks along the way are those who have fallen from grace.[4] William Peden calls Cheever "a wry observer of manners and mores [who] is more saddened than amused by the foibles he depicts with understanding and grace."[5] Cheever attempts to define "the quality of American life" or "How We Live Now." His stories, according to Alfred Kazin, are "a demonstration of the amazing sadness, futility, and evanescence of life among the settled, moneyed, seemingly altogether domesticated people in [Suburbia]."[6] John Aldridge finds Cheever "extraordinary in his power to infuse the commonplace and often merely dyspeptic metaphysical crises of modern life with something of the generalizing significance of myth."[7] Cheever's people, latter day neighbors of Irving's and Edith Wharton's, in class and consciousness closer to Howells's and Sinclair Lewis's, are revealed in the mode of Hawthorne, with the insight of F. Scott Fitzgerald.

II

One of Cheever's most famous, striking, and original stories, "The Swimmer," elucidates his characteristic artistry as well as his version of American existence. The basic situation is well known: Neddy Merrill's impulsive decision to swim eight miles home via a series of pools. But by the time he has finished, years have passed and his house is deserted. Neddy's arrival home is an example of Cheever's suburbanite, here falling through the surface into the abyss over which his life has been precariously structured, while in other stories there are magical transformations. This abyss is the gulf between the fantasies Americans live by and the actualities they live in. Neddy makes the once-in-a-lifetime discovery that he has won the race but lost his "life." The apparently self-confident conformist whose life-style is identified with his environment, he is a thorough creature of his culture. Neddy is, moreover, athletic in a culture that admires the summer of youth and innocence and suppresses the winter of age and decline. He has "the especial slenderness of youth. . . . He might have been compared to a summer day, particularly the last hours of one, and while he lacked a tennis racket or a sail bag the impression was definitely one of youth, sport, and clement weather" (54–55). The purpose of his swim is to enhance the beauty of the summer day, but his experience turns out to be closer to Housman's Athlete Dying Young than to Shakespeare's young man. His newly discovered route home will be named the Lucinda River (to honor his wife), but it is actually to be a celebration of his own fading youth and an expansion of diminished possibilities.

The narrative begins on "one of those midsummer Sundays when everyone sits around saying: 'I *drank* too much last night.' " Sunday, an exception to the weekly routines and rituals, is a day of special peril in Cheever's fiction. It is the day people fall through the cracks in their lives.[8] Like Irving in "Rip Van Winkle" Cheever describes "magical hues": "It was a fine day. In the West there was a massive stand of cumulus cloud so like a city seen from a distance—from the bow of an approaching ship—that it might have a name. Lisbon. Hackensack" (54). Cheever's protagonist, along with Rip, is an avatar of the amiable good fellow, the shallow American who drinks too much and "lives" too little. He is first seen with one hand in the water of a pool and the other around a glass of gin. Not the lazy dropout, Neddy is an escapist and a dreamer (and part-time "pool bum"). He has material abundance, but that, he finds, is not enough; he shares with many of Cheever's protagonists a vague discontent. His escape from cares and responsibilities and from time is similar to Rip's, the cocktail party Ned's equivalent for Rip's pub. Rip's dream of a perpetual men's club has its correspondence in Ned's dream of a permanent poolside party. Both go on to have extraordinary experiences in the "enchanted mountains," in a dream world of the past, the unconscious, and the imagination. There both men meet regional "natives" whose "hospitable customs and traditions . . . have to be handled with diplomacy" (56). Rip's overnight sleep covers two decades; Ned's long day's journey compresses several years. The Big Sleep becomes the Big Hangover, each signifying the central hollowness of each man's middle years, that American emptiness between Pepsi-Cola and Geritol.

Rip's encounter and sleep and Neddy's suburban swim are mythic experiences that have indexes in both psychology and reality. On one level, Rip's afternoon in the mountains and Neddy's swim saga epitomize their lives, each experience significantly initiated with drinking. While Rip has an aversion to all profitable work, Ned represses all unpleasant facts from his consciousness. Both time-travellers desire escape because of similar psychological inabilities to face adult responsibilities and to commit themselves to dull actuality. They want to leave behind everyday existence, domestic troubles, loneliness, advancing age. Like generations of Americans they have taken to the woods—to hunt, to fish, to camp out, to contemplate the wilderness, and/or to find the "real America." Neddy's swim is obviously just a more domesticated form of woodcraft. He leaves Technopolis for Arcadia, the suburban for the sylvan, history for pastoral; but now the machine itself has been set up in the garden (in the form of the pool filter).

Irving's storied Hudson is replaced by the fantasied Lucinda, a "river" of swimming pools. Both "Rip Van Winkle" and "The Swimmer" contain mythic thunder storms and cyclic seasonal imagery. For Ned the starting point is a fine midsummer day at the Westerhazy's. Cheever, like Irving, moves from the mimetic to the mythic, managing subtle and skillful shifts from actual time and place to the world of nature and the imagination, time measured by sun and season instead of clocks and commuter trains. But the key to meaning in Nature's rhythms and rituals is lost to Ned as it had been to Rip. At the first pool where the apple trees are in bloom, Ned has already gone back even further than spring—to Eden which had been a "world of apples." From here he progresses to the Bunkers' party where he is welcomed, to the Levy's where the party is over and the maple leaves are red and yellow, to the Lindley's riding ring overgrown with grass. Then the Welchers' pool is dry, the bathhouse locked, and the house "for sale," prefiguring the end of his journey. Ned's most difficult portage is the highway where the motorists harass and ridicule him, but by then he has reached the point of no return. His desire for a drink is mocked when he is assailed by an empty beer can. To mobile Americans (as H. L. Mencken prophesied) Nature has become a place to toss beer cans on Sunday afternoons. But all those cars on the Turnpike are—if we believe Paul Simon—looking "for America."

At the crowded, regimented Recreation Center the pool reeks of chlorine (in contrast with the pure waters of private pools) and Ned is subjected to the lifeguard's rebukes. America's natural resources have become crowded, polluted, and "collectivized," trout-streams cut up and sold by the yard (as at Richard Brautigan's Cleveland Wrecking Company). Next, at the Hallorans, the beech hedge is yellow; Ned is cold, tired, depressed, and his trunks feel loose. It is definitely autumn with falling leaves and woodsmoke. At the Sachses he barely finished his swim and, desperately needing a drink, he heads for the Binswangers. The Merrills had always refused their invitations, but now Ned finds that he is the one to be snubbed. In addition, the dark water of the pool has a "wintry gleam." Then after his former mistress refuses his request for a drink, he is exhausted and for the first time he has to use the ladder in getting out of a pool. Moreover, the flowers and constellations are unmistakably those of autumn (66–67). He is unable to dive into the last pools. Miserable, cold, bewildered, he weeps. He has been "immersed too long." The temporal drift is ever downward, with summer, the time of physicality and material prosperity, giving way to the season of decline and decay. During his odyssey Ned loses a sense of time just as "his gift for concealing painful facts let him forget that he had sold his house, that his children were in trouble, and that his friend [Eric Sachs] had been ill" (64). His affair with Shirley Adams had been terminated "last week, last month, last year. He couldn't remember" (66). As he progresses only the journey itself has immediate reality.

During Neddy's swim, he loses everything—wife, children, home, friends, mistress, job, investments, youth, hopes, self. At the end he "had done what he wanted, he has swum the country" (67), but his house is dark, locked, and empty, recalling Rip who discovered his house abandoned and in decay and found himself alone in the world, puzzled by "such enormous lapses of time." The Lucinda River, like the Hudson, represents time and change; the waterway of "light" and new beginnings becomes the river of darkness and despair. Cheever has carried the identity-loss, which Irving ultimately averted, to its finale. The constituents of actuality have slipped away. All that he thought he had is lost; all relationships have come to naught. He is left with emptiness. "Everything" was never enough: now it is nothing. While Irving's tale ranks not only as a classic but as a national resource for cultural reference, "The Swimmer" is no less rich and includes areas beyond Irving's attention.

Neddy is the depthless dreamer and organization man, but he also acts out the frontier myth of exploration, independence, endurance, and self-reliance. He even sees himself "as a legendary figure" (55). "Making his way home by an uncommon route gave him the feeling that he was a pilgrim, an explorer, a man with a destiny" (56). Another Columbus, he has only imaginary charts to follow. A pioneer, he confronts the challenge of nature alone. And as a pilgrim, his journey recalls Bunyan's figure who has numerous American facsimiles. His journey takes him westward, that most American and symbolic of directions. Neddy, however, faces not the primitive forces of the wilderness but pools, gardens, and highways. His pool expedition is a Madison Avenue packaging of Emerson's call to "enjoy an original relation to the universe," his naturism just as ersatz as the nudist Hallorans reading the *Times*. By the 1960s the Frontier is something not lived but read about, a vision enriched by memory. Ned desires to go back in time and space, to move outward and inward, while an onerous world moves forward and downward.

Cheever omits the final movement of the archetype (Rip's reconciliation with the new life of the town), but he plays out the full, darker implications. The everyday world, re-established at the conclusion of "Rip Van Winkle," is irretrievably lost at the end of "The Swimmer." Irving created a legendary past (based on European myths) to enrich the texture of a raw, new present. Cheever imagined a mythic alternate to explode an unreal present. Irving's dream-world is, finally, not believed in, while for Cheever myth, dream, and the unconscious have more "reality" than objective existence. After 140 years, Cheever has replaced history, Irving's primary allegiance, with mystery. According to Richard Poirier the most interesting American writings are an image of the creation of America itself: "They are bathed in the myths of American history; they carry the metaphoric burden of a great dream of freedom—of the expansion of national consciousness into the vast spaces of a continent and the absorption of those spaces into ourselves."[9] By taking his protagonist outside of society and by moving his fiction into myth, Cheever has earned a place in the major tradition of American literature. Through action, image, and allusion he creates a literary, mythic, and cultural context. The Hudson, Concord, Mississippi, Thames, Rhine, Nile, and Ganges mingle in the creative consciousness.

III

In his fiction Cheever presents the symptoms of contemporary anxiety and ennui but only implies the causes. His men suffer from that American inability to make sense out of life that derives from a failure to recognize the unreality of their lives. They are, however, evidently tired of an existence that does not fulfill, of living without imagination. All of their life-pursuits—success, status, sex—ignore reality and are in fact fantasies. Freedom, happiness, achievement, and popularity are illusions. Substance is frittered away through absorption in detail. The suburbanite, above all, dwells in cultural deprivation, in a synthetic environment, with "neither the beauty and serenity of the countryside, the stimulation of the city, nor the stability and sense of community of the small town."[10] Ned has the civilized man's psychic need to rebel against his plastic surroundings and the organized world of logic, reason, and technology. Wanting to escape the familiar routines that have shaped his life, he seeks adventure, freedom, and peace in nature. Filled with euphoria and wanderlust, a need to expend energy and experience a richer mode of response, he wants to re-establish contact with life. "To be embraced and sustained by the light green water was less a pleasure, it seemed, than the resumption of a natural condition" (55). His attempt at renewal is analogous to mythicized sex, "the supreme elixir, the painkiller, the brightly colored pill that would put the spring back into his step, the joy of life in his heart" (66). His swim, moreover, expresses an artistic impulse, the attempt to do something unusual, to create an alternate reality. It illustrates the subconscious knowledge Cheever described in "the Seaside Houses": ". . . we are, as in our dreams we have always known ourselves to be, migrants and wanderers" (180). Neddy's swimming the "quasi-subterranean stream that curved across the county" (55) seems like a movement through the womb-like unconscious, the element of metamorphosis and rebirth.

There is also nostalgia for an old innocence, for the "forest primeval" and the "green breast of the new world." Ned wants to start again, to make a new beginning and would swim nude if he could. His epic swim, like his morning slide down the bannister, is an attempt to slow down the encroachment of age. Youth is, as Cash Bentley in "O Youth and Beauty" believed, the best time—the brightest and most blessed. With a typically American inability to accept imperfection, Ned wants neither to grow old nor to grow up; he regrets lost youth and fading *machismo*. His athletic prowess is his last valuable possession. A return to nature ("In the woods is perpetual youth," according to Emerson, and going to the woods was, to John Muir, "going home") also betokens a return to the "childhood" of America and to a simpler, more "real" existence. Neddy feels the need to believe in the myth of a Golden Age, a legend accepted as fact, and has the optimist's faith that all problems have solutions. Similarly the Lucinda River, like the Northwest Passage, exists, and all he has to do is swim it to make it real. The American, alone with a continent, invents his own environment, a self-sufficient New World of the mind. Leaving the here and now for the bye and bye, the American looks forward to the past and backward to the future. Eighteenth- and nineteenth-century visions of coming possibilities are translated into twentieth-century dreams of past actualities, past visions are accepted as real, present facts are rejected as false. In fine, dream and reality are not reconciled but confused.

In "The Swimmer" the American Dream becomes the creation of one's own reality—the dream of living out one's imagination. In the present the only way to start anew is via the imagination. With the closing of the Frontier, the dreamer-explorer is left with nowhere to go except "passage to more than India," no guide to follow except the Transcendentalist injunction: "Build therefore your own world." Ned shuts exterior malice out of his personal wonderland—a neighborhood Disneyworld sufficient to satisfy a middle-class "capacity for wonder." He creates a myth of private satisfaction to counter a public despair. Though Thomas Merton did not have Neddy's plight in mind, his comment is applicable: "An investigation of the wilderness mystique and of the contrary mystique of exploitation and power reveals the tragic depth of the conflict that now exists in the American mind. . . . Take away the space, the freshness, the rich spontaneity of a wildly flourishing nature, and what will become of the creative pioneer mystique? A pioneer in a suburb is a sick man tormenting himself with projects of virile conquest."[11]

Cheever's story, probably the most important use of the swimming pool in American literature, is an imaginative vision of American reality in its interplay of person and object. (To Cheever's people, of course, the pool is an index of affluence and status.) In Fitzgerald's *The Great Gatsby* the swimming pool is also connected with the protagonist's character and quest.[12] Gatsby and Neddy are the lustrous but naive American fools doomed by time, mortality, and history. Both wish to achieve the transcendent moment when dream and reality are one. But both attempts at transcendence are foiled by transience, water in the pools symbolizing flux and mutability. Neddy's swim, like Gatsby's final plunge, is an encounter with that new world, but one already fallen. The dreamer is betrayed by reality and by his own dream. "The Swimmer," like *Gatsby* ends with a deserted house in a Paradise garden overgrown with weeds. Gatsby's mansion is not only the millionaire's palace with an obscenity scrawled on the steps but also an epitome of Western culture. Neddy's, on the other hand, is the family domicile; it is revelatory, however, to recall that his swim included parties, neighbors, friends, and a mistress, but only casual references to his family, with whom his concern had been as shallow as Rip's with his. Ned suffers a contemporary *Angst;* having spent too much for recognition and success, he cannot face failure. His intended romantic escape from limiting reality moves from exhilaration to exhaustion to a painful confrontation with an inner void: empty house/empty life.

Neddy's personal dilemma has both psychological and cultural roots. His crisis of consciousness is shared by his culture for "The Swimmer" probes a trauma deep in the national character. The story of the American is, like the many adaptations of "Rip Van Winkle," an "unfinished" story still awaiting its "final imaginative re-creation."[13] "The Swimmer" is neither rewriting nor updating of "Rip," any more than "The Enormous Radio" is a modernization of "Young Goodman Brown;" both stories are re-visions of archetypal Americans and situations which link the destiny of characters with the meaning of American history. Like Irving's classic, Cheever's tale endures in the reader's memory with its artistry, its psychological impications, its cultural resonance, and its penetration of the currents of existence. Cheever, moreover, gives the reader many of the rewards of traditional fiction along with the peculiar pleasures of contemporary meta-fiction. There is more in this story about · "How We Live Now" than in any other work of comparable length. Swimming has become a new metaphor for the westering impulse, as walking, trekking, floating, running, riding, fishing, and driving had served other writers. The quest for the real America (if one exists) is again an exploration of inward shores. Neddy's westward swim is into the eternal country of the imagination.

Cheever's characteristic stance, a mixture of apocalypse and celebration, despair with much of the contemporary world along with joy in nature and the imagination, may be seen encapsulated in a passage from "The Country Husband:" "The village hangs, morally and economically, from a thread; but it hangs by its thread in the evening light."[14] *Falconer*, Cheever's prison-novel, a seeming deviation from his usual locale, objectifies dramatically his central idea of confinement. As with Dostoevsky, the prison is an epitome of society, but for Cheever the suburban town itself is a metaphoric prison: "spiritually, financially, we were the prisoners of our environment although if we had enough money we could have flown to some other . . . part of the world."[15] But it is not money that offers escape. As an answer to confinement in suburban artificiality, conformity, and dullness Cheever has offered the imaginative quest for pastoral freedom. His debut-story, "Expelled," projected a Thoreauvian search for a natural alternative for society. And the first story in his first collection, *The Way Some People Live*, proposed swimming as an escape from social pressures. Cheever consistently associates the values of nature and the imagination, simple physical pleasures and dreaming because of their connection with primal reality.

IV

Cheever's aesthetic credo requires that he present not the facts but "the truth;" his role is not that of the historian but that of the storyteller recapitulating "the verities." His novels and stories are, therefore, less a depiction than an expression of his time. The fictions in *Some People, Places, and Things That Will Not Appear in My Next Novel* explicitly concern the writer's problem in rendering modern life in fiction:

> Fiction is art and art is the triumph over chaos (no less) and we can accomplish this only by the most vigilant exercise of choice, but in a world that changes more swiftly than we can perceive there is always the danger that our powers of selection will be mistaken and that the vision we serve will come to nothing. We admire decency and we despise death but even the mountains seems to shift in the space of a night and perhaps the exhibitionist at the corner of Chestnut and Elm streets is more significant

than the lovely women with a bar of sunshine in her hair, putting a fresh piece of cuttlebone in the nightingale's cage. Just let me give you an example of chaos and if you disbelieve me look honestly into your own past and see if you can't find a comparable experience. . . .[16]

The absurd events which he narrates in "The Death of Justina," Cheever claims, could "only have happened in America today." "The Brigadier and the Golf Widow," the first and titular story in the volume containing "The Swimmer," begins: "I would not want to be one of those writers who begin each morning by exclaiming, O Gogol, O Chekhov, O Thackeray and Dickens, what would you have made of a bomb shelter ornamented with four plaster-of-Paris ducks, a birdbath, and three composition gnomes with long beards and red mobcaps?" (1).

"A Miscellany of Characters That Will Not Appear" in his next novel includes, as examples, the pretty girl at the Princeton-Dartmouth Rugby game, all parts for Marlon Brando, all homosexuals, and all alcoholics: "Out they go, male and female, all the lushes; they throw so little true light on the way we live" (*Some*, 169). The narrator of "A Vision of the World," who finds that the externals of life have "the quality of a dream" while his reveries have "the literalness of double-entry bookkeeping" (217), wants "to identify . . . not a chain of facts but an essence . . . to grant [his] dreams, in so incoherent a world, their legitimacy" (218). He finally accepts the world in which he lives as a dream and the dreams he has as real. In Cheever's view, fiction is that intersection of "reality" and the imagination.

With increasing persistence he has commented on the challenges that the American fictionist faces today, suggesting that the "trumped-up" stories of generations of storytellers can never "hope to celebrate a world that lies spread out around us like a bewildering and stupendous dream" (*Some*, 175). In his later work the discernible progress is into more innovative techniques and a bleaker vision. He has moved deeper into the darkness of the American funhouse. Many of his best later stories are self-conscious, reflexive, metafictional. Prose narrative forms, which date from about the same time as explorations of the New World, have always been journeys of discovery: new worlds and new modes of perception and new forms. Fiction is, as Lionel Trilling has said, "a perpetual quest for reality."[17] And for the postmodernist writer who gives new twists to the perennial conflict between ideal and real and to the "modern" concern with illusion, Reality itself is the primary theme.

The success of Cheever's fiction is dependent on his skill in placing fantastic incidents within a plausible context (or, sometimes, conversely) and in juxtaposing Westchester and Wonderland. His work, if read attentively, can alter the way we think about ourselves. Every incident is set within the history of a culture, a country not yet a nation, not quite completed, like the unfinished pyramid on a dollar-bill. He charts the demise of a life-style in a long day's dying. But Cheever sees the present blighted cityscape not as "the ruins of our civilization" but as a construction site, "the temporary encampments and outposts of the civilization that we—you and I—shall build" (*Some*, 3). John Cheever follows in the line of fabulist and mythopoeic writers, participating in the chief business of American fiction: the creation of American Reality. America—and Reality—are composed of change, flux, chaos, contradiction; Reality sometimes seems like a comedy of the Absurd.[18] The American experience has been an existential encounter with the dark territory of a continent, with history, and with the self.

American itself is an absurd creation. Our writers have asked: Is it a place? a people? a fact? a faith? a disease? a nightmare? an idea? a moral condition? To Fitzgerald, France was a land, England a people, America an idea. Brautigan, who like Cheever, always writes about "America" suggests that it is "often only a place in the mind," echoing Emerson's America: "a poem in our eyes." At the conclusion of "Boy in Rome," Cheever has his young American, whose planned return home has been foiled, remembering an old lady in Naples "so long ago, shouting across the water [to a departing ship], 'Blessed are you, blessed are you, you will see America, you will see the New World,' and I knew that large cars and frozen food and hot water were not what she meant. 'Blessed are you, blessed are you,' she kept shouting across the water and I knew that she thought of a place where there are no police with swords and no greedy nobility and no dishonesty and no briberies and no delays and no fear of cold and hunger and war and if all that she imagined was not true, it was a noble idea and that was the main thing" (*Some*, 161–162). From the coast of Europe "across the water" to the unexplored inner shores of America, the cycle begins again: from vision to reality to dream to fiction.

Notes

1. Lewis Nichols, "A Visit with John Cheever," New York *Times*, 5 January 1964, p. 28.

2. "The Swimmer," *The Brigadier and the Golf Widow* (1964; rpt. New York: Bantam Books, 1965), p. 65. Henceforth all parenthetical page references will be to this volume. After completing the present study I discovered that Frederick Bracher had already suggested the "Rip"-parallel. See Cortland F. Auser's citation in "John Cheever's Myth of Man and Time: 'The Swimmer,'" *CEA Critic*, 29 (March 1967), 18–19.

3. This view of Howells is that of George Carrington in *The Immense Complex Drama: The World and Art of the Howells Novel* (Columbus: Ohio State University Press, 1966).

4. Quoted in *Time*, 27 March 1964, p. 67.

5. William Peden, *The American Short Story: Front Line in the National Defense of Literature* (Boston: Houghton Mifflin, 1964), p. 55.

6. Alfred Kazin, "O'Hara, Cheever & Updike," *The New York Review of Books*, 20 (19 April 1973), 16.

7. John W. Aldridge, *The Devil in the Fire: Retrospective Essays on American Literature and Culture 1951-1971* (New York: Harper's Magazine Press, 1972), p. 236.

8. Lynne Waldeland, *John Cheever* (Boston: Twayne, 1979), p. 95.

9. Richard Poirier, *A World Elsewhere: The Place of Style in American Literature* (New York: Oxford University Press, 1966), p. 3.

10. Philip Slater, *The Pursuit of Loneliness: American Culture at the Breaking Point* (Boston: Beacon Press, 1970), p. 9.

11. Thomas Merton, "The Wild Places," *The Center Magazine,* 1, No. 5 (July 1968), 43.

12. See Milton Stern, *The Golden Moment: The Novels of F. Scott Fitzgerald* (Urbana: Univ. of Illinois Press, 1970), pp. 166, 169. One of Cheever's "Metamorphoses" narrates the transformation of a "nymphlike" young woman into a swimming pool.

13. Constance Rourke, *American Humor: A Study of the National Character* (1931; rpt. New York: Doubleday Anchor Books, 1953), p. 181.

14. *The Housebreaker of Shady Hill and Other Stories* (1958; rpt. New York: MacFadden-Bartell, 1961), p. 67.

15. *Falconer* (New York: Knopf, 1977), p. 80. See also John Hersey, "Talk with John Cheever," New York *Times Book Review,* 6 March 1977, pp. 1, 24.

16. *Some People, Places, and Things That Will Not Appear in My Next Novel* (New York: Harper and Brothers, 1961), p. 2. Hereafter cited as *Some* in parenthetical references.

17. Lionel Trilling, *The Liberal Imagination: Essays on Literature and Society* (New York: Doubleday Anchor Books, 1950), p. 206.

18. See Richard B. Hauck, *A Cheerful Nihilism: Confidence and "The Absurd" in American Humorous Fiction* (Bloomington: Indiana Univ. Press, 1971).

The Symptomatic Colors in John Cheever's "The Swimmer"

Nora Calhoun Graves*

A close reading of John Cheever's "The Swimmer,"[1] reveals many angles for study, but an emphasis which proves intriguing is the use of color. Since "The Swimmer" deals primarily and figuratively with water, the chief color is one esthetically and normally associated with water—green with some variants.

The story begins at the Westerhazys' pool. Here the water exhibits "a pale shade of green," fed as it is "by an artesian well with a high iron content" (603). A few lines later Neddy Merrill, the main character, sits "by the green water" (603) as he attempts to strengthen his body by imbibing gin, a temporary solution which adds dimension to his already nagging drinking problem. When Merrill finally succumbs to the spell of the pool, he enjoys his crawl and the feel of the buoyancy "embraced and sustained by the light green water" (604) far less than normal. For at this time the sheerest joy for him would be a swim *au naturel,* a delight temporarily postponed but later executed at the Halloran pool.

Merrill plunges on in his desire to complete a "cross country" via the

*This essay was written specifically for this volume and is published here for the first time with permission of the author. An earlier version appeared in *Notes on Contemporary Literature,* (March 1974).

pools of his shallow, and often surface, acquaintances. The Bunkers' pool showed an unusual extravagance and luxury because of its "sapphire-colored waters" (605).

Continuing on his fruitless and humiliating journey, Neddy cannot go back, actually or even in memory; his mind is even hazy concerning the Westerhazys' pool. He cannot "recall with any clearness the green water" or "the friendly and relaxed voices" (607). At the recreation center, Neddy notices that the pool is commercial and chlorinated—a sharp contrast to the Bunkers' "sapphire water." The commercial taint seems to surface. The Hallorans' pool is quite different. The Hallorans are older and wealthier than most of Neddy's friends. It is appropriate that the waters of their pool are "opaque gold" (608). Neddy's final plunge[2] is in the pool owned by his former mistress, Shirley Adams. There he finds "lighted, cerulean water" (611) but no longer any hospitality or satisfaction. He weeps.

It is interesting to note that even though Cheever uses special shades of green and blue in describing Merrill's aquatic journey,[3] there is the exception already mentioned: the senior Hallorans' pool is "opaque gold." This exception in describing water, however appropriate, might suggest that Cheever has used variants of gold kaleidoscopically and naturally as he describes select people and things.

We discover several illustrations. Neddy, youthfully exuberant, smacked the bronze backside of Aphrodite (603). From the goddess to Shirley Adams is a long way but Shirley is described as having brass colored hair (611). One of the guests at the Bunkers' party, not socializing but drifting in the pool, was Rusty Towers (605). The word rusty is repeated at the end of the story in regard to the rusty handles on the garage door (612). Neddy noticed too that the "beech hedge was yellow" (608). Variants of gold are mentioned not only explicitly but also suggestively. As Neddy left Shirley Adams' home, there is perhaps meaning in his smelling chrysanthemums and marigolds.

One may conjure suggestive colors from the reference to "flowering apple trees" which bordered the Westerhazys' and the Grahams' property (604) as well as from the reference to Mrs. Hammer among "her roses." In addition there are splashes of color which Cheever uses: "a green tube for the NEW YORK TIMES," a circling, cavorting "red de Haviland trainer" (605) and a naked maple tree divested of its "red and yellow leaves" which are now settled in the grass and in the water (606).

Even though shades of gold, bronze, rust, and yellow figure prominently and other colors are mentioned and suggested, the dominant color Cheever uses is one normally connected with water: the color of green and its variants of sapphire and cerulean, but the array of colors, delicate and soft, daring and flamboyant, garish and somber, have sketched the life of Neddy Merrill as he lived in the past and as he exists in the present.

When Neddy Merrill, showing stages of exuberance then exhaustion, has completed his cross country swim, his triumph was shallow and worthless; he discovered a dark, locked house, a dangling rain gutter and rusty handles on locked garage doors. Home was as empty as he. In effect, the color range from green to gold, with a splash of red, suggests the vigor and enthusiasm of Merrill's untamed extravagancies prior to his contamination and finally illustrates his growing insensitivity and his personal erosion which led to his loss of family and home—a condition which mere "swims" cannot lave or a loss of memory re-create.

Notes

1. John Cheever, "The Swimmer," in *The Stories of John Cheever* (New York: Alfred A. Knopf, 1978), pp. 603–612. Subsequent references are parenthetically indicated. My first discussion of this work appeared in NCL, IV, No. 2 (March 1974), 4–5. My present revision is contributed by permission.

2. Although Merrill had two more pools to swim, his debilatory condition necessitated his "hobbled sidestroke" in the Gilmartins' pool and a paddle stroke in the Clydes' pool.

3. The watery journey included fifteen actual pools; one pool was dry, the Welchers' pool.

Cheever and Hawthorne: The American Romancer's Art

Samuel Coale*

> Looking back at the village we might put ourselves into the shoes of a native son (with a wife and family in Cleveland) coming home for some purpose—a legacy or a set of Hawthorne . . .
>
> *The Wapshot Chronicle*

When on 9 September 1979 at the MacDowell Colony in Peterborough, New Hampshire, John Cheever became the twentieth recipient of the Edward MacDowell Medal, annually given for "outstanding contribution to the arts," Elizabeth Hardwick, in the principal speech in honor of the occasion, observed that in re-reading many of Cheever's stories, "I began to see some kind of symbolic approach closer to Hawthorne than to, say, Fitzgerald whom he once might have reminded us of."[1] Cheever has always been too easily aligned with *The New Yorker* "school" of writers, to that clutch of novelists of suburban manners, such as John O'Hara and J. P. Marquand, and only recently have critics and scholars begun to see in his work something far greater than was at first apparent. The comparison with Hawthorne and his "symbolic approach" to literature is precisely where a reassessment of Cheever's work should begin.

*This essay was written specifically for this volume and is published here for the first time with permission of the author.

Hawthorne was, to say the least, a trail-blazer in American literature in terms of his creation of psychological romance. Puritanism itself provided the background of Hawthorne's interest, and in the more secular world of the nineteenth century, when the existence of God himself was beginning to be questioned—let alone the prior existence of a divine design carefully crafted—the power of Evil and the power of Light seemed to break free in their own dualistic duel from any thought of or belief in reconciliation and fusion. Hawthorne's great contribution to American literature was to internalize the warring opposites of the degenerate Puritan faith into the individual human psyche.

Hawthorne's is an essentially Manichean vision founded on or reduced to certain psychological truths. The battle between darkness and light or the interpenetration of each occurs first in the depths of the self before recurring in the outward realm of society and history. Such a vision produces a fictional form of episodic tableaux, within which the self exists *in extremis:* "The mind's positioning is the poetic action . . . of the individual in his isolated present moment trying to interpret the immediate by a direct reference to the eternal."[2]

In all of Hawthorne's romances, the reader is always aware of the distance between the narrator and his story, whether the voice is Hawthorne's in *The Scarlet Letter, The House of the Seven Gables*, and *The Marble Faun,* or Coverdale's in *The Blithedale Romance.* The narrator is immediately present as a personal voice exploring his own material. He may use allegory, myth, Christian morality, whatever as devices or interpretations that deal with the material at hand. The reader is supposed to join the narrator in this process of investigation. Hawthorne suggests many allegorical interpretations of a single scene—and after all, the process of allegory was "sanctioned by his literary culture"[3]—in order to arrive at some ultimate significance, and in doing so consciously involves his reader in that process. The tone he achieves in his style, according to Hoffman, remains

> both detached and committed, both amused and serious, both dubious and affirmative. Its commitment, seriousness, and affirmation, however, all point to something other than the literal context of its assertions; toward that the style indicates detachment, amused tolerance, dubiety. What is seriously affirmed is that something was signified . . . a multiple truth larger than either of the partial truths . . . the world of fact is an hieroglyph of the spirit, and the language of the spirit is beyond the capacity of either unassisted belief or unassisted reason to read aright.[4]

The themes, form, style, and vision of John Cheever's fiction reflects Hawthorne's. The Manichean pattern and theme can be seen in Cheever's use of two brothers as alternative visions of reality in his short stories and in all of his novels. Cheever's characters often view themselves as shaped by the social demands of their environment, whereas Cheever, in his fragmentary plotting and episodic structure, undermines this superficial "suburban gloss," reduces suburbia to a state of mind, and thereby presents it as one more psychological projection of man in an infinite state of flux. If his characters feel that they are products of an infinite network of social obligations, status-seeking, money-making, and object-consuming, Cheever reveals them as trapped in certain psychological states, bordering on the traditional patterns of Puritan guilt and evil. In such a realm reality easily slips between the visible physical world and the dream world, between suburban splendors and nightmarish visions, and Cheever's episodic structure emphasizes exactly that. In most of his fiction Cheever's own personal voice and style are apparent as he himself considers his characters and the world around them; he relies less on allegory, more on mythic allusions, Christian symbols, and Biblical references, but the distance between himself and his tale emphasizes his consideration of it and our complicity in that consideration. Finally Cheever's acknowledgement that, in his New England boyhood in Quincy, Massachusetts, Calvin's "presence seemed to abide in the barns of my childhood and to have left me with some undue bitterness," reflects Hawthorne's own Puritan conflicts.

Cheever's use of two apparently different brothers in his fiction to express opposite visions of reality can be explored in biographical, psychological, thematic, and structural terms. Cheever's own brother, Frederick, who was seven years older and who died an alcoholic, became in Cheever's eyes "the strongest love of my life."[5] After his expulsion at seventeen from Thayer Academy, Cheever went to live with his brother Frederick in Boston, and they both took a walking tour of Germany in the summer of 1929. Cheever has admitted to fantasizing about killing his brother at times and that, perhaps because of their father's desertion of the family, there grew up between them "an unseemly closeness";[6] theirs was in effect "a Siamese situation."[7] He relied upon his brother before striking out on his own and going to New York during the Depression to write.

In the short story, "The Brothers" (1937), Cheever writes about Tom and Kenneth Manchester, two brothers who have sought each other out after the divorce of their parents. They cling to this intense affection "as if sharing it with others would be some betrayal of their pleasure." The collapse of their family "brought the brothers still closer together . . . cherishing their habitual round, their aimless comings and goings, the little certainty they had rescued from the wreck of their home." They both have an extremely intense appreciation of family and place, of "the familiar hills" that now seem desolate but hardy in the autumn of "the New England of their fathers."

Finally Tom realizes that their own present refuge in each other cannot continue: "It was the first time it had occurred to Tom that their devotion to each other might be stronger than their love of any girl or even than their love of the world." He realizes that theirs is "a love that held no jealousy and no fear and no increase," that their mutual devotion might deform them and turn their sanctuary into some place of sterile affection. Consequently Tom decides to move to New York.

On "one of the first great nights of autumn [when] the wind tasted of winter and of the season's end and moved in the trees with the noise of a conflagration," Kenneth "felt the pain that Tom had brought down on both of them without any indignation; they had tried to give their lives some meaning and order, and for love of the same world that had driven them together, they had had to separate." He is left "like a stranger at the new, strange, vivid world." Maturity, the recognition of separate selves, the interposition of sexual completion and need, all have emerged to sever the boyhood refuge and brotherly closeness. A deep sense of loss and loneliness accompanies the necessary split. It is a loss that most Cheever characters carry with them and that can never be healed.

In "The Lowboy" (1959) and especially in "Goodbye, My Brother" (1951) the psychological split between brothers widens. In allegorical fashion one brother expresses a love of natural beauty, an appreciation of humanitarian values and social/religious ceremonies, and reveals an enlightened spirit and a sense of decorum and grace. The other gloats on the decay and ugliness of the world, embodied as they seem to be in a brutalized materialism and his own rootless selfishness, and on the forces of destruction which can undermine all illusions of decorum and grace. In "The Lowboy" the "bad" brother, Richard Norton, radiates the "aura of smallness" and selfishness of the "spoiled child." He has risen from a sad and chaotic past "into a dazzling and resplendent respectability," which he wishes to maintain at all times. He insists on having the lowboy which the narrator, the "good" brother, at first wishes to have, since it is a family heirloom. Richard demands it; the narrator surrenders it. Richard takes it home and sets it up exactly as it had been in the family, complete with silver bowl "on its carpet of mysterious symbols."

Richard's "wayward attachment" to the lowboy, however, transforms him. In the narrator's mind, because it is linked to a chaotic and sorrowful family past, "the fascination of the lowboy was the fascination of pain." Richard becomes quarrelsome and argumentative. The narrator, noting the transformation that has taken place—"Oh, why is it that life is for some an exquisite privilege and others must pay for their seats at the play with a ransom of cholers, infections, and nightmares?"—returns home to smash all the family heirlooms that remain and exclaims: "We can cherish nothing less than our random understanding of death and the earth-shaking love that draws us to one another. . . . Cleanliness and valor will be our watchwords. Nothing less will get us past the armed sentry and over the mountainous border."

At first the psychological conflict is clear: Richard views life in its darker terms, having "committed himself to the horrors of the past"; the narrator delights in the "green-gold" light of a spring day: "It was astounding in its beauty, and seemed . . . a link in a long chain of leafy trees beginning in childhold." And yet it is the narrator after all who tells the story, who seems entranced by his brother's darker visions. It is the narrator who conjures up the entire nightmare vision in his story of family ghosts returned on a dark and rainy night to observe the lowboy in Richard's house. It is the narrator who evokes the drunks and the suicides and the cripples in his family tree and confines Richard's position "to observation." Even on that burgeoning spring day the narrator admits "it was the shadow that was most mysterious and exciting, the light one could not define." His tale of his brother's transgressions is in effect his own personal exorcism; the "dark" brother becomes a psychological projection of his own darker obsessions and his need to triumph over them by proclaiming "cleanliness and valor." His is a vigorous—and as we shall see, stylistic—attempt to get beyond the sentry and the mountains into a realm of light and transcendental vision, and his brother's failure to do so almost assures and is necessary for his own.

The same is true for the marvelously constructed "Goodbye, My Brother." Lawrence Pommeroy conjures up a bigoted and narrow universe, steeped in its own decay and gloom. His world feasts on the same kind of "spiritual cannibalism" that motivated his Puritan ancestors. He reminds the narrator of a "Puritan cleric" with his "habits of guilt, self-denial, taciturnity, and penitence." "His baleful and incisive mind" embodies that Calvinistic New England legacy of "undue bitterness" which resides in Cheever's fiction. The narrator is determined "to trace some moral chain of being." He admires "the harsh surface beauty of life," those "obdurate truths before which fear and horror are powerless," and records his sensuous moments: the roses smelling like strawberry jam, the grapes smelling of wine, the sky filled with "continents of shadow and fire." The Pommeroys gather at their summer house at Laud's Head and more or less systematically run Lawrence out of the family.

And yet once again the narrator admits that he and Lawrence are "very close in spirit." The phrase looks in both directions at once, for it suggests both that they are not really close at all and that they are extremely close. For all his railing against the vestiges of Puritanism in Lawrence, the narrator reads as much "significance and finality into [his] every gesture" as he does in Lawrence's, even though his own he considers blessed and Lawrence's, "sordid." The narrator sees the world in terms of signs, portents, revelations, and religious ceremonies: swimming becomes a ritual baptism, an "illusion of purification" where the family can "shed our animus in the cold water." His use of the word "illusion" suggests that he may suspect the foundations of his own good faith in the beauty of life, and when he goes to meet the summer ferry on the island and discovers that for all its whistles and clangings and smell of brine, it is "a voyage of no import," he realizes all too swiftly that "I had hit on exactly the kind of observation that Lawrence would have made." Throughout the story he ascribes certain dark feelings and thoughts to Lawrence by using such phrases as "it must have occurred to him" or "as if he saw" or "I knew that the buoys . . . would sound to him like half-human, half-drowned cries." As last fed up with Lawrence's gloom, his inability to enjoy himself, his acidic remarks about the family and a party at the club (the men dress up in their old football uniforms, the women in their bridal gowns, for the "come-as-you-wish-you-were" party) the narrator strikes him on the beach with a root. It is a repetition of a similar incident twenty-five years before when the narrator hit his brother with a rock. This visionary Cain strikes out at the Puritanical Abel.

Lawrence, stunned, leaves the Pommeroy clan once and for all. He will not return to Laud's Head for summer vacations. His goodbye is one more in a long series of goodbyes, or so the narrator describes it. For a man intent on denying the reality of Lawrence's gloomy vision, the narrator spends a lot of time re-creating the depth, the imagery and the scope of that vision. But his own lyric appreciation of the world around him triumphs, once the darker brother has been exorcised. The story ends with that lyric vision completely in control, with its poetic rhythms and mythic overtones, but it is a vision which in this case has been earned by the narrator's wrestling with his own Puritan heritage. The last two sentences, re-arranged, can be seen as an effective poem:

> My wife and my sister were swimming
> —Diana and Helen—
> and I saw their uncovered heads,
> black and gold in the dark water.
> I saw them come out
> and I saw that they were naked,
> unshy, beautiful, and full of grace,
> and I watched the naked women
> walk out of the sea.

In Cheever's four novels—or, more accurately, romances—his creation of the two antagonistic brothers becomes not only the major psychological focus but also the major thematic and structural one as well: "A mythology that would penetrate with some light the density of the relationship between brothers seems to stop with Cain and Abel and perhaps this is as it should be." "Mysterious polarities" dictate the major pattern of Cheever's fiction; the darker brother proves to be "one of those figures who stand outside the brightly lighted centers of our consciousness and defeat our love of candor and our confidence in the sweetness of life." Such psychological states, represented by the opposing brothers—a romantic patterning of obsessive, symbolic, and allegorical types, in place of fully realized, well-rounded novelistic characters—reflect Cheever's larger themes, "the clash between night and day, between the head and the groin." As he makes explicit in *The Wapshot Scandal*,

We are born between two states of consciousness; we spend our lives between the darkness and the light, and to climb in the mountains of another country, phrase our thoughts in another language or admire the color of another sky draws us deeper into the mystery of our condition . . . here is a whole new creation of self-knowledge, new images for love and death and the insubstantiality and the importance of our affairs.

Cheever's "condition" clearly reflects the Manichean oppositions of Hawthorn's fiction.

In *The Wapshot Chronicle* and *The Wapshot Scandal* Coverly and Moses Wapshot enact the episodic drama of spirit and flesh. Coverly clearly posses "an alert and sentimental mind"; he is Icarus, "something mysterious and unrestful" to his father Leander; he suffers the extreme rootlessness of the modern age and nostalgically longs for the more traditional (however illusory) confines of St. Botolphs; yet to him is granted "a searing vision of some golden age . . . a vision of life as hearty and fleeting as laughter and something like the terms by which he lived." Moses on the other hand, the more sensual of the brothers, basks in his "judicious and tranquil self-admiration." His "taste for the grain and hair of life" underscores "the kind of good looks and presence that sweeps a young man triumphantly through secondary school and disappointingly enough not much farther." "He was the sort of paterfamilias who inspires sympathy for the libertine," given the frigidity of his own code of decency and his hypocritical philandering when it comes to "sexual commerce." Coverly's awe in the face of life, his appreciation of the beauties of the natural landscape and his own father's sacramental and "unobserved ceremoniousness of his life", and his Christmas dinner for the blind contrast with Moses' petty adulteries with the widow Wilston at the Viaduct House on Christmas Eve and his cynical belief that "the brilliance of light, the birth of Christ, all seemed to him like some fatuous shell game invented to dupe a fool like his brother while he saw straight through into the nothingness of things."

The Coverly-Moses, the enlighted spirit and selfish sensuality conflict, is reproduced in *Falconer*, Cheever's latest novel, in which Ezekiel Farragut, the Coverly brother, accidentally murders his brother Eben: "They looked enough like one another to be taken for twins." Eben is an alcoholic, abusive and cruel; he summons waiters by clapping his hands, and "his marriage could be dismissed, if one were that superficial, as an extraordinary sentimental and erotic collision." Ezekiel, heroin addict and murderer, yet celebrates "the simple phenomenon of light— brightness angling across the air—" which strikes him "as a transcendent piece of good news;" he continually marvels at the "invincible potency of nature" within a ceremonial sense of traditional religion and form. Ezekiel strikes Eben with a fire iron, when Eben exclaims that their father really wanted to have their mother have an abortion and prevent

Ezekiel's birth. Ezekiel's dark night of the soul comes to an end when he hides himself in the burial sack of the dead prisoner Chicken and manages to be re-born into freedom.

Cheever's most apocalyptic and allegorical brothers are not brothers at all, yet they represent most clearly the conflict between social order and decency and individual chaos and dark dreams. In *Bullet Park* Eliot Nailles represents the perfect suburbanite, assured of his own sense of duty and decency, having "less dimension than a comic strip" in his solidly monogamous relationship with Nellie, viewing his love for his wife and son Tony as "a clear amber fluid that would surround them, cover them, preserve them and leave them insulated but visible like the contents of an aspic." He "thought of pain and suffering as a principality, lying somewhere beyond the legitimate borders of western Europe." His fragile suburban insulation is first threatened by Tony's spiritual paralysis— "There is a tendency in your income group to substitute possessions for moral and spiritual norms. A strict sense of good and evil, even if it is mistaken, is better than none"—and by Paul Hammer's kidnapping and attempted crucifixion of his son. Hammer, Nailles's nemesis—Nailles believes in "the mysterious power of nomenclature . . . nothing short of death could separate John and Mary. How much worse was Hammer and Nailles"—is an illegitimate child; his very existence is already "a threat to organized change." He's a creature of his own mysterious dreams and believes that "the nature of man was terrifying and singular and man's environment was chaos." Moral prerogatives and duties appear to him as no more sturdy than a fragile kite string in the wind. He threatens "whole artificial structures of acceptable reality," such as Nailles's suburban existence, sees no genuine emotion or value in Nailles's existence whatsoever, listens to his mother's railing against the selfishness and vacuousness of American civilization—"Never, in the history of civilization, has one seen a great nation singlemindedly bent on drugging itself"—and decides that he will crucify Tony Nailles to "wake that world."

If Cheever's Manichean characters represent the warring factions within the human heart—"the human heart in conflict with itself" is how Faulkner described his subject—they also serve as the structural polarities of the basic form of American romance, which Cheever re-creates. The realm of Cheever's world exists, like Hawthorne's, somewhere between the actual and imaginary realms of human experience: Cheever's St. Botolphs, Bullet Park and Falconer Correctional Facility reflect certain states of mind—states of spiritual confinement and nostalgic and moral commitments—which are both conjured up and shattered. Both Hawthorne and Cheever create romances of disenchantment which contain momentary glimpses or "spells" of celebration and communal vision. Both romancers are more interested in concentrating on the nature of men's motives and desires in their creation of stylized characters, in determining "to trace some moral chain of being" within the universe or in man's experience of it, than in re-creating the social environment and carefully observed manners of the literary realist. Cheever's observation of suburban manners often reflect his concern with moral duty and choice, but in many cases the manners are themselves responsible for the lack of moral choice in their practitioners. Finally both Hawthorne and Cheever rely upon a variety of forms in which to spin their tales—allegories (most insistent in Hawthorne's case, obviously), myths, legends, psychological fantasies, dreams—thus opening up the experience of their characters, beyond the "social reality" of day-to-day life. And each relies on a series of emblematic episodes to reveal his vision.

In the opening paragraph of *The House of the Seven Gables* Hawthorne at once establishes his setting, his mood, and his relationship with the reader. The romantic spell is at once conjured up. The setting is an old New England town, steeped in age and shadows from the past. The meditative mood implicitly reveals the strong and mysterious influences of the past upon the present, thus creating an atmospheric medium of mellow lights and shadows unlike the broad daylight world of realistic novels. Hawthorne's old Pyncheon house, "rusty," "huge," and "weather-beaten," suggests the romantic precincts of old castles and mouldering ruins. At the same time Hawthorne consciously includes the reader in his created spell, speaking of "*our* New England towns" and revealing immediately the effect of the old house on him during "*my* occasional visits to the town aforesaid." He at once elicits the reader's sympathies and includes him in his own quest toward "tracking down" the mysteries hidden in the old house. The reference to "antiquities" promotes a certain nostalgia for the shadowy past as well, a fascination with long-ago times and dream-like, legend-haunted landscapes.

Cheever conjures up St. Botolphs in *The Wapshot Chronicle* and *The Wapshot Scandal* in similar fashion. St. Botolphs is "an old place, an old river town." It exudes "an aroma of the past" and suggests "an impression of unusual permanence" on its green. The snow falling on Christmas Eve in the opening paragraph of *The Wapshot Scandal* exhilarates and refreshes old Mr. Jowett, the stationmaster "and drew him—full-souled, it seemed—out of his carapace of worry and indigestion." The snow's "whiteness seems to be a part of our dreams." Setting and mood compliment Hawthorne's own, and Cheever immediately includes the reader in "*our* dreams."

The differences between Hawthorne's and Cheever's opening paragraphs, however, are more immediately apparent. With every reference to the "then" of the past and the impression of permanence which only seems permanent, Cheever immediately drops his reader into the "now" of the modern world. Cheever's mood of romance appears far more fragile than Hawthorne's: burdened with nostalgia for a lost Eden that may or may not have existed, Cheever's characters—and readers—are swiftly made aware of the discrepancy between human yearning and the realities of modern guilt, rootlessness, and disconnection. Thus if St. Botolphs was once a great inland port, now it displays only a table silver factory. Windows that first strike one "as delicate and reproachful as the windows of a church," are in reality looking out from a dentist's office and an insurance agent's office. St. Botolphs now looks prosperous only when an Independence Day parade is forming. Similarly old Mr. Jowett is singing "Oh, Who Put the Overalls in Mrs. Murphy's Chowder" on Christmas Eve, "although he knew it was all wrong for the season, the day and dignity of a station agent, the steward of the town's true and ancient boundary, its Gates of Hercules." That last Herculean image appears both ironic and romantic, at once part of Mr. Jowett's own self-inflation and Cheever's comic exaggeration, and as part of a genuine conjuring up of an old New England village on the snowy, legendary eve of Christmas.

In Cheever's four romances Cheever's own creation of suspended, enchanted moments at the beginning of each book grows less and less romantic. St. Botolphs in *The Wapshot Chronicle* is presented in a full-bodied, historical manner: the village exists in the "real world" just as he describes it. In *The Wapshot Scandal*, however, Cheever announces his own separation from the Wapshots and their world: "It was always in their power to make me feel alone, to make it painfully clear that I was an outsider." By the end of the novel he announces his decision never to return to St. Botolphs again, and the village itself dissolves into "nothing at all." By the time of *Bullet Park* the mood of the opening paragraph has become far more plaintive and somber, and the romantic reverie is now clearly a solitary thing: "Paint *me* a small railroad station. . . ." The setting is still "at the heart of the matter," the reader is still included in the reverie—"*You* wake in a pullman. . . . *We* travel by plane . . ."—and "your country" still suggests that strange, romantic aura—"unique, mysterious, vast"—but the world looks lonely and empty, a place of weary travellers coming and going. "The spirit of our country seems to have remained a country of railroads," and although that spirit is not entirely rootless and transient, "a somber afterglow" permeates the opening of the novel.

Finally, in the opening paragraph of *Falconer*, Cheever seems to have done away with the aura of romance altogether. His concentration upon the escutcheon over the main entrance to the prison, with its fatalistic and lethal images of arrows, swords, blindness, and pikes, leads him to dwell on this "last emblem" the prisoners will see before they go to their separate cells. That emblem suggests to him "man's endeavor to interpret the mystery of imprisonment in terms of symbols." Cheever's distance from his emblem, his more or less objective description of it, drained of much of the romantic and legendary aura of his first three novels, reminds us in tone of Hawthorne's opening scene in *The Scarlet Letter* and of the opening paragraph in *The Marble Faun*. He too is observing his own creation more removed from the realm of mystery and romance, when he spies "the pretty figure of a child, clasping a dove to her bosom, but assaulted by a snake" and views it in stark allegorical terms as "a symbol . . . of the Human Soul, with its choice of Innocence or Evil close at hand." Both writers seek refuge in an immediate emblematic statement, though Cheever's still suggests an ultimate "mystery"—the true province of romance, perhaps—in place of Hawthorne's unrelenting allegorical interpretation.

Both writers create a dream texture in their tales, suggesting that "reality" exists in some "neutral territory" between the visible, physical world and the interior, imaginary one. Cheever suggests that "the mind itself is such a huge and labyrinthine chamber that the Pantheon and the Acropolis turn out to be smaller than we had expected." Man is indeed "a microcosm, containing within himself all the parts of the universe. . . . The distillations and transmutations release their innate power." More explicitly he describes St. Botolphs as "a place whose streets were as excursive and crooked as the human mind."

All Cheever's romances—and many of his best short stories—are crammed with dreams, nightmares, reveries, memories, omens, spells, and epiphanies. Consciousness invests everything with a nagging, ghostly uncertainty: visions undermine the explicit codes of suburban manners. Transformations suddenly occur. The social environment becomes not a strait-jacket of independent rules and regulations but a state of mind, forever shifting and shimmering, in no way as permanent and exclusive as the inmates of Shady Hill and Proxmire Manor would have it. The world becomes "something mysterious and unrestful," a bewildering dreamscape of loneliness and rootlessness. Reality becomes "no more inviolable than the doors and windows that sheltered her." Even morality may become a fragile manner "influenced by landscapes and kinds of food." Rites and ceremonies tremble and shudder in a world where "total disaster seemed to be some part of the universal imagination." A primordial chaos threatens everything. Tony Nailles can only be "rescued" by a mysterious Swami who regards himself as a "spiritual cheerleader" and chants his litanies, which appear as artificial yet as mesmerizing as a game of Grandmother's trunk or an adolescent's howl damning the suburban world. The world embodies "the landscape for some nightmare or battlefield" in which old men sell "phallic symbols and death's heads." Only in *Falconer* does Ezekiel Farragut, if only momentarily, break free of a dark, imprisoned world and rejoice at the genuine revelation of light.

Critics have often argued about the episodic nature of Cheever's longer fictions, viewing them as clumsy attempts to stitch together random short stories and odd bits and pieces culled from the imagination of a writer, essentially, of short stories. In fact such episodic notation mirrors the emblematic form of the romance that Hawthorne employed. Hawthorne's persistent use of allegorical symbolism in Cheever's fiction is often replaced by Cheever's similar use of the manners and mores of suburbia: both conventions help tie the various episodes and fragments together. Each episode in a Cheever book can be seen as an emblem of the entire theme and vision of the book: each incident repeats, comments upon or embroiders the basic vision or situation of Cheever's fictional world. The experience of loneliness, isolation, nostalgia, moral conflicts with good and evil surface in each of Cheever's separate events. His plots are not so much incremental as spasmodic, dreamlike (thus matching the dreamlike texture of his tales), and quirky. These fragments reflect the actual modern experience of characters' lives and help to break up and subvert the cocoon of manners and illusions of suburban permanence these people seek refuge in.

Cheever's novels of manners are actually romances in search of modern man's moral identity, and the wild and wonderful nature of his eccentric episodes, the mingling of the marvelous and the actual, reveal the psychological complexities of a fragmented world. Truth may lie "at the center of the labyrinthine and palatial structures" of Cheever's quixotic plots and that truth may be the acknowledgment that all events in modern life seem to take "such eccentric curves that it was difficult to comprehend." In each episode the self *in extremis*, however comically rendered, resembles Hawthorne's allegorical scaffold scenes in *The Scarlet Letter*: monologue may replace emblem, but the intent and effect remain the same.

Hawthorne's personal voice as authorial intruder occupies all his romances: the reader is ushered into exploring his fictional material with him. The same is true with Cheever. When Hoffman described Hawthorne's style as "both detached and committed, both amused and serious, both dubious and affirmative,"[8] he could just as easily have been describing Cheever's. And when he suggests that the style, whether affirming or denying, points "to something other than the literal context of its assertions," the same can be said of Cheever's. In relying on allegorical signs, Hawthorne suggests both multiple significances and the possibility that there may ultimately be no significance at all. In comparing the "fabled then" of our nostalgic American heritage and the "prosaic now" of our contemporary American experience, Cheever uses all kinds of allegorical, mythic, legendary, Christian images and yet suggests that all may be ultimately chaotic and empty. "Nothing at all" remains in *The Wapshot Scandal*; Eliot Nailles goes off to work wonderfully drugged at the end of *Bullet Park*, suggesting that no matter how decent and decorous suburbia may be it cannot handle or deal with real suffering; only in *Falconer* does Ezekiel Farragut rejoice, his love of light carefully supported by traditional Christian imagery and ritual. In *The Wapshot Chronicle* Leander Wapshot's earthy, ceremonious love of natural beauty and rites of human passage, circumscribed carefully by the often eccentric traditions and habits of an old New England village, helps see Coverly through, and even though Farragut views his Wapshot-like family unsparingly without the soft focus of sentiment and legend—they "were the sort of people who claimed to be sustained by tradition, but who were in fact sustained by the much more robust pursuit of a workable improvisation, uninhibited by consistency"—he yet admires their "pure, crude and lasting sense of perseverance."

Cheever consistently plays off romantic images against more mundane ones. His texts are filled with heraldic, archaic, Biblical, abstract moral images connected with fables and myths and old traditions against which are juxtaposed the common, ordinary images of everyday existence. The style therefore reflects in its "distilled dissolution," in its constant downward movement "from fable to floor,"[9] the over-all vision of decay and collapse, the experience of disenchantment, which underlies all of Cheever's fiction. As Hawthorne suggests in *The House of the Seven Gables*:

> . . . if we look through all the heroic fortunes of mankind, we shall find this same entanglement of something mean and trivial with whatever is noblest in joy or sorrow. Life is made up of marble and mud. . . . What is called poetic insight is the gift of discerning in the sphere of strangely mingled elements, the beauty and the majesty which are compelled to assume a garb so sordid.

One should explore more precisely the tone of Cheever's style. If the style of the American psychological romance often reaches the intensity of poetry (one thinks most often of Faulkner), if it strives to achieve a heightened consciousness with exaggerated effects and reveals a fascination for an atmosphere of mystery, of light and dark, and mixes the marvelous and legendary with the mundane and ordinary, then Cheever's style matches that of the romance. It is his tone, however, that is very different from other romancers' styles.

Cheever believes that decorum is "a mode of speech." His lucid, careful language reflects a certain propriety of behavior and observance of "good manners" which in no way reflects the over-heated, zealous prose of a Faulkner. His is similar to the neoclassic sense of propriety and "rightness," the same cool, even-tempered prose style that suggests in its tone Hawthorne's. Cheever's tone at all times is dignified, formal (one constantly must recognize how, in many ways, *Falconer* is both a stylistic and thematic breakthrough in Cheever's fiction) and sharp-eyed: he seems determined to maintain a stoical sense of duty in the face of any disaster or nightmare.

The reader is as constantly aware of Cheever's handling and shaping his material to find revelation in it as he is of Hawthorne's. But Cheever's coolly controlled prose achieves a comic tone that Hawthorne's usually does not. Cheever maintains a comic distance toward present chaos in a mock-heroic manner. Episodes such as the apocalyptic Easter egg hunt in

The Wapshot Scandal, the discovery of Coverly's possible homosexuality in *The Wapshot Chronicle*, the tribal rites and passions of suburbia in *Bullet Park*, and the rigors of prison life in *Falconer* share this careful blend of human desire, frustration, and that gentle comic distance and observation that make us laugh at our human foibles.

Cheever's laughter is a gentle one, a sympathetic one, for his characters, trapped in their own images of suburban convention and social regulation, often are trying to re-capture and portray whatever shred of dignity and decorum they can muster. Cheever approves of their attempts, however foolish, sympathizes with their failures, however self-generated, and mocks them for their hankering after objects and status and the last refuge of the scoundrel, respectability; his style alerts us to his own decorum in the light of contemporary confusions, to his characters' gropings toward some vision of the same light, and to the dark awareness that the strength of their yearning may produce nothing finally but fragmented fury and a wistful, misplaced ideal of a lost sanctuary.

In many ways Cheever's style contradicts the fragmented and episodic structure of his romances and short stories. His decorous tone, which can be mistaken for the glossy finish of suburban conventions in those tales seemingly mesmerized by the comfortable crises of *New Yorker* fictions, is often the result of a lyric and graceful repetition of images and objects; his plots, which reveal modern psychological existence as essentially chaotic and disconnected, are the results of the romancer's technique and vision that is intent upon breaking through the public display of social conventions and peering more deeply into the nature of man in both his moral and psychological dimensions. When style and plot seem too much at war with one another, then Cheever does seem to be engaged in the "soft sell of disaster,"[10] of not taking the very visions he conjures up seriously enough. His best tales are perhaps those in which the lyric style and lyric vision complement one another, or in which dream, meditations and digressions open up the surface of the tale and allow for Cheever as author and as involved participant in the story to "think out loud" about the ramifications of his art, his search for a moral chain of being, and his pursuit of a lasting, recognizable vision. "The World of Apples" and "Angel of the Bridge" suggest the first kind of tale, as do the epiphanies within the romances; "The Death of Justina" suggests the latter.

The story of "The Death of Justina" is a comic one in which suburban conventions conflict with higher, more necessary duties. The narrator's wife's old cousin, Justina, expires in her chair after lunch. The narrator lives in Zone B of Proxmire Manor: no one can be moved or buried there; Zone B doesn't recognize death. Proxmire Manor has excluded it from its glossy suburban precincts. The narrator finally makes a deal with the mayor, and Justina is finally buried in a place like a dump to which the dead "are transported furtively as knaves and scoundrels and where they lie in an atmosphere of perfect neglect."

The vision of "The Death of Justina" embraces a wider territory. Cheever observes the American landscape of a "half-finished civilization," seeing only "utter desolation"; Proxmire Manor exists as a sanctuary in a wasteland, where the homes of friends are "all lighted and smelling of fragrant wood smoke like the temples in a sacred grove, dedicated to monogamy, feckless childhood, and domestic bliss but so like a dream." Americans seem atrophied in consumerism, relying upon Elixircol tonic to rid them of all maladies, victims of apocalyptic commercialism in the narrator's dream of a strange supermarket. In this modern American scene disappointment exists everywhere; a "terrifying bitterness" stares out of the "anthracite eyes" of a melting snowman on the hill. The narrator momentarily surrenders to the nostalgic image of his grandmother and sleigh bells, when in fact she worked as a hostess on an ocean liner before her death. The realization of death hovers in the air, in Justina's sudden demise, in the narrator's forced surrender of smoking and drinking. Elixircol will not rout it, nor will Justina's undertakers who mask the reality of death with "a violet-flavored kiss. . . . How can a people who do not mean to understand death hope to understand love, and who will sound the alarm?" And finally even the efficacy of art itself is doubted: certainly "fiction is art and art is the triumph over chaos (no less), and we can accomplish this only by the most vigilant exercise of choice, but in a world that changes more swiftly that we can perceive there is always the danger that our powers of selection will be mistaken and that the vision we serve will come to nothing." Cheever admires decency and despises death, but in the world of "Justina," can this be enough?

In the course of the story Cheever relies upon mediations, dreams, memories, visions, digressions, and Biblical quotations to express the various dimensions of his concerns, his questions about modern suburban morality, consumerism, our recognition of the fact of death, our psychological disconnection and uncertainty. The tale opens with Cheever's own meditations on the nature of his art. This is followed by the narrator's meditations on the state of his health, on the conventions of his social environment—"death is not the threat that scandal is"—and on his own unsettling ideas and dreams, that the soul lingers in the body after death and that he sees a face in his English muffin, "a pure force of gentleness and censure." The concerns between Cheever and the narrator are obviously similar, but the narrator is more specifically a product of his social milieu, and Cheever is standing outside and above that milieu, raising the wider question of chaos and change and its effect upon us and art in general.

The narrator's return to Proxmire Manor is acknowledged as "a digression and has no real connection to Justina's death but what followed could only have happened in my country and in my time and since I was an American traveling across an American landscape the trip may be part of the sum." No "real connection" perhaps in terms of the bare bones of the plot or fuller body of social conventions but connected of course to the very essence of Cheever's vision of art, death, and the American psyche. Cheever parodies the slick television commercials for Elixircol and replaces the final one, which the narrator must write, with the complete Twenty-third psalm: in that tight, succinct litany of faith must come man's true acknowledgment of need and the dispelling of his own grief. For the vision of the apocalyptic supermarket, a scene of nightmarish guilt drowning in darkness, Cheever creates a dream, at first beyond the scope of and disconnected from the fact of Justina's death, yet again another dimension of his vision. This strange scene, which Cheever describes as "the strangeness of a dream where we see familiar objects in a unfamiliar light," suggests one more emblematic encounter with Cheever's vision of loneliness, moral blight and eventual death.

All these various forms—dreams, meditations, authorial intrusions, digressions—are the romancer's stock in trade, his mingling of the marvelous and mundane, his fictional "tricks" to open up the placidly seeming world of Proxmire Manor and reveal the psychological interior of man's distressed and discordant soul. Justina's death becomes the object of these fantasies and hallucinatory asides. It suggests the fanciful delight Hawthorne takes circling the corpse of Judge Pyncheon. Stunned by the fact of death, Cheever weaves his tale out of the fabrics of romance and swells his vision of contemporary disenchantment.

Both Hawthorn and Cheever share the similar literary tradition of the American romance, as fashioned by Hawthorne. They share the basic elements of the romance form in general: the stylized characters, the atmospherics, the elements of prophecy and transformation, allegorical patterns, perilous journeys, "a penchant for the marvelous," the use of legends, myths, and fables as stylized patterns to "get at" the mysterious roots of human motive and desire. Cheever shares with Hawthorne the particular form of the American psychological romance as well, in which the self, not society or social forces, stands at the center of the fictional realm, marked as it is by the distinctly Manichean conflict between good and evil, light and darkness, both of these as equal and ominous combatants, both at times hopelessly intermingled and confused. Both Hawthorne and Cheever create fictions mixing dreams and actuality, creating that psychological landscape of mind and matter which the isolated self occupies. Their episodic structure reflects the emblematic quality of incidents and images; these become miniature epiphanies of an entire theme or vision. Both authors visibly explore their own material, either from Hawthorne's more tragic or Cheever's more comic perspective, creating their own distance from it in order expressly to invite the reader to join them in their quest. Finally Cheever's fiction—and the fiction of John Gardner, John Updike, Flannery O'Connor, William Faulkner, William Styron, Paul Theroux, to name just a few—reflects and extends Hawthorne's form of the psychological romance in modern American fiction. That form continues to thrive and expand. Hawthorne's exploratory and successful work has not been in vain.

Notes

1. Elizabeth Hardwick, quoted by Michiko Kakutami, "In a Cheever-Like Setting, John Cheever Gets MacDowell Medal," *The New York Times*, 11 September 1979, p. C7.

2. John F. Lynen, *The Design of the Present: Essays on Time and Form in American Literature* (New Haven: Yale, 1969), pp. 76, 31.

3. Daniel Hoffman, *Form and Fable in American Fiction* (New York: Oxford University Press, 1961), pp. 173–4; Cited below as Hoffman.

4. Hoffman, pp. 173–4.

5. John Cheever, quoted by Jesse Kornbluth, "The Cheever Chronicle," *The New York Times*, 21 October 1979, p. 29; Cited below as Kornbluth.

6. Kornbluth, p. 103.

7. John Cheever, quoted by Samuel Coale, *John Cheever* (New York: Frederick Ungar, 1977), p. 3.

8. Hoffman, p. 173.

9. Beatrice Greene, "Icarus at St. Botolphs: A Descent to 'Unwanted Otherness,' " *Style*, Vol. 5, 1971, pp. 120, 123.

10. John W. Aldridge, "John Cheever and the Soft Sell of Disaster" in *Time to Murder and Create* (New York: David McKay, 1966).

John Cheever and the Promise of Pastoral

Frederick R. Karl*

In both his short and longer fiction, John Cheever has taken on a major American theme, that of the persistence and, ultimately, the failure of pastoral. Although we associate pastoral chiefly with nineteenth-century writers—Emerson, Thoreau, Hawthorne, Whitman, Melville—it is no less insistent a force in postwar fiction, having become, if anything, more ambiguous. Whereas earlier it might have been perceived as a form of salvation, now it is wrapped in irony, paradox, irresolvable conflict. Like so many of his contemporaries, Cheever, in the two Wapshot books, boldly challenged the pastoral theme, only to find by the time of *Bullet Park* and *Falconer* that pastoral is as complicated, even self-defeating as every other idea which the postwar novelist must decipher. The promise of pastoral succumbs to Kafkan enclosure, salvation to burrows.

*This essay was written specifically for this volume and is published here for the first time with permission of the author. Parts of it are based on sections of the author's *American Fictions, 1940–1980*, forthcoming from Harper & Row, 1982.

Whether represented realistically, sentimentally, or fantastically, pastoral has the quality of "ideal realms" implicit in it. Emerson's sense of "angelic use," in which large spaces could join with inner possibilities and poetic imagination, finds its meaning in the pastoral experience. The City of Man and the City of God had to be merged with each other for Emerson, and in that juncture we have the meeting ground of an ever-running American theme, where pastoral allows for the immanence of both, interconnected. Emerson's warning that the individual can destroy himself outside of a context meant he foresaw the dangers of ego-worship and self-indulgence which so characterize our postwar era. Yet excesses are the price we pay for the individual's right of freedom from the limitations of the past. Recognizing this, Emerson also tried to bring the individual back to a sense of history, to a balance between social past and present self.

Pastoral works toward this end, although it is never really successful as an ideological mode in American thought. It works better as a fictional idea, as an image, as a fantasy interlarded with real people and events. At its worst, it becomes an "Easy Rider" vision, a perversion of its real qualities in which self-indulgence can be justified by space and countryside. Those who express pastoral values there are infantile, while those who foreclose the dream altogether are contemptible.

The farm may have been a "holy emblem" to Emerson, but farms now are desolate places; land is too expensive to be tilled and given over to food. People have replaced the "holy emblem" of growth and development. William Whyte's description of the organization man in Lake Forest, Illinois, fits well into the idea of a "pleached pastoral:" given over to group suburbia. In his description, we observe how pastoral purity has given way to belief in the group and faith in technology as the means to achieve a sense of belonging. With this, the nineteenth-century dialectic between pastoral and machine is finished; pastoral lost. De Toqueville warned that conformity would undermine the unique American genius; that a social ethic or social consensus would be destructive, even fatal. The perfect machine rather than a pastoral memory would become our emblem of Eden, and with that a social consensus achieved. "Paradise Lost," in Emma Rothschild's use, ironically becomes the breakdown of the automotive age, not the decline of a human value system.

Kenneth Keniston speaks of "unprogrammatic alienation," a condition which he finds unique, for it involves "dissent without a fully articulated foundation," or rebellion without a cause. He was writing in 1965, before Civil Rights movements and the Vietnam War provided the causes; but his point does cover a general malaise that began to reveal itself in the 1950s. Our fiction in its stress on frenetic space, on the counterfeit and factitious, on futile attempts to recall Eden and pastoral moments seems to reflect qualities associated with alienation: "distrust, pessimism, resentment, anxiety, egocentricity, the sense of being an outsider, the rejection of conventional values, rejection of happiness as a goal, and a feeling of distance from others."

While malaise was generally a world-wide response, we must stress that such feelings were speeded up in America, were more massive, if our fiction is a valid reflection of underlying national attitudes. Behind the malaise is that broken association of self and nature, of individual and community; that loss the individual suffers when he recalls a once-Edenic existence, the hostility he senses toward ideas that remain only fantasies. A good part of the problem is our paradoxical need for Edenic memories even as we recognize they are mythical, that is, no longer visible, even if irresistible.

Keniston found that among his alienated students there was a constant: they cultivated sentience and solitude, and they associated those qualities which sustained them with a pastoral past, a whiff of Eden, the myth of the "hut dream"; so that Thoreau at Walden or communes based on Brook Farm remained as generating ideas or images. In this respect, our students are not alienated, but mainstream: they have, despite their passivity and disdain for an active or adventurous life, found agreement with the larger America, the America we find in our fiction. Its reflection of pastoral paradoxes is not marginal, "crazy," or exaggerated, but loyally American.

Those images of broken lives, dislocated individuals, fragmented existences are not simply examples of decline; they are images of how a life must be structured when it lives with paradoxes and fantasies. We need only contrast what we made of the West in an earlier generation and how we view California now, in terms of what Edwin Fussell has called "a condition of the soul [rather] than as a physiological region." The West has become a mythical place, especially since its depiction in novels and stories came from Easterners, who could "invent" its qualities unobserved. Like Eden, the West remained out of sight for those who wrote about it; and its physical aspects, whether prairies, settlements, lakes, communities, could become part of mythology instead of reality. Cheever's St. Botolphs, while East, not West, fits this pattern.

When Turner drew his line at the "frontier" and pronounced that it had vanished, he was really speaking of something mythical and imaginary. He was saying, in effect, that American civilization has overtaken Eden, that the line between civilization and undeveloped nature no longer existed. He was not clarifying the myth, but exploiting it; so that our writers became even more frenzied about an Edenic past, as it seemed to have receded. Thoreau foreshadowed this "frenzy" and in "Walking" perceived the West as "the wild" (its original title), as a place of absolute freedom, a contrast with civilization and its constraints.

None of this transformation of realities into myth and then living with the myth rather than the reality is a break with our history; it is, rather, a continuation of some of our earliest attitudes, embedded deep in the Puritan past. The Indian was for the Puritans a very complex phenomena which they had to master ideologically as well as physically. For the Indian represented nature, which the Puritans associated with an adversary relationship to civilization; and, therefore, the Puritans had to discover ways in which the Indian became significant or representative of what civilized man should *not* be or become. Yet the Puritan could not forsake nature, which included Indians, as part of the God-patterned universe in which all men lived. It was necessary for the Puritans first and then their successors to formulate a theory which established a new order which excluded the Indian. Part of this was accomplished by identifying the Indian with Satan, so that the struggle with the Indian became not an example of colonialism, but "a sign of earthly struggle and sin," a "religious enterprise." To grab Indian land, to kill Indians, to exclude them by way of reservations and other deprivations were ways of containing Satanism and carrying out God's divine plan.

With this thread running through our history and implicit in our history books (as Frances Fitzgerald has shown), the Indian, the West, development, colonialism, et al., come together as myth; and this myth is associated with an Edenic past, a pastoral rite, a sense of ever-receding time and space. A young country's life is extended back to the beginning of time, to the cosmogony itself. We must become aware of how our youthful country is transformed by our sense of space and time, so that we recall the Garden, which is where our frontier really ends (or begins).

Not surprisingly, in the 1960s, when so much of our past and so many of our myths were being reexamined, the Indian reemerged. Several nonfiction studies of Indians include Vine Deloria, Jr.'s *Custer Died for Our Sins*, Alice Marriott and Carol K. Rachin's *The American Epic*; fiction, Kesey's Chief Bromden in *One Flew Over the Cuckoo's Nest*, Heller's Chief White Halfoat in *Catch-22*, Berger's *Little Big Man*, Matthiessen's Meriwether Lewis in *At Play in the Fields of the Lord*, and numerous others.

The American action in Vietnam increasingly focussed attention on the Indian, since the destruction of one inevitably recalled the destruction of the other. Even our "safe zones" for Vietnamese friendlies had in them the idea of Indian reservations. But many of the novels and studies preceded our awareness of the Vietnam conflict—Berger, Heller, Kesey, for example. We are, therefore, involved far more deeply in a cultural development than in a simple application of one phase of history to a previous one. We are present at a deeply embedded cultural theme, one that I have identified with a persistent pastoralism.

For these books, in one way or another, circle around to Indian forms of existence as ways of responding to the very qualities that civilization is proud of quieting. After the display of civilized values represented by the fifties, that mixture of imitation, counterfeit, economic advances, personal aggrandizement, that confusing display of American might and pusillanimity, we needed something simpler or purer or less contrived. Indian life and values seemed worth recalling, and that memory, we observe, was never too distant from our sense of an Edenic past. The "savage Indian" now becomes the purest form of civilization. The myth remains, however deformed.

Every American writer wishing to enter the mainstream of fiction must arrive at what Empson called some "versions of pastoral." Most of our major writers began their careers with such incursions, although in their later fiction they may have moved to other matters. Yet some careers have been so closely identified with pastoral modes that they cannot be perceived otherwise. It is, it is worth stressing, the matter of America.

Cheever's two Wapshot novels, along with many of his short stories by implication, are shadowy existences of Hawthorne's sense of the flawed pastoral. Hawthorne, in *The Scarlet Letter* and elsewhere, observed men as living in a "dispossessed garden," that is, in a garden of potential perfection upset by man's own imperfections. Hawthorne's sense of the mode is almost as archetypically American as is Emerson's "ideal realm," the latter leading to fantasies, the former to waste lands. For Hawthorne, the "perfect place" can never be free of evil or sin; the ideal must always be balanced by the dysfunctioning human, beset by some demonic force which he or she cannot resolve. Cheever's adaptation of this removes much of the fierce intensity, the fire of madness we perceive in Hawthorne's vision, and turns the material into a comically dispossessed pastoral: life remains appetizing although profoundly disturbed. He is concerned with "American dreams," or "American nightmares," whereas Hawthorne stressed unexpungeable scars.

Cheever's dispossesed pastoral is St. Botolphs, an old river town, an inland port in the great days of the Massachusetts sailing fleets;[1] now, it has been diminished to a small factory town, with a factory that "manufactured table silver and a few other small industries." Yet even so St. Botolphs has within it key pastoral dimensions, so that proximity to nature as an unthreatening environment still obtains. There the Wapshot family lives in uneasy balance: Leander and his captaincy of the riverboat *Topaze*, Mrs. Sarah Wapshot, and their two sons, Coverly and Moses. The names of the latter suggest the pastoral dimension, as well as the Hawthorne tradition.

When Moses and Coverly leave St. Botolphs for New York and Washington, respectively, their point of reference is not just home, represented by St. Botolphs, but a locale signifying for them a prior existence associated with Edenic, not just idyllic, life. Their memories include alternating trips with Leander into the wilderness where they fish for trout and live in squalor. For the sake of the Edenic setting, they accommodate themselves to desperate camp conditions. Yet the period has its magical dimensions: they are reliving, within distance of St. Botolphs, a wilderness life that contains no threat, no women, no social life—simply Leander and one son cooking hamburgers on a pot lid and trolling for trout, separate from the world, in a Garden of their own making, untouchable from the outside. That camp is like being present at the creation.

Withal, everything is decaying. Deep in the wilderness, there is a reminder that Eden is ephemeral. "Everything was dead; dead leaves, and branches, dead ferns, dead grass, all the obscenity of the woods death, stinking and moldy, was laid thickly on the trail. A little white light escaped from the clouds and passed fleetly over the woods, long enough for Moses to see his shadow, and then this was gone." (1957; Bantam Ed., 1958, p. 58) Yet even against this sense of dying and sere nature, there is the wonder of the present. It has its Indian overtones, the "savage life" superior to the civilized. On one trip, Coverly takes a cookbook to camp, because his mother has said that Leander does not know how to cook. When he starts to read it, Leander grabs it and tosses it "out into the night." Coverly feels he "had failed himself and his father by bringing a cookbook to fishing camp; he had profaned the mysterious rites of virility and had failed whole generations of future Wapshots . . ." (p. 60).

The boys strike out to make their fortunes, but a kind of magnetic force turns their inner life back toward St. Botolphs. Although the town is seriously flawed—Leander is a wastrel, a Byronic poseur, Mrs. Wapshot caught in a marriage that has long since gone sour, old cousin Honora lost in a time zone without relationship to present events—even so, it is "some reminder of paradise—some happy authentication of the beauty of the summer countryside. . . . It was all real and they were flesh and blood" (p. 19).

Personal dimensions broaden into socio-political when Cheever contrasts Coverly's background with the places he is sent as a taper. As a man involved in computers, he is himself systematized, sent by way of a preselected program to locations he knows nothing about, then further programmed into government villages also standardized. This institutionalization of life finds its lateral movement in the destruction of the *Topaze* on the rocks—Leander's quest for Byronic experience is dashed on the shoals; and in the flawed quality of Clear Haven, the castlelike home where brother Moses pursues his fair Melissa. Thus, all three locations are faulted, with St. Botolphs the most resistent to the ravages of civilized change.

Clear Haven, despite recalling that "first place," is a prison of sorts, where Justina, Melissa's old aunt, rules as a dictator, keeps all the inmates in thrall to her, and tries to prevent Melissa from functioning as an individual. Before Moses has insight into the castle, he sees it as a perfect place for the early months of his marriage. Since his perception of love and a relationship is intensely associated with sexual fulfillment, his dreams of paradise are filled with lovely women. Fair Haven is a refuge for comely people: ". . . for even the benches in the garden were supported by women with enormous marble breasts and in the fall his eye fell repeatedly on naked and comely men and women in the pursuit of the glow of love" (p. 264).

But like everything else beyond the domain of St. Botolphs, life is infected by ego, self-indulgence, power games. Justina boasts of her own power: ". . . I could be all these things [wicked, rude, boorish] and worse and there would still be plenty of people to lick my boots." As she smiles sweetly on Moses, he "saw for once how truly powerful this old dancing mistress had been in her heyday and how she was like an old Rhine princess, an exile from the abandoned duchies of upper Fifth Avenue and the dusty kingdoms of Riverside Drive" (pp. 267–68). Moses perceives more than Eve; he sees, as if for the first time, evil.

The novel is of an ideological piece with Cheever's stories. For unlike Updike, with whom he can be superficially compared, Cheever is very conscious of the darkening sky that lies just beyond every endeavor to live and/or expand. The promises of pastoral exist to be broken. The suburban railroad which runs through the center of so many of his stories is a monster of civilization, a freak which becomes indispensable, and a deceptive element in the life of every commuter. For while it is a lifeline, it is also a passage into anonymity. The railroad connects two forms of life: St. Botolphs, based on illusions, and its morbid replacements, Clear Haven and government villages. Near the end of the novel, a new cycle is about to begin, with the death of Leander by drowning and the birth of sons for Coverly and Moses. Leander's death clears the way for another round of illusions based on pastoral dreams. For the new generation, St. Botolphs will prove a magnet for their dreams; and they will repeat that alternation of refuge and escape which gives them vitality.

When Cheever returned to the Wapshot chronicle in *The Wapshot Scandal*, published six years later in 1963, everything that disconnects the individual from St. Botolphs has within it forms of death, usually by way of machinery and technology. The Garden and the Machine are in deadly conflict, and illusions based on pastoral promises gain in significance. In a key episode, Coverly has become attached to the team of Cameron, a man whose scientific achievements have made him an arbiter over life and death for much of the world. Yet Cameron is himself woefully incomplete, lacking a dimension, the archetype for Cheever of those who have made no progress "in solving the clash between night and day, between the head and the groin" (Perennial Ed., 1973, p. 141).

Thrust into the world without any clear sense of himself or that world, his attachment to Cameron's team fortuitous, part of a computer error, Coverly checks into a hotel where the team is housed, where he listens to talks on interstellar space, one by a Chinese on the legal problems attendant on such a move, another on sending a man into space in a sack filled with fluid. The talks drone on, and Coverly tries to comprehend what they have in common with actual life. They seem segments of a conceptualization that has nothing to do with man and his appetites. ". . . but how could he square the image of a man in a sack with the small New England village where he had been raised and where his character had been formed? It seemed, in this stage of the Nuclear Revolution, that the world around him was changing with incomprehensible velocity but if these changes were truly incomprehensible what attitude could he take, what counsel could he give his son?" (p. 142).

Coverly's dilemma is how to behave in a society which has retreated from recognizable values, from forms of behavior he can assimilate. Old cousin Honora, also, no longer recognizes social functions and must flee St. Botolphs in disgrace. When she plugs her old curling iron into the ship's electrical system, she blows the two generators and the ship is becalmed. Honora for the moment stills time, retrieves pastoral; but of course her triumph is temporary and futile.

Cheever is neither intense nor tragic about such conflicts between individual behavior and a world in which values no longer matter. But in his suburban manner, he is attempting large American themes, what we find more intensely and comprehensively in books as different as *Giles Goat-Boy* (only a few years removed from the second *Wapshot*) and *Gravity's Rainbow*. Barth and Pynchon are more panoramic novelists, but they limn similar sensibilities. And if we dip back into Barth's earlier career, before *Giles*, we see in his *The Floating Opera* and *The End of the Road* a similar kind of world to what Cheever has illuminated.

Although Coverly is not a victim, women are particular prey of this riven sensibility. While Honora has enough of the old-fashioned in her to survive, someone like Gertrude Lockhart is the anonymous victim. Her downfall is a gradual one connected to the breakdown of the machinery in her home; whatever is expected to work fails to operate, and she is reduced to cave woman status amidst the decline of her home. Since technology has displaced pastoral, she is caught between systems and takes her life.

The end of the novel is a rounding off, with Christmas in St. Botolphs; the way *Scandal* began, it will end. Coverly and Moses welcome a busload of blind people into the former's house, and the seeing and blind sit down to dinner together. With that, the omniscient narrator indicates that it is time to pull out. He leaves on an incantatory note, to the effect that all will fade, St. Botolphs and whatever it stands for—like Eden itself: "I will never come back, and if I do there will be nothing left, there will be nothing left but the headstones to record what has happened; there will really be nothing at all" (p. 244). Leander's final message, that man's soul is able to "endure every sort of good and every sort of evil," will become an idle fancy. Once the illusions pass, the Machine has triumphed. This we note in *Falconer*, where the promise of pastoral has given way to a Kafkan enclosure.

The Kafkan vision, which suggests the disintegration of a solid reality, does provide a metaphor for American life: the loss of Eden, the fear that one might not be among the elect, the need for and yet fear of isolation. What was Biblically the Tower of Babel has become for us the Pit of Babel; what was beguilingly melodic for Odysseus when he passed the Sirens is for us a great silence which closes us off from melody—and we do not even hear the silence when the Sirens stop singing; what Gregor has found as a gigantic insect is that he is more alive than he was as a functioning and dutiful son in the Samsa family. Rebellion has led, not to heroism, but to dimunition. Pastoral has been enclosed by a castle fantasy or a "trial" room.

The serious American prison novel—as apart from prison literature and the popular detective story—is rare, since the enclosed aspect of prison life strips away one of the traditional weapons of the novelist, his use of spatiality and, by implication, the pastoral dimension. *Falconer* is of interest not only because of what Cheever has created but because of a conservative novelist's attempt to move beyond a dispossessed pastoral. His Farragut (a solid American name, an admiral in the Civil War) is a kind of updated Rojack, from Mailer's *An American Dream. Falconer* is, in fact, like a satirical imitation of Mailer's book, with Farragut a fratricide, an extension of Rojack, who has murdered his wife. The American dream for Farragut has ended up as drugs, murder, prison, homosexual love, loss of freedom—the other side of Rojack's "dream."

Since Farragut's experience or journey has ended in prison—the negation of space and, therefore, the negation of traditional American pastoral—his sexual quest has disoriented him even more than it has Rojack. In one of the more curious passages, Cheever locates man's identity (as did Mailer) in his sexual powers, citing the penis as the mode by which men are differentiated from each other:

> Considering the fact that the cock is the most critical link in our chain of survival, the variety of shapes, colors, sizes, characteristics, dispositions and responses found in this rudimentary tool are much greater than those shown by any other organ of the body. They were black, white, red, yellow, lavender, brown, warty, wrinkled, comely and silken, and they seemed, like any crowd of men on a street at closing time, to represent youth, age, victory, disaster, laughter and tears. There were the frenzied and compulsive pumpers, the long-timers who caressed themselves for half an hour, there were the groaners and the ones who sighed, and most of the men, when their trigger was pulled and the fusillade began, would shake, buck, catch their breath and make weeping sounds, sounds of grief, of joy, and sometimes death rattles. (Ballantine Ed., 1977, p. 125)

This is, in its way, the ultimate disconnection; so that the organ, a mass of tissue backed up by desire, becomes synecdochal, the erectile tissue standing in for the entire sexual experience. The narcissism here would surprise even Rojack, but it is all part of a disengagement from space—the traditional form of salvation for the American male. Emotional engagement, thought, even complicated desire and will are eliminated in favor of the organ itself. It becomes, in this view, a pumping machine: "the trigger was pulled," and that sets off the mechanism. We recall Indian-Puritan life—trigger, fusillade, death rattles—disengaged from pastoral hope. One feels Cheever should intend satire, that Farragut is possibly a figure of mockery, a parodic Rojack. On the contrary, Cheever keeps to neutral ground, where there is little tonal variety; everything is accepted for what it is, without differentiation. Every crime, state of loneliness, sexual act, rebellious move is charted with a standard tone. All behavior become homogeneous, apparently, and within that context the penis as erectile tissue, a stand-in for sex, is the ultimate release, escape, expansion into space.

Falconer very possibly takes its odd shape from the fact that Cheever has no space in which to move his character. The prison, the "Falconer" of the title, much like Sing-Sing in Ossining, New York, turns all spatiality into Kafkan walls, lanes, cubby holes. The sole spatial component comes in the form of Farragut's dreams, reveries, fantasies, nightmares; and at the end of the novel when he escapes and "rejoices" because he has lost his fear of falling. The main body of his experience, however, involves enclosed space, as befitting a prison, a prison as both a physical fact and a matter of mind. Now we have not only a dispossessed garden but an antipastoral.

Cheever is concerned with the energy that can be discharged within a situation that calls for enervation, passivity, even anomie. Thus he has a typical American theme: the attempt to achieve spatiality in a situation that permits little of it. Yet his attempt to create tensions between space and negation of space is unattainable in the format he has designed, and the novel achieves neither enclosed suffocation nor frustrated spatiality. Cheever's removal from even a problematical pastoral—the area of his strength as a writer—has led to confusion. Because of the lack of differentiation of experience, because of tonal fatigue, the novel is neither Kafkan nor American, neither within a recognizable tradition nor self-defining. The opposition between society and individual which should generate the comic interplay (*Falconer is* a comic novel) is dissipated by the spatial movement, here a prison space. Ideologically, that leaves the novelist bereft, for he has lost the interplay, the tension, the driving dramatic movement which running or escaping dissipates. Comedy cannot function in a social vacuum.

Cheever's dilemma is that of the postwar American novelist. Driven even deeper into paradoxes, unable to see any way out, he would like to nullify complexity by means of running, sensation, sensory perception. Yet Arcadia also beckons, that memory of Garden perfection embodied in the pastoral experience. Even while hearing the call of the forest bird, the writer would nevertheless like to transform childlike fantasies and observations into the lines and rhythms of his own needs. According to this, all the old myths are outdated; nothing holds, because there is no center. Not only is the ceremony of innocence lost, all ceremony is emptied out. Only "I" remains. Everything becomes fodder for sensation; nothing can be believed, for all has turned to deception and loss. The mode is Kafkan, but the "promise of pastoral" cannot be eliminated; the dilemma becomes the novelist's cross.

Notes

1. The obverse of St. Botolphs would appear to be Bullet Park of Cheever's 1969 novel of contemporary suburbia. There, Eliot Nailles and Paul Hammer are caught in a mythical struggle that belies the typical American town of the setting. But Bullet Park is in actuality an extension of St. Botolphs; only in the later book the pastoral vision has darkened, the relationship of self and environment has intensified, the dispossession grown greater. Hammer is the suburban "Indian," Nailles the Puritan settler; a showdown is inevitable. The means of salvation for Nailles' son, Tony, is a chain saw used to cut open a locked church door. The complex of images—hammer, nails, chain saw, church (chancel and pew), suburban context—reinforces that confusion of realms caused by the pastoral theme.

The Passion of Nostalgia in the Short Stories of John Cheever

Burton Kendle*

"it is a passion of nostalgia"

Henry James, letter to
William Dean Howells, 1904

The passionate attempt to retain and foster an image of an innocent past unifies the rich and varied fictional world in the stories of John Cheever.[1] His characters obsessively pursue this image of lost innocence, often their own, sometimes simultaneously registering the painful reality that motivates this nostalgia. Different characters may view the world through contrasting perspectives; the dual vision may exist within a single character; the tone of a story may imply an image of reality that clashes with that of the main character or narrator. Whatever the terms of this split, the dual vision defines the distance between aspiration and actuality for Cheever's protagonists.

"O Youth and Beauty!" contrasts the perspectives of travellers, who see the suburb of Shady Hill "in a bath of golden light" (p. 215), and of the protagonist, who has a more sober view: "Louise, tonight, is a discouraging figure. The lamp picks out the gray in her hair. Her apron is

*This essay was written specifically for this volume and is published here for the first time with permission of the author.

stained. Her face seems colorless and drawn." A similar tension between antithetical visions dominates Cheever's stories and explains why many characters find unacceptable a world that apparently satisfies others, and why this dissatisfaction leads to a quest for a private eden.

Shifting perspectives may battle within a single consciousness, as when the husband in "The Ocean" mistakes his wife for her mother, "a harsh-voiced blonde of about seventy, with four scars on the side of her face, from cosmetic surgery," and then attempts to comfort his wife," "I'm *terribly* sorry, darling. . . . It was the dark" (pp. 569–71). However amusingly prophetic the episode, it underscores the husband's growing awareness of the subjective nature of reality. Such subjectivity, a crucial aspect of Cheever's fiction, can isolate people from the world and each other and, when the inevitable confrontation occurs, make them vulnerable to the realities they have ignored. But, conversely, this subjectivity in its most attractive form is the love, ultimately family love, that enables characters to endow wives, children, and ordinary life with those qualities that make the necessary facts of existence desirable. Cheever's husbands frequently invoke private systems of standards by which they hope to impose their subjective visions on a resisting reality.

Tension between two characters can mirror an unacknowledged uneasiness within the protagonist. The unnamed narrator of "Goodbye, My Brother" laments his brother Lawrence's inability to share "the illusion, when we are together, that the Pomeroys are unique" (p. 3), and that family loyalty is the key to order and happiness. The family summer place on a Massachusetts island typifies the many coastal refuges which allow characters to retain their image of an idyllic world because such settings not only suggest the sea's power to restore innocence[2] but also encourage recollections of a happier past: "The sea is our universal symbol for memory." ("Percy," *Stories*, p. 634) "Goodbye, My Brother" begins with a reference to the father's drowning in a sailing accident ("The Day the Pig Fell Into the Well" drowns a young sailor in an equally lethal Pacific). But the narrator rejects this frightening picture of the sea, despite Lawrence's warnings that the family home will fall into the sea, warnings that shade into a general prophecy of family doom, delivered with the ominous flatness characteristic of Cheever's truthtellers: "Diana is a foolish and promiscuous woman. So is Odette. Mother is an alcoholic. If she doesn't discipline herself, she'll be in a hospital in a year or two. Chaddy is dishonest. He always has been" (p. 19). The narrator can respond only by violently attacking Lawrence with a root significantly "heavy with sea water" (*ibid.*), an action that ironically confirms Lawrence's view of the family's hidden corruption (and foreshadows the murder of brother by brother in *Falconer*).

That the narrator partly shares Lawrence's vision is clear when he imagines Lawrence's grim meditations on the depths of the sea. Yet the narrator negates this imagined scene with a description of his swimming wife and sister emerging from the sea "naked, unshy, beautiful, and full of grace" (p. 21), an image reinforcing the vivifying power of water. These conflicting sea images imply the unadmitted division within the narrator, desperately trying to sustain his positive view of the ocean and of his family's safety within a nourishing past. If the narrator is a special pleader, Lawrence is a special prosecutor, and truth must lie somewhere in between; but the story ultimately supports the narrator, whose love can justifiably soften or even distort the truth to make life attractive and occasionally permit an epiphany beyond the power of Lawrence. Lawrence's omission of love distorts to the point of caricature and makes existence unendurable. Only rarely can a character, like the elevator operator in "Clancy in the Tower of Babel," acknowledge and successfully harmonize such warring visions: "Clancy was struck with the strength and intelligence of his son's face, but he guessed that a stranger might notice the boy's glasses and his bad complexion. . . . this half-blindness was all that he knew himself of mortal love" (p. 127). Appalled by the moral nihilism and pain of the residents of his building and, presumably, of all New Yorkers, Clancy can ultimately neither rebuke nor forgive the sinners, but finds his survival only in the illusory sanctuary of family goodness, the crucial refuge in Cheever's stories. Lacking the harmonizing power of such love, Cheever's characters, like the Westcotts in "The Enormous Radio,"[3] often fail to sustain their nostalgic illusions and fall from a belief in the innocence of their own lives to a painful confrontation with "the deposits of silver polish on the candlesticks" (*Stories*, p. 35), and a previously unacknowledged awareness of their own sinfulness. This story, an archetypal version of the loss of the vision of an innocent world, reveals that both vision and loss can occur in a Manhattan apartment, though Cheever's short fiction shows them as more frequent in New York suburbs or on New England coasts, and possible even in Europe. The Westcotts' willed innocence appears in Irene's "wide, fine forehead upon which nothing at all had been written," and in Jim's "intentionally naive" manner and determination to "feel younger" (p. 33) than he was. Like the mother-in-law's plastic surgery in "The Ocean," the Westcotts' refusal to accept the cycle of human existence is unconnected to Cheever's touchstone of family love and seems a negative version of the desire for a timeless Eden. Their new radio that looks "like an aggressive intruder" (p. 34) is the serpent in this Eden. Through its ability to broadcast conversations from neighboring apartments, the radio alerts the couple to the suffering and moral weaknesses of others and, ultimately, of themselves. Jim's final speech reveals the unstable basis of the idyllic world they had inhabited at the beginning of the story and catalogues their half-buried sins, especially Irene's abortion that symbolizes a denial of family love. Such recollections produce no pleasurable *frisson*, but condemn the

Westcotts to a future of bickering, ironically their chief link with Adam and Eve. Jim and Irene can neither accept the world to which they have been exiled, nor can they reenter their illusory paradise.

Like the disillusioned Westcotts, Cheever's New York residents or visitors generally feel mocked by reminders of Eden, symbols of the failure of previous questors or of themselves. The paranoid narrator of "The Ocean," who painfully seeks the possibility of goodness in both Bullet Park and New York, experiences the perversion of the ideal in a decaying tenement ironically named the Eden, from which he hopes to rescue his daughter: ". . . I entered Eden like an avenging angel, but once under the Romanesque arch I found a corridor as narrow as the companionway in a submarine" (p. 579). Painfully aware of traditional patterns, but lacking real religious or moral authority, he allies himself with the fallen world by attempting to bribe his daughter's lover into freeing her from his parody of Eden. The compassionate building manager of "The Superintendent" also suffers from the moral failures of his residents and seeks guidance from his own traditional version of the ideal, a belief that the City of God is accessible even behind city clouds: "But the sky told him only that it was a long day at the end of winter, that it was late and time to go in" (p. 177). The context of a fallen world makes a mockery of the implied promise of coming spring, and the superintendent, unable to recall his youthful vision, will not translate his concern into action.

This bleak truth about New York does not discourage those outsiders who envision an urban Eden and are invariably disappointed, like the pathetic midwesterners (natives would know better) who seek Manhattan success in "O City of Broken Dreams," or like Ohio-born Jack Lorey of "Torch Song," whom the city slowly destroys. Those suburban wives who also invade the city to fulfill themselves by appearing nude in off-Broadway plays ("The Fourth Alarm") or who seek adulterous affairs in the safety of an anonymous urban setting and buy children's toys to assuage their guilt ("The Geometry of Love") are similarly victims of an erroneous belief in an urban Eden. But like the midwesterners who define the good life in terms of business success, these women have a shallow conception of paradise as an arena for self-gratification and no thought for the love which is the essential element in such visions.

In some stories Europeans or the children of expatriate Americans view all of America as edenic. An old Neapolitan woman in "Boy in Rome" shouts encouragement to an emigrating friend: "Blessed are you, blessed are you, you will see the New World" (p. 456), and the heroine of "Clementina" enjoys "a sort of paradise" (p. 446) in a Washington suburb. The children of American exiles, "the real expatriates," who may have never seen the States, "have a sense of being far, far from home that is a much sweeter and headier distillation than their parents ever know" (p. 308). Conversely the expatriate mother of "The Bella Lingua" developed her version of Europe as a paradise when, as an unhappy midwestern child, she saw on a cracked theater curtain:

> A vision of an Italian garden, with cypress trees, a terrace, a pool and fountain, and a marble balustrade with roses spilling from marble urns. She seemed literally to have risen up from her seat and to have entered the cracked scene, for it was almost exactly like the view from window into the courtyard of the Palazzo Tarominia where she lived. (p. 305)

Like many of its American parallels, this European paradise was imperfect from its flawed, gaudy inception.

Despite these interesting variants, however, Cheever's Eden generally involves returning to the original suburban or coastal setting of remembered happiness, or moving to a similar area which promises a renewal of the former good life. Cheever's fiction embodies this desire, essentially a middle-class desire, in Mr. Selfredge, who

> had retired from the banking business—mercifully, for whenever he stepped out into the world today he was confronted with the deterioration of those qualities of responsibility and initiative that had made the world of his youth selective, vigorous, and healthy. ("The Trouble of Marcie Flint," p. 296)

Often, as in "The Season of Divorce," this middle-class "ability to recall better times" focuses primarily on economic loss:

> Lost money is so much a part of our lives that I am sometimes reminded of expatriates, of a group who have adapted themselves energetically to some alien soil but who are reminded, now and then, of the escarpments of their native coast. (p. 137)

This nostalgia for a vanished past connects with the homesickness of those exiles who lead unsatisfactory lives in Europe or those in "The Scarlet Moving Van" who flee their failed visions in American suburbs.

Whatever its economic or psychological origins, this same nostalgia produces ironical versions of paradise. That the Selfredges and their neighbors keep a public library out of Shady Hill from fear of attracting outsiders and disseminating subversive ideas suggests a necessary, if unattractive, attempt to avoid those dangers that helped destroy the original Eden. But that two small children almost die of poison in a Shady Hill garden implies that the efforts of the Selfredges are futile. Similarly, in "The Ocean" the protagonist's boss, an aspiring suburban Adam, dies from a bee sting while gardening. Despite this negative coloration, however, Cheever's gardens exert a profound nostalgic force on escapees from the urban present. Paul Hollis of "The Summer Farmer" experiences a violent "sense of homecoming" (p. 80) when he returns to his family summer property with its pasture called "Elysian, because of its unearthly stillness" (p. 82). Along with this nostalgia, Paul acknowledges that the purchase of pet rabbits for his children pains the son of the farmer who sells them and that Kasiak, Paul's hired man, will eat the rabbits in the Fall (the seasonal implications of this Eden make clear that Paul's nostalgia must restrict itself to very narrow limits). Paul's concept of a transient Eden clashes with the Russian-born Kasiak's vision of "the birth of a just and peaceable world, delivered in bloodshed and arson" (p. 82). Their moral struggle over the mysterious poisoning of those same crucial rabbits results predictably in Paul's "loss of principle" (p. 88) with no compensating promise of the redemption possible for the original Adam. Paul's willingness to accept the consequences of a limited Eden, a sign of his awareness of the unchangeable power of the real world, undercuts the force of his commitment and dooms his venture.

A more complex attitude toward rural edens emerges in Jim, protagonist of "The Common Day," who "is so accustomed to the noise and congestion of the city that after six days in New Hampshire he still found the beauty of the country morning violent and alien" (p. 22). This New England setting with "the magnificent vegetables that [the gardener] had watered with his sweat" (p. 25), a man killed by lightning, and "other perils of the country," (p. 32) seems closer to the world of the exiled Adam than to Eden, though Jim and his wife Ellen feel the beauty of the country morning transport them to "the excitement of their first meetings" (p. 28). The belief in a recoverable Eden is stronger in Ellen, who searches old farms for a permanent haven. Characteristically Cheever contrasts the visions of husband and wife: "Where she saw charm and security, he saw advanced dilapidation and imprisonment." While understanding her vision and impelled by love and residual nostalgia to attempt to share her desire, Jim's rural experience ultimately forces him to view elements from past country life negatively. The existence they symbolize seems vanished beyond recall, though characters in this and other stories go painfully through the motions of trying to recapture it.

Even when Cheever satirizes suburban or coastal settings, inhabitants with sufficient commitment to traditional or private ideals can achieve a kind of balance. The urgency to regain or establish the good life symbolized by suburban living is most extreme in "The Death of Justina" and "A Vision of the World." The former describes suburban Proxmire Manor, part of a world "where even the cleaning women practice the Chopin preludes in their spare time" (p. 432), and where zoning ordinances apparently permit neither dying nor burying: "How can a people who do not mean to understand death hope to understand love, and who will sound the alarm?" (p. 437). Yet, even in the context of this suburb and of a Manhattan advertising job that similarly denies death and other realities, the narrator can reaffirm his commitment to the good life by typing the 23rd Psalm. In "A Vision of the World," set "in another seaside cottage on another coast" (p. 512), the narrator finds a buried note from a young man who vows "if I am not a member of the Gory Brook

Country Club by the time I am twenty-five years old I will hang myself."
With slightly less vehemence the narrator declares that though he might
survive without his wife and children, "I could not bring myself to leave
my lawns and gardens" (p. 514). He spends an evening investigating the
would-be suicide at Gory Brook, where the nostalgic music suggests
another unsuccessful aspiration for permanence: "We seemed to be dancing on the grave of social coherence." Though he partly acknowledges the
failure of his Eden, the narrator still desires "to grant my dreams, in so incoherent a world, their legitimacy" (p. 515). His awakening that night
from a dream of women in old-fashioned clothing to a literally cleansing
rain (the familiar linking of the past with rain in Cheever) enables him to
reassert his commitment to his personal ideals: "Valor! Love! Virtue!
Compassion! Splendor! Kindness! Wisdom! Beauty!" (p. 517). The
strength of this commitment, though his stridency may imply some uncertainty, should allow him to retain that illusion of being "contented and at
peace with the night" which Cheever characters continually seek in their
suburban edens.

Such balance, however precarious, is comparatively rare in
Cheever's suburban world. More representative is the satirical image of
the "wildlife preserve where the leader of the Audubon group was suffering from a terrible hangover" (p. 603) in "The Swimmer." On a more
serious level "The Hartleys" dramatizes the attempt of an unhappy couple
to recapture the illusion of their past good life by returning to their New
England honeymoon site. Mr. Hartley spends much of his time nostalgically describing his family, but his wife bitterly attacks this obsession with
past happiness:

> Why do we have to make these trips back to the places where we thought
> we were happy? What good is it going to do? What good has it ever done?
> We go through the telephone book looking for the names of people we
> knew ten years ago, and we ask them for dinner, and what good does it
> do? What good has it ever done? (p. 63)

The accidental death of their daughter at this resort reaffirms the difficulty of reeentering past edens. The dead or threatened children who
populate Cheever's stories make clear that the world their elders inhabited has decayed to the point where the innocence that children embody no longer protects them but makes them vulnerable to both the
dangers of ordinary existence and to the nostalgic experiments of their
parents.

The nostalgic ideal does not always depend on a specific physical setting. Characters sometimes rely on a reversion to behavior or attitudes
reminiscent of an idyllic past. The vacationers of "Goodbye, My Brother"
dress up in football uniforms and bridal gowns for their club dance, and
most of the men, in a studied attempt to act with the thoughtlessness of
youth, dive off the club dock for the requisite purifying swim. The ageing

athlete of "O Youth and Beauty!" similarly tries to recreate the feats of his college career, his one period of fulfillment, with fatal results. However touching these stories, their characters envision a shallow conception of the good life. Characters with somewhat higher aspirations continually lament Wordsworthian "vanishings," intuitions that they have "lost or forgotten something" (p. 138). The frustrated wife of "The Season of Divorce," who mourns her neglected linguistic and intellectual skills suggests some of the specific components of this vision of the good life. Sometimes the loss is more general, more anguished: an unhappy friend in "The Jewels of the Cabots" periodically calls the narrator to demand rhetorically: "We were happy, weren't we?" (p. 686).

Appropriately, because of the middle-class backgrounds of most Cheever characters, their visions of a lost golden age seem synonymous with recollections of actual lost gold. The nostalgia of Mrs. Beer in "Just One More Time" is representative: "Her father . . . had lost millions and millions and millions of dollars. All her memories were thickly inlaid with patines of bright gold . . ." (p. 248). Though recollections of high bridge stakes and Daimlers threaten to link her nostalgia with the reveries of former athletes for the days of their football glory, Mrs. Beer's vision is powerful enough to help recreate her lost world, however shallow it appears, and however cynical the viewpoint of the narrator. The success of the Beers may stem partly from the strength of their devotion to their past and to each other. Sometimes, even when members of this class retain their money, the moral universe it once made possible has vanished, and the nostalgia plays with these lost codes: Mr. Bruce of "The Bus to St. James's" sees his class as bewildered and confused in principle, too selfish or too unlucky to abide by the forms that guarantee the permanence of a society, as their fathers and mothers had done" (p. 284). Through a few adroit background details and through an exploration of the minds of selected characters, Cheever manages to suggest the changing economic, social, and ethical history of the American middle class.

Not surprisingly, the passionate nostalgia of Cheever residents is selective and necessitates the suppression of elements from the past, public or private, that might threaten their idylls. Just as Shady Hill dwellers prevented the establishment of a free public library in "The Trouble of Marcie Flint" because it might disrupt their community, in "The Country Husband" they seem "united in their tacit claim that there had been no past, no war—that there was no danger or trouble in the world" (p. 331). The protagonist keeps silent about an important wartime incident because the issues the story embodies would disturb without educating his townsmen. This limited use of the past motivates the narrator's brother in "The Lowboy" to "desire one solid piece of furniture, one object I could point to, that would remind me of how happy we all were, of how we used to live . . ." (p. 405). He ignores the family's actual history and is unaware that "the fascination of the lowboy was the fascination of pain"

(p. 410) and that he has "committed himself to the horrors of the past" (p. 411). Insight into his brother's obsession causes the narrator to smash various heirlooms of his own and, like the protagonist of "A Vision of the World," to reaffirm his commitment to the standards that should underlie an idealized world: "Cleanliness and valor will be our watchwords" (p. 412). This story and others present a negative image of the family past and its effect on the present. While family love may be the chief means for Cheever's characters to survive a chaotic present and to recreate a new eden, the family history, especially that of father and son or brother and brother, frequently makes such an escape necessary and impossible.

On occasion, familiar Cheever abstractions are made flesh, as when the loved wife and sister who emerge Venuslike at the end of "Goodbye, My Brother" seem to embody the narrator's conception of family love. In a variant of this, the protagonist of "The Pot of Gold," who spends years seeking the literal gold, with its promise of the good life, that obsesses the imagination of many middle-class characters, finally achieves a special vision of his wife as the embodiment of the treasure: "Desire for her delighted and confused him. Here it was, here it all was, and the shine of the gold seemed to him then to be all around her arms" (p. 117). In "The Cure," a husband who desperately attempts to embody his ideals of love and community in a less than perfect family and town to compensate for the horrors of the ordinary world ultimately claims success: "We've been happy ever since. . . . Everyone here is well" (p. 164). Though his triumph, like that of other protagonists, may seem too sudden or fortuitous to be convincing, the story suggests that the capacity to love permits a seizing and exploiting of the slightest hint as the basis for a powerful illusion. Another figure with such capacity is the alcoholic father of "The Sorrows of Gin." Unaware that his young daughter has learned of "the pitiful corruption of the adult world" (p. 208), and perhaps incapable of admitting such corruption himself, he still believes in the possibility of suburban paradise: "How could he teach her that home sweet home was the best place of all?" (p. 209). Mixed with Cheever's irony is the implication that the strength of paternal love, tested here for perhaps the first time, may authenticate the illusion for a while at least. Johnny Hake, "The Housebreaker of Shady Hill," similarly escapes his accumulated miseries by "no more than the rain on my head—the smell of it flying up to my nose—that showed me the extent of my freedom" (p. 268). This power to free himself from the dark side of his past is as mysterious to Johnny as it may be to the reader:

> And it was no skin off my elbow how I had been given the gifts of life so long as I possessed them then—the tie between the wet grass roots and the hair that grew out of my body, the thrill of my mortality that I had known on summer nights, loving the children, and looking down the front of Christina's dress. (p. 268)

This ability to fuse the sensations of the rain with positive recollections of his family into an acceptance of the world that acknowledges but does not dwell on its "dark" side enables Johnny to end his adventures "whistling merrily in the dark" (p. 269). Thus, human love, with its memories of flawed, but still desirable relationships, domesticates visions of paradise and reconciles characters to a less than perfect present. This love either displaces nostalgia or, more often, coexists symbiotically with it.

Powerful nostalgia for a shared family past makes possible the mother's epiphany that ends "The Day the Pig Fell into the Well." At their summer home, as members of the Nudd family recall the events of a day long past, in the context of the present, the mother wonders: "What had made the summer always an island, she thought; what had made it such a small island? What mistakes had they made? What had they done wrong?" (p. 235). Yet, the very act of remembering mitigates, temporarily at least, her sense of loss: "The story restored Mrs. Nudd and made her feel that all was well . . . The room with the people in it looked enduring and secure, although in the morning they would all be gone." Such a vision of a safe world, coexisting with an awareness of its transience, is pe‑haps all that family memories and a commitment to love can offer such seekers of paradise.

In some stories the characters' belief that they have approximated paradise counterpoints the cynical attitude of the narrator, who seems blind to the workings of family love or other mysterious sources of happiness. "The Worm in the Apple" shows how the suspiciously contented Crutchmans' who live "happily, happily, happily, happily" (p. 288), continually confound the narrator's assumptions that their existence is seriously flawed. Cheever's recent story, "The Island," one of the few that does not depend on family love to generate its paradise, sets up a similar tension as the narrator learns that once famous people who, according to statistical probability, should have suffered unattractive fates, are now inhabiting a modified paradise: "The climate of the place was pleasant, but 10t so desirable as to put it on any cruise route or to support any hotels. Gale winds blew . . . in April or May, but this was evidently the only serious inclemancy."[4] The story is one of a small group in which entry i1to Eden depends not on family love but on some equally mysterious good fortune or innate capacity for happiness that allows the islanders to "have an easy time of it, reading the classics and eating shellfish." Tension between the worldly or even cynical narrator's viewpoint and the unquestioning happiness of fulfilled family members or of dwellers on miraculous islands emphasizes that such achievements are rare enough in Cheever's world to generate disbelief and mock conventional expectations.

Even rarer is the ability of the artist to restore a vision of innocence to both himself and a responsive audience. "A World of Apples" focuses on an aged American writer living in Italy, Asa Bascomb, whose "work seemed an act of recollection" (p. 615) and embodied the healing power of memory. Bascomb achieved fame with his book *The World of Apples*, "poetry in which his admirers found the pungency, diversity, color, and nostalgia of the apples of the northern New England he had not seen for forty years" (p. 613). Because of Bascomb's reliance on the past, prolonged absence from these New England roots explains his cycle of obscene dreams, his compulsion to write pornography, and his conviction that the world has forever lost its innocence, but this painful experience does not destroy his belief in absolutes: with the characteristic divided vision of Cheever's characters, he sees a soliciting male whore as "angelic, armed with a flaming sword that might conquer banality and smash the glass of custom" (p. 618). This idealism explains Bascomb's desire to regain his youthful vision by visiting the shrine of a more authentic local angel who "can cleanse the thoughts of a man's heart" (p. 620). In a conclusion that seems to recapitulate all the key themes of Cheever's stories, the Protestant Bascomb visits the Catholic shrine, sees a single ray of light emerge from the clouds and, like other protagonists, invokes his private pantheon: "God bless Walt Whitman, God bless Hart Crane . . . Dylan Thomas . . . William Faulkner, Scott Fitzgerald, and especially Ernest Hemingway" (p. 622). The next day, his prayers apparently answered, he sees a waterfall reminiscent of one in Vermont where, as a boy, he had watched an old man "undress himself with the haste of a lover" and enjoy a kind of ritual cleansing, an old man Bascomb finally recognized as his father. After repeating the same ritual immersion, the aged Bascomb is able to write "a long poem on the inalienable dignity of light and air that, while it would not get him the Nobel Prize, would grace the last months of his life" (p. 623). The past, especially viewed through the sensibility of an artist and focusing on family love and an erotically rich bath, can renew Bascomb and reconcile him to the present, though as is usual in Cheever, it is a present this side of the Nobel Prize. Bascomb's ingenuity in fusing elements from his New England past, his literary career, and the Catholic context in which he now lives into a private code of existence typifies the spiritual eclecticism of Cheever's protagonists.

Bascomb's "paradise within," transient because it exists in the consciousness of a dying man, exhibits neither the dependence on physical locale nor the reversion to youthful frolicking of some seekers of Eden. The mind of the artist is itself the source of its freedom and can dispense with even the proximity of loved ones that Cheever's fathers and husbands require, however elevated their commitments.

The "passion of nostalgia," of Cheever's questors, both lovers and artists, is, at its most profound, a desire not only for the ease and delights of Eden, but also for the moral purity of prelapsarian man. Like Bascomb, or Francis Weed of "The Country Husband," some protagonists willingly undertake rigorous disciplines to renew their visions. Another perceptive observer of the human scene, the narrator of "Brimmer," sums up this view of "life as a perilous moral adventure. It is difficult to be a man, I think; but the difficulties are not insuperable" (p. 391).

Notes

1. With the exception of two uncollected pieces, *The Stories of John Cheever* (New York, 1978) is the source of all citations from Cheever's fiction.

2. Water exerts a strong effect on Cheever's characters, sometimes tempting them with the illusion of a baptismal cleansing or womblike peace they can no longer attain, sometimes satisfying these desires. For "Artemis, the Honest Well Digger," "water was his profession, his livelihood as well as his passion. . . . Water was love" (p. 650). And the story begins and ends with "the healing sound of rain" (pp. 650, 671). Beach scenes in "Montraldo" remind the narrator "more forcibly than classical landscapes of our legendary ties to paradise" (p. 564). The suburban husband in "The Swimmer," who plans to swim his way home via the pools of his neighbors, defines his desired intimacy with water as a form of creative homage: "The day was beautiful and it seemed to him that a long swim might enlarge and celebrate its beauty" (p. 604). That the swimming is a doomed attempt to recreate the illusion of happiness with his family in a presumably idyllic setting becomes increasingly clear to both reader and character. His failure echoes that of another husband in "The Seaside Houses," who feeling "painfully depraved, guilty, and unclean" (p. 488), hopes that swimming will restore him to past innocence. Recollected water scenes in "The Trouble of Marcie Flint" have a strong erotic component: "now mixed up with my memories of the sea island was the whiteness of Marcie's thighs" (p. 295). Similar erotic connotations enrich the episode in "Metamorphoses" involving Nerissa, the repressed spinster who grieves so much because of her forbidden love that she turns into the swimming pool, "this watery home sweet home" (p. 547), where she and her lover had innocently swum. Though the narrator of the uncollected story, "The National Pastime," stresses the practical significance of the rain that signals his freedom from traumatic baseball games, his imagery suggests the rich connotations of water: "A single drop of rain would have sounded like music." (John Cheever, "The National Pastime," *New Yorker*, [26 September 1953] 33). The story's climactic scene links the recollection of even violent rain to the vision of an idyllic refuge from pain: "the grainy light of a thunderstorm, when the clearness of the green world—the emblazoned fields—reminds us briefly of a great freedom of body and mind." (*Ibid.*, p. 35) These few selections suggest the rich pattern of water references in Cheever's stories.

3. For a detailed attempt to read this story as an ironic version of the Eden myth, see: Burton Kendle, "Cheever's Use of Mythology in 'The Enormous Radio,' " *Studies in Short Fiction*, 4 (Spring 1967), 262–64. A differing view appears in Henrietta T. Harmsel, " 'Young Goodman Brown,' and 'The Enormous Radio,' " *Studies in Short Fiction*, 9 (Fall 1972), 407–408.

4. John Cheever, "The Island," *New Yorker*, 27 April 1981, p. 41.

Of That Time, of Those Places:
The Short Stories of John Cheever

Richard H. Rupp*

In the 1978 edition of his collected short fiction, John Cheever arranged the sixty-one stories chronologically, and it makes sense to read them that way. These stories span a generation of writing, from the mid-forties to the early seventies. "Their order is, to the best of my memory, chronological and the most embarrassingly immature pieces have been dropped."[1] They chronicle the social, spiritual, and geographical mobility of Cheever's people—the eastern Protestant middle class—and they chronicle loss and change: "These stories seem at times to be stories of a long-lost world when the city of New York was still filled with a river light, when you heard the Benny Goodman quartets from a radio in the corner grocery store, and when almost everybody wore a hat." Not only places but people have changed: "Here is the last of that generation of chain smokers who woke the world in the morning with their coughing, who used to get stoned at cocktail parties and perform obsolete dance steps like 'the Cleveland Chicken,' sail for Europe on ships, who were truly nostalgic for love and happiness, and whose gods were as ancient as yours and mine, whoever you are" (p. ix).

Of that time, of those places: Cheever's stories dramatize rites of passage, the ceremonies of youth and middle age, a life style that changes and vanishes to be succeeded by another. They chronicle the ephemeral and the eternal in American life—what has passed, what is passing, what is to come. The places are New York City, suburbia (apotheosized in innocent Shady Hill and its sinister neighbor, Bullet Park), Rome, and Italy, St. Botolphs and the Massachusetts islands. As he traces the passions and wanderings of his fellow Americans, Cheever gives us a comprehensive, compassionate account of the way some people live.

John Cheever is a middle-class writer who describes middle-class experience: the relocation from urban origins to suburban disenchantment. Cheever's heroes are less individuals than types or versions of the same experience; his innocents are either born into or move into a specious Eden. Discovering there a corruption both personal and social, they struggle toward some spiritual reintegration, usually through marriage and the family. Frequently the Cheever hero faces up to some universal human quirk or ailment and accepts himself and his life as he finds it. His experience is illustrative, representative, and communal—for Cheever is writing, as Emerson wrote, of representative men. His voice as he speaks to us—and he characteristically comments on the situations he creates—is wry, compassionate, and detached, that of the sympathetic observer.

*This essay was written specifically for this volume and is published here for the first time with permission of the author.

Much of the appeal in these stories derives from Cheever's perceived relationship with his readers. Like another great New Yorker before him, he speaks of Americans and for them:

> Walt Whitman, a kosmos, of Manhattan the son,
> Turbulent, fleshy, sensual, eating, drinking, and breeding,
> No sentimentalist, no stander above men and women or apart
>   from them,
> No more modest than immodest.
>
> Unscrew the locks from the doors!
> Unscrew the doors themselves from their jambs![2]

Although he claims to be a provincial writer in his Preface to these stories, Cheever treats America's soul as well as its suburbs. Wherever Americans have grown up in cities and fled to the uneasy Edens outside them, there stands John Cheever, like Walt Whitman.

His audience, then, is not restricted to New Yorkers and *New Yorker* readers; he speaks to civilized Americans everywhere. As Cheever posits him, the reader is intimately familiar with America's upward mobility and footloose life style. Like his characters, Cheever's reader was born in a small town, has spent some of his working life in a big city, and now lives in a suburb. He has traveled to Europe—preferably by boat—is married, male, middle-aged, commutes to work by train, belongs to the Episcopal Church, drinks too much; vexed by his own sexuality he wanders an erratic path between fidelity and infidelity (but always back again); is literate, bemused, ironic, and nostalgic for the better time and place that never was. Not since J. D. Salinger discovered American teenagers has a writer so identified and identified with his audience. At his best, Cheever's reader shares the community of his fellow sufferers on the five-forty-eight.

Finally, the ideal reader, like the characters, is himself capable of violence, insanity, even cruelty to animals. He is deterred from the abyss of isolation and egoism only by the bizarre, the unique, the unexpected in his own character. He is strengthened if at all by an appetite for life, an eye for its pied beauty, a taste for the eccentric. Cheever's narrator, like a slightly drunken celebrant, weaves towards the high altar of American innocence to offer there a sacrifice of praise for the goodness and vitality of this life, here and now; for, at heart, Cheever knows his America to be decent, pious, loving, committed to the eternal verities of love, family, and community.

His stance is basically religious and conservative. He has inverted the transcendentalism of his spiritual forbears, Hawthorne and Emerson, opting instead for the immanence of salvation in the here and now, for the community of love in the temple of Mammon. A brief look at some of these stories will, I hope, bear out these extravagant contentions.

The stories invite classification by setting. The New York stories seem to fall into two groups, early and late. In the earlier group, Cheever's characters live in Manhattan apartment buildings—vertical conclaves where community is at best difficult. In the later group, New York is no longer a place to live but only an arena for bizarre actions. The two suburbs, Shady Hill and Bullet Park, are similarly demarcated between apparent community and grim isolation. Rome and Italy offer interesting variations on the theme of American isolation, while St. Botolphs and its offshore islands chronicle the strains inherent even in real communities.

To begin with the "early" New York stories, let us consider "The Enormous Radio," "O City of Broken Dreams," "Torch Song," and "Christmas Is A Sad Season for the Poor." Cheever knows and gives us the rituals of the elevator and the lobby, the quirks of diverse tenants, the balkiness of machinery. Typically, Cheever finds a simple, natural action and enlarges it to absurd dimensions for both comic and pathetic effects. A major source of his comic effects can be found in what Henri Bergson has called "mechanical inelasticity."[3] Whenever humans begin to act like simple machines, we laugh at them.

"The Enormous Radio," for instance, shows the effect of a strange, balky machine on a susceptible, lonely housewife, who becomes in effect its human extension. Irene Westcott listens with increasing horror and fascination to the domestic affairs of her neighbors, thereby bringing the sorrows of the world into her marriage to Jim:

> "Don't, don't, quarrel with me," she moaned, and laid her head on his shoulder. "All the others have been quarreling. They're all worried about money. Mrs. Hutchinson's mother is dying of cancer in Florida and they don't have enough money to send her to the Mayo Clinic. At least Mrs. Hutchinson says they don't have enough money. And some woman in this building is having an affair with the handyman—with that hideous handyman. It's too disgusting. And Mrs. Melville has heart trouble and Mr. Hendricks is going to lose his job in April and Mrs. Hendricks is horrid about the whole thing and that girl who plays the 'Missouri Waltz' is a whore, a common whore, and the elevator man has tuberculosis and Mr. Osborne has been beating Mrs. Osborne." She wailed, she trembled with grief and checked the stream of tears down her face with the heel of her palm. (p. 45)

From external to internal sorrow is only a short, inevitable step. Accusations about mishandled money, stolen jewels, and an aborted child fly between the Westcotts while the newscaster on the enormous radio speaks in noncommittal tones about a railroad disaster in Tokyo and a fire in a Buffalo hospital, extinguished by nuns. Like Young Goodman Brown, the Westcotts have lost an illusory faith and must begin again to find a real one with each other. Cheever enlarges on this catalogue of woes to incorporate the Westcotts in the community of suffering.[4]

"O City of Broken Dreams" speaks to another American myth, that of the young man from the provinces.[5] In this case Evarts and Alice

Malloy bring his unfinished play from Wentworth, Indiana, to Tracy Murchison, a New York producer who lectured in Wentworth about the lack of young playwrights. Industrious, simple, hard-working Americans, the Malloys are strung along by the Murchisons, get lost in the city, processed by a high-roller theatrical agent, betrayed and sued for libel by Mama Finelli from Wentworth and by Tracy Murchison. In the process Evarts and his beautiful play are ground to powder. We last see them westbound on the train for the splendid promise of Hollywood. Unlike Hawthorne's Robin, however, the Malloys have an untroubled faith in a mythical Major Molineux.

"Torch Song" also speaks to the perverse innocence of American dreams. The setting is New York during the late thirties and forties. Jack Lorey and Joan Harris "came from the same city in Ohio and had reached New York at about the same time in the middle thirties." (p. 105)

Over the years Joan drifts in and out of Jack's life as they drift from one job and one lover to another. They meet at odd and unexpected moments. Joan is always with a different man—first a drug-addicted Swedish count, then with a brutal German, then with a succession of drunken and doomed men: with Philip, an RAF pilot; with Pete, an aspiring ad man; with Ralph, a music-loving heart specialist; with Stephen, an English anthropologist; with Stanley, who kept a filthy room in Chelsea. Finally, after the war, a failed marriage, and failing health, Jack meets Joan again, dressed always in black. Sweet, patient, innocent as always, the Black Widow has come for him at last, and her visit frightens him out of self-pity and lassitude:

> "Does it make you feel young to watch the dying?" he shouted. "Is that the lewdness that keeps you young? Is that why you dress like a crow? Oh, I know there's nothing I can say that will hurt you. I know there's nothing filthy or depraved or brutish or base that others haven't tried, but this time you're wrong. I'm not ready. My life isn't ending. My life's beginning. There are wonderful years ahead of me. There are, there are wonderful, wonderful, wonderful years ahead of me, and when they're over, when it's time, then I'll call you. Then, as your old friend, I'll call you and give you whatever dirty pleasures you take in watching the dying, but until then, you and your ugly, misshapen forms will leave me alone."
> (p. 121)

The pattern of mechanical inelasticity this time has gone beyond the comic to the grotesque. Joan Harris, like Chekhov's Darling, drains the life from her lovers. Joan's affinity for doomed Europeans may suggest a wider significance as well. This is Cheever's parable of World War II, and Joan is the Angel of Death.

A final example from the early New York stories, "Christmas Is A Sad Season for the Poor," satirizes American abundance and self-pity. It concerns an elevator operator in Sutton Place who feels sorry for himself at Christmas time and lets the tenants know it: "It isn't much of a holiday for me, Mrs. Gadshill," he said. "Christmas is a sad season if you're poor. You see, I don't have any family. I live alone in a furnished room" (p. 154).

Carried away by self-pity and a meretricious sentimentality for poor kids everywhere, Charley invents two dead children and a crippled wife, alternating this specious identity with that of the lonely bachelor as the spirit and his passengers move him. His self-pity invites their confidence, but their own woes leave him unmoved. His alleged sufferings do not go unrewarded, however. The food and the loot fill his locker while Charley swoops up and down at full speed. Charley has become one of Bergson's simple machines. But he terrifies Mrs. Gadshill with his swooping, and she has him fired by the superintendant. Taking heart, Charley thinks of his landlady and her three skinny children in their basement room. He stuffs his presents into a big burlap sack and hurries home, a drunken Santa Claus. Unknown to Charley, the local Democratic Club has fed and provided presents for the landlady and her children. Once he is out of sight, she remembers the Shannons, poorer than herself, and rushes off into the twilight burdened with Charley's presents.

In this story Charley dramatizes the manifest compulsion of it all. But underneath the sentimentality and the farce his characters seem to realize a communal obligation to lessen the sadness of Christmas for the poor, stumbling as they do towards inept generosity. Cheever blunts his satire with compassion, but the comic pattern remains—an exaggerated, repeated action, arising out of mechanical inelasticity, produces its comic and pathetic effects.

The later New York stories focus less on apartment living than on experiences in the city at large. New York in the fifties and sixties has become less a place to live than a place to make a living. Put simply, New York is now the stage for some human action, ridiculous, mythical, or strange, which dramatizes the plight of deracinated man. Three examples will serve: "The Angel of the Bridge," "Metamorphoses," and "The Fourth Alarm."

The first of these describes a miraculous action, and miracle is never far from the realistic surface of Cheever's stories. The narrator's family, transplanted from St. Botolphs, Massachusetts, consists of the narrator's seventy-eight-year-old mother who ice skates at Rockefeller Center and fears airplanes, his older brother, who fears elevators, and himself, seemingly normal. The narrator, who may be Coverly Wapshot, develops acute pontophobia, however, while crossing the George Washington Bridge in a thunderstorm. He imagines the bridge collapsing and hurling "the long lines of Sunday traffic into the dark waters below us" (p. 582).

> The truth is, I hate freeways and Buffalo Burgers. Expatriated palm trees and monotonous housing developments depress me. The continuous music on special-fare trains exacerbates my feelings. I am deeply troubled by the misery and drunkenness I find among my friends. I abhor the dishonest practices I see. And it was at the highest point in the arc of a

> bridge that I became suddenly aware of the depth and bitterness of my
> feelings about modern life, and of the profoundness of my yearning for a
> more vivid, simple, and peaceable world. (pp. 584–85)

This I take to be vintage Cheever. The bridge symbolizes a disaffection of man for his creations, a disaffection so deep as to induce paralysis.
The city of man is almost Augustinian in its iniquity. With its airplanes,
its elevators, its bridges, the city has become literally oppressive and
threatening.

The miracle occurs on the approaches to the Tappan Zee Bridge. He
thinks he might negotiate something at water level, but as he approaches
the bridge, he cannot go through with it. He pulls off to the side, utterly
distraught, and imagines himself in a psychiatric ward, "screaming that
the bridges, all the bridges in the world, were falling down" (p. 586).
Then she appears at the door, this nameless angel of the bridge, a young
girl with long, straight brown hair, a cardboard suitcase, and a harp,
hitch-hiking. As they start up again, she plays the harp and sings "The
Riddle Song" ("I gave my love a cherry. . . .")

> She sang me across a bridge that seemed to be an astonishingly sensible,
> durable, and even beautiful construction designed by intelligent men to
> simplify my travels, and the water of the Hudson below us was charming
> and tranquil. It all came back—blue-sky courage, the high spirits of
> lustiness, an ecstatic sereneness. Her song ended as we got to the toll sta-
> tion on the east bank, and she thanked me, said good-bye, and got out of
> the car. (p. 587)

The miracle is not the heavenly being but the earthly touch, the sense
of community, however fleeting, that makes the girl's song an act of ritual
praise for creation. The story stands in dramatic contrast to Joan Harris's
torch song. It instances the immanence of God's love for the narrator and
enables him to relate to his terrified brother and mother. Things haven't
changed—he has. He can accept his family's frailties without condemning
them. "My brother is still afraid of elevators, and my mother, although
she's grown quite stiff, still goes around and around and around on the
ice" (p. 587).

The second story, "Metamorphoses," shows Cheever in an Ovidian
mood.[6] The four otherwise unrelated segments exemplify the changes that
result when people are deliberately excluded for human community.
Larry Actaeon, an investment banker, is torn apart by his own hounds
after surprising a senior partner with another partner's widow in venereal
intimacy. This Diana takes her revenge only after he has been mistaken
for a waiter and for a bartender, however. Even his wife doesn't know it
is Larry who has been metamorphosed into a human stag.

In segment two, Orville Betman, a Madison Avenue Orpheus, sings
television jingles extolling the virtues of toothpaste and peanut butter. But
he cannot move Victoria Heatherstone, with her sick, scholarly father (a

Trollopian), to live with him. They marry secretly, but that is not recognition enough. So Orville comes like young Robert Browning to confront a tyrannical Mr. Barrett on an upstate island. He sings Handel arias under her window and sweeps his Eurydice away, only to have her die in an auto wreck beside him as he contemplates her beauty behind the wheel. Nothing remains for him but to metamorphose into a disembodied voice, singing irresistably of table polish, bleach, and vacuum cleaners.

In segment three, Mrs. Peranger, a society matron, refuses to allow her dowdy, virginal daughter Nerissa to marry the local veterinarian. While she is haughtily refusing the application of the *declasse* Pentasons for the inclusion of their daughter in the next debutantes' ball, Nerissa metamorphoses into a swimming pool.[7]

In segment four of the story Mr. Bradish, a divorced man and a reformed smoker, begins to pride himself on his newly-discovered will power. But he goes to a cocktail party, where he is overcome by gin and by desire for a young woman "wearing a light sack or tube shaped dress, her long hair the color of Virginia tobacco" (p. 653). He attacks her and is thrown out of the party. In the elevator he stands next to a stranger "whose brown suit looked and smelled like a Havana Upmann"; the elevator operator smells like a cheap tobacco blend that was popular in the fifties. The doorman smells like a Burley mixture. On the street the passing parade conjures up images and smells of pipes, tobaccos, and cigarettes:

> It was a young woman—really a child—whom he mistook for a Lucky Strike that was his undoing. She screamed when he attacked her, and two strangers knocked him down, striking and kicking him with just moral indignation. A crowd gathered. There was pandemonium, and presently the sirens of the police car that took him away. (p. 654)

Here metamorphosis becomes a habit of mind, developed out of a specious sense of superiority which isolates Bradish from those of his kind and allows his cravings unbridled rein over his actions. By now the pattern becomes clear. Cheever is developing characters who in their zeal for half truths destroy their sense of balance and relation. Mechanical inelasticity, whether found in thought, deed, or attitude, jeopardizes one's humanity.

In the third story from the late New York group, "The Fourth Alarm," a man is forced to choose between his identity and his wife. The protagonist, a patient, decent, middle-aged suburbanite, must come to terms with his stage-struck wife, Bertha, who has landed a starring role in the all-nude review, *Ozamanidas II.*

At the climax of the show—one hesitates to use the word—the cast invites all the audience to shed their clothes and join them on stage in a group grope. At first the narrator cooperates, but he carries his wallet, wristwatch, and keys with him towards the stage. One actor, then the whole cast encourage him to "put down his lendings." But to do so would involve a surrender, not just of money and the certainty of getting home to the suburbs, but of his very identity:

> The voices of the cast were loud and scornful, and there I was, buck naked, somewhere in the middle of the city and unwanted, remembering missed football tackles, lost fights, the contempt of strangers, the sound of laughter from behind shut doors. I held my valuables in my right hand, my literal identification. None of it was irreplaceable, but to cast it off would seem to threaten my essence, the shadow of myself that I could see on the floor, my name. (p. 767)

And so he puts his clothes on and goes home.

In contrast to the Sutton Place stories of New York at mid-century, these three give us vignettes of a fantastic, unlivable environment. If we are to take the action of "The Fourth Alarm" as illustrative, the best a sane man can manage is a strategic withdrawal. New York is no longer habitable.

Although he began his writing career in the thirties with stories about New York life, Cheever first reached national prominence in the late fifties and early sixties with the Wapshot novels. By the time he won the National Book Award, he was writing of Shady Hill, an idealized Westchester suburb. A consideration of his two suburban settings, Shady Hill and Bullet Park, reveals the same kind of contrasts observable in his New York stories—a gradual darkening of vision as the possibilities of full, authentic life in contemporary America seem to lessen. At the same time, his outlook has become more clearly and specifically religious.[8]

Shady Hill first appears in "O Youth and Beauty!" Once again Cheever employs the pattern of the simple action, repeated to the level of absurdity, which so often characterizes his comic imagination in these stories. The protagonist, Cash Bentley, feels compelled to defend his youth and beauty at the tag end of cocktail parties. While Trace Bearden fires his starter's gun out the window, Cash runs the high hurdles over the living room furniture: "There was not a piece of furniture in Shady Hill that Cash could not take in his stride. The race ended with cheers, and presently the party would break up" (pp. 249–250).

The Bentleys cling precariously to their suburban life; beset with unpaid bills and high expenses at the country club, Cash drinks too much and quarrels with Louise, his wife. The obstacle races are his tenacious claim on a receding youth. At the Farquarsons, Cash catches his foot on a piece of furniture and falls, gashing his head and breaking his leg. His fall is also a fall from grace. Once popular, Cash now sits at home beside Louise, "who is sewing elastic into the children's underpants" (p. 255). Cash begins to turn jealous of young lovers, grows moody, drinks too much. His youth and beauty are passing.

Then one night the Bentleys return to the country club with the Beardens; after too many drinks Cash begins the obstacle race once more. He clears all the furniture in the lounge but collapses on the floor at the other end. His public appearances are over—but not his career. The next night, at home, he drags the furniture into the shape of the race course. Louise is called upon to fire the starter's pistol, which she has never done before.

> "Hurry up," he said, "I can't wait all night."
> He had forgotten to tell her about the safety, and when she pulled the trigger nothing happened.
> "It's that little lever," he said. "Press that little lever." Then, in his impatience, he hurdled the sofa anyhow.
> The pistol went off and Louise got him in mid-air. She shot him dead.
> (p. 259)

This passionate clinging to a passing stage of life is fatal. Cheever seems to be re-writing "The Short Happy Life of Francis Macomber" as a cautionary tale for aging suburbanites.

Another such tale is "The Five-Forty-Eight." The story manifests the effects of thoughtless egoism on its hero, a middle manager ironically named Blake. Blake's problem is a former secretary named Miss Dent, a shy, troubled young woman who has apparently worked nowhere else. Blake takes sexual advantage of her, fires her, and feels uneasy late one afternoon when he sees her follow him to Grand Central. She sits beside him and pokes a pistol in his ribs, forcing him to take an interest in her raving, rambling love letters that she addresses "Dear Husband."

Blake looks around the swaying railroad car for help but finds none. Mr. Watkins, his next-door neighbor, is asleep. He has insulted Watkins, a corduroy and scandal-clad artist who has violated the sumptuary code of Shady Hill. No one is interested in Blake's predicament. As the stations roll by, he is forced to listen to Miss Dent's confused and compulsive self-revelation. She has been in hospitals; she is lonely; he has poisoned the minds of all prospective employers against her. " 'All I've wanted in life is a little love,' she said. She lightened the pressure of the gun" (p. 291).

They get off at Shady Hill; Miss Dent forces him out of the light and into the darkness. There she forces him to kneel on the ground. She tells him that she will not harm him. She wants to help him, but he is beyond help. No matter how good and loving and sane she might be, he would not listen to her or be worthy of her. She concludes, rightly enough: "Oh, I'm better than you, and I shouldn't waste my time or spoil my life like this. Put your face in the dirt. *Put your face in the dirt!* Do what I say. Put your face in the dirt" (p. 294). Blake does so, and this ritual abasement saves his life. But it does not enlighten him. Cheever gives us a parable here, that of the Shady Hill pharisee and a demented publican. Only the publican, cleansed of her compulsions, goes away justified. Hers is the authentic, passionate life. Blake, a creature without even the grace of a first name, has never lived and never will.

"The Housebreaker of Shady Hill" suggests that not all the denizens of the town are so spiritually dark, however. Johnny Hake, for one thing, knows where he was born and raised, where he belongs, and despite his frailty under financial pressure, what he believes in. He is tested early. When called upon to fire the boss's front man, he cannot bring himself to do it. His visit to the bedside of Gil Bucknam is warning enough for the man, however; as soon as Bucknam pulls himself together, he fires Johnny. Johnny strikes out on his own, does miserably at soliciting sales over the phone, and resorts to stealing nine hundred dollars from a sleeping neighbor's trousers.

> Oh, I never knew that a man could be so miserable and that the mind could open up so many chambers and fill them with self reproach! Where were the trout streams of my youth, and other innocent pleasures? The wet-leather smell of the loud waters and the keen woods after a splashing rain; or at opening day the summer breezes swelling like the grassy breath of Holsteins—your head would swim—and all the books full then (or so I imagined, in the dark kitchen) of trout, our sunken treasure. I was crying.
> (p. 306)

Johnny Hake has broken "all the unwritten laws that hold a community together." With the stolen money he is able to pay his bills—bills were smaller in those days—but the financial reprieve has left him spiritually bankrupt. Once his eyes are darkened, however, he sees theft everywhere—a customer takes a thirty-five cent tip from a lunch counter; a friend offers to "steal" money from a trusting customer; he remembers stealing fifty dollars from his father's pocket in a New York hotel room; the newspapers are suddenly replete with accounts of international thefts and swindles. Like Irene Westcott and Goodman Brown before him, Johnny Hake has fallen from innocence.

But he will not succumb to self-pity. He echoes one of the cardinal tenets in Cheever's code of conduct, the need to seize one's identity and to live it out regardless of consequences: "If there is anybody I detest, it is weak-minded sentimentalists—all those melancholy people who, out of an excess of sympathy for others, miss the thrill of their own essence and drift through life without identity, like a human fog, feeling sorry for everyone" (p. 314).

That identity, even though it includes housebreaking, stands him in good stead. Ultimately the old man at Parablendum dies, and Gil Bucknam calls him back to his job. He takes an advance on his salary, repays the Warburtons (a Jamesian echo), and whistles his way back home past the Shady Hill police. Thus corporate bonds are only a special form of communal bonds; Johnny's bonds with Parablendum restore him to financial and spiritual health. The essential principle here and throughout Cheever's stories is belief in self-worth and respect for the communal obligation which derives from that belief.

Francis Weed, the Country Husband, is another version of the troubled suburbanite—beset this time not by the need for money, but by a crash landing in a Pennsylvania cornfield, by a tearful wife and squabbling children, and by a sad Nausicaa named Anne Murchison. Francis feels the ache of lust for the babysitter and plans to seduce her with a bracelet. But he never gets the opportunity. With unconscious wisdom, Julia keeps her out of his way. Desperately trying to cope with his sexual frustrations, Francis takes the analyst's advice and turns to woodworking. It works. The perilous peace of Shady Hill, founded on the illusion of harmony, descends on Francis Weed as well. Dogs, children, commuter trains, and local characters assume their wonted roles in his ordered life. "Then it is dark; it is a night when kings in golden suits ride elephants over the mountains" (p. 410).

One last story will exemplify this perilous balance between order and chaos in Shady Hill. Moses Coverly, the narrator of "The Death of Justina," proclaims his credo early in the story:

> Fiction is art and art is the triumph over chaos (no less) and we can accomplish this only by the most vigilant exercise of choice, but in a world that changes more swiftly than we can perceive, there is always the danger that our powers of selection will be mistaken and that the vision we serve will come to nothing. (pp. 505–6)

This time the mechanical inelasticity which so plagues Cheever's people is external, in the vexations of work and in the zoning regulations. Moses is forced to write an Elixircol commercial while trying to bury his wife's cousin Justina, the mysterious and exotic witch of *The Wapshot Chronicle;* she has the misfortune of dying in Zone B, where death is not permitted.

Moses coerces the mayor into making a risky exception to the zoning laws, which have the force of the Decalogue in Proxmire Manor. Only death is obscene there, so in defiance of the Decalogue Moses transports the corpse across interzone lines for burial on the outskirts of town. This attention to the filial pieties—and Cheever is the most Roman of our writers—is bought at some cost. The Elixircol commercial somehow functions as an extension of the zoning regulations. Its requirements are equally inflexible. So an exasperated Moses strikes back as best he can, by burlesquing the language of advertising and addressing its hidden appeals directly. His first draft frightens and indicts the reader for his greed, his sexual excess, and his fear of death. The second draft reproaches him for his barely disguised lust. The third and absolutely unusable draft is the Twenty-third Psalm: *"The Lord is my shepherd; therefore can I lack nothing. . . .*" The story ends with a prayer, a plea for sublime common sense to preserve human dignity.

"The Death of Justina" is the funniest and the best of the Shady Hill stories, even though it is set in Proxmire Manor, a place where nothing ever happens (by deliberate design). It is unusual again in combining the themes of the search for identity and the need for community with the character of Moses Coverly, resurrected from the Wapshot novels. Chronologically it falls between the two novels, before Moses' utter collapse at the end of the *Scandal*.

If innocence, forgiveness, and community serve to support the continuity of life in Shady Hill, no such meliorating forces are at work in Bullet Park. Man is isolated, unsupported by marital love, family, or a strong community. Even the climate seems to have turned colder. Bullet Park is, first of all, the setting for Cheever's third novel. The story of Mr. Hammer and Mr. Nailles recapitulates the sacrifice of Isaac and the crucifixion of Christ. Bullet Park witnesses no resurrection, however; it is a grim place which deprives its inhabitants of that community they need to come fully alive.

The place has its comic moments, of course. The narrator of "The Ocean" suspects that his wife is putting pesticide on his cutlets. He has lost his job after successfully negotiating a takeover by a larger company. His daughter Flora has dropped out of college and lives in Greenwich Village with her unemployed boyfriend, pasting costly butterflies on a skeleton. The narrator seeks refuge in dreams and memories. He remember's Cora's beauty when he married her. He wakes beside her at three in the morning, seized by the desire to love all those who have slighted him. He sees a green meadow and a sparkling stream, thatched-roof cottages and a square Saxon church tower. He looks for his wife and daughter in the village but cannot find them. He falls into a deep sleep on the grass, like Piers Plowman. Perhaps he will wake to love, but the prospects are not promising.

"The Swimmer" offers us even less by way of promise. Neddy Merrill, another compulsive athlete like Cash Bentley, decides to swim home one midsummer day through the chain of backyard pools he calls the Lucinda River, after his wife. He sets off in the full bloom of youth, an alcoholic Odysseus. Although the pattern of his progress is uncertain at first, it gradually clarifies. Once the alcohol wears off, people aren't as friendly as they once were. His mistress snubs him; a hostess accuses him of gate crashing. His progress through each pool becomes more difficult. His body wears down. The weather is changing. In his fleeting encounters Neddy hears surprising allusions to events in his life, events of which he is unaware. He has financial problems, marital difficulties, trouble with his daughters. When he finally swims home, aging and sober, the cold winds of October are blowing on his bare body.

The place was dark. Was it so late that they had all gone to bed? Had Lucinda stayed at the Westerhazys' for supper? Had the girls joined her there or gone someplace else? Hadn't they agreed, as they usually did on Sunday, to regret all their invitations and stay at home? He tried the garage doors to see what cars were in but the doors were locked and rust came off the handles onto his hands. Going towards the house, he saw that the force of the thunderstorm had knocked one of the rain gutters loose It hung down over the front door like an umbrella rib, but it could be fixed in the morning. The house was locked, and he thought that the stupid cook or the stupid maid must have locked the place up until he remembered that it had been some time since they had employed a maid or a cook. He shouted, pounded on the door, tried to force it with his shoulder, and then, looking in at the windows, saw that the place was empty. (pp. 724–25)

In "The Swimmer" Cheever conveys the effects of drink and the passing years through the simple but powerful metaphor of Neddy's swim through the pools of Westchester County. But at least Neddy has reached a point where he can see himself as he is, and live, perhaps for the first time—if he can find the strength to do so.

"Another Story" plays a variation on the theme of bare, unaccommodated man. The narrator has befriended a threadbare Italian prince, Marcantonio Parlapiano ("Mark Anthony, speak softly"), who generally goes by "Boobee." Boobee is transferred by his company from Verona to New York with his American wife, Grace. Boobee has a language problem, though, and doesn't adapt well to American ways. While his neighbors speak of balky machines (rotary lawn mowers) and of chemical fertilizers, Boobee "praises the beauty of the landscape, the immaculateness of American women, and the pragmatism of American politics, and spoke of the horrors of a war with China. He kissed me goodbye on Madison Avenue. I think no one was looking" (p. 739).

The medium of Boobee's confusion is language. He has not and seemingly cannot learn the language of the tribe. To compound his confusion, Grace decides to take up opera. Boobee thinks she is mad but finds no solace from the narrator, who tells him that American husbands do not complain about their wives. Shortly after this scene, Boobee is injured in an automobile accident. When the narrator goes to see him in the hospital, he learns that Boobee and Grace are separated. He cries as he recounts the ultimate indignity: Grace wants him to change his name. Rather than do that, he decides to return to Verona, where unhappy love is a long tradition.

The coda offers a parallel experience. The narrator runs into a friend in Moscow. At the airport he hears a story about the friend's ex-wife, who found her identity as a terminal announcer at Newark Airport. Unfortunately she brings the language and intonation of the terminal home to the dinner table. This loss of language destroys their intimacy and their marriage:

> Well, we stayed together for another six months, but that was really the end of it. I really loved her. She was a marvelous girl until she began to give me this feeling that I was a dumb passenger, one of hundreds in some waiting room, being directed to the right gate and the right flight. We quarreled all the time then, and I finally left, and she got a consent decree in Reno. She still works at Newark, and I can hear her telling Mr. Henry Tavistock to please report to American Airlines ticket counter.... (p. 749)

In each of these Bullet Park stories, a marriage has failed. In each, people are cut loose from their moorings and drift on the ocean of life without direction, without love, without community. Like the later New York stories, Cheever's Bullet Park evidences a darkening of vision, a reduction of hope, an awareness of the fragility of love and the confusion of life against which art is only a momentary stay. One thinks again and again while reading these stories of another New Englander, Wallace Stevens, for whom the writing of poems is the pressing back of the imagination from within against the pressure of news from without. We are not far in either case from art as desperation.[9]

Cheever is no suburban Celine, however. Balance is everything for him. Balance, and humor, and an appetite for life, and a capacity to celebrate the world and the individual. He seems to find a partial order between the individual and his world in the Italian stories—but that order does not include expatriated Americans, with rare exceptions. Having lived there for some time in the fifties, Cheever loves Rome and Italy. The country offers tangible evidence that man has lived on harmonious terms with his world for centuries.

"The Bella Lingua" is an example of a kind of Italian order from which Americans are excluded. Wilson Streeter—the name sounds suspiciously like Lambert Strether—is an expatriate statistician, divorced, who wants to learn the beautiful language. He finds a succession of Italian teachers no help to him. Finally he comes upon Kate Dresser, who is willing to teach him. He comes weekly to an Italian palace for his lesson. Periodically a group of aging Italian nobles shuffle through the apartment on the way to tea at the Baronessa Tarominia's, at the other end of the palace.

Kate, a widow, has a fifteen-year-old son, Charlie, who has found some companionship with Embassy children. All of them are aggressively American. They wear blue jeans and black leather jackets; they carry baseball mitts. "They are Embassy children, and the children of writers and oil-company and airline employees and divorcees and Fulbright Fellows. Eating bacon and eggs, and listening to the jukebox, they have a sense of being far, far from home that is a much sweeter and headier distillation than their parents ever know" (p. 365).

Streeter, on the other hand, thinks that he has acclimated himself to Italy. He visits friends in the country and enjoys the song of an Italian peasant girl with flowers in her hair, but he still doesn't understand what she is singing. He makes halting progress with his Italian lessons, but his knowledge of the language is only secondary and literary. The American counterpart of Boobee, he knows not the language of the tribe.

Into this world comes Uncle George, from Krasbie, Iowa. Uncle George serves as a catalyst and foil to Streeter. George is tricked, robbed, and exasperated by Italians, but his innocence is inviolable. Streeter, by contrast, is fooling himself. His pathetic efforts to acclimate himself to the bella lingua and to Roman life takes him nowhere. Seeing a whore, a corpse, and a churl who is feeding firecrackers to stray cats, Streeter knows that he does not want to die in Rome.

It is Uncle George then, and not Streeter, who comes as the ambassador to take Charlie home with him. Kate will have her Rome if she insists and so will Streeter, as Strether had his Paris before him, but all the life, the vigor, and the future are drained from that life when Uncle George (the name is surely symbolic) takes Charlie back to Krasbie. Streeter and Kate begin the study of Dante, but the great *Commedia* is only a linguistic substitute for the life of Americans in America. Cheever implies that America's future lies less in Bullet Park than in Krasbie. It certainly doesn't lie in Rome, with its threadbare aristocrats.

Not all Romans are so pathetic, though. "The Duchess" recounts the progress of a simple woman, sole offspring of a crippled Italian Duke and a Cockney nurse, through the pitfalls of interminable courtships. Donna Carla is a genuine gentlewoman—simple, humble, pious, and practical. She spends her time supervising the twenty shops on the ground floor of the palace, the leaky plumbing, the accounts of her peasants in Tuscany. One by one her suitors come seeking her fortune and her palace; one by one she entertains and discourages them, with infinite tact and practicality. In the end Donna Carla marries her English clerk, Cecil Smith.

> They returned to Rome, and she took an office adjoining his, and shared the administration of the estate and the work of distributing her income among convents, hospitals, and the poor. Their first son—Cecil Smith, Jr.—was born a year after their marriage, and a year later they had a daughter, Jocelyn. Donna Carla was cursed in every leaky castle in Europe, but surely shining choirs of angels in heaven will sing of Mrs. Cecil Smith. (p. 424)

Surely they will. Unlike American expatriates, sad, footloose wanderers that they are, Donna Carla has found her place in Rome and in society, which, even though it rejects her, benefits from her steady ministration to its needs. Mrs. Cecile Smith lives an authentic existence.

Another authentic character is Asa Bascomb, an old Yankee poet who lives in a villa below the hill town of Monte Carbone, south of Rome. He is eighty-two, the son of a Vermont farmer and the only survivor of a poetic group whose other four members die suicides. Bascomb relies on his memory, which brings continuity to centuries of Italian history. Cheever makes him the custodian of civilization.

By being only a man, Asa Bascomb is beset by human weakness, specifically lust. He struggles with his desires in orderly fashion, however, writing his poems in the morning, and pornographic stories and dirty limericks in the afternoon. Western civilization includes not only Saracen towns and twelfth-century churches, but the sexual merriment of Petronius and Juvenal as well, so he turns to them for solace. He reconsiders his life, his public position as poet laureate, struggling to resolve his reputation and his desires. "He seemed to hold the crown, hold it up into the light, it seemed made of light and what it seemed to mean was the genuine and tonic taste of exaltation and grief" (p. 733).

To exorcise his imagination, Bascomb makes a pilgrimage to Monte Giordano, where he sees an Italian family on a picnic, meets an old man looking at a stamp album, and leaves a gold medal with a Russian inscription, his Lermontov medal, at the feet of the olive-wood angel. He falls to his knees and prays a litany for dead writers: "God bless Walt Whitman. God bless Hart Crane. God bless Dylan Thomas. God bless William Faulkner, Scott Fitzgerald, and especially Ernest Hemingway" (p. 736).

On his way home the next day, Bascomb steps into a mountain waterfall, remembering his old father, who once stepped into another waterfall at the edge of his Vermont farm, bellowing with joy. The experience is a ritual cleansing for Bascomb, a resolution of the forces of lust and joy that have troubled his life. "His return to Monte Carbone was triumphant and in the morning he began a long poem on the inalienable dignity of light and air that, while it would not get him the Nobel Prize, would grace the last months of his life" (p. 737).

"The World of Apples" celebrates the joyous reconciliation of conflicting tendencies that beset every man's life. If one is to live authentically, he makes a similar reconciliation, thus fulfilling the potential of his own life. Such a reconciliation involves a harmony between man and his world with its waters, its mountains, its light, and air. Cheever's Asa Bascomb emerges from his ordeal as the worthy son of great poetic sires—Walt Whitman, Prospero, and St. Francis. He observes the filial pieties with reverence, and his reward is joy in life.

One final locale for Cheever's stories deserves attention, St. Botolphs. It figures prominently in *The Wapshot Chronicle*, less so in *The Wapshot Scandal*. Few of these stories are set in Massachusetts, but those that are shed light on the mythic origins of Cheever's imagination. Three of them at least deserve consideration for their emphasis upon the continuity of family life. They are "Goodbye, My Brother," "The Lowboy," and "The Jewels of the Cabots."

The first of these begins the 1978 collection. It deals with a family vacation at Laud's Head on one of the Massachusetts Islands—in all likelihood, Martha's Vineyard. The family problem is the youngest brother, Lawrence. Lawrence is a stingy, mean-spirited, moralistic philistine. He attacks the family house—and through it, the family itself—as impractical, in danger of destruction from the sea, extravagant. Gradually he dissipates the patience and good will of his sister, brothers, and widowed mother.

Finally the narrator can take it no longer. He accuses Lawrence of excessive gloom and hears him dismiss each family member as promiscuous, alcoholic, dishonest, or foolish. Exasperated, the narrator picks up a tree root and hits Lawrence on the back of the head with it. (Then he keeps him from being sucked out in the undertow.) He is alive, all right, but the blow precipitates his departure. Taking his wife and two unhappy children away from the family, Lawrence goes on "to do important things." Cheever's narrator comments on the situation:

> Oh, what can you do with a man like that? What can you do? How can you dissuade his eye in a crowd from seeking out the cheek with acne, the infirm hand; how can you teach him to respond to the inestimable greatness of the race, the harsh surface beauty of life; how can you put his finger for him on the obdurate before which fear and horror are powerless? The sea that morning was iridescent and dark. My wife and my sister were swimming—Diana and Helen—and I saw their uncovered heads, black and gold in the dark water. I saw them come out and I saw that they were naked, unshy, beautiful, and full of grace, and I watched the naked women walk out of the sea. (p. 23)

In turning his back on the family, Lawrence has cut himself off from the source of life itself.

The second of these three St. Botolphs stories is in many ways a reworking of "Goodbye, My Brother." This time the brother's name is Richard, and he is in every way a small man. The family dispute centers on a lowboy, a family heirloom that the narrator has received from Cousin Mathilda. Richard wants the lowboy and comes to make his claim. His desire is simply greater, thus more authentic than the narrator's. He must have the piece, so the narrator gives it to him.

Unfortunately, the piece is damaged. The man who repairs the splintered leg discovers that this is the famous Barstow lowboy, made by the celebrated Sturbridge cabinetmaker in 1780: it is worth ten thousand dollars. As time passes, Richard reconstructs both the lowboy and the room in Cousin Mathilda's house, with another Turkish carpet, heavy brasses, and a silver pitcher to cover the water stain left by the pitcher.

It would seem that Richard is paying his pieties to the family, but he is not. In his idolatry of heirlooms, he has underestimated the lives which they were made to enhance, and those lives come back in ghostly procession to haunt him. The narrator watches this parade of prickly individualists who will not be reduced to the status of furniture custodians. First comes Grandmother De Lancey, who campaigned for women's rights and cheered fire engines. Then Aunt Louisa, who painted huge canvases and smoked cigars (like Amy Lowell). Then Timothy, a child pianist who played with an orchestra at twelve and killed himself at fifteen. Uncle Tom, whose conquests numbered in the thousands, appears, carrying his crippled son up the stairs. Next comes Aunt Mildred, the poet who took a lover and left Uncle Sidney with the housework. Sidney himself, stinking of liquor, sits beside Richard on the sofa. He spills whiskey, inflames it with his lighted cigarette, and watches the whole macabre Christmas fantasy go up in flames.

Richard learns nothing from the masque. He has committed himself to the lowboy. At Thanksgiving Dinner he quarrels with his wife and children, sending the narrator home to smash and discard all the heirlooms that have hedged his own life:

> Out they go—the Roman coins, the sea horse from Venice, and the Chinese fan. We can cherish nothing less than our random understanding of death and the earth-shaking love that draws us to one another. Down with the stuffed owl in the upstairs hall and the statue of Hermes on the newel post! Hock the ruby necklace, throw away the invitation to Buckingham Palace, jump up and down on the perfume atomizer from Murano and the Canton fish plates. Dismiss whatever molests us and challenges our purpose, sleeping or waking. Cleanliness and valor will be our watchwords. Nothing less will get us past the armed sentry and over the mountainous border. (p. 487)

Like Asa Bascomb's mountain stream, this vigorous housecleaning is a ritual cleansing of the imagination which frees the narrator to live.

"The Jewels of the Cabots" is the last story in the 1978 collection. Like the first one, "Goodbye, My Brother," the last one is set in St. Botolphs. The occasion is the funeral of Amos Cabot, murdered by his wife for moving in with Mrs. Wallace across the river. But the murder scarcely matters to Coverly Wapshot, who takes the occasion to recall his brief love for Molly, Amos's daughter. (Coverly remembers the day that Mrs. Cabot's diamonds are discovered missing. Geneva, the older daughter, has taken them from the lawn where they were drying in the sun. She sails to Alexandria, becomes a Moslem, and marries an Egyptian noble.) The trouble began with a quarrel at home, after which Amos Cabot left. Coverly comments on these troubles in a brief reflection on his art:

> Children drown, beautiful women are mangled in automobile accidents, cruise ships founder, and men die lingering deaths in mines and submarines, but you will find none of this in my accounts. In the last chapter the ship comes home to port, the children are saved, the miners will be rescued. Is this an infirmity of the genteel or a conviction that there are discernible moral truths? Mr. X defacates in his wife's top drawer. This is a fact, but I claim that it is not truth. In describing St. Botolphs I would sooner stay on the West Bank of the river where the

houses were white and where the church bells rang, but over the bridge there was the table-silver factory, the tenements (owned by Mrs. Cabot), and the Commercial Hotel. At low tide one could smell the gas from the sea inlets at Travertine. . . . (pp. 812–13)

Coverly goes on to muse about the gratuitous ugliness of life, of spiritual nomads, marital misfits, and the inept struggles of his father to carve the Sunday roast. Not for him the obscene tantrums of uprooted women. Coverly knows his roots, mildly regrets his preference for a traditional, orderly, ceremonial style of life. The family offers the natural confines for the vagaries of love, and even if they lead to murder, those vagaries are at least understandable within those confines. Violence outside the family occurs in a vacuum and is therefore unintelligible.

So the family and marital love are first and last Cheever's subject, the magnetic north of his compass and ours. He calls attention to his limitations but doesn't apologize for them. Not for him the world of, say, Joyce Carol Oates. His stories are parables, fairy tales for grown-ups, but they celebrate love, the wonders and beauties of the natural world. He portrays the contrary forces at work within this world of love, to be sure. His characters struggle for balance between a vigorous individuality that threatens to warp itself in grotesque isolation and a need for community that may degenerate into mindless defense of the zoning regulations. Balance is not easily won, but it is everything.

Cheever has placed himself squarely in the New England tradition of our national literature. His roots go back to Emerson, Thoreau, and Hawthorne and beyond them to his colonial forbears.[10] He reminds us that not only Jewish-American writers have families; tradition and filial piety apply to Yankee stock as well.

Individuality may be rugged, bizarre, or pathetic, but it does evidence the struggle towards identity which all of us must undergo. The community may be idealized and increasingly difficult to find, particularly in the later stories, but it is there nonetheless—most of all in the community of understanding that Cheever projects with his readers. For through it all, the ugliness of individual acts is muted by the charm of the narrative voice—beguiling, understanding, bemused, generalizing, incantatory.

Perhaps the most remarkable of Cheever's achievements is his simple conviction that he will be read and understood. He speaks to our need for heroes and heroism, our desire to affirm ourselves, to find harmony between our inner and outer landscapes. In reading him sympathetically, we see ourselves and our America, imperiled not so much by violence without as violence within—the loss of faith, the loss of hope, the loss of love.

John Cheever celebrates our mortality in these stories, as his fellow New Englander Wallace Stevens celebrates it in "Sunday Morning." As recurrent as are his New York, his Shady Hill, his Bullet Park, his Rome, and his St. Botolphs, they instance not so much clinical analyses of places and mores as glimpses of an ideal; not places and times, but an attitude of accommodation, of compassion, of a celebration both sacred and profane. Cheever raises them in a wry, tongue-in-cheek, hand-curled-around-the-glass toast to the human frailties that are our fate and our glory.

Notes

1. *The Stories of John Cheever* (New York: Alfred A. Knopf, 1978), p. ix. All page references cite the Ballantine paperback edition (New York, 1980).

2. Walt Whitman, "Song of Myself," *The Collected Writings of Walt Whitman*, ed. Harold W. Blodgett and Sculley Bradley (New York: W.W. Norton Company, 1965), p. 52.

3. Henri Bergson, "*Les attitudes, gestes et mouvements du corps humain sont risibles dans l'exacte mesure óu ce corps vous fait penser à une simple mecanique.*" "Le Rire," *Oeuvres*, 2nd ed., ed. Henri Gouhier (Paris: Presses Universitaires de France, 1963), p. 401.

4. See Henrietta Ten Harmsel, " 'Young Goodman Brown' and 'The Enormous Radio,' " *Studies in Short Fiction*, 9 (1972), 407–08.

5. Daniel Hoffman identifies the characteristic of this genre in his analysis of "My Kinsman, Major Molineux," in *Form and Fable in American Fiction* (New York: Oxford University Press, 1961), pp. 117–118.

6. Alwyn Lee's cover story on the occasion of *The Wapshot Scandal*'s publication was entitled "Ovid in Ossining." See *Time*, 83 (27 March 1964), 66–72.

7. "The fifty Nereids, gentle and beneficient attendants on the Sea-goddess Thetis, are mermaids, daughters of the nymph Doris by Nereus, a prophetic old man of the sea, who has the power of changing his shape." Robert Graves, *The Greek Myths*, (Baltimore: Penguin Books, 1955), 1:127.

8. George Hunt makes this clear in his review of the collection: "Just as Cheever is not a strict satirist he is not a moralist either. And yet, his work, as his last novel *Falconer* made evident, is deeply Christian in sensibility. Few of his stories, apart from cleverly inserted Biblical allusions, are obivously religious in design. But Cheever's sympathy for his characters' fallen state together with their vague yearings of personal rebirth, for a virtuous life possibly untrammeled by life's more sordid confusions, betray his sincere Episcopal beliefs. Every artist's endeavor demands an implicit faith-commitment to a world he hopes will reward it, but Cheever has been more religiously specific. He has said in an interview, 'The religious experience is very much my concern, as it seems to me the legitimate concern of any adult who has experienced love. . . . The whiteness of light. In the church, you know, that always represents the Holy Spirit. It seems to me that man's inclination toward light, toward brightness, is very nearly botanical—and I mean spiritual light. One not only needs it, one struggles for it. It seems to me that one's total experience is the drive toward light.' " "A Style Both Lyrical and Idiosyncratic: Beyond the Cheeveresque," *Commonweal*, 106 (19 January 1979), 21–22.

9. See Wallace Steven's conclusion to "The Noble Rider and the Sound of Words": "The mind has added nothing to human nature. It is a violence from within that protects us from a violence without. It is the imagination pressing back against the pressure of reality. It seems, in the last analysis, to have something to do with our self-preservation; and that, no doubt, is why the expression of it, the sound of its words, helps us to live our lives." *The Necessary Angel: Essays on Reality and the Imagination* (New York: Vintage Books, 1965), p. 36.

10. "His combination of attention to the individual and awareness of the facts and powers of society connect him more with classic American authors like Hawthorne, James,

and Fitzgerald [than with his contemporaries]; and despite his own New England background and East Coast life-style, he has resisted the post-World War II tendency of American writers to divert American fiction toward a narrow exploration of their own individual religious, racial, or geographical roots." Lynne Waldeland, *John Cheever* (Boston: Twayne, 1979), p. 143.

Cheever's Expatriates

John L. Brown*

Reviewers of *The Stories of John Cheever* (1978) kept reminding us, time after time, that Cheever is "our Chekhov of suburbia." But another, less familiar, but nevertheless significant aspect of his work has largely escaped the attention of commentators: that part of it dealing with the European-American relationship. Samuel Coale[1] notes that Cheever "spent a year in Italy with his family in 1956"—*e basta*. Lynne Waldeland[2] remarks that "the Italian stories are considerably less successful," and goes on to make brief and perfunctory remarks on "The Duchess," "The Golden Age," and "Boy in Rome."

Cheever, of course, was never, in any sense, "an expatriate writer" in the tradition of the twenties. His contacts with the Old World were brief and generally, it would seem, rather superficial. As a young man he "took a walking tour in Europe." In the Army during World War II, he witnessed, in a Norman village, an incident of which many who took part in the invasion had seen the like. A girl who had slept with the Germans is being punished by the townspeople. Her hair is cut off and she is paraded naked through the streets, reviled, spat upon, and stoned. Cheever uses this incident in "The Country Husband."[3] Much later, in 1964, he spent six weeks in Russia on an official exchange program. A section of "Artemis, the Honest Well Digger" (pp. 650–71) recalls some of his impressions of this visit. Artemis wants to get away from his New England village for a while, to avoid the lustful assaults of a determined matron who had engaged him to dig a well, but who expects him to provide other services as well. A travel agent sells him "a package" to the Soviet Union—he didn't care where he was going, as long as it was a good distance away. As a well digger and presumably a member of "the American proletariat," he is welcomed at an official ceremony and is provided with an attractive interpreter, with whom he promptly falls in love and goes to bed. Leaving her apartment, he is halted by a policeman, who tells him that he is leaving for the United States the next morning. The two lovers begin to correspond, but their letters, of course, are monitored

*This essay was written specifically for this volume and is published here for the first time with permission of the author. An earlier version appeared in *World Literature Today* (Autumn 1979).

by both governments and their amorous *bavardage* is interpreted as a code for the transmission of strategic information. Artemis, summoned to Washington, is informed that the State Department wants him to send to Natasha, "in their code . . ." the information, or rather the misinformation" they wish to transmit to the Russians. He declines and leaves "feeling worse than he had felt in Moscow and singing the unreality blues." Although he continues to write to Natasha, he never hears from her again.

So much for the casual transmutation of personal experience abroad. However the European experience that contributed most directly to Cheever's work was the year he spent in Italy in 1956. In the post World War II years, Italy, to a certain degree, had replaced Paris as the favorite haven of the American expatriate. Many of them came and went—Tennessee Williams, Gore Vidal, Robert Fitzgerald, Eleanor Clarke, and Robert Penn Warren, Allen Tate, William Styron, William Demby among many others. More than a dozen of the collected stories are either set in Italy or make some reference to the Italian experiences of the characters. They represent, perhaps, an attempt to break out of the narrowness of suburbia, to try new paths, to explore a more spacious, more richly allusive domain. In them, Cheever tries his hand at a theme which has challenged many of our writers in the past, from Henry James onwards—the theme of "the American abroad," of the expatriate life. In Cheever's case, as we might suspect, the eye which observes so unerringly, with such murderous accuracy, the shady side of Shady Hill, focusses less sharply on the Italian scene.

It is always risky for a highly specialized craftsman, adept in depicting a well-defined sector of his native turf, to venture on an alien terrain, one with which he is acquainted only briefly and largely by hearsay. Even though he had an extensive tourist's knowledge of Europe, Henry James' descriptions of Paris "high life" (as, for example, in *The American*) seem the work of an outsider, straining to catch a glimpse, from the windows on the street, of what is going on inside. Cheever, so sure of himself in suburbia, seems to share something of the bewilderment of his own expatriates when confronted with the more ancient wickednesses of Italy. Like them, he is at first attracted to the great name, to the grand but decaying palace, to the storied castle. But those readers who have a smattering of Italian may be somewhat disconcerted by the farcical labels he affixes (with ironic intent?) to his aristocratic characters. In "Boy in Rome" (pp. 452–67) we are introduced to a royalty with the incredible moniker of Princess Tavola Calda (Steam Table). The Anglo-Italian noblewoman in "The Duchess" (pp. 347–58) bears the name of Carla Malvolio-Pommodori—an appellation that suggests "wicked tomatoes." Spurning princely offers, she marries her lower-class English estate manager and they settle down in their vast Roman palace to live simple lives and to distribute most of her income to charity. In other tales, Cheever seems to be consciously holding his bluebloods up to ridicule by giving them such titles as the Duke of Ricotto Sporci (which brings to mind dirty—"sporca," cheese—"ricotta"). Indeed, many of the Italian characters remain unidimensional, even verge on caricature. And although Cheever's gift for the telling phrase and the witty judgement seldom deserts him, these tales sometimes take on the flavor of exemplary fables, of demonstrations, rather too predictable demonstrations, of certain stereotyped situations of the expatriate life.

Several of them deal with Americans like Streeter in "La Bella Lingua" (pp. 302–18). He is "keenly conscious of the fact that he was making his life in a country that was not his own." He imagined that "his sense of being an outsider would change when he knew the language." So he embarks on the study of "la bella lingua" with a series of eccentric teachers, beginning with an ancient lady who will do nothing but read *Pinocchio* to him and ending with a cultivated American Foreign Service widow from Iowa. She is madly in love with the Old World, but her adolescent son hates Italy and is only too happy to return to the Middle West with his grass-roots uncle. (The uncle behaves like a character out of *Innocents Abroad* and is horrified by all the naked statues he sees in Rome, although he is secretly attracted by dirty post-cards.) As Streeter, under the devoted tutelage of the cultivated widow, becomes more competent in the language, the bitter truth is borne in upon him that he simply better understands, that he can never hope *really* to understand. Even the loveliest moments, such as an evening in a villa at Anticoli, bring only "a borrowed, temporary, bittersweet happiness." He cannot forgive the gratuitous cruelty that these supposedly "sensitive" people inflict so callously on man and beast. Seeing a hit and run victim dying in the street, surrounded by a garrulous and unfeeling crowd, he wondered why it was that "they regarded a human life as something of such dubious value." He encounters a young man offering to one of the thousands of the famished cats that live in the ruins a piece of bread in which was concealed a lighted firecracker and laughing uproariously when it exploded and the animal "let out a hellish shriek." On the way home that evening, he passes a hearse, whose driver had "the face of a drunken horse-thief." It rattled over the paving stones so violently that "the poor soul it carried must have been in a terrible state of derangement." The mourners' carriage that followed was empty. "The friends of the dead man had probably been too late or had got the wrong date or had forgotten the whole thing as was so often the case in Rome" (p. 310). Streeter, after all his efforts, was really no closer to "understanding Italy" than the freshly arrived tourists, staring out of the windows of the bus taking them from Naples to Rome, "separated only by a pane of glass from a life that was as strange to them as life on the moon." He could fully share their feelings of frustration and disappointment: "Oh, I wish that I'd never come," said one old lady to another. "I just wish I'd never left home. . . ."

Those rare Americans who succeed in making the adjustment to a foreign society are usually not the better for it. Brimmer, a professional expatriate (pp. 386–95) whom the narrator meets on the crossing from New York to Naples has the leering face and the goatlike eye of an old satyr. Europe had liberated him from every vestige of Puritan morality and he leads a life singlemindedly devoted to fornication. Listening to the lovemaking, in the cabin next to his, of Brimmer and a French lady he had picked up that morning, the narrator recognized that "there was no inclination to internationalism in my disposition" and that "he was no European." And such depravity, alas, goes unpunished. The following summer, spearfishing at Porto Santo Stefano, he sees the face of Brimmer staring subaqueously up at him from the page of a waterlogged copy of *Epoca*. The old satyr had just married a starlet half his age.

The returning expatriate in "Mene Mene Tekel Upharsin" (pp. 554–60), who has the illusion of finding literary texts inscribed in unexpected places on the walls of railroad stations and of restrooms, is told by his American associates that "you've simply been away too long. You're out of touch." And the narrator himself, as he prepares to go back to Europe, seems half convinced that he has been away too long and that he is really "out of touch with decency and common sense." In "Montraldo" (pp. 561–66), a rather thin, contrived little piece, another expatriate, who flees his native shores after having pulled off an ingenious robbery at Tiffany's holes up in an obscure village on the Tyrrhenian coast. He takes a room in a dilapidated villa, where the owner, a refined and thoroughly ruined old Roman aristocrat, is outrageously abused and exploited by her maid, who, it is revealed on the noblewoman's deathbed, is her illegitimate daughter.

The American who arrives, hat symbolically in hand, to render a barbarian's homage to an old, superior culture, is soon disabused in the booming, money-mad "New Europe" that has emerged from the War. Seton (pp. 396–403), an American television writer, and his family rent a picturesque castle overlooking an isolated seaside village, where he hopes that they will be able to escape "from the barbarism and the vulgarity" of the world of the tube. Naive illusion. He soon discovers that the "unspoiled natives," "their bladders awash with Coca-cola" are mad for TV which "has begun to transform them from sailors into cowboys, from fishermen into gangsters, from shepherds into juvenile delinquents." He becomes a village celebrity when it is learned that he is the author of a soap opera, "La Famiglia Tosta," a nationwide success in its Italian version, rather than simply "il poeta" he had represented himself to be. The mayor himself arrives, accompanied by a delegation of the village notables, to do honor to their distinguished guest. "And can you imagine, Signor, that we thought that you were merely a poet!" Seton, like so many others, discovers that the "Old World" of his dreams has been "cocacolonized" and replaced by a society which avidly seeks to acquire everything he had despised at home.

The perceptive expatriate soon reaches the conclusion that no matter how hard he may try he will never really belong. "A Woman Without a Country" (pp. 423–28), a rich American, "one of those tireless wanderers who go to bed night after night to dream of bacon, lettuce, and tomato sandwiches" had fled the United States after being involved in a scandal more comic than tragic. She was determined to cast off her former identity and become Italian. She cultivated a slight accent in English. She labored over the language. She strained to "pass" as a native. But the inevitable result was that "she was not so much here in Italy as that she was no longer there in America."

The children of expatriate parents often suffer an even more profound sense of alienation. "I don't know why it is that expatriate children should seem underfed, but they often do," remarks the narrator in "An Educated Woman" (pp. 521–35), "and Jill, with her mixed clothing and her mixed languages gave the impression that the advantages of her education had worked out in her as a kind of pathos." "Boy in Rome" (pp.452–66) recounts another of these cases. The boy and his widowed mother live in a historic Roman palazzo, where they have luxury and no comfort, where none of the conveniences functions, and where they are always cold. He is fed up with hearing people in the streets singing about the sunny South. They should be singing instead, he thinks, about "the burst pipes and the backfired toilets and how the city lies under the snow like an old man with a stroke." "My mother has many American friends who speak fluent Italian and who wear Italian clothes—everything they have is Italian, including the husbands sometimes—but to me there always seems to be a little funny about them, as if their stockings were crooked or their underwear showed and I think that is always true about people who choose to live in another country." He becomes involved, through his mother's boyfriend, Tibi, an American writer who is "too tired" to write, in an operation to smuggle out of the country a picture, "a national treasure," which Tibi has arranged to acquire from the Princess Tavola Calda and which he plans on selling at a huge profit on the American market. The boy consents to carry the picture in his luggage (who would suspect a teenager to be in possession of a museum piece?), since he is so homesick that he is willing to try anything to get back to the States. But the old Princess Tavola Calda was too crafty for her would-be exploiters. When the boy is followed and apprehended in Naples for attempting to abscond with a national treasure, it is discovered that "the treasure" is only a piece of cardboard. The Princess has kept the picture—as well as the money she received for it. And as he prepares to take the train back to Rome, the boy remembers a scene he witnessed on the docks of Naples. An old lady kept shouting to her relatives departing for the USA: "Blessed are you, blessed are you. You will see America." And he begins to share with us his (or rather Cheever's) elevated reflections: "I knew that large cars and frozen foods and hot water were not what she meant . . . I knew she thought of a place where there are no police with swords and no greedy nobility and no dishonesty and no briberies and no fear of cold and hunger and war and if all she imagined were not true, it was a noble ideal and that was the main thing" (p. 466). Here Cheever, the moralist, yields to the temptation of intervening in the narration in order to make comments of his own which cannot convincingly be ascribed to the character.

"World of Apples" (pp. 613–23) suggests the experience of those many distinguished Anglo-American poets, from Landor to Ezra Pound, who spent their last years in "the golden light" of Italy. Asa Bascombe had long since left his native Vermont for Monte Carbone, a hill town south of Rome. It is curious that this "Cézanne of poetry," whose most popular work, "The World of Apples," celebrated the simplicities of New England, should have chosen to settle on the shores of the Tyrrhenian. Very frequently, in these later stories, even when they do not specifically deal with Italy, there occur references to the Italian scene, which are allusions to presumably personal impressions. In "A Miscellany of Characters . . ." (p. 471) the boarded-up palaces of the Grand Canal look like "the haggard faces of the grade of nobility that shows up for the royal weddings in Hesse." The twittering of the swallows in the Roman twilight "seems like light, as the light of day loses its brilliance" (p. 689). A popular song "Marito in città" provides the title for the tale of a lonely husband whose family is away on vacation. Such examples could be multiplied.

Cheever also deals with the reverse situation: that of the Italian who has been exported to the New World. Clementina (pp. 438–51), the servant of an American diplomatic family who has brought her back to the States with them, is enchanted with her new life. She loves all those marvelous gadgets, the roaster, the toaster, the washer, the dryer, the mixer, which do all the work and which give her a sense of power besides. So enchanted, in fact, that when her temporary visa runs out, she enters into a loveless marriage (which shocks her idealistic American employers) with an Italian milkman three times her age, in order to be able to remain in the country. And she settles down blissfully to stuff herself and grow fat, to watch TV morning, noon, and night, to go shopping in the supermarket for all those fine things ("much finer things than the Pope himself possessed"), remembering only intermittently the harshness and the cruelty of her remote Abruzzi village and "that darkness that she knew to lie at the heart of life." Another uprooted Italian, the impoverished Prince Parlapiano, saddled with one of those outlandish names that Cheever invents for his nobility, adjusts less easily (pp. 624–33). Married in Rome to a beautiful but severe young woman from the American consulate, he and his bride come to live in Bullet Park. The Prince's manners are all wrong. On arrival, he greets the narrator with kisses on both cheeks, definitely not the thing to do in a suburban station at eight o'clock in the morning. "Several people looked away. One friend turned pale." The princely accent everywhere inspired hilarity, disdain, and even suspicion; his noble distinction seemed ridiculous in an alien setting. "He might be the Prince Parlapiano in a place like the Plaza, but struggling with the menu at Chock Full O'Nuts he was an untouchable." Finally, rejected by the entire community and divorced by his wife, who discovers that she wants "a career of her own," the saddened Prince returns to his native Verona.

Cheever, it is clear, as we can see from his loving descriptions of seaside villages, of Tuscan landscapes, of villas in whose ancient gardens the nightingales still sing, perceived and appreciated all the traditional beauty of Italy. But as a moralist in whose veins flowed the blood of Wapshot ancestors, firm in his attachment to the Protestant and democratic values of his own country, he is even more aware of the decay, the poverty, the cruelty of an old and played-out society, in which the American expatriate can expect nothing better than "a borrowed, temporary, bittersweet happiness." The great palaces, once you get inside them, turn out to be dirty and neglected and evil-smelling. And the ruined princesses who live in them hide the cheese parings left over from lunch in their bags and are forced to borrow a few lire from their servants. Italy, the Old World, certainly offers no promise of deliverance from "that darkness at the heart of life" of which Cheever is always so deeply aware. And Rome indeed, behind a facade of a millenary culture, can be just as sad and sinister, evil and tawdry as Shady Hill behind its facade of a plasticized well-being.

Notes

1. Samuel Coale, *John Cheever* (New York: Ungar, 1977), p. 7.

2. Lynne Waldeland, *John Cheever* (Boston: Twayne, 1979), p. 87.

3. John Cheever, *The Stories of John Cheever* (New York: Knopf, 1978), p. 330. "He asked Nellie Farquarson who she was. . . . Nellie said the maid had come through an agency and that her home was near Trenon in Normandy. . . . Francis realized that he had seen her before. It had been at the end of the war. He had left a replacement depot with some other men and had taken a three day pass in Trenon. On their second day they had walked out to the crossroads to see the public chastisement of a young woman who had lived with the German commandant during the Occupation." All subsequent references to *The Stories* will be incorporated in the text.

Witchcraft in Bullet Park

John Gardner*

When in 1969 John Cheever turned from the lovable Wapshots to the weird creatures who inhabit Bullet Park, most reviewers attacked or

*Reprinted with permission of the author from *New York Times Book Review*, 24 October 1971, pp. 2, 24.

dismissed him. They were, it seems to me, dead wrong. The Wapshot books, though well made, were minor. "Bullet Park," illusive, mysteriously built, was major—in fact, a magnificent work of fiction.

One reason the book has been misunderstood is that it lacks simple message. No man who thinks seriously about the enormous old questions can reduce his thought to a warning sign like BRIDGE OUT. Another reason is that Cheever is right about evil: it comes quietly, unannounced by thunder or screeching bats—comes like the novel's well-dressed man getting casually off a train 10 minutes before dark. Talking of the oldest and darkest evil, Cheever speaks softly, gently, as if casually. Suspense is not something he fails to achieve in "Bullet Park" but something he has avoided. The novel moves as if purposelessly, like its bland-minded, not very likable protagonist, and from time to time gives a nervous start at the blow of a distant axe.

Cheever's subject is chance—but more than that. Chance is a vehicle that carries the book into darker country. The opening lines present a setting—a train station—designed to suggest the whole human condition in this mysterious, chance-riddled universe. A temporary planet whose architecture, like that of the station, is "oddly informal, gloomy but unserious;" a place of isolation where chance seems to rule even art. "Paint me a small railroad station then," the novel begins—as if any other setting would do as well. (But: "The setting seems in some way to be at the heart of the matter," says Cheever, sly. Art, like life, may start with chance, but chance shrouds something darker.)

The harmless looking man who steps from the train meets a real estate agent named Hazzard—"for who else will know the exact age, usefulness, value and well-being of the houses in town." By chance, days later, the harmless looking man will be standing on the platform with Eliot Nailles, the novel's hero, when another man is sucked to his death by an express train. The stranger has nothing to do with the accident; he's buried, at the time, in his newspaper. But the skin crawls. We learn later that by a series of accidents the stranger has become, unbeknownst to himself, a center of demonic malevolence.

We've been told repeatedly that the universe is gloomy and frightening, random. Brute existence precedes essence and also sometimes follows it, as it does in Nailles's good Christian mother, reduced by senility to a human doll in a nursing home. Ah, yes, ah, woe, we are tugged by cosmic strings, dolls all! Or are we? Cheever reconsiders the idea of chance, remembering psychic and psychological phenomena, the claims of good and bad witches. What emerges is a world where hope does exist (magic is real and can cure or kill), a world in a way even grimmer than Beckett's because here love and sacrifice are realities, like hope, but realities in flux, perpetually threatened, perishing.

The novel says yes-and-no to exitentialists, who can account for all but the paragnost. Cheever, in other words, sees the mind in its totality—sees not only the fashionable existential darkness but the light older than consciousness, which gives nothingness definition. Partly for the sake of this wholeness of vision, Cheever in "Bullet Park" abandoned the fact-bound novel of verisimilitude, which is by nature impotent to dramatize the mind's old secrets, and turned to dependence on *voice*, secret of the willing suspension of disbelief that normally carries the fantasy or tale.

Cheever's voice—compassionate, troubled, humorous—controls the action, repeatedly calling attention to itself in phrases like "at the time of which I'm writing." Where his voice fades out, character voices come in. Without explanation or apology, he shifts, early in the novel, to the cry of an unnamed and never-again-to-be-heard-of adolescent, a cry against suburban hypocrisy. ("Oh damn them all, thought the adolescent.") Later, telling how Eliot Nailles nearly murdered his son, Cheever shifts to Nailles's own voice as Nailles goes over the incident in his mind. With similar abruptness he introduces the voices—or, sometimes, centers of consciousness—of Nailles's wife, neighbors, a zodiac-trapped French teacher, a Negro swami and the harmless looking stranger, mad Paul Hammer.

Hammer decides to murder Nailles—at first Eliot, later his son, Tony. The decision is without explicit motivation, based mainly on "the mysterious binding power of nomenclature." Cheever could have explained the whole thing, black magic as psychosis (the magic of names), and would have done so in a Wapshot book. But how do you *render* a thing so strange? Instead of explaining, he inserts Hammer's journal. With a mad man's objectivity, Hammer sketches the story of his life.

The coldness of tone (even when the scene is comic), the flat description of his enfeebled quest for relationship, his survival by flight into symbolism (yellow rooms, a dream-castle, pieces of string) explains magically what the fact-bound novel would turn to the dry unreality of a case study. The motive for the projected murder is coincidence—a correspondence of names, two pieces of string. We learn that Paul Hammer has murdered before, without knowing it himself, to get a yellow room. But the rendered proof of his demonic nature is his voice, a quiet stovelid on terror and rage.

As in all first-rate novels, the form of "Bullet Park" grows out of its subject. More here than in his earlier writings, Cheever depends on poetic (which is to say, magical) devices—rhythm, imagistic repetition, echo. Instead of conventional plot, an accretion of accidents. Far below consciousness, the best people in Bullet Park are mirror images of the worst: they live by magic, correspondence.

On the level of consciousness, Nailles lives by sugary, foolish opinions and declares his life "wonderful"—but he cannot ride his commuter train except drugged. Out of touch with his son, governed partly by ethical clichés and partly by the normal frustration of the blind—ruled in other words by chance—he throws out his son's beloved TV and starts the child on the way to mental illness. By the chance combination of his middle-class values, his son's slight willfulness, an argument with his wife, and an accidental meeting with black-jacketed boys whose faces he cannot see, Nailles tries—in what could pass for inexplicable rage—to murder his son on a miniature golf course. (The mechanistic universe writ small. The symbolism of place is always grim in "Bullet Park.") Though Nailles's putter misses his son's skull, the black-magic selfish rage in his attack leaves the son psychologically crippled—in fact, dying of murdered will—savable only by a swami.

An accidental meeting with a man in a bar and a chance echo when Nailles returns home makes Nailles distrust his faithful wife—faithful because, by accident, her would-be seducers were confounded by, respectively, a fire, a cold, an attack of indigestion. In short, Nailles, a tragicomic fool, is simply lucky. By accidents of his childhood, he is in touch with Nature: he cuts down diseased elms with a comically typical suburban chain-saw and shoots, in his undershorts, a century-old snapping turtle (naked man against the dinosaur). Hammer, by accidents of childhood and bastardy, is cut off from Nature and himself. Nailles's blessing is that he is married to a good woman and has a son, whereas Hammer is married to a bitch and is childless. Nailles's luck means that he's faintly in touch with the higher magic of the universe—the magic of love, creative force—whereas Hammer is in touch only with lower magic, correspondence.

Magical coincidence, echo, repetition. When images recur or correspondences appear, they are causes, benevolent or harmful. From his psychic, wholly self-centered mother, Hammer gets his witchy idea of drugging and immolating some innocent victim to "wake up" drugged America. When Rutuola, the gentle swami, makes magic, the result is ritual. Both are attempts to draw in the power of the universe. Both work, sometimes. Both are crazy. ("I know it's crazy," Tony says, raised from despair by the swami's chant of Love, Love, Love, "but I do feel much better.")

Benevolent witchcraft, ritual, assumes that the universe contains some good and that men in groups can reach harmony with it. (Rain or shine, Nailles drives with his windshield wiper on, because that's his silly congregation's sign of faith in the resurrection.) Malevolent witchcraft, on the other hand, assumes cosmic forces attendant to the will of the witch. Neither side wins decisively. (Selfless men contain selfishness, and even Hammer has impulses toward love.) The mainly benevolent have their marginal advantage because in times of crisis they tend to work together. Out of lonely arrogance Hammer spills his plan to the swami, and from love the swami warns Nailles.

But though Tony is rescued—Nailles rising to that strange trance-state in which nothing can go wrong (a dazzling piece of writing)—Nailles's existence is merely salvaged, not redeemed. Nailles at the start called his drab life "wonderful." When Rutuola brought Tony from despair, "everything was as wonderful as it had been." Now, when the murder has been blocked, with the help of that ridiculous chainsaw, Cheever closes: "Tony went back to school on Monday and Nailles— drugged—went off to work and everything was as wonderful, wonderful, wonderful, wonderful as it had been."

There, it may be, is the underlying reason that reviewers were annoyed by "Bullet Park." The novel is bleak, full of danger and offense, like a poisoned apple in the playpen. Good and evil are real, but are effects of mindless chance—or heartless grace. The demonology of Calvin, or Cotton Mather. Disturbing or not, the book towers high above the many recent novels that wail and feed on Sartre. A religious book, affirmation out of ashes. "Bullet Park" is a novel to pour over, move around in, live with. The image repetitions, the stark and subtle correspondences that create the book's ambiguous meaning, its uneasy courage and compassion, sink in and in, like a curative spell.

John Cheever's *Bullet Park:*
A Key to His Thought and Art

Lynne Waldeland*

The work of John Cheever that has come to seem most pivotal to an understanding of his career to date is the novel *Bullet Park*, published in 1969. It was a work which was considerably misunderstood and undervalued when it appeared, probably for a variety of reasons, not the least of which is its yoking verisimilitude of place together with entirely fantastic events. However, it is a work which stands in a definable relationship to Cheever's previous fiction and which clearly looks forward to the startling developments in *Falconer* (1977).

No work of Cheever has been received with less critical consensus or so much out-and-out disapproval as *Bullet Park*. When it appeared, Cheever's prestige was sufficient to warrant the lead in the *New York Times Book Review*, but Benjamin DeMott, who reviewed the book, generally discounted the achievement of the novel. He was unmoved by Cheever's handling of subject and characterization and very troubled by the structural problem he perceived, calling the book "broken-backed" and "tacked together."[1] Mary Ellmann charged Cheever with writing about "fashionable pain" and the "moral insufficiency of power mowers and martinis" in the novel.[2] Samuel Coale, while acknowledging that this

*This essay was written specifically for this volume and is published here for the first time with permission of the author.

is Cheever's most experimental and carefully created novel, complains that the book is too episodic in structure and that the style is too light for the darkness of the vision it communicates.[3] The most favorable and, I think, perceptive review that appeared at the time of the novel's publication was one in which the *Time* magazine reviewer saw immediately that the novelist was much less interested in the manners and morals of suburbia than in ancient religious and philosophical concerns with good and evil, chance and accident, will and fate.[4]

It remained for John Gardner, in a retrospective essay published in 1971, to begin to give *Bullet Park* its rightful place in Cheever's *oeuvre* and in twentieth-century fiction. Announcing that the critics who had dismissed the novel were "dead wrong," he asserts: "The Wapshot books, though well-made, were minor. *Bullet Park*, illusive, mysteriously built, was major—in fact, a magnificent work of fiction." He suggests several reasons as to why the novel was misunderstood, including its refusal to present a simple message; because "Cheever is right about evil; it comes quietly, unannounced by thunder and screeching bats;" and because it is a philosophical novel about chance, not a novel of manners about contemporary suburban life, despite its setting. Gardner pinpoints Cheever's handling of *voice* as the technical device which most contributes to the novel's power and success and, in a final guess as to why reviewers were annoyed by the novel, sums up his sense of its value:

> The novel is bleak, full of danger and offense, like a poisoned apple in the playpen. Good and evil are real, but are effects of mindless chance—or heartless grace. . . . A religious book, affirmation out of ashes. . . . The image repetitions, the stark and subtle correspondences that create the book's ambiguous meaning, its uneasy courage and compassion, sink in and in, like a curative spell.[5]

Gardner is right in his assessment of the novel's meaning and importance. *Bullet Park* is not marred by serious structural problems; far from taking a chic potshot at the easy target of suburban life, it is not even *about* life in the suburbs and when it does discuss that life, it rejects simplistic criticism. The style seems perfectly suited to the novel's content, especially in the terms Gardner proposes: Cheever's handling of the storytelling voice. It is as well-constructed, thematically provocative, and fictionally successful a novel as Cheever has written to date. Furthermore, because of its relation to Cheever's previous and subsequent work, it provides a valuable key to an understanding of his major themes and techniques.

Some initial difficulties do confront any reader who innocently picks up *Bullet Park* and may even bother readers who know Cheever's earlier work. Some may be troubled by the amount of violence, both physical and psychological in this novel, especially since the setting seems to be an ordinary American suburb in which life is, if anything, dull. But

Cheever's previous novel, *The Wapshot Scandal*, had prepared us for the destructiveness of American life as it affects citizens of the bucolic St. Botolphs. Several stories in *The Brigadier and the Golf Widow* also deal directly with the increasing danger and dislocation of life in our times. But *Bullet Park* is the farthest step toward the depiction of a downright ominous world. We have travelled from the relative calm and restorable tranquility of Cheever's first fictional suburb, Shady Hill, to the more violently named Bullet Park, where madness and death are more prominent than ever before in Cheever's fiction. He has not, in this novel, relinquished the sense of the promise of life which characters apprehend in the ordered suburban world of his earlier works, but the elements which legislate against happiness, and even survival, are more present and more terrible. Some characters in this novel try to sustain a belief in life in Bullet Park as paradisaical, but the world of this suburb is, as Samuel Coale says, a "Lethal Eden."[6]

There are other difficulties for readers in trying to come to grips with this novel. For one thing, the main characters are named Hammer and Nailles, a device which struck many readers and reviewers as gimmicky and which worked against the seriousness with which they were then willing to take the novel. The plot involves the mysterious illness of Nailles's son Tony, who refuses to get out of bed one morning, and its equally mysterious cure by a swami; the plan of Hammer to crucify Nailles on the altar of Christ Church, a plan later revised, for no apparent reason, to make Tony the victim; and the sudden phobia about riding commuter trains that turns Nailles, the seemingly best-adjusted character in the novel, into a drug addict. This plot makes it hard for readers to feel themselves on firm, serious ground. Is it an allegory? Is it a joke? Fate has intervened before in Cheever's suburban world; certain accidents, some happy, some unfortunate, have befallen many of his suburban characters; but the circumstances have not usually been so bizarre, or the consequences so dire. However, Cheever does manage to control these elements which could threaten the novel's coherence. For one thing, he sets these coincidences, mad plots, and potential tragedies within a world which is presented to us with a high degree of verisimilitude so as to make us reasonably comfortable about the element of *place*, at least. Also, although he retains the high degree of omniscience that marks his story-telling mode, except for Part Two of the novel which is turned over entirely to Hammer's first-person journal, he allows us more insights than usual in his fiction into the characters' minds, backgrounds, dreams, and motives. The effect of this knowledge of the interior nature of the characters, especially of Hammer and Nailles, is to make much of what occurs in the novel seem humanly possible if not always logically plausible.

The attempt to provide the reader with the security of a verisimilar world begins on the novel's opening pages:

Paint me a small railroad station then, ten minutes before dark. Beyond the platform are the waters of the Wekonsett River, reflecting a somber after glow. The architecture of the station is oddly informal, gloomy but unserious, and mostly resembles a pergola, cottage or summer house although this is a climate of harsh winters. The lamps along the platform burn with a nearly palpable plaintiveness. The setting seems in some way to be at the heart of the matter. (p. 3)[7]

The rest of the first chapter involves the arrival by train of a man, Hammer, who will be shown around Bullet Park by a real estate agent. This device allows the reader to tour Bullet Park with them and to get a sense of its physical layout as well as its social dimensions. Throughout the novel, Cheever continues to cite the routines of suburban life—parties, commuter trains, volunteer fire companies, chain saws, Sunday mornings in church—to keep the reader comfortable with some sense of a credible world in which the novel's events *could* occur.

Far from using his suburban setting to poke cheap fun at the excesses of suburban life as several critics charge, Cheever presents a distinctly complex view. In the first chapter, he provides the critical view of a disgruntled adolescent:

Damn the bright lights by which no one reads, damn the continuous music which no one hears, damn the grand pianos that no one can play, damn the white houses mortgaged up to their rain gutters, damn them for plundering the ocean for fish to feed the mink whose skins they wear and damn their shelves on which there rests a single book—a copy of the telephone book bound in pink brocade. (p. 5)

The excessiveness of the language of this passage undermines it, and, for good measure, the narrator explicitly rejects this view, saying that "the adolescent, as adolescents always are, would be mistaken." (p. 6) However, Cheever does touch on some excesses of suburban life through comic exaggeration. For instance, there are the Ridleys—

a couple who brought to the hallowed institution of holy matrimony a definitely commercial quality. . . . They were not George and Helen Ridley. They were "the Ridleys." One felt that they might have incorporated and sold shares in their destiny over the counter. "The Ridleys" was painted on the door of their station wagon. There was a sign saying "The Ridleys" at the foot of their driveway. In their house, matchbooks, coasters and napkins were all marked with their name. They presented their handsome children to their guests with the air of salesmen pointing out the merits of a new car in a showroom. The lusts, griefs, exaltations and shabby worries of a marriage never seemed to have marred the efficiency of their organization. One felt that they probably had branch offices and a staff of salesmen on the road. (pp. 100–101)

Or there is Tommy Lewellen, invitations to whose parties read: "The Amalgamated Development Corporation and Mr. and Mrs. Thomas

Lewellen cordially request the pleasure . . ." so that he can deduct the party's cost from his income tax.

But despite his fondness for these caricatures, Cheever's attitude toward the suburbs is not negative in this novel. His real view is expressed in this statement made by Nailles to his son:

> When you go to the theater they're always chopping at the suburbs but I can't see that playing golf and raising flowers is depraved. The living is cheaper out here and I'd be lost if I couldn't get some exercise. People seem to make some connection between respectability and moral purity that I don't get. For instance, the fact that I wear a vest doesn't necessarily mean that I claim to be pure in heart. . . . All kinds of scandalous things happen everywhere but just because they happen to people who have flower gardens doesn't mean that flower gardens are wicked. (p. 66)

Nailles is not Cheever's spokesperson in the novel, and, in fact, his loves and enthusiasms are often simplistic; but the sanity of his view that the suburbs are simply places to live that offer certain options for the use of one's time rather than symbols of moral probity or hypocrisy seems to represent Cheever's view throughout the novel. Cheever's primary focus in the novel is not on suburban life, but he has chosen this suburb as the carefully presented arena for his story. Its recognizable qualities help intensify the impact of the intrusion of accident and evil into such an everyday, ordinary setting.

Along with his placement of the admittedly fabulous events in a believable setting, Cheever gives credibility to the novel by revealing the interior of his major characters to a degree unprecedented in his fiction; the reader concludes that even if the characters' behavior appears incredible in the normal course of events, it proceeds plausibly from their own inner workings. The main developments in the lives of the two main characters are that Nailles becomes a drug addict, while Hammer plans and tries to execute a sacrificial murder. Oddly enough, thanks to Cheever's technique, it is almost easier to believe the latter than the former. His handling of Hammer's point of view reveals that character's near insanity and hence a certain mad logic in his behavior that does not exist to help us understand Nailles.

Hammer arrives at his mental instability by an understandable route. He is born the illegitimate son of a wealthy socialist, who never acknowledges him, and Gretchen Schurz, a midwestern girl who was his father's secretary. He is raised by his paternal grandmother. (While trying to decide on a legal name for her grandson, the grandmother happens to look out the window as the gardener walks by carrying a hammer; she settles on Paul Hammer.) He does not see his father, and his infrequent visits with his mother are unsatisfactory as she becomes increasingly crazy, convinced that she hears Brahms concertos in the noise of airplane engines and that she can ascertain the nature of the people who occupied hotel rooms before she did. In one of her rambling monologues, she suggests to Paul that he crucify a comfortable suburbanite in order to wake up a drugged world. Hammer struggles on alone through adolescence and early manhood, one day waking up in the grip of a "cafard," a palpable despair, resulting in an obsession with finding and living in a room with yellow walls. After an international search, he spots his salvation in a house in Blenville, Pennsylvania. The divorcee who owns the house is killed in an accident that is in an ambiguous way Hammer's fault, and he buys the house and moves in. He falls in love with a woman in the neighborhood; their marriage isn't happy because she will only sleep with him during thunderstorms or other convulsions of nature or history. He and Marietta move to Bullet Park, where she, like Gee-Gee, a character in an earlier story, "The Scarlet Moving Van," uses social occasions to denounce the hypocrisy of suburban life. Remembering his mother's suggestion, he begins to plot the crucifixion of Eliot Nailles. Later, he decides to kill Tony instead, for no clearer reason.

Hammer is somewhat aware of his degree of alienation, and he longs for a world with meaning and order. There is an internal logic to much of what Hammer does, as well as moments at which his life could have gone differently had chance led in another direction. The degree of chance in the events which lead to his final act—from his birth and upbringing to his marriage to his moving to Bullet Park and meeting a man named Nailles—is very strong. Furthermore, the way in which we receive the details of Hammer's life strengthens our sense of his madness; most of our knowledge of him is presented through his first-person journal, the tone of which is cold and matter-of-fact when, in the face of the events of his life, we might more readily expect anger, pain, and perhaps some guilt. As Gardner says: "The rendered proof of his demonic nature is his voice, a quiet stovelid on terror and rage."[8] Part Two of *Bullet Park*, entirely given over to the journal, is effective because it creates some sense of motivation for what is otherwise an almost inexplicable act and also because the manner of the telling, in its inappropriate calm in the face of violence and murder, increases the horror.

On the surface, Eliot Nailles seems to be as lucky in the circumstances of his life as Paul Hammer was unlucky. Born, raised, and educated more conventionally than Hammer, he loves his wife, his son, his work, his house, Bullet Park, driving the volunteer fire truck, cutting wood with his chain saw. The opposition of their names signals some other contrasts between the protagonists. In addition to the marital and family happiness of Nailles in contrast to the lack of those things in Hammer's life, Nailles is also in touch with nature, where Hammer is not. Nailles loves the changes of seasons, fishing, and his aged hunting dog, Tessie, while Hammer, seeing the infirmity of the dog, suggests that she should be shot. Nailles seems to be an appreciative, creative participant in the world, while Hammer is the perennial outsider.

However, on closer scrutiny, we see certain limitations of character and vision in Nailles, as well as some dark and violent impulses. His limitations are primarily of perception; he is a simple man, thrown by complexity and suffering with which, until the events of the novel, he has had little experience. We are told that "Nailles thought of pain and suffering as a principality lying somewhere beyond the legitimate borders of Western Europe. The government would be feudal and the country mountainous but it would never lie on his itinerary and would be unknown to his travel agent" (p. 50). We learn not only of this ignorance of the darker sides of life, but of another sort of simplicity in Nailles: "One of Nailles' great liabilities was an inability to judge people on their appearance. He thought all men and women honest, reliable, clean and happy and he was often surprised and disappointed" (p. 53). In the novel, Tony's mysterious but life-threatening illness ends Nailles' inexperience with pain and grief, and in his attempt to deal with this blow, he is brought out of this state of prelapsarian innocence which has led him to believe simplistically in the goodness of all people, the predictability of life, and the solidity of the earth itself.

Furthermore, as Nailles moves away from the simple faith that has guided his life, certain parallels with Hammer emerge, much to our surprise. The compulsiveness of Hammer has a parallel in Nailles's suddenly one day being unable to complete his trip to the city on the commuter train. A doctor prescribes tranquillizers, and by the end of the novel, Nailles is dealing with a drug pusher in order to be able to get to his office and earn a living. The seriousness of this sudden phobia is that it undermines Nailles's sense of coherence and reason as the governing powers of the world. The fact that he develops a phobia about trains may be precipitated by his seeing a neighbor fall or jump under the wheels of a train one day; but it is really the mysterious illness of his beloved son that destroys Nailles' sense of order and tranquillity. Thus, Nailles, who seems at first the opposite of Hammer, comes to share with him a degree of irrational psychological behavior. Another more surprising link develops between the two men. Although Hammer is the one who plans and almost succeeds in a murder, Nailles, on four different occasions, contemplates killing someone; and in three of the instances, the emotion is clearly murderous. The first time, embarrassed by the drunken antics of his father in front of a school friend of his, he wishes his father dead. Another time—from humane motives—he contemplates smothering his mother with a pillow as she lies unconscious in a nursing home, never to recover from the stroke that has felled her. The third—and most serious—instance occurs in a quarrel with his son; the boy taunts him with the meaninglessness of his work, and Nailles strikes at him with a golf putter, missing splitting his skull only because Tony ducks and runs away. Lest we wrongly assume that this is only a threatening gesture, Nailles continues:

"So there I was on this ruined miniature golf course having practically murdered my son but what I wanted to do then was to chase after him and take another crack at him with the putter. I was very angry. I couldn't understand how my only son, whom I love more than anything in the world, could make me want to kill him." (p. 118)

Far too simple to understand the psychological relationship of love and hate in the human psyche, Nailles is prey to angers that mystify him, the last manifestation of which occurs when Hammer suggests that Nailles shoot his aged dog. For a moment Nailles wants to murder Hammer. All of these violent emotional impulses of Nailles lead us to Cheever's real intention in his handling of his characters in *Bullet Park*. Rather than intending them to be some sort of stick-figure opposites, the two men are closer to being alter-egos. Murderous impulses may reside in any human heart, as they do in the heart of Nailles; but Hammer, because of the insanity which renders him impervious to the restraining effects of society and human community, is the one who acts upon such impulses while Nailles does not. Hammer is an uncontrolled version of what most people, Nailles included, may have it in them to be at their worst moments. He is also—along with Tony's illness and his train phobia—a mysterious visitation in Nailles' life, the chance entrance into an orderly, happy life of the reality of violence and malevolence.

The plot of the novel emphasizes chance, although it gives some occasional clues as to causality that in their inadequacy are almost more frustrating than is blind chance as an explanation for dire events. For example, in racking his memory to think what might have caused Tony's refusal to get out of bed, a refusal that seems likely to lead to atrophy and death, Nailles remembers the night he threw the television set out of the house because Tony watched it too much, the day that Tony was pulled off the football team because of low grades, and, of course, the fact that he had struck at him with a golf putter, an event that occurs the night before Tony's strange malady strikes. All of these events could add up to some explanation, but Tony himself brings up none of them, saying only that he feels sad. After doctors and psychologists have failed to cure him, Tony's parents call in a swami recommended to them by a former cleaning lady; the oddness of such an act for people in their social milieu underscores their desperation. Tony is healed in a matter of hours. The murder attempt on Tony is also handled in a way that emphasizes the role of chance. Why Hammer chooses Tony as his victim after having previously settled upon Nailles as a typical suburbanite to crucify is never explained. Then Hammer inexplicably reveals his plan to the swami, who rushes to warn Nailles. Nailles arrives at Christ Church to find the doors locked and to hear Hammer say that he will burn Tony on the altar as soon as he finishes smoking a cigarette. This gives Nailles time to rush home and get his chain saw and cut through the church door to rescue his son. The fact that both the choice of victim and the victim's salvation are so totally a matter of chance is the sobering truth that underlies this almost unbelievable series of events.

It should be clear by now that Cheever is not occupying himself or the reader with one more attack on the suburban way of life. The suburb of Bullet Park provides a workable, because believable, setting for the story he planned to tell, but it is not itself the focus. The novel's real subject is societal to the extent that it indicates the value of society as a restraining force on the human being's darkest possibilities. But the most important subject of the work is the presence of good and evil or, perhaps in this novel, just evil. Evil is shown to be powerful; in *Bullet Park*, what goes wrong with the characters is a life-and-death matter. Several lives are lost, and those of the main character, Nailles, and his son are threatened. But evil is also random, coming from nowhere, choosing its victims by chance, and leaving its mark. It is made more terrible by its appearance in a world where there is also a degree of love, order, and tranquillity. As John Gardner says: "What emerges here is a world where hope does exist (magic is real and can cure or kill), a world in a way even grimmer than Beckett's because here love and sacrifice are realities, like hope, but realities in flux, perpetually threatened, perishing."[9] In other words, a world depicted as without love or hope is less tragically susceptible to the entrance of evil than a world populated by people who try to sustain love and hope in their lives. Also, the novel deals, through the portrayal of Nailles, with the effects of an initiation into a knowledge of evil on a person previously unacquainted with it. While Nailles is allowed to save his son at the end of the novel, there is no suggestion that he has been enabled to do this by his experience with suffering; his love for Tony at the outset is so great that he would have done the same thing at the story's beginning. The novel does not suggest that Nailles' suffering has been redemptive. It ends with this line: "Tony went back to school on Monday and Nailles—drugged—went off to work and everything was as wonderful, wonderful, wonderful, wonderful as it had been" (p. 245). Readers may be reminded, as the *Time* reviewer was, of the five repetitions of the word *nothing* at the end of *King Lear*. The repetition of *wonderful* undercuts and finally erases the meaning of the word. Cheever does not suggest that Nailles is better off for his suffering; indeed the implication is that he is permanently scarred. What affirmation there is in the novel lies in the fact that a simple, optimistic man, with relatively limited resources of perception, has been able to assimilate grief and suffering and an awareness of evil without being totally destroyed; it is the affirmation of survival rather than of transcendence.

The structure of the novel is very simple but neither "broken-backed" nor overly episodic. Benjamin DeMott, in his criticism of the structure, was apparently troubled by the fact that Part One is devoted to Nailles, Part Two completely to Hammer, and Part Three, briefly, to the attempted murder. But Part One subtly prepares us for the importance of

Hammer in the story; he figures in four chapters, despite the emphasis on Nailles. He is, in fact, the first person we meet in the novel, the man who comes to look at houses in Bullet Park in Chapter One. He appears at church where he is introduced to Nailles and discovers the conjunction of their names; he invites the Nailles to dinner, a dinner at which the unhappiness of his marriage is revealed; and he is on the train platform the day the man is killed and he rides into town with Nailles after the death. He is a significant enough person in Part One that we are prepared for his centrality in Part Two and his role in the events of Part Three. Furthermore, the novel is episodic only in that the characters systematically think back over events in the past in an attempt to understand the present. In Part One, Nailles tries to reconstruct the events of Tony's life for a clue to the cause of his illness, but it is the illness itself which dominates Part One and unifies these reminiscences. In Part Two, Hammer's journal also reconstructs the formative events of his life, all with an eye to explaining how it happens that he is about to embark upon a premeditated murder. Far from being loosely structured, the novel achieves considerable unity, more than in either of the Wapshot novels which preceded it.

The charge that the style is inadequate to the subject matter, too lyrical or too light for such serious events, overlooks Cheever's managing of the element of voice in the novel. There is first of all the voice of the narrator, whose commentary on events stands quite apart from the judgments which Nailles and Hammer make on those same events. He is the one who sets the scene, rejects the narrow criticism of the adolescent in Chapter One, and tips us off to the novel's final meaning by the use of too many "wonderfuls" in the last line of the book. His distance, his judgments, and his irony, when he wishes it, are always clear. Cheever has always made extensive use of a high degree of omniscient narration, and it works with great impact in *Bullet Park*. The lyricism in the novel is primarily a function of the viewpoint of Nailles. When the lyricism seems disproportionate, it can be traced to the fact that Nailles is sentimental. He waxes poetic about his wife, his son, nature, even his chainsaw, but his lyricism is unimaginative. And Part Two of the novel, Hammer's journal, is written in an entirely different voice, cold, matter-of-fact, with the logic of madness. This section possesses neither the reflective distance of the narrator nor the sentimental lyricism of Nailles; it is a controlled handling of point of view which underlines frighteningly the character of the person telling his story. Cheever here is more in charge of point of view and voice than he has ever been in the novel form, and his achievement adds considerably to the impact of the novel. Despite the realistic texture of *Bullet Park*, Cheever has avoided the usual story-telling mode of the realistic novel with its preference for showing over telling. He *tells* the story, relying, as Gardner says, on voice, "secret of the willing suspension of disbelief that normally carries the fantasy or the tale."[10] This story is not finally a fantasy, and that fact adds to its horror, but it asks us to believe in events that strain our credulity. It is the assured voice of the author-narrator which convinces us to put aside our doubts and enter the dangerous world of *Bullet Park*.

Bullet Park was followed by the publication of a volume of short stories, *The World of Apples* (1973), and then by another novel, *Falconer* (1977). Though favorably reviewed, *Falconer* was for the most part regarded as an astonishing change of direction for Cheever. Instead of the familiar New England towns or suburbs of other Cheever fiction, *Falconer* is set in a prison. The tension between brothers which has been an issue in Cheever's work boils over into murder in this novel. The main character, Ezekiel Farragut, despite an upbringing similar to that of most of Cheever's major characters, is a fratricide and a drug addict who becomes involved with a homosexual while in prison. On top of all of this, the novel is abundantly, unequivocally religious in its values and its final meaning. Cheever's readers were startled, though fascinated, by these developments. But a careful reading of *Bullet Park*—which it did not receive from many when it first appeared—shows that most of these subjects were rolling around in Cheever's consciousness long before *Falconer* was written. Farragut, who kills his brother in a moment of overpowering rage, is not hard to connect with Nailles of *Bullet Park*. Nailles has the same murderous impulses but perhaps because he has less imagination and vitality, perhaps because drugs have a lesser hold on him, perhaps because he has no brother whose hostility over the years has worn down his resistance, fails to act upon them. Drug addiction as a possibility in the lives of well-educated, middle class people is not new to *Falconer*. Nailles becomes addicted in the course of *Bullet Park* and remains so at the novel's end. And, although *Bullet Park* is not overtly religious in its meaning as *Falconer* is, it examines moral categories and theological concepts with a directness unusual in the contemporary novel. *Falconer* actually proceeds logically from the investigations Cheever began in *Bullet Park*. It is as though Nailles, given a brother and a finer intelligence, were put through a more severe set of trials—drug addiction, imprisonment, a range of human temptations—so as to learn that if there is to be any salvation, it lies in the putting of a fairly orthodox Christian theology into practice in one's daily life. Retrospectively, we can see that *Falconer* is considerably prepared for by the achievement of *Bullet Park*. *Bullet Park* is the work which must be considered to comprehend fully John Cheever's career.

Notes

1. Benjamin DeMott, "A Grand Gatherum of Some Late Twentieth Century Weirdos," *New York Times Book Review*, 27 April 1969, p. 40.

2. Mary Ellmann, "Recent Novels: The Language of Art," *Yale Review*, 59 (Autumn 1969), 111–12.

3. Samuel Coale, *John Cheever* (New York: Ungar, 1977), pp. 103–05.

4. "The Portable Abyss," *Time*, 25 April 1969, p. 109.

5. John Gardner, "Witchcraft in Bullet Park," *New York Times Book Review*, 24 October 1971, pp. 2, 24.

6. Coale, p. 95.

7. John Cheever, *Bullet Park* (New York: Alfred A. Knopf, 1969), p. 3. Pages references are to this edition and appear in parentheses in the text.

8. Gardner, p. 2.

9. Gardner, p. 2.

10. Gardner, p. 2.

John Cheever and the Development of the American Novel

Theo D'haen*

Richard Chase, in *The American Novel and its Tradition*, argues that the romance is the characteristic American novel form, rather than the novel "proper" which he considers the typically European form.[1] The European and, above all, the English novel reflect a European reality ruled by complicated social relationships. That is also why the rise of the European novel is narrowly linked to the emergence of the bourgeoisie as the ruling class in most European countries.[2] In many ways American reality, and certainly in the nineteenth century, is more primitive than its European counterpart. It is not the social struggle that dominates the American scene, but the struggle with nature, with the elements, and with the Indians. Consequently the American experience—especially in New England where the ideas of the Puritans show strong Manichean tendencies—acquires a mythical dimension.[3] In literature this takes the form of a return to allegory and symbolism, literary techniques that in Europe antedate the rise of the novel proper, but that are better suited to give expression to the elementary struggle—between good and evil, between man and nature—as it manifests itself in the American experience. That is why the romance often situates itself in the uncharted territories between civilisation and wilderness, as in the works of Cooper, or between the real and the imaginary, as in the work of Hawthorne. Henry James, in a series of prefaces to his novels, sought to define and clarify the difference between the romance and the novel. In short, the novel aims to picture relationships, to elaborate characters and trace their develop-

*A version of this essay originally appeared in Dutch in the journal *Maatstaf* (July 1978). This new essay was written specifically for this volume and is published here with permission of the author, who acknowledges herewith the considerable assistance given by R. G. Collins in the preparation of this English version.

ment, to describe characters in contact with their social environment, and to maintain a logical plot development. In James' own practice the privileged means of access to the world of the novel is one character's experience (the famous "point of view"). The touchstone for the import of the novel then becomes its verisimilitude, its validity in experientially reflecting reality. In passing it should be noted that, although they are usually Americans, it is only in the dealings and contacts of the protagonists with the European culture—in all respects more rigidly structured and "socialized"—that the novels of James find their true subject: the so-called "international theme." Implicitly, the fact that even James himself needed such a framework to portray his characters as "social creatures," points to the suitability of the romance for dealing with indigenous American themes. Moreover, some of James' own novels, such as *The American*, show clear signs of romance influence. The romance tradition, notwithstanding the impressive *oeuvre* of Henry James based on opposition to it, has been and still is one of the most vital currents of American literary history; the best work of countless American novelists tends to the romance rather than to the novel proper. Cooper's Leatherstocking tales are a case in point, as are Melville's *Moby Dick* and the best work of Faulkner. So, too, is the work of John Cheever.

Virtually all Cheever's novels relate to New England. Although they seem to be taking place sometime after the Second World War, via flashbacks they reach back to the end of the nineteenth century. Still, Cheever's New England is not the real New England; fully in accordance with the romance tradition, the setting of Cheever's novels acquires a symbolic character. The romance works by polar opposition: it contrasts various symbols and consequently also the values these symbols stand for. In Cheever's world this technique fastens upon a myth—one also used by Hawthorne—the myth of America as paradise regained, of the New World as a New Garden of Eden, a myth which Leo Marx, in his *The Machine in the Garden*, shows to have been part of the Western reaction to America ever since the continent's discovery.[4]

According to this myth, America is an unspoiled land of promise to the Europeans, a land where they can build a just society, in freedom and in harmony with nature. All through the nineteenth century this idealistic view of America nourished American literature; it is Emerson who summed up the characteristics and values typical of this ideal pastoral society with the term "self-reliance." A sense of justice, a sense of enterprise, respect for a man's character rather than for his wealth, respect for native traditions over the slavish imitation of foreign fashions, and above all the courage to be an individual rather than a cog in the social machine: these are the essential ingredients of self-reliance. Even as late as the mid-twentieth century Robert Frost articulated this myth in his poetry.

In *The Wapshot Chronicle* the myth of the American Eden is embodied in life on West Farm, the hereditary domain of the Wapshot family, and in St. Botolphs, an imaginary little town in Massachusetts. In Cheever's books and stories the Eden myth intrudes via the characters' reminiscences of the New England youth which they all have in common. Drawing upon classical American literature for examples, Leo Marx has argued that a major theme of that literature is the confrontation of the pastoral-idyllic myth with intruding technology. For Marx, *The Great Gatsby*, with its impressive description of nature as regimented in suburban garden plots, together with concrete wilderness and the waste that are inevitable by-products of our megalopolitan civilization, announces the final victory of technology over nature. Cheever's fictional world rests on a similar confrontation: the idyllic naturalness of St. Botolphs and of West Farm forms a sharp contrast with the artificial hell of New York's dormitory towns, following New England the alternate setting of Cheever's work. Cheever's protagonists move between these two worlds: mythical paradise, and a far more concrete hell.

Because of the romance form and its reliance on stark contrasts, the protagonists of these novels, using E. M. Forster's typing from *Aspects of the Novel*, are "flat" rather than "round." Either they are stereotypes, like Leander or Honora Wapshot, or, like Moses and Coverley Wapshot, they are "coathangers" around whom situations and events are draped. It is not the characters themselves that are of real interest but, rather, the contrasts between the situations and the values they symbolize. Moreover, Cheever's careful manipulation of narrative distance ensures that the reader never fully identifies with any one of the characters. If occasionally a change occurs in a character's psyche, this is never the result of a gradual psychological development, but always of an epiphanal event, a sudden insight. In the title story from *A World of Apples*, for instance, Asa Bascomb, an old poet settled in Italy, suddenly achieves a form of self-acceptance after a pilgrimage, and after he has performed the same ritual he saw his father do a half century before in Northern New England, the region of his birth. Only in *Falconer* does Cheever arrive at a fully elaborated psychological character, in the person of the protagonist Farragut.

St. Botolphs is the American Eden, and suburbia, the galaxy of dormitory towns in New York, Connecticut, and New Jersey that Cheever describes with wit and acerbity, is its counterpole. The real subject of Cheever's work—and given its Biblical overtones a theme better suited to Puritan New England is hard to imagine—is the expulsion from Paradise. If the myth of Paradise and the exile from Paradise are closely linked to the New England spirit, the concrete elaboration of this theme in Cheever's books is firmly rooted in New England's dire socio-economic reality. The immediate and apparent cause of the exile of Moses and Coverley from West Farm is the seduction by Moses of a (willing) girl who, after a car accident, came to stay with the Wapshot family. The real cause, however, lies deeper. Instrumental in bringing about the exile of the brothers is Honora Wapshot, a cousin of Leander. She is the owner of the family fortune, of West Farm, and of the Topaze, the ferryboat with which Leander makes his living, and from which he derives his self-respect. Honora secretly witnesses the seduction of the girl, and she demands that Moses and Coverley leave West Farm and prove their ability to support themselves. Only after each of them have produced male offspring will Honora, by testament, leave them the family fortune. Only then Leander and his wife Sarah will be allowed to live out their days carefree at West Farm. To survive in the outside world, to find a wife, and to found a family, Moses and Coverley have to live by the rules of modern American society. They have to give in to their employers' whims, and their lives become routine patterns of due dates, installment payments, cocktail parties, neighbors' fights, and visits to psychiatrists. In short, they are forced to renounce all "self-reliance" and to join suburbia.

The real reason, then, for Moses' and Coverley's departure from Paradise is sheer economic necessity. At first sight, even this necessity seems to arise from the arbitrariness of an eccentric old woman. However, in the second Wapshot book, *The Wapshot Scandal*, we learn that Honora's fortune exists of inherited capital on which she has never paid taxes. That is why Honora herself has to go into self-exile from St. Botolphs in order to flee the tax collector. The Eden of West Farm turns out to be built on quicksand.

If, initially, the Wapshot books seems to chronicle the fall of one New England family, careful analysis reveals that the fate of the Wapshots really is that of New England itself. It also becomes clear that Cheever undermines the pastoral myth of America as the New Eden even when he seems to be applying it straightforwardly: West Farm and St. Botolphs are not true paradise, but only its distant shadow. When Leander was young, or even earlier, in the nineteenth century, St. Botolphs was self-reliant. In those days its inhabitants sailed the seven seas and traded their way from pole to pole. In those days the little town was a bustling metropolis. Now it is only a sleepy little tourist town, a day trip for city people. In the past West Farm was a working farm; now it is only, as a visitor remarks, a quaint run-down old house. The only function left to St. Botolphs, and by implication to New England, is to grant the real America, suburban America, a peek into the past. St. Botolphs and West Farm have been reduced to relics.

Leander's self-respect derives from his job as captain of a ferry boat, transporting day visitors to and from an island fun fair. When Sarah, after the Topaze has sunk, converts the raised wreck into a souvenir shop, Leander realizes his own uselessness. He swims out into the sea, and disappears into the waves. For Frederick Bracher, in "John Cheever and Comedy," Leander is the real hero of the Wapshot chronicle.[5] According to Bracher, Leander has mythical and legendary qualities: he embodies traditional values and skills, such as the art of felling a tree or of cleaning a rifle. However, the irony of the situation, and the tragedy of Leander, is that these values and skills are utterly useless in suburbia, the place where Leander's sons have to spend their lives. Leander rigidly applies the norms by which he has lived, and the loss of which he laments in the present-day world, and he chooses to disappear into that element which gave him his last grain of self-respect: the sea. It is hardly a coincidence that nineteenth-century New England, in the guise of St. Botolphs, also derived its self-reliance from the sea. While Bracher sees Leander as a bridge between generations, I see him as the very end of a particular way of life. With Leander, a world sinks into the ocean.

The exile of Moses and Coverley, which initially seemed due to an old lady's whim, and which later proved to have economic causes, mirrors the literal socioeconomic plight of New England itself. The loss of economic potential as a result of the increasing economic importance of the American South and West, the deterioration of such traditional industries as paper, textiles, and the shoe factories, the ever increasing concentration of the shipping and transport industries, the decrease and mechanization of the fishing industry, the huge areas of former farmland now lying idle because of the superior competitiveness of western farming: all these have contributed to the exile of countless New Englanders to the belts of satellite towns ringing Boston and New York. After their exile, Moses and Coverley, the younger generation, are integrated into suburbia. Honora, the older generation, chooses differently. After an extended stay abroad, she returns to St. Botolphs and, her entire view of things hopelessly unsettled, starves and drinks herself to death. In both cases the conclusion is identical: the American Eden exists no longer, and the order it represented can now only be kept alive artificially, a curiosity for tourists, a nostalgic relic, a memory of youth. Here, too, the real tragedy of New England and of the United States reveals itself: Emerson's self-reliance, incorporating the Jeffersonian ideal of the United States as a new, free and simple society, no longer exists. Although softened by graceful wit, Cheever's books convey a message of sorrow and despair for a lost land of opportunity.

The Wapshot novels explicitly posit the theme of the conflict between Eden and suburbia. In Cheever's other books, this theme is implicitly raised. *Bullet Park*, in the eponymous novel, is a dormitory town close to New York. The senselessness of life in such a community is illustrated by the lives of the two protagonists: Eliot Nailles and Paul Hammer. As their names indicate, fate has put these two characters in a very special relation. The entire book works toward a climax in which Hammer intends to sacrifice Nailles' son on the altar of a local church, but Nailles succeeds in preventing the sacrifice. In this book, too, the characters function as symbols rather than as psychologically realistic people. The description of the phobias from which the characters suffer creates an atmosphere of emptiness and senselessness. For instance,

Nailles, in order to overcome his distaste for his daily commuter train ride to and from his job in New York, starts taking tranquillizers. Finally, owing to the open prescriptions of a doctor who blatantly disregards the law, he becomes a drug addict. Hammer, on the other hand, from an early age has been suffering from insane delusions. Notwithstanding his phobias, Nailles is the stereotype of the "successfully integrated personality." Because of his paradigmatic quality, and because of the exemplary senselessness of his job—although he calls himself a chemist he really makes his living by promoting a mouthwash—Nailles is chosen by Hammer as his victim for a ritual sacrifice. In this way Hammer wants to open the eyes of the world to the regimented insanity of suburban life as symbolized by Nailles, and by Bullet Park. However, when the crucial moment arrives, Hammer lacks the courage to carry out his intention. He is relegated to an insane asylum. Nailles' son returns to school, and Nailles himself swallows his daily dose of pills and goes off to work. The logic of senselessness has triumphed once again. Regardless of its humorous overtones, *Bullet Park* is Cheever's most pessimistic vision of America. If the Wapshot books explicitly pointed to the demise of a world and its values, they also kept alive the memory of that world and of the myth behind it. In *Bullet Park* the "American Dream" has lost all mythical dimensions.

In *Falconer* Cheever for the first time orders an entire novel around one central character, a character moreover that psychologically develops throughout the novel. Still, *Falconer* does not constitute a radical break with the earlier work. In a sense, Cheever here picks up where he left off eight years before with *Bullet Park*. The protagonist of *Falconer*, Farragut, is a typical dweller in suburbia. He is a university professor, and during the Second World War had become addicted to drugs to the point where he is now an officially registered heroin addict. Whereas in *Bullet Park* Hammer intended to commit a ritual sacrifice, Farragut has effectively committed one by impulsively murdering his brother, a typical exponent of modern city life in all its senselessness. Via flashbacks we learn that Farragut's background resembles that of Moses and Coverley Wapshot. For the reader acquainted with Cheever's earlier work, the opposition between pastoral myth and suburbia is *a priori* incorporated into *Falconer*. Convicted for fratricide Farragut is sent to a penitentiary: Falconer. There he gradually overcomes his drug addiction, albeit without his knowing so, by being administered ever smaller doses. Slowly he changes from an outsider among the prisoners to their leader, and he actively involves himself in prison life. Finally, he concerns himself with the fate of a fellow prisoner and eases the older man's dying hour. By this act of grace Farragut regains contact with the deepest wellsprings of his own humanity. When the old man's body is being removed for burial, Farragut takes his place and in this way escapes from Falconer. He is reborn into a new and brighter life.

As in his earlier works, Cheever sees the solution to the dilemmas facing the characters as self-knowledge and self-acceptance. In *Falconer*, though, self-knowledge and acceptance result from the psychological growth of the protagonist himself, and not from a mystical epiphanal experience. As a result, *Falconer* shows a greater coherence than Cheever's earlier work, and gains in realism and credibility. At the same time, this change in technique implies that with *Falconer* Cheever has at least partly abandoned the romance tradition. Nevertheless, for readers acquainted with the earlier work, the symbolism and the contrasts typical of the romance remain active, albeit on a deeper level. Like a two-faced Janus, *Falconer* looks in two directions: on the one hand it harks back to and summarizes Cheever's entire career in the romance tradition; on the other hand, it is a resolute step toward the novel "proper." The loss of symbolic and allegoric depth in *Falconer* in comparison to Cheever's earlier novels is compensated by the gain in psychological depth resulting from the treatment of the protagonist as a "social creature."

We can conclude that Cheever's entire work bears out Chase's hypothesis of the American novel's gradual development toward realism, though not without continually rediscovering and incorporating the possibilities offered by the romance. For Chase, feelings of alienation, cultural contradictions and a sense of loss of balance are at the root of American ambivalence toward the novelistic genre. Cheever's work appears to be inspired by similar feelings and ideas, by a similar unease. At the same time Cheever's fiction illustrates the history of that America which he himself knew from oral memory and by personal experience: New England from the 1880s to the present day. Cheever's future work will indicate whether the optimism of *Falconer's* ending, and the evolution toward the novel proper are constant features on the road toward a more optimistic vision of America.

Notes

1. Richard Chase, *The American Novel and Its Tradition* (New York: Doubleday Anchor, 1957).

2. See for example, my "Robinson Crusoe and *La Jalousie*" in *Revue des langues vivantes/Tijdschrift voor levende talen* 1 (1978), 28–36.

3. See, for example, Perry Miller's *Errand into the Wilderness* (Cambridge, Mass.: Harvard University Press, 1956).

4. Leo Marx, *The Machine in the Garden* (New York: Oxford University Press, 1967).

5. In *Critique* 6, No. 1 (1963).

A Cheever Bibliography Supplement, 1978–1981

Dennis Coates*

[Editor's Note: The most comprehensive bibliography available on Cheever was that of Dennis Coates "John Cheever: A Checklist, 1930–1978" in *Bulletin of Bibliography*, 36 (Jan.–Mar., 1979), 1–13, 49. Numbering approximately 630 items the Coates bibliography is essential for scholars in the field. The following Supplement includes items inadvertently omitted from the earlier list as well as an updating of it.   RGC]

I. PRIMARY SOURCES

A. Books

The Wapshot Chronicle. New York: Harper & Row, 1979. (With *The Wapshot Scandal* in one volume.)

Falconer. Boston: G. K. Hall, 1977. (Adult Ser. Large print Books)

The Stories of John Cheever. New York: Ballantine (rpt.), 1980.

Oh What a Paradise It Seems. New York: Alfred Knopf, 1982

B. Short Stories

"The Night Mummy Got the Wrong Mink Coat." *New Yorker*, 56 (21 Apr. 1980), 35.

"Island." *New Yorker*, 57 (27 Apr. 1981), 41.

C. Short Stories (Anthologies)

"Homage to Shakespeare" (1937)—*Great Short Stories of the World.* Eds. Whit and Hallie Burnett. London: Souvenir, 1970.

"The Enormous Radio" (1947)—*Timeless Stories for Today and Tomorrow.* Ed. Ray Bradbury. New York: Bantam, 1970.

—*Big City Stories by Modern American Writers.* Eds. Tom and Susan Cahill. New York: Bantam, 1971.

—*The Light Fantastic.* Ed. Harry Harrison. New York: Scribners, 1971.

"Goodbye, My Brother" (1951)—*Counterparts.* Ed. Dean Fowler. Greenwich, Conn.: Fawcett, 1971.

"The Five-Forty-Eight" (1954)—*Points of View.* Eds. James Moffet and Kenneth R. McElheny. New York: New American Library, 1966.

*This bibliography was prepared especially for this volume and is used with the permission of the author.

"The Country Husband" (1954)—*Fiction 100*, 2nd Edition. Ed. J. Pickering. New York: Macmillan, 1978.

"The Housebreaker of Shady Hill" (1956)—*The Art of Fiction/3*. Eds. R. F. Dietrich and Roger H. Sundell, New York: Holt, Rinehart & Winston, 1978.

"The Chimera" (1961)—also in *Short Story International #4*. Ed. Sylvia Tankel. International Cultural Exchange, Oct. 1977.

"The Swimmer" (1964)—*Experience and Expression*. Ed. J. L. Kimmey. Glenview, Ill.: Scott, Foresman, 1977.

"The World of Apples" (1966)—*Major American Short Stories*. Ed. A. Walton Litz. New York: Oxford, 1980.

"The Jewels of the Cabots" (1972)—*Fiction's Journey*. Ed. Barbara McKenzie. New York: Harcourt, Brace & Jovanovich, 1978.

"Falconer" (1976)—also in *Best American Short Stories, 1977*. Ed. Martha Foley. New York: Houghton Mifflin, 1977.

D. Essays, Reviews and Articles

"Why I Write Short Stories." *Newsweek*, 92 (30 Oct. 1978), 24–5.

"Fiction Is Our Most Intimate Means of Communication." *U.S. News and World Report*, 86 (21 May 1979), 92.

"My Daughter, the Novelist." *New York*, 13 (7 Apr. 1980), 53.

"In Praise of Readers." *Parade*, 28 December 1980, p.6.

E. Drama

"The Shady Hill Kidnapping." An original play to be televised by the Public Broadcasting Service in 1982.

II. ADAPTATIONS

Gurney, A. R., Jr. *O Youth and Beauty!* A teleplay for the Public Broadcasting Service's *Great Performances* series, adapted from the story (first appeared 31 Oct. 1979).

McNally, Terrance. *The Five-Forty-Eight*. A teleplay for the Public Broadcasting Service's *Great Performances* series, adapted from the story (first appeared 7 Nov. 1979).

Wasserstein, Wendy. *The Sorrows of Gin*. A teleplay for the Public Broadcasting Service's *Great Performances* series, adapted from the story (first appeared 24 Oct. 1979).

III. SECONDARY SOURCES

A. Books

Bosha, Francis A. *John Cheever: A Reference Guide.* Boston: G. K. Hall, 1981.

Waldeland, Lynn. *John Cheever.* Boston: G. K. Hall (Twayne Series), 1979.

B. News Articles and Biographical Notices

"Academy Institute to Elect Head." *New York Times,* 23 Jan. 1979, p. C20.

Breslin, John B. "John Cheever in the Critics' Circle." *America,* 140 (17 Feb. 1979), 115–16.

Broyard, Anatole. "Mysterious Short Story." *New York Times Book Review,* 1 Mar. 1981, p. 35.

"Cheever, John." In *Current Biography Yearbook 1975.* Ed. Charles Moritz. New York: H. W. Wilson, 1975, pp. 74–76.

Feron, James. "Festival in Ossining." *New York Times,* 13 Jan. 1980, Sec. 22, p. 2.

"14 to Get $4,000 Awards For Literature on May 21." *New York Times,* 24 Apr. 1980, p. C27.

Kakutani, Michiko. "In a Cheever-Like Setting, John Cheever Gets Mac-Dowell Medal." *New York Times,* 11 Sept. 1979, p. C7.

Kihiss, Peter. "Shepard Takes Pulitzer for Drama, Baker of Times Wins for Comment." *New York Times,* 17 Apr. 1979, p. A1.

Kornbluth, Jesse. "The Cheever Chronicle." *New York Times Magazine,* 21 Oct. 1979, pp. 26–29, 102–05.

Lask, Thomas. "Publishing: When a Small Press Becomes Popular." *New York Times,* 2 Feb. 1979, p. C22.

Mitgang, Herbert. "Behind the Best Sellers." *New York Times Book Review,* 28 Jan. 1979, p. 36.

Mitgang, Herbert. "National Book Awards Announce Nominations." *New York Times,* 19 Mar. 1979, p. C13.

Mitgang, Herbert. "National Book Critics Prize to 'Stories of John Cheever.' " *New York Times,* 16 Jan. 1979, p. C9.

"Notes on People." *New York Times,* 2 Dec. 1980, p. C18.

O'Connor, John J. "TV: A Series of Stories by John Cheever Begins." *New York Times,* 24 Oct. 1979, p. C28.

O'Connor, John J. "TV: Cheever Puts Terror on the 5:48." *New York Times*, 7 Nov. 1979, p. C32.

O'Connor, John J. "TV: Cheever's 'O Youth and Beauty!' on WNET." *New York Times*, 31 Oct. 1979, p. C31.

Shepard, Richard F. "WNET to Do Plays By U.S. Novelists." *New York Times*, 8 Feb. 1979, p. C13.

"Sketches of Winners of the Pulitzer Prizes in Journalism, the Arts and Letters." *New York Times*, 17 Apr. 1979, p. B8.

Smilgis, M. "John Cheever." *People* 11 (23 Apr. 1979), 78–80.

Tyler, Ralph. "How a Trio Of Cheever Stories Made It to TV." *New York Times*, 14 Oct. 1979, p. B1.

D. Interviews

Brans, Jo. "Stories to Comprehend Life: An Interview With John Cheever." *Southwest Review*, 65 (Autumn 1980), 337–45.

Callaway, John. Interview with John Cheever on "John Callaway Interviews," first televised by the Public Broadcasting Service on 15 Oct. 1981.

Cavett, Dick. Two interviews with John Cheever on *The Dick Cavett Show*, televised by the Public Broadcasting Service on 16 Nov. 1977 and 21 Mar. 1978.

Collins. R. G. and Jacqueline Tavernier-Courbin, "An Interview With John Cheever." *Thalia: Studies in Literary Humor*, 1, No. 2 (1978), 3–9.

Prokopova, Părvoleta. "Utresnijat den na sueta trjaba da băde po-dobăr!" *Slavjani* (Sofia), Sept. 1977, 8.

E. Criticism

Baldicyn, P. V. "Osobennosti realističeskoj prozy SŠA 60-x godov i tvorčestvo Džona Čivera." *Filologičeskie Nauki*, No. 1 (1978), 37–46.

Coates, Dennis E. "John Cheever: A Checklist, 1930–1978." *Bulletin of Bibliography*, 36 (Jan.–Mar. 1979), 1–13, 49.

Detweiler, Robert. "John Cheever's *Bullet Park:* A World Beyond Madness." In *Essays in Honour of Professor Tyrus Hillway*. Ed. Erwin A. Stürzl. U. of Salzburg: Inst. für eng. Sprache & Lit., 1977, pp. 6–32.

D'haen, Theo. "John Cheever en de Amerikaanse roman." *Maatstaf*, 26, No. 7 (1978), 61–67.

Gardner, John. "Moral Fiction." *Saturday Review*, 5 (1 Apr. 1978), 29–33.

Griffin, Bryan F. "Literary Vogues." *Harper's Magazine*, 258 (June 1979), 90–93.

Hamano, Shigeo. "Cheever no *Falconer* to Kogaizoku." *Eigo Seinen*, 123 (1977), 342–44.

Hyman, Stanley Edgar. *Standards: A Chronicle of Books for Our Time.* New York: Horizon Press, 1966, pp. 199–203.

Idol, John L., Jr. "Responses of Contemporary Novelists to *Look Homeward Angel.*" *The Thomas Wolfe Newsletter*, 3 (Fall 1979), 2–8.

Kazin, Alfred. *Bright Book of Life: American Novelists and Storytellers from Hemingway to Mailer.* N.Y.: Little, Brown & Co., 1973).

O'Hara, James. "Cheever's *The Wasphot Chronicle:* A Narrative of Exploration." *Critique*, 22, No. 2 (1980), 20–30.

Pawlowski, Robert S. "Myth as Metaphor: Cheever's 'Torch Song'." *Research Studies*, 47 (1979), 118–21.

Sizemore, Christine W. "The Sweeney Allusion in John Cheever's 'Enormous Radio'." *Notes on Contemporary Literature* 7, No. 4 (1977), 9.

F. Reviews

Falconer

Brown, T. "*Falconer.*" *The New Review*, 4 (Sep. 1977), 56.

Iyer, Pico. "A Nice Reliable Chevrolet: Aspects of John Cheever." *London Magazine*, 17 (Nov. 1977), 41–48.

Oates, Joyce Carol. "*Falconer.*" *The Ontario Review*, 7 (Fall–Winter, 1977–78), 99–101.

Tyler, Anne. "Chocolates in the Afternoon and Other Temptations of a Novelist." *Book World (Washington Post)*, 4 Dec. 1977, p. E3.

The Stories of John Cheever

Bell, Pearl K. "Literary Waifs." *Commentary*, 67 (Feb. 1979), 67–71.

Boeth, Richard. "The Poet of Shady Hill." *Newsweek*, 92 (30 Oct. 1978), 96.

Bradbury, Malcolm. "Better Times." *New Statesman*, 97 (29 June 1979), 956–57.

Brown, John L. "That Darkness at the Heart of Life: The Collected Stories of John Cheever." *World Literature Today*, 53 (Autumn 1979) 624–25.

Buffington, Robert. "Speak Mnemosyne." *Sewanee Review*, 88 (July 1980), 423–31.

Cunningham, Frank R. "Cheever's World: Seeing Life Whole." *Chronicle of Higher Education*, 17 (11 Dec. 1978), R6–R7.

De Santana, Hubert. "In the World of Orchards." *Macleans*, 91 (4 Dec. 1978), 61–62.

Fuller, Edmund. "A Pride of Short Story Collections." *Wall Street Journal*, 30 Oct. 1978, p. 24.

Gray, Paul. "Inescapable Conclusions." *Time*, 112 (16 Oct. 1978), 122, 124, K11.

Guereschi, Edward. *"The Stories of John Cheever." Best Sellers*, 38 (Feb. 1979), 337.

Hunt, George. "Beyond the Cheeveresque." *Commonweal*, 106 (19 Jan. 1979), 20–22.

Irving, John. "Facts of Living." *Saturday Review*, 5 (30 Sep. 1978), 44–46.

Kapp, Isa. "Cheerless World of John Cheever." *New Leader*, 61 (11 Sep. 1978), 16–17.

Kennedy, Eugene. *"The Stories of John Cheever." Critic*, 37 (15 Feb. 1979), 4, 8.

King, Francis, "Making It New." *Spectator*, 242 (23 June 1979), 29–30.

Leedom-Ackerman, Joanne. "Cheever's Stories Jump the Suburban Fence." *Christian Science Monitor*, 23 Oct. 1978, p. B18.

Leonard, John. "Books of the Times." *New York Times*, 7 Nov. 1978, p. 43.

Locke, Richard. "Visions of Order and Domestic Disarray." *New York Times Book Review*, 3 Dec. 1978, pp. 3, 78.

Mason, Kenneth C. "Bookmarks." *Prairie Schooner*, 53 (Spring 1979), 92.

Mason, Michael. "Gilt-edged Investments." *Times Literary Supplement*, 7 Dec. 1979, p. 103.

McPherson, William. "Cheever By the Dozen." *Book World (Washington Post)*, 22 Oct. 1978, pp. E1, E6.

Meisel, Perry. "The World of WASP." *Partisan Review*, 47, No. 3 (1980), 467–71.

Meyer, Arlin G. "A Garden of Love After Eden." *Cresset*, 42 (June 1979), 22–28.

Nicol, Charles. "The Truth, The Impractical Truth." *Harper's Magazine*, 257 (Oct. 1978), 93–95.

Rickenbacker, William F. "Visions of Grace." *National Review*, 31 (13 Apr. 1979), 491–93.

Schickel, Richard. "Cheever Chronicle." *Horizon*, 21 (Sep. 1978), 28–33.

Shaw, Robert B. "The World in a Very Small Space." *Nation*, 227 (23 Dec. 1978), 705–07.

"The Stories of John Cheever." Choice, 15 (Feb. 1979), 1662.

"The Stories of John Cheever." Kirkus Reviews, 46 (15 Aug. 1978), 906.

Swift, John N. "Stories." *Shenandoah*, 30 (Fall 1978), 91–96.

Towers, Robert. "Light Touch." *New York Review of Books*, 25 (9 Nov. 1978), 3–4.

Tyler, Anne. "Books Considered." *New Republic*, 179 (4 Nov. 1978), 45–47.

Williams, Joy. "Meaningful Fiction." *Esquire*, 90 (21 Nov. 1978), 35–36.

Yardley, Jonathan. "All in the Family." *Commonweal*, 106 (11 May 1979), 265.

INDEX